FRAGONARD

MARIE-ANNE DUPUY-VACHEY

Cover
La Liseuse,
c. 1789, oil on canvas, 81x 65 cm
Washington, National Gallery of Art.

Editorial Director: Anne Zweibaum
Editorial Coordination: Christine Marchandise
Translation: John Tittensor
Design: Sandrine Roux/Caroline Keppy
Picture Research: Hélène Orizet
Copy Editor : Nastasha Edwards
Photo Engraving: Grafiche Zanini, Italy

Publication N° 331
ISBN: 2-87939-301-9
Printed in Italy.

MARIE-ANNE DUPUY-VACHEY

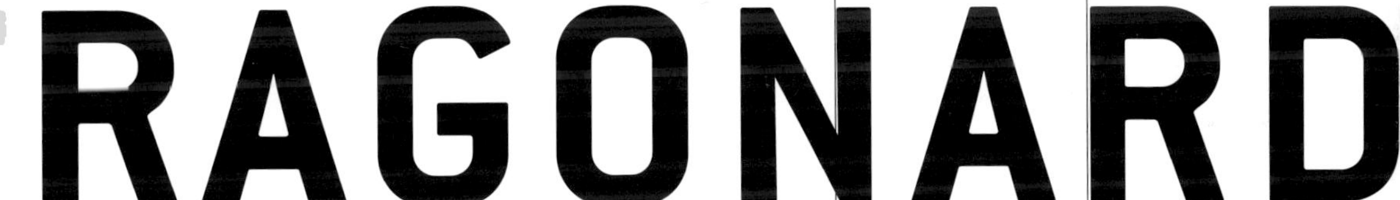

FRAGONARD

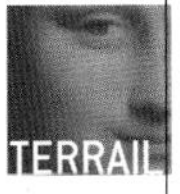

I

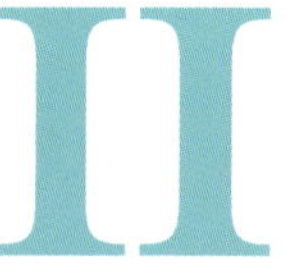

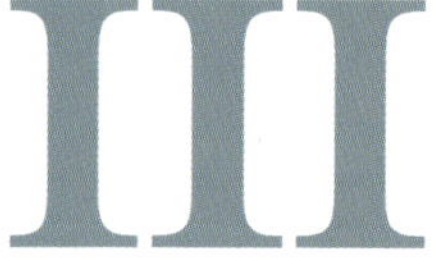

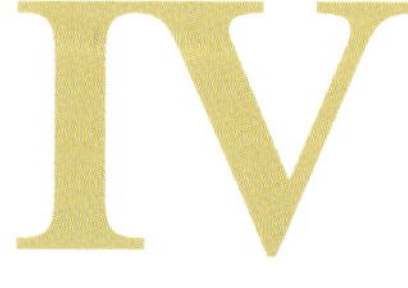

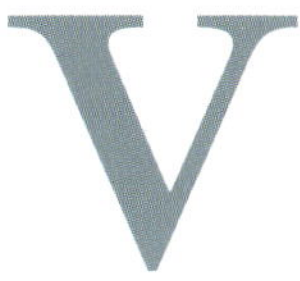

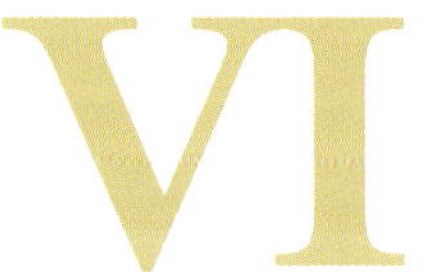

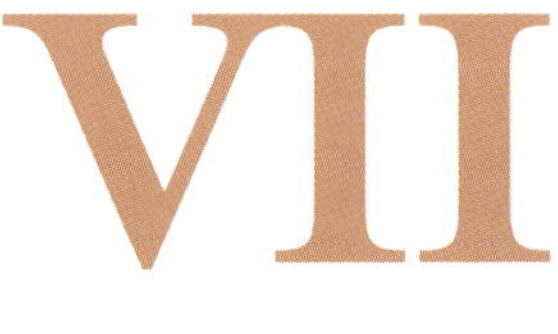

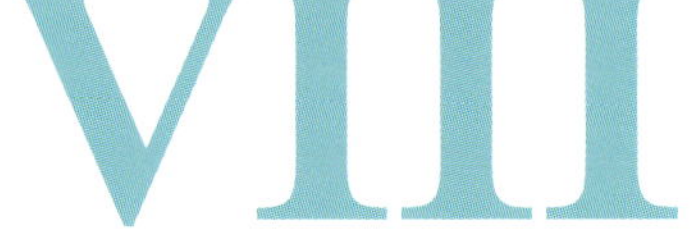

I

A Provençal's

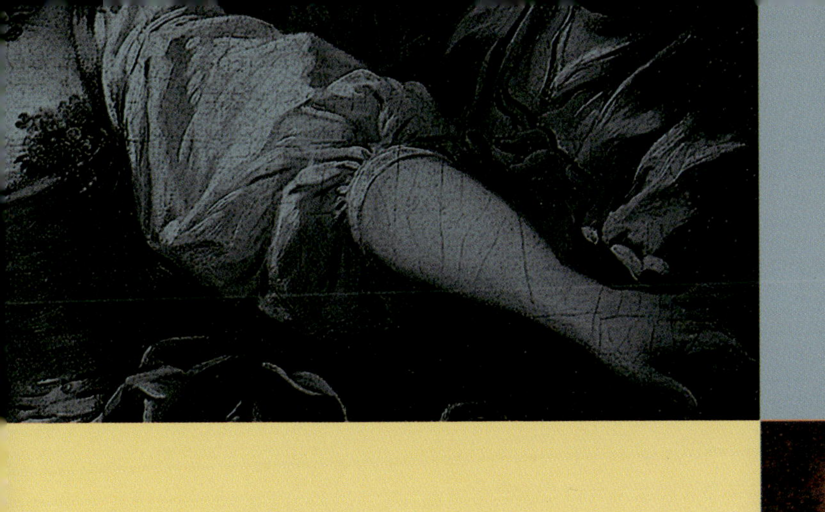

Progress

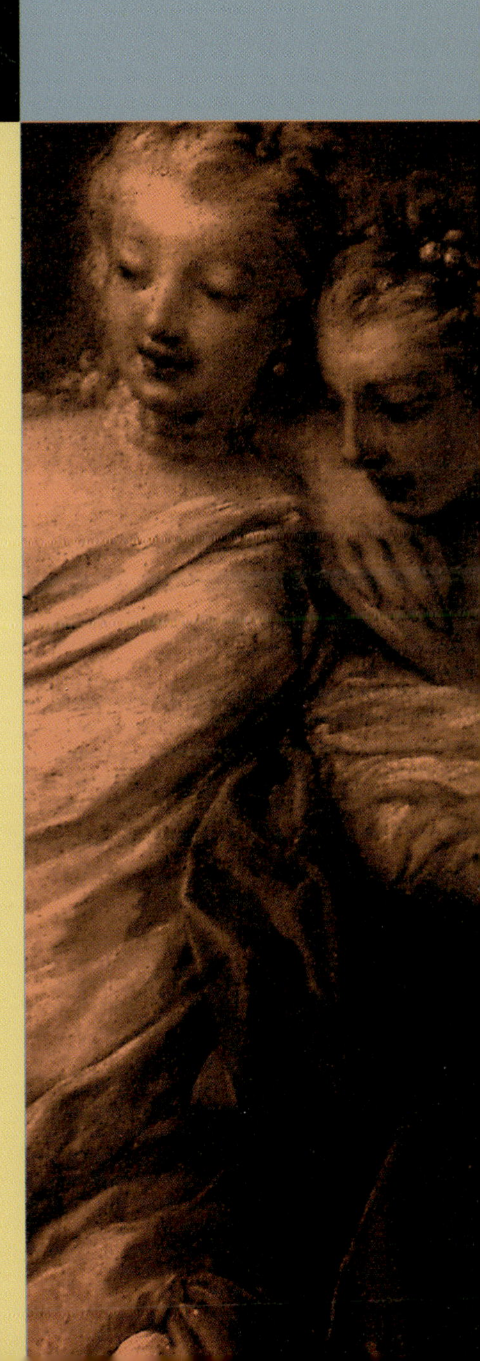

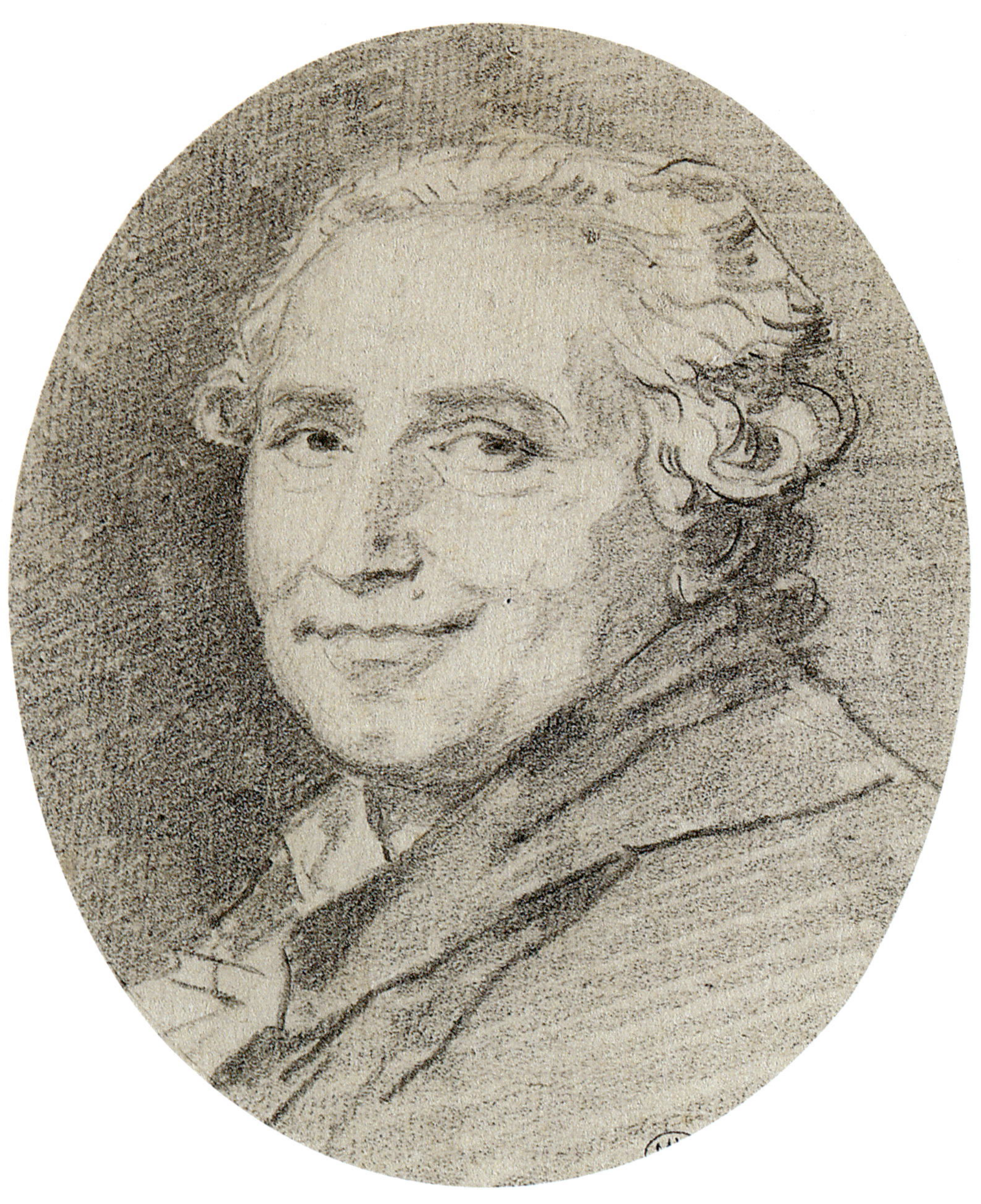

Self-portrait of Jean-Honoré Fragonard,
c. 1780, black chalk, 15.6 x 15.3 cm
Paris, Musée du Louvre.

Jean-Honoré Fragonard was born in Grasse, southern France, on 4 April 1732—during the reign of Louis XV—and died in Paris in August 1806, just a few weeks before Napoleon's defeat of Prussia at Jena. His was a life marked out by events and upheavals that included the Seven Years' War, the accession of Louis XVI, the emergence of the Empire out of the chaos following the French Revolution, and a change of centuries. Lasting until the dawn of the 19th century, those seventy-four years seem to embrace a long career, yet this was far from the case: as his grandson put it, "Fragonard's fall from favor came when he was not yet fifty. One could say he outlived his public by twenty-five years."

A Portrait of the Artist

Théophile Fragonard (1806-76) never knew his grandfather, who died the year Théophile was born. However, the disclosures he made in the mid-19th century to a number of historians and writers—notably the Goncourt brothers—include the reminiscences of Marie-Anne Fragonard (the painter's wife), Alexandre-Evariste (Fragonard's second child and Théophile's father), and Théophile's great-aunt, Marguerite Gérard. What makes these revelations so precious is the dearth of archival information on the painter's career: of an oeuvre comprising over four hundred works, perhaps fifteen can be dated exactly and fewer than twenty bear a signature sometimes abridged to an offhand "Frago".

We face the same problem when it comes to what Fragonard looked like. He seems to have set no great store by his own image and no convincing evidence has been advanced concerning the canvases in which he is said to appear. The only known portraits deserving of any credibility are three late drawings that at least do not contradict the terse description provided by the certificate of citizenship issued to Fragonard during the French Revolution: "Four feet eleven inches tall, round face, high forehead, gray hair, gray eyes, gray eyebrows, normal nose, average mouth, round chin, pockmarked features." People who knew the artist during his last years spoke of someone small, "quite chubby"—the official record of his death has him "extraordinarily plump"—and with "a tangle of gray hair. He habitually wore a cloak of the *houppelande or roquelaure* type, made of salt and pepper cloth like the habit of the Gray Sisters." He was, added his studio neighbors at the Louvre, "spry, alert and always cheerful."

Unlike many of his painter colleagues, Fragonard

did not come from an artistic family. His father, François Fragonard, is mentioned in documents as a "glovemaker's assistant"—a way of saying he worked with leather. Indeed, tanning hides was the dominant industry in Grasse, until it was replaced by perfume-making in the late 18th century. Much has been made of the links between Fragonard's oeuvre and the "city of perfumes", as if the myriad flowers that bring such colorful voluptuousness to his canvases could have had no other inspiration but his home town. It should be remembered, however, that the Grasse of the time was a modest city of less than ten thousand people—it now has over thirty-five thousand inhabitants—whose mesh of narrow, winding alleyways was rank with the foul odor of the local tanneries. We know, moreover—from the same certificate mentioned above—that when Fragonard was only six he moved to Paris with his family. He doubtless returned more than once, but no stay in Grasse is recorded before 1790.

Prentice Years

For an account of how the painter made his way in the Paris art world, we must once again rely on Théophile Fragonard, even if some of the "facts" smack more of legend than of true biography. According to the grandson's version, the young Jean-Honoré found a post as a notary's clerk, but was soon dismissed on the grounds that he spent all his time drawing. His mother, however, was perceptive enough to take her son to see the painter François Boucher (1703–70), whose star was then at its zenith, but Boucher displayed little enthusiasm for the youngster's drawings. Ultimately Fragonard would learn the basics from Jean-Baptiste Chardin (1699–1779), painter of spare, simple interiors and still lifes full of a hushed poetry. The pupil profoundly admired his master and was

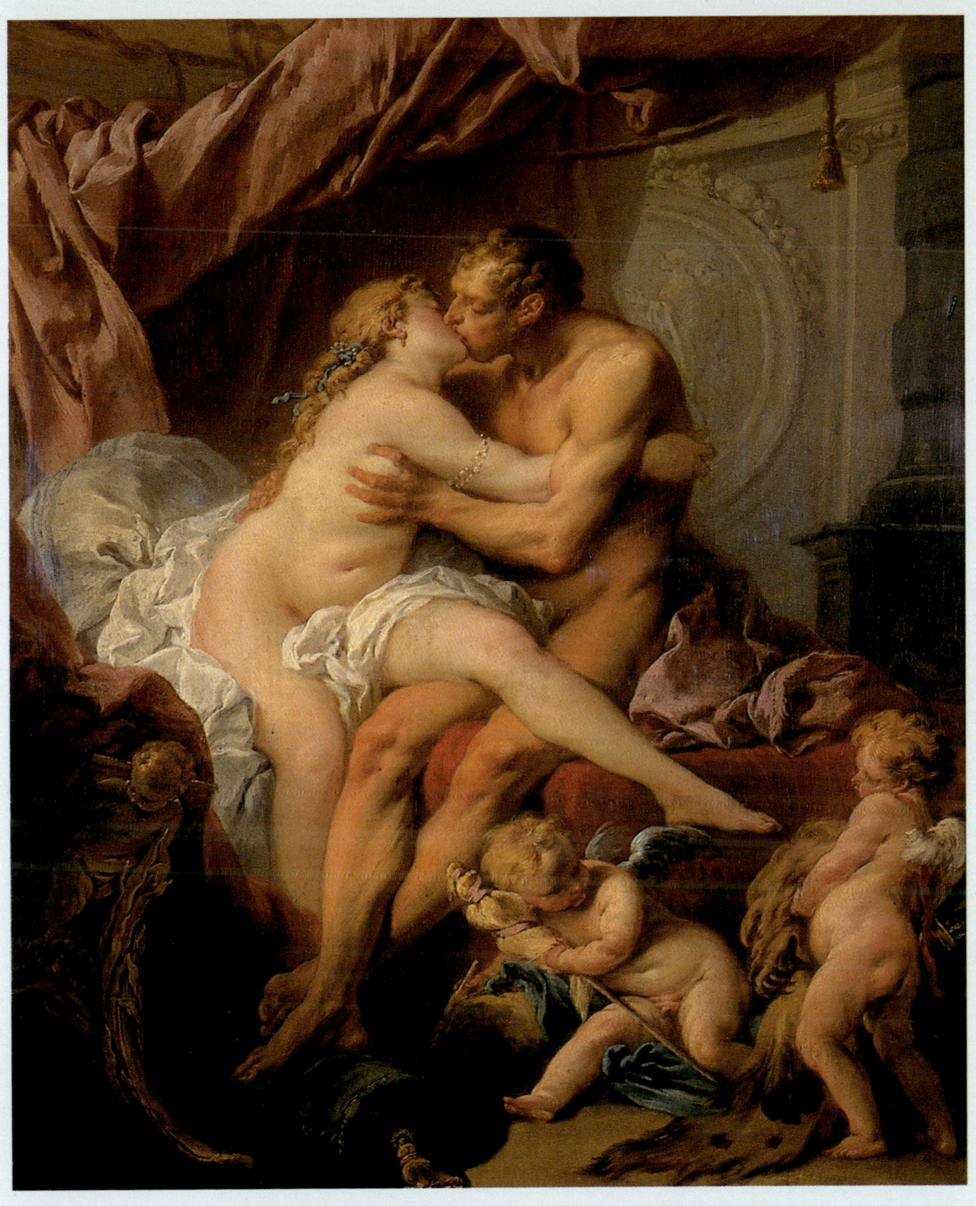

François Boucher,
Hercules and Omphale,
c. 1731-34, oil on canvas, 90 x 74 cm
Moscow, Pushkin Museum.

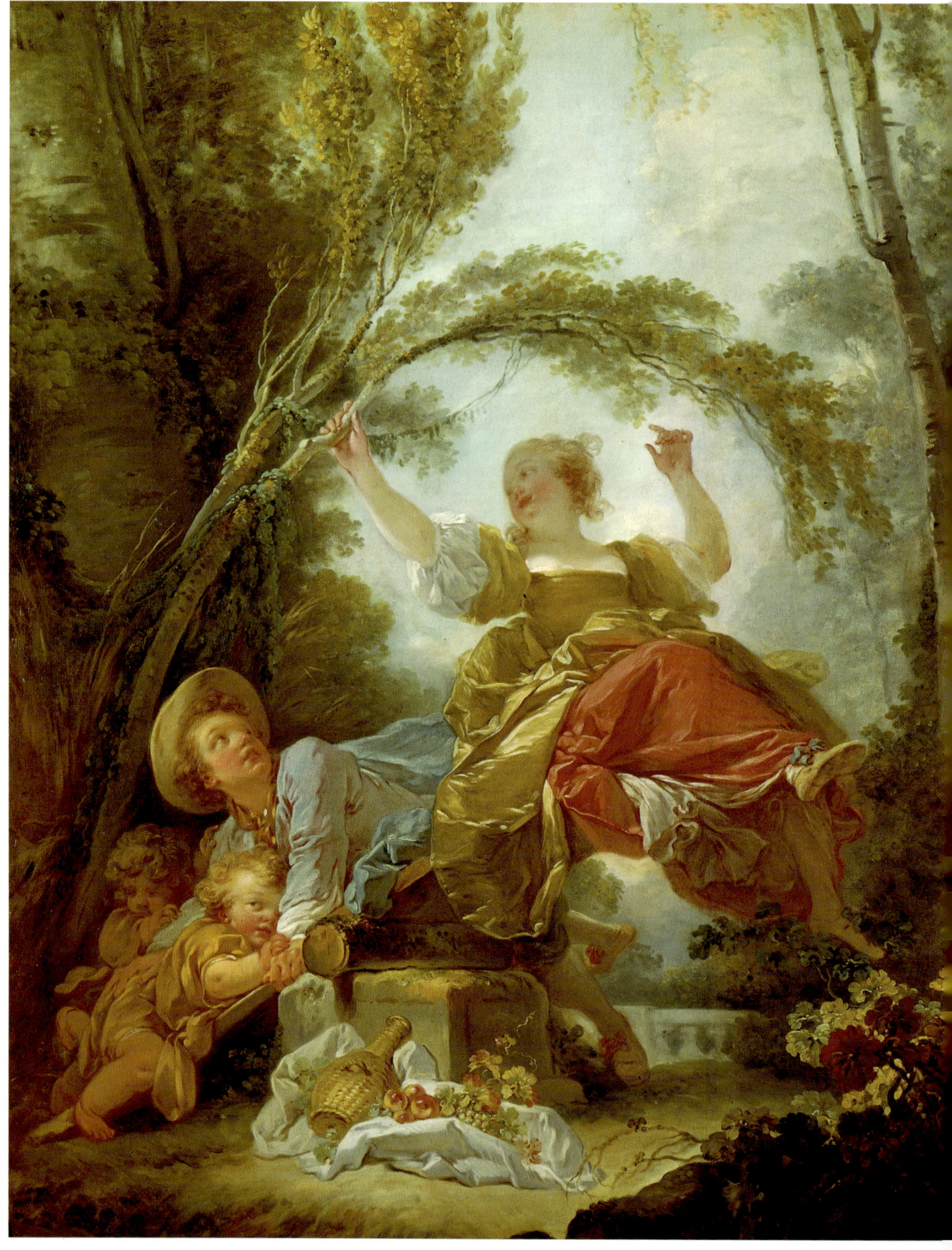

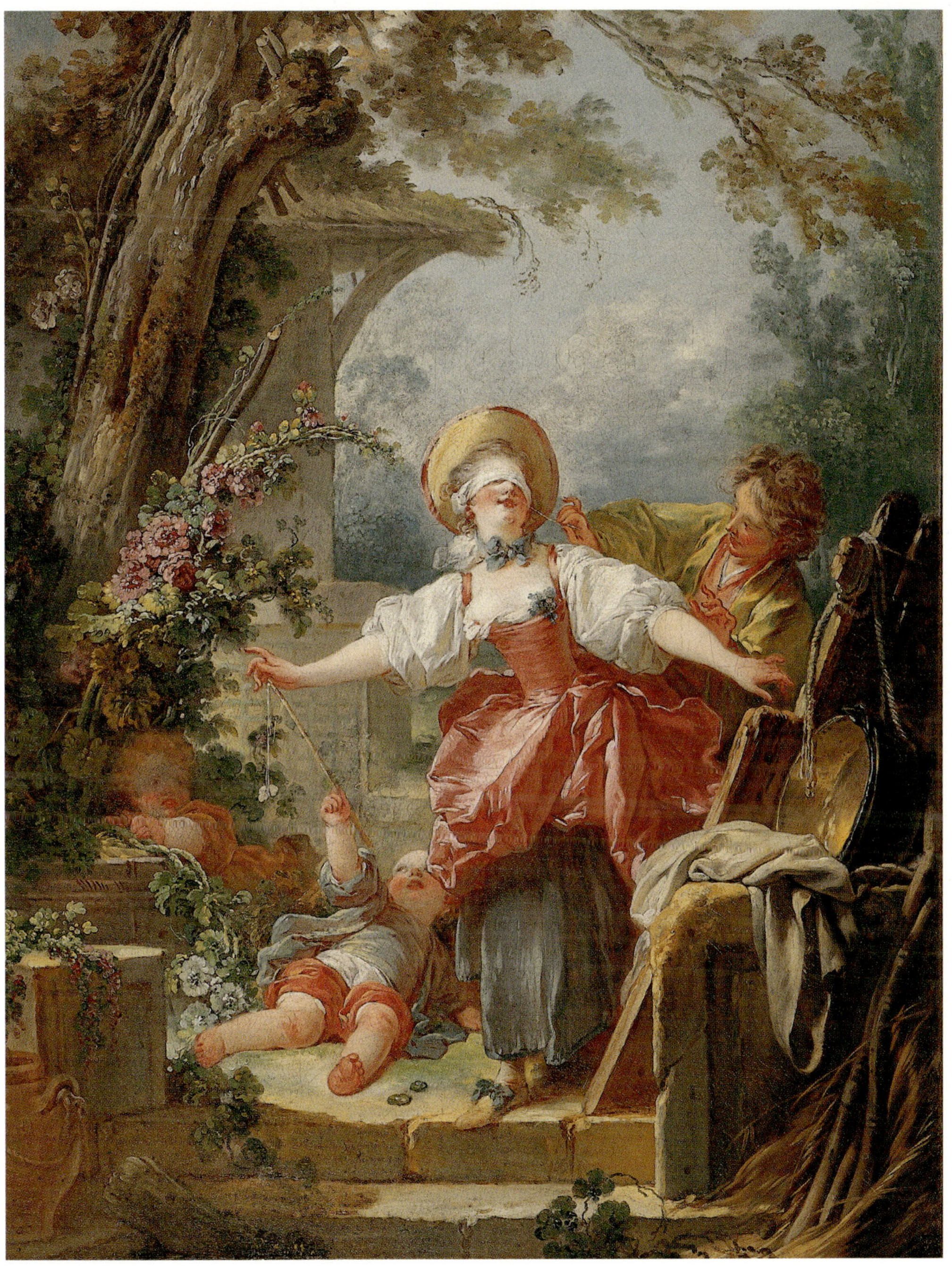

The Seesaw,
c. 1755, oil on canvas, 120 x 94.5 cm
Madrid, Thyssen-Bornemisza Collection.

Blindman's Buff,
c. 1755, oil on canvas, 117 x 91.5 cm
Toledo, Ohio, Toledo Museum of Art.

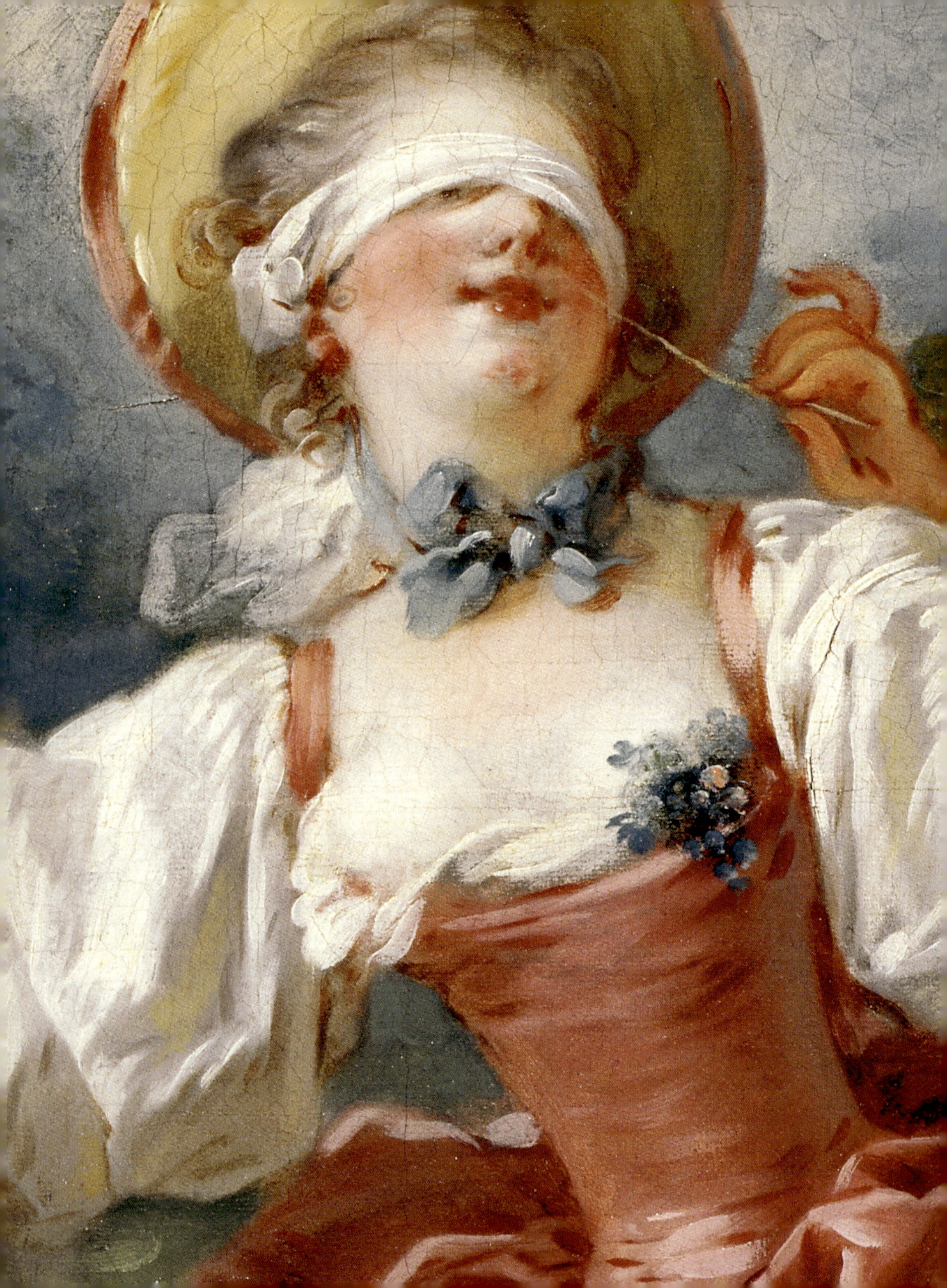

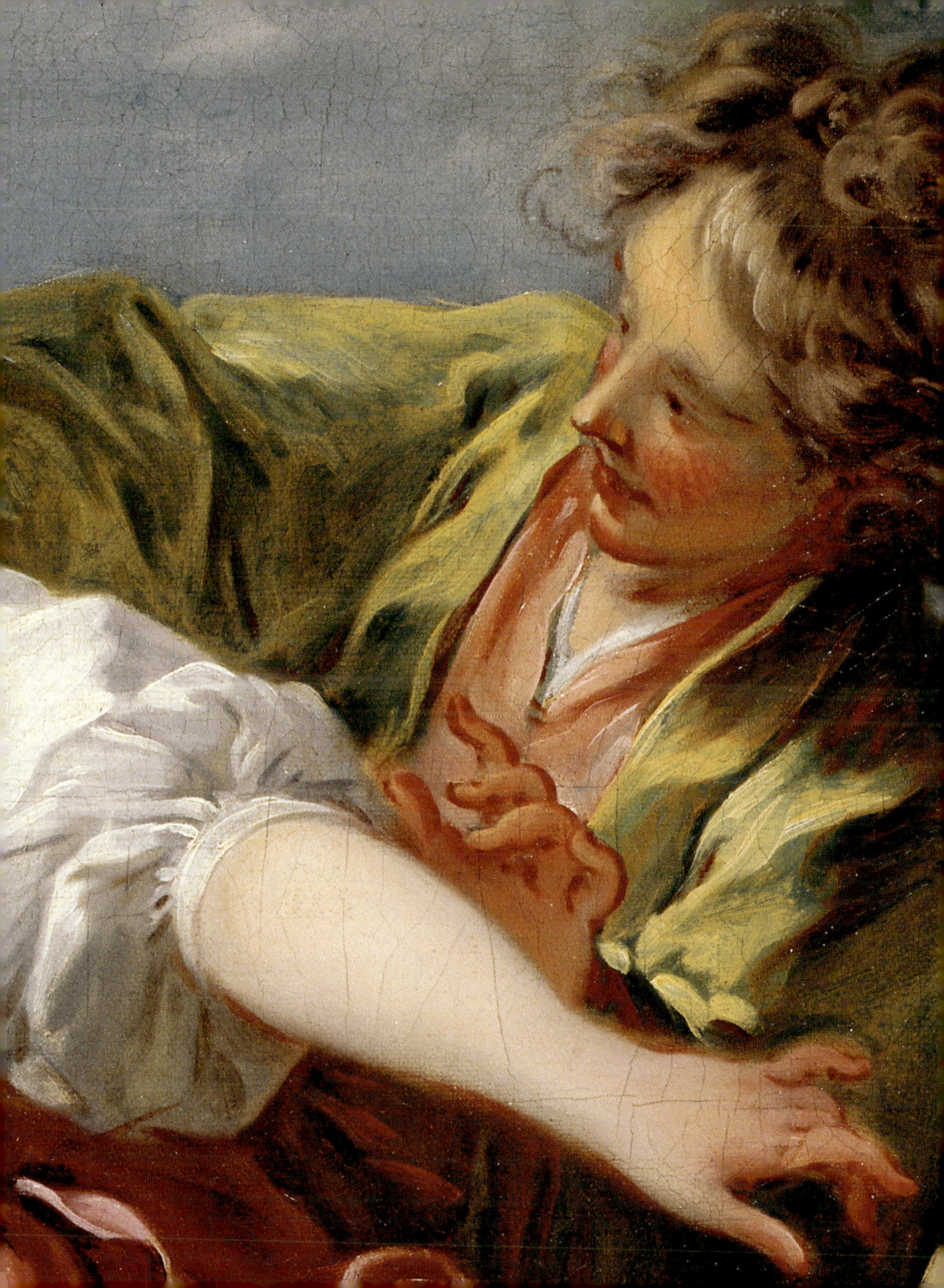

enormously grateful for the freedom he was given to work as he wished, but—still according to Théophile—could not confine his lively imagination to the depiction of vegetables...

And so it was back to Boucher, now clearly impressed by the progress he saw. The result, for the apprentice painter, was a radical, decisive change, as he soaked himself in Boucher's deliciously artificial Rococo style, with its blue-tinged vegetation, theater sets, silk-clad shepherds and shepherdesses with flocks of beribboned sheep, and mythological deities frolicking naked amid plump little cupids. Fragonard even went so far as to make a full-size copy of the passionate embrace of Boucher's early *Hercules and Omphale*. The teacher's influence would show through in many of the young painter's decorative works, notably in the borrowing of pastoral subjects and youthful physical types. A now-separated pair of paintings, *Blindman's Buff* and its pendant *The Seesaw* (c. 1750–52) testify to an affinity so close that it misled the painters' contemporaries: in engravings made in 1760 they were initially attributed to Boucher, the error only being rectified in later proofs. The freshness of the colors and the liveliness of the brushwork, however, clearly belong to Fragonard.

In 1752—and even though he was not a student at the Academy—the twenty-year-old artist presented for the Prix de Rome scholarship. With both Boucher and Chardin on the jury, he took out first prize with the biblically-inspired *Jeroboam Sacrificing* to Idols, and theoretically from then on the classical career awaited him: after the stay in Rome provided by the scholarship, he would be summoned to join the Academy, membership of which was imperative for all those seeking to make a name for themselves in the arts. Founded in 1648, the Academy in its 18th-century version had a staff of thirty: a director and a chancellor, four rectors, twelve teachers, eight counselors, teachers of perspective and anatomy, a secretary, and a treasurer.

Before being admitted, an artist had first to be approved on the basis of a work presented to the Academy jury; then, in a period usually of six months to two years after such approval, he would submit a second work—his "reception piece"—and become a fully-fledged Academician. Only Academicians and those having received the initial approval could show at the Salon, that other key institution on the art scene of the time. Named after its venue, the Salon Carré on the first floor of the Louvre, the event took place every two years, opening on 25 August, the King's feast-day, and closing as a rule late in September. Admission was free and the public came in droves to admire, criticize and compare the latest works of contemporary painters, sculptors and engravers.

Once received into the Academy, an artist could pursue his rise by becoming a counselor, a teacher's assistant, a teacher and ultimately rector. The upper echelons, however, were open only to artists admitted as "history painters": from the outset the Academy had imposed a strict classification on modes of representation, and the summit of this hierarchy was occupied by history painting, the "grand genre" covering subjects drawn from mythology, the Bible and classical literature. Lower down the scale came, in order, the portrait, the "genre scene" taken from everyday life, the landscape and the still life. The primacy accorded history painting had its roots in the criteria of the time: the "grand genre" called for more imagination and inventiveness from the artist than the other fields, considered inferior on the grounds that they required no more than a talent for "imitation".

When approval came for Fragonard, the king's First Painter, Charles Coypel (1694–1752), had just died. This office entailed playing the intermediary between one's Academy colleagues and the Superintendent of the Royal Buildings—the Minister of the Arts as it were—in the matters of arranging commissions, choosing subjects, allotting of works, ruling on admissions, etc. In the absence of a successor to Coypel, the post was held for the next ten years by the engraver Charles-Nicolas Cochin (1715–90), while the powerful Superintendent of the Royal Buildings was Madame Pompadour's brother the Marquis de Marigny (1727–81). Under their combined direction history painting loomed larger than ever, as witness the high prices the category commanded compared to much less expensive portraits.

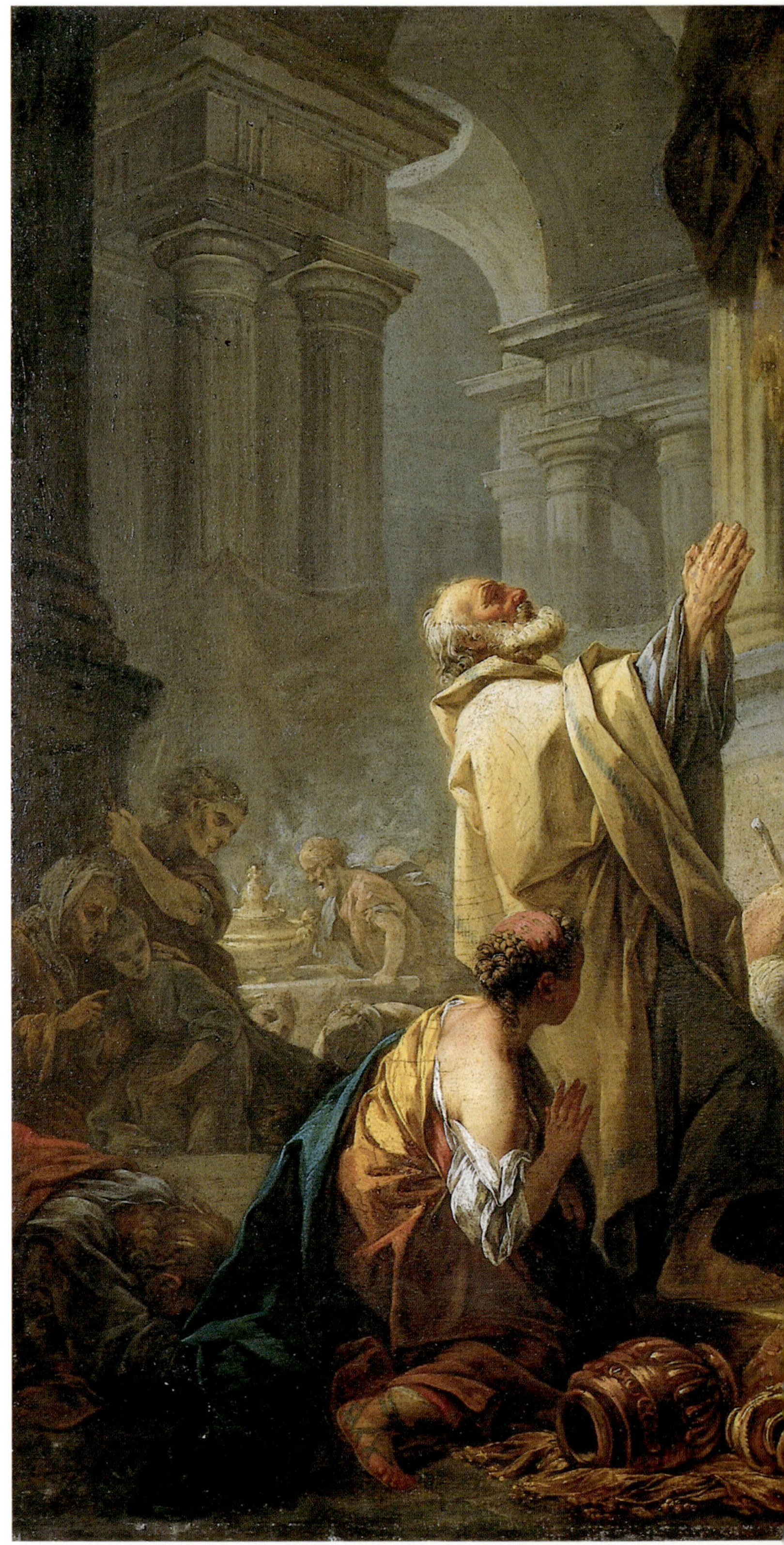

Jeroboam Sacrificing to Idols,
1752, oil on canvas, 111.5 x 143.5 cm
Paris, École Nationale Supérieure des Beaux-Arts.

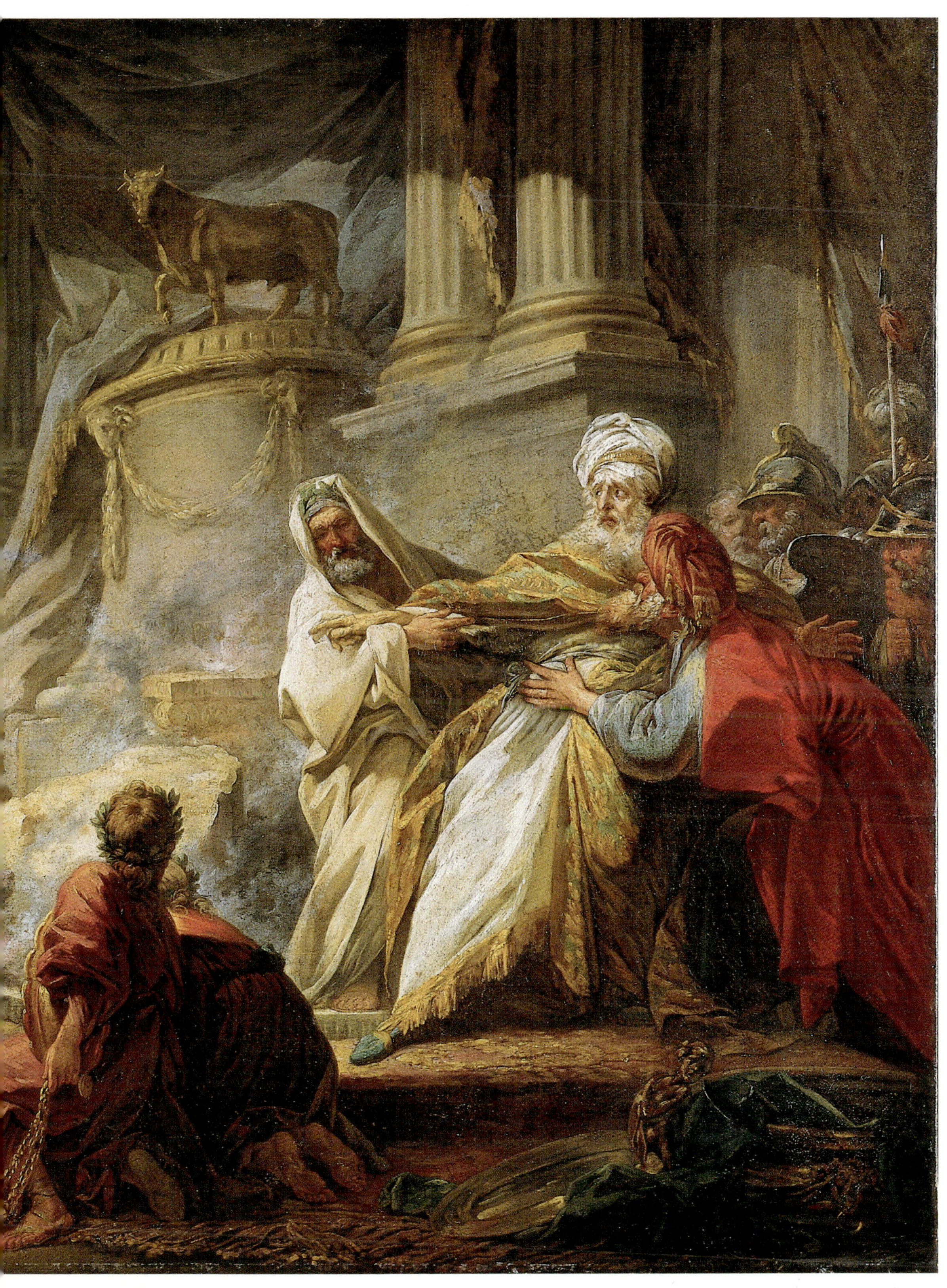

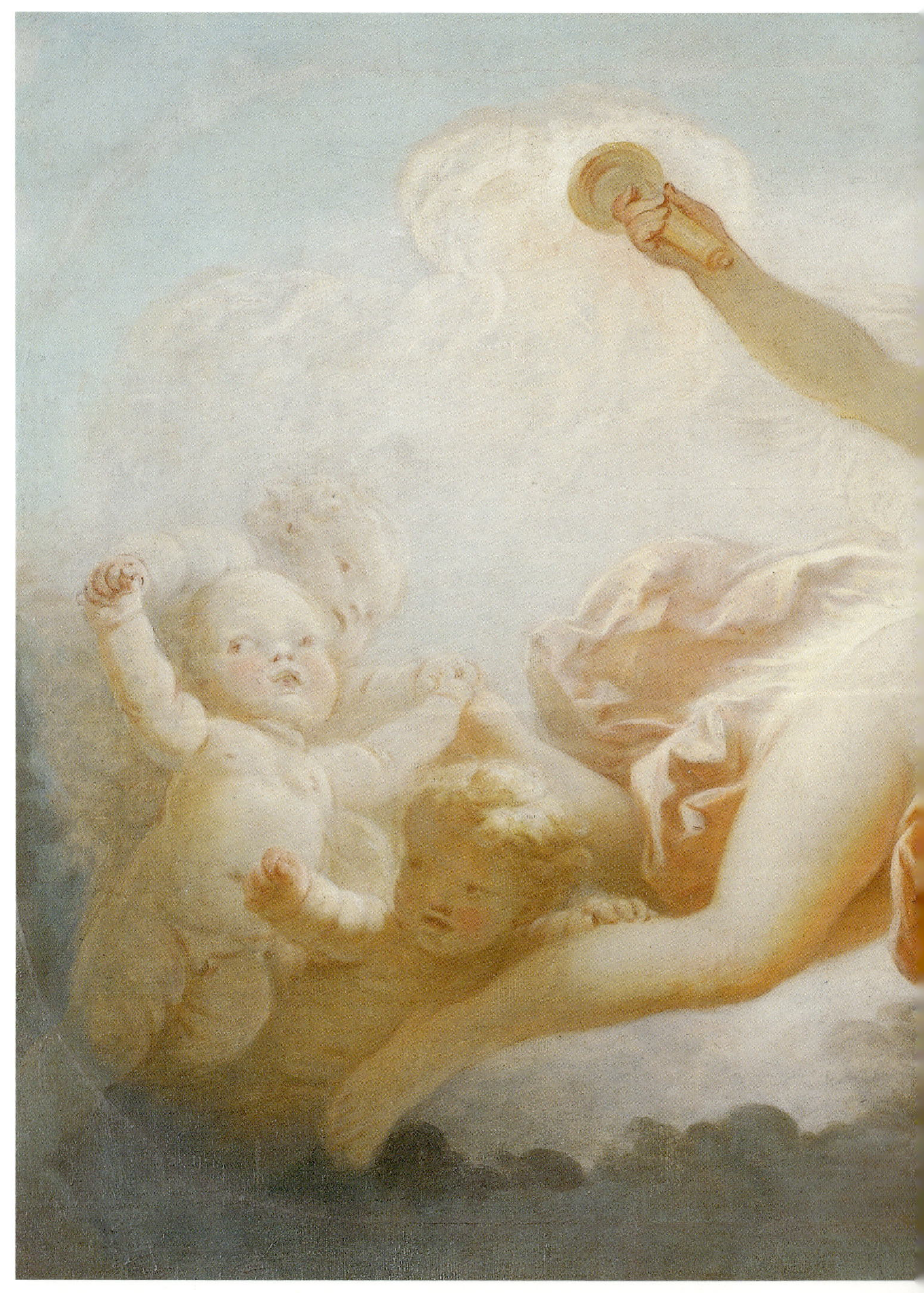

Love Setting the World Aflame,
c. 1765, oil on canvas, 116 x 145.4 cm
Toulon, Musée des Beaux-Arts.

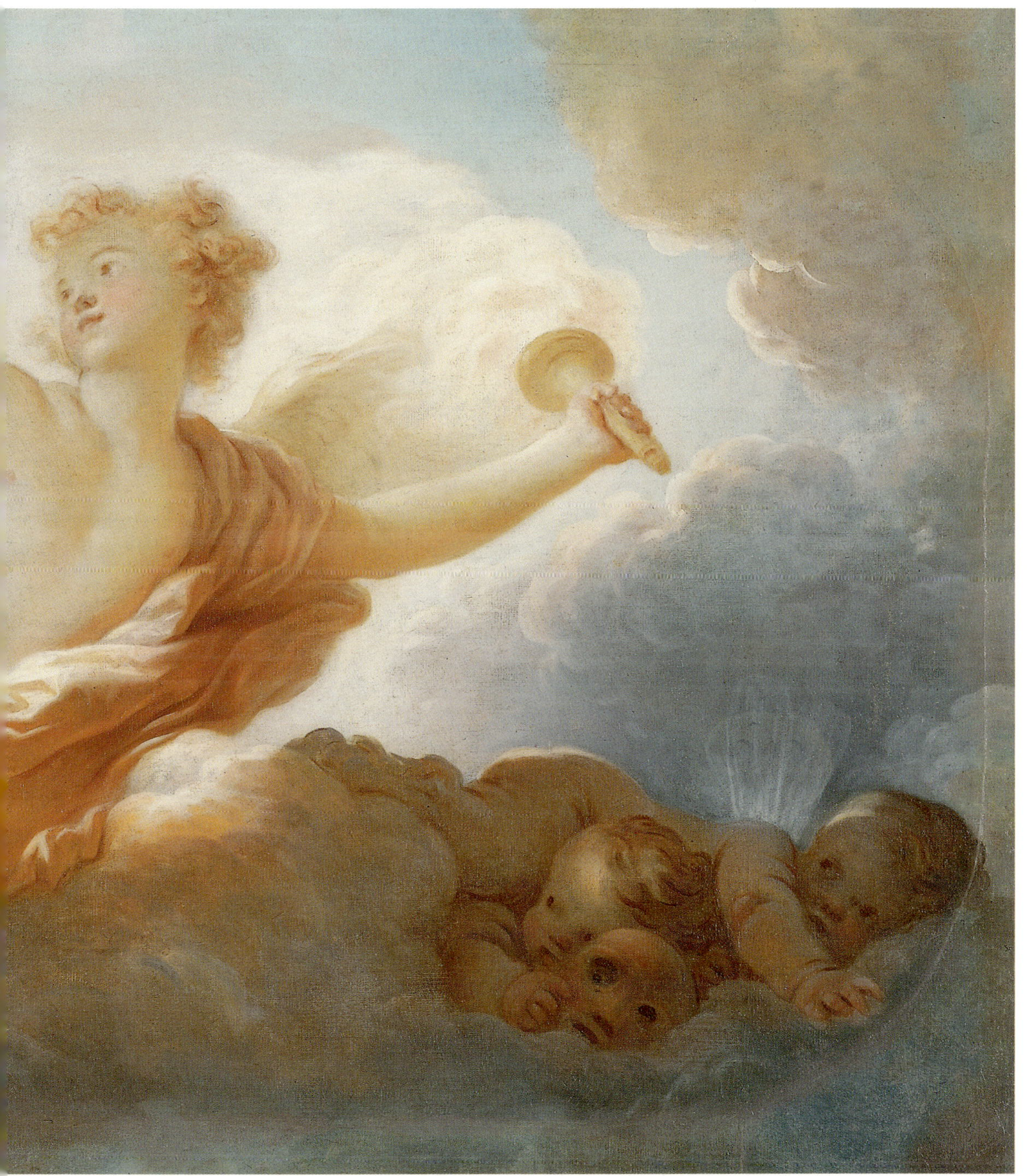

The Ecole Royale des Elèves Protégés, Threshold of the French Academy in Rome

It was natural, then, that Fragonard should set his sights on a career as a history painter. Before being sent to Rome, scholarship laureates had to take three years of classes at the Ecole Royale des Élèves Protégés, a school founded some years earlier for prizewinners to fill in the gaps in their education. The art program as such was complemented by courses in history, geography, literature, perspective and anatomy, and each year the six pupils had to present a composition of their choice to the king, at Versailles. Fragonard had no sooner begun at the Ecole Royale than he embarked on a large painting titled *Psyche Shows Her Sisters the Presents She Has Received from Cupid*. The episode is taken from the 2nd-century Latin writer Apuleius: Psyche has been wafted to an

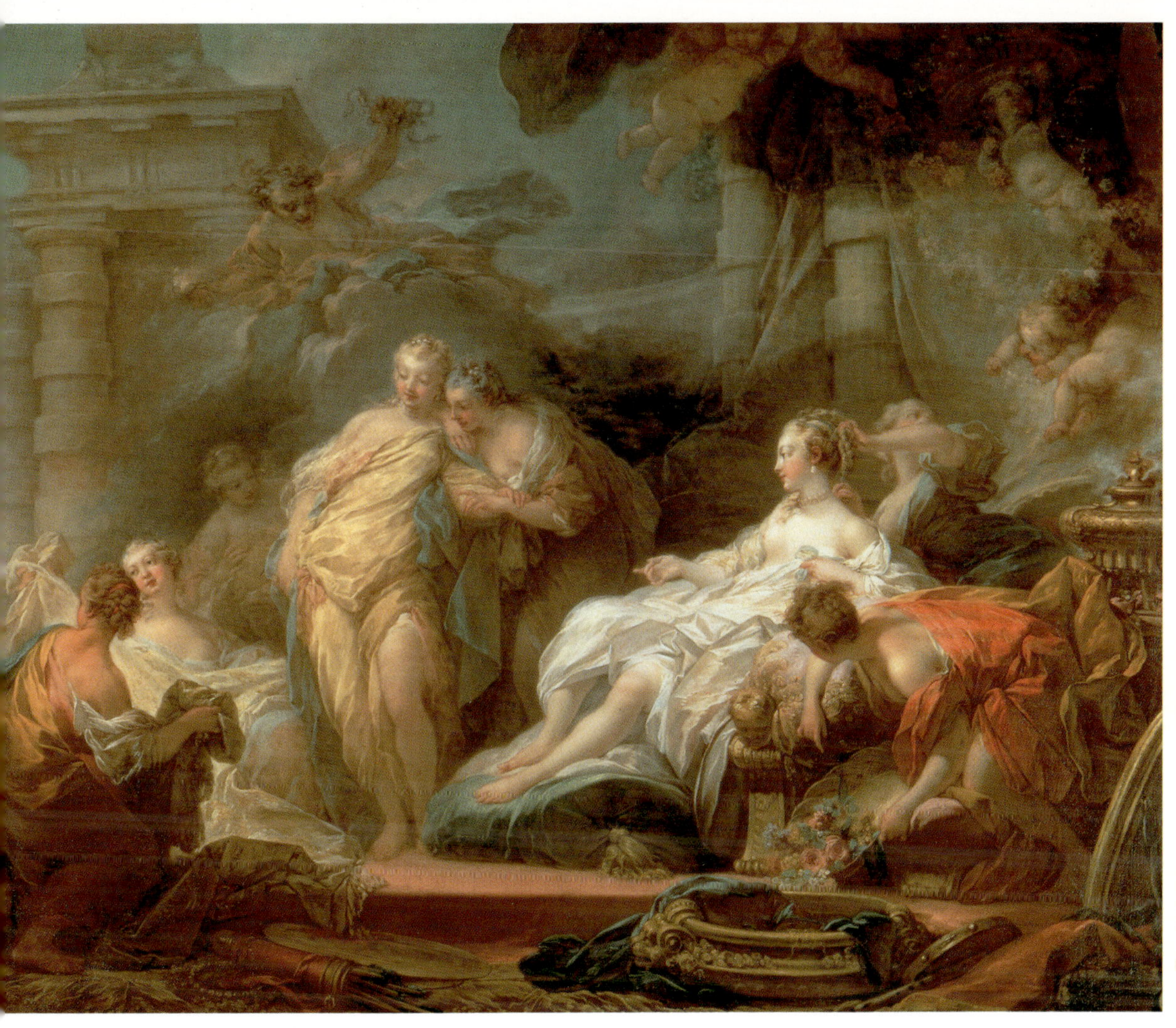

Psyche Shows Her Sisters the Presents She Has Received from Cupid,
1753–54, oil on canvas, 167 x 192 cm
London, National Gallery.

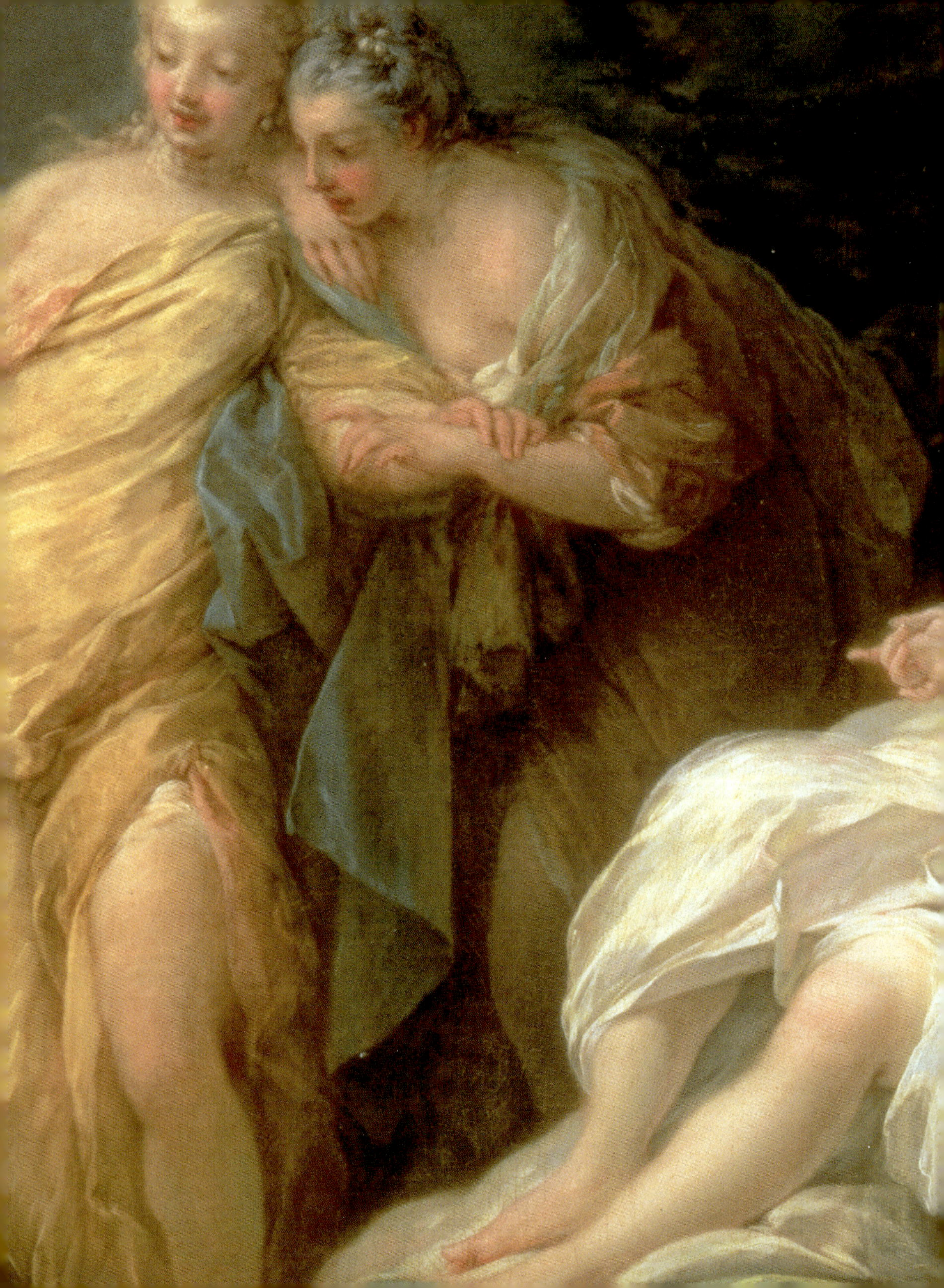

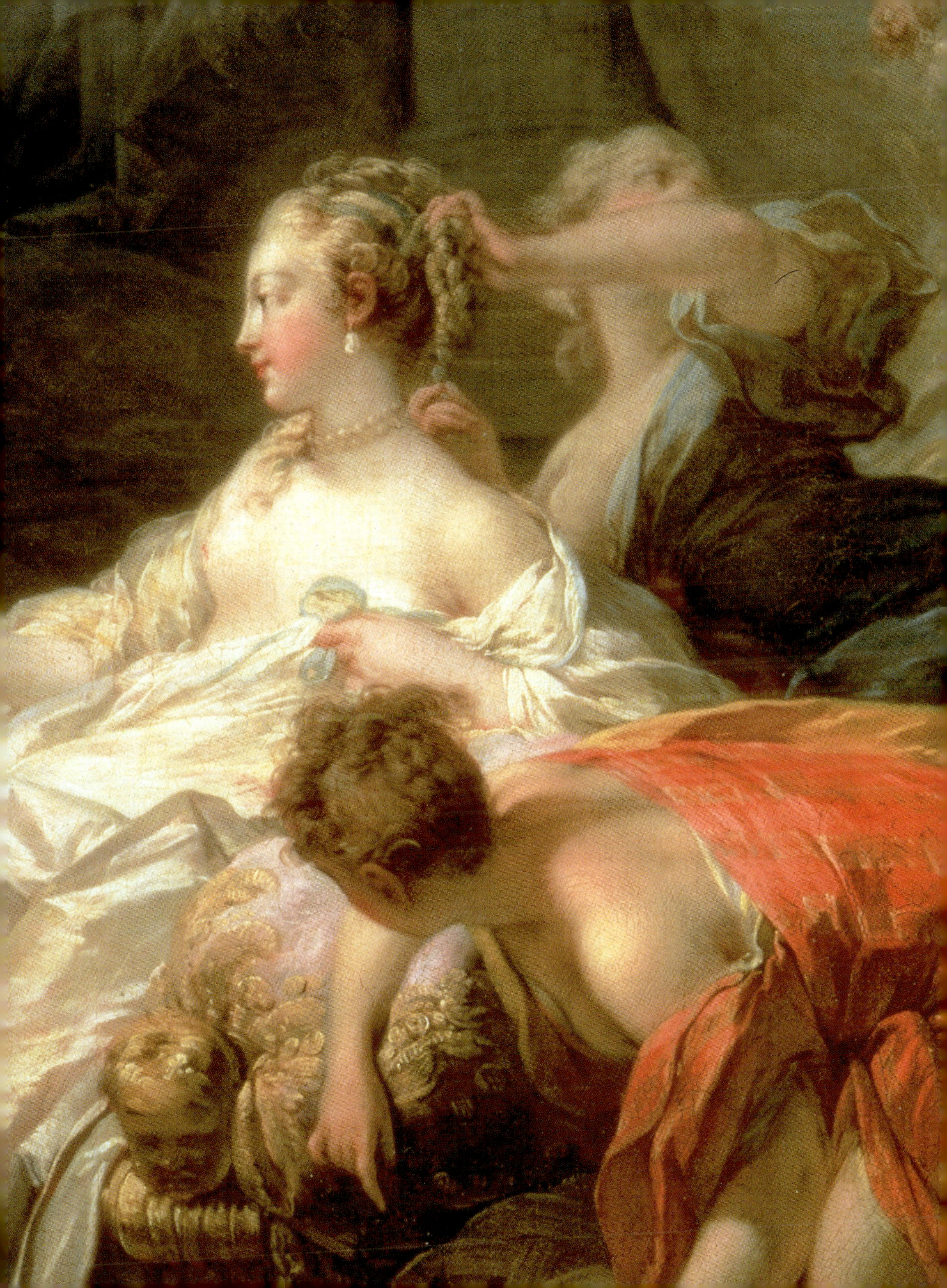

enchanted palace by Cupid, who promises her eternal happiness if she does not seek to know the face of the lover who covers her with gifts. In the sky hovers the figure of Envy, brandishing venomous snakes that symbolize the jealousy gnawing at Psyche's sisters.

Regrettably lacking part of its left-hand side, this canvas betrays the influence not only of Boucher but also of Carle Van Loo (1705–65), then director of the Ecole Royale des Elèves Protégés. Appointed rector of the Academy in 1754, Van Loo was widely regarded as the foremost painter in the kingdom, if not in Europe. His influence on his pupils was considerable, especially in the case of Fragonard: born in Nice, Van Loo shared the latter's Provençal background. His counsel was so valued that Fragonard and his fellow students requested an extra year at the school, thereby postponing their departure for Rome.

Fragonard took advantage of this time bonus to paint a religious scene, *Christ Washing the Feet of the Apostles*. The work was commissioned by the Brotherhood of the Blessed Sacrament in Grasse, whose members were keen to have their altar painting executed by a local boy whose success in Paris had filtered through to his hometown. As in the earlier paintings, Fragonard has yet to assert the full breadth of his personality, but he reveals an acute sense of color and lighting and an indisputable mastery of composition in a powerfully structured scene following the line of columns in the newly built chapel on the south side of Grasse cathedral. This ability to design a work in perfect harmony with an existing setting was already an intimation of the master-decorator to come. The painting was presented to Louis XV on 13 April 1755, but no record remains of the reactions it caused. In the following year the Marquis de Marigny signed the certificate allowing Fragonard to leave for Rome.

Christ Washing the Feet of the Apostles ,
1754–55, oil on canvas, 398 x 292 cm
Grasse, Cathedral.

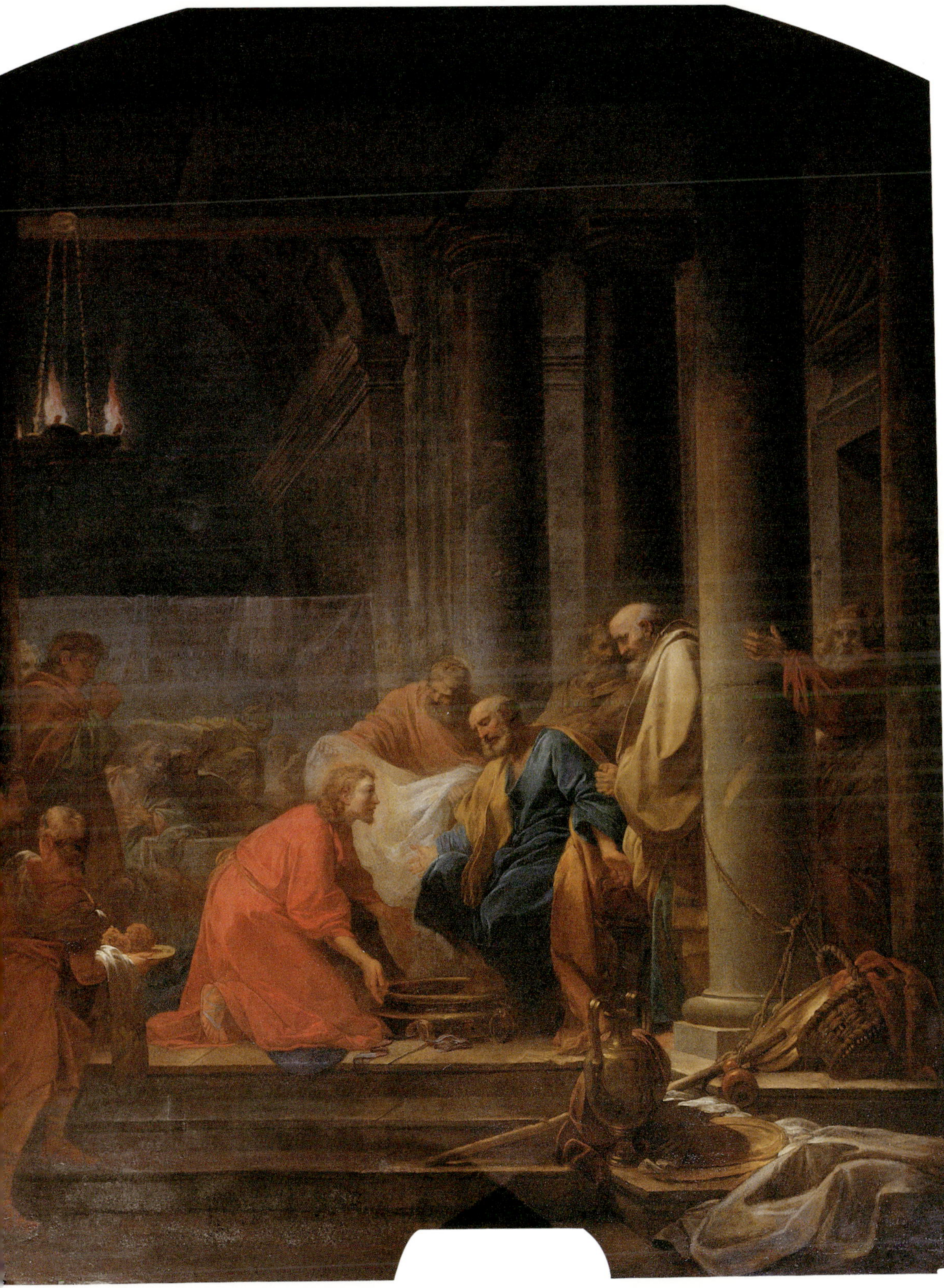

II

Two Experiences of

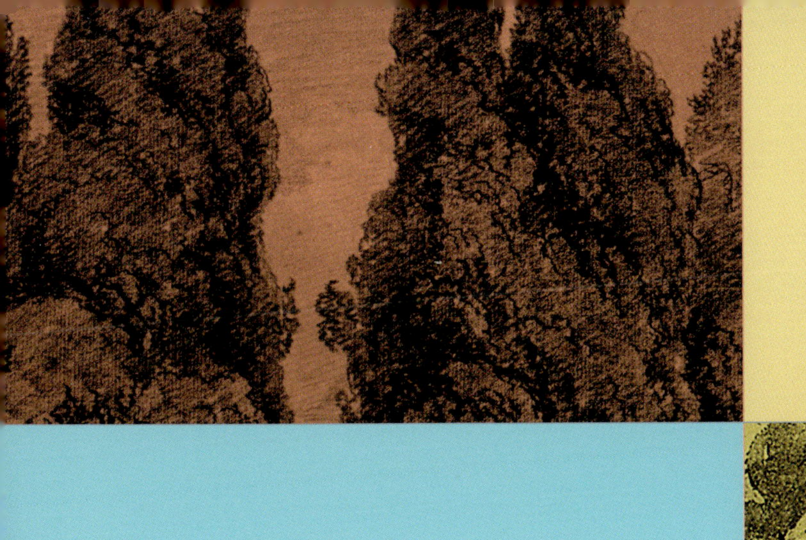

Italy

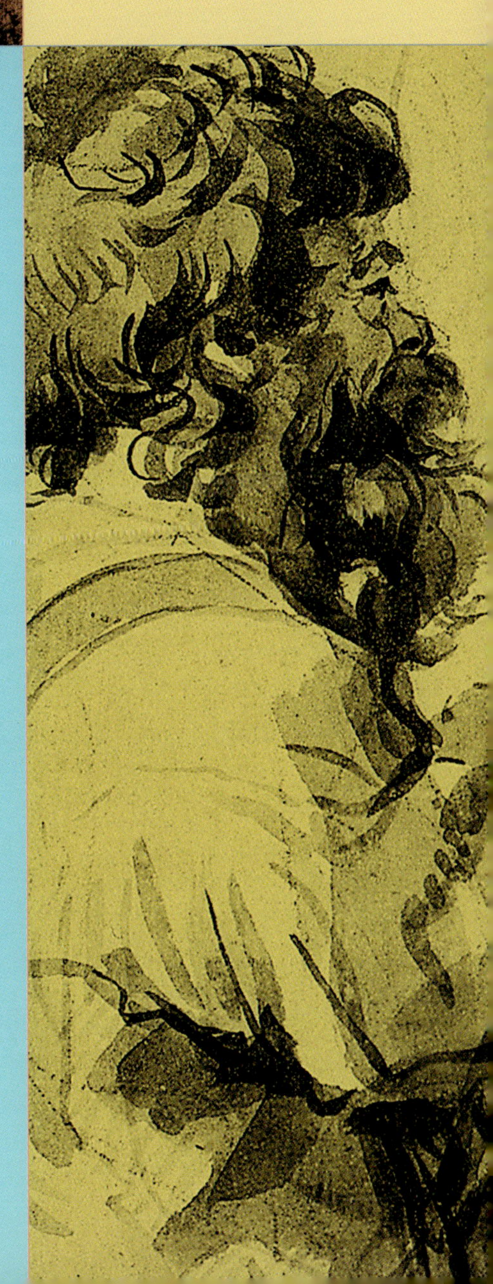

Italy had long been a homeland for artists. With the Renaissance came not only the archeological revelation of the marvels of Antiquity, but also the masterworks of contemporary painters, sculptors and architects working in the service of popes and princes; all in all a host of things to discover, study and contemplate that made the country a potent drawcard.

For France's artistic community, the opening of an annexe of the Academy in Rome in 1666 endowed the visit to Italy with an official framework: artists who had given clear proof of their abilities and passed the Academy's competitive examination in Paris could now be rewarded with a three-year residence in the Eternal City and a living allowance from the king. Surrounded by the cultural riches of centuries—of which they were expected to produce copies—they would round out their training under the eagle eye of the director. Since 1725 the French Academy in Rome had been housed in the Palazzo Mancini, among the handsomest buildings on the Corso, that long avenue stretching through the heart of the modern city. For artists who had not followed the official study program, there was sometimes the possibility of finding a well-heeled patron and thus making a "pilgrimage" by then considered obligatory.

In the century of the Enlightenment the "Grand Tour" became a kind of ritual, not only for artists looking to further their education and test themselves against the masters, but for all wealthy, cultivated Europeans. There was more at stake, however, than the glorious past, than simply paying one's respects to the emblematic works left by the geniuses of the Renaissance: for in the course of time new stopping-places had been added to the journey, and works dating from the previous century—by the great painting innovators, in Bologna in particular—had become an absolute must. Then there were the archeological discoveries being made in and around Naples, and the marvelous decorative work of the Tiepolos in Venice: all added attractions for a voyage from which one could not help but return a changed person.

First Stay (1756-61): an Artist in Search of Himself

Fragonard reached Rome a few days before Christmas 1756. Had he taken the time to stop over in Grasse before crossing the border? He may well have wanted to: so as to call on his parents, but also to see the *Christ Washing the Feet of the Apostles* he had dispatched to the cathedral there—the cathedral in which he had been baptized—the previous year. We cannot be sure, however, that the visit was possible, for he was not traveling alone: with two colleagues—sculptor Jean-Baptiste d'Huez (c. 1728–93) and painter Charles Monnet (1732–c. 1808)—he was escorting, as far as Turin, Christine Somis (1724–85), wife of Carle Van Loo and a singer and harpsichordist of renown. And meanwhile in Rome, the director of the French Academy there, the painter Charles-Joseph Natoire (1700–77), was impatient to get to know his new lodgers and set them to work: far from being left to their own devices, Academy residents were presented with a tight program in which their work was laid down and closely supervised by the director.

Natoire took his duties very seriously, dedicating himself to looking after his residents and vigorously encouraging them to travel all over Italy. A significant feature of his time as director was his emphasis on drawing as part of their obligatory work: to the usual studies of nude and clothed models he added landscape drawing, urging his pupils to work from nature. What he called his "hermitage"—the house he had bought on the Monte Palatino, behind the Campo Vacino—had become a hub for artists, art lovers and scholars from France and Italy, and for foreigners passing through. The garden was dotted with moldings in the antique style, the resultant mix of vegetation and ancient architecture providing an imaginative springboard for the artists whose skills the director was seeking to foster in the domain of picturesque landscape.

For Fragonard and the other alumni of the Ecole Royale des Elèves Protégés, discipline at the Academy cannot have seemed overly strict. Moreover, in comparison with many of his fellow residents, the young Provençal probably found his new life facilitated by some knowledge of Italian: more than likely his childhood in Grasse—a few miles from the border, and not far from Savoy, long under Italian domination—would have given him a nodding acquaintance with the language. Even so, like many other foreign artists, he was to find himself deeply unsettled by his discovery of Rome and its treasures. Nothing had prepared him for an experience of this magnitude: neither the program at the Ecole Royale des Elèves Protégés, nor his study of the many Italian paintings in the royal collection;

Charles Natoire,
The Artist's Garden and "Villa" in Rome,
1760, pen and sepia ink, watercolor, 28.1 x 42.5 cm
Weimar, Schlossmuseum.

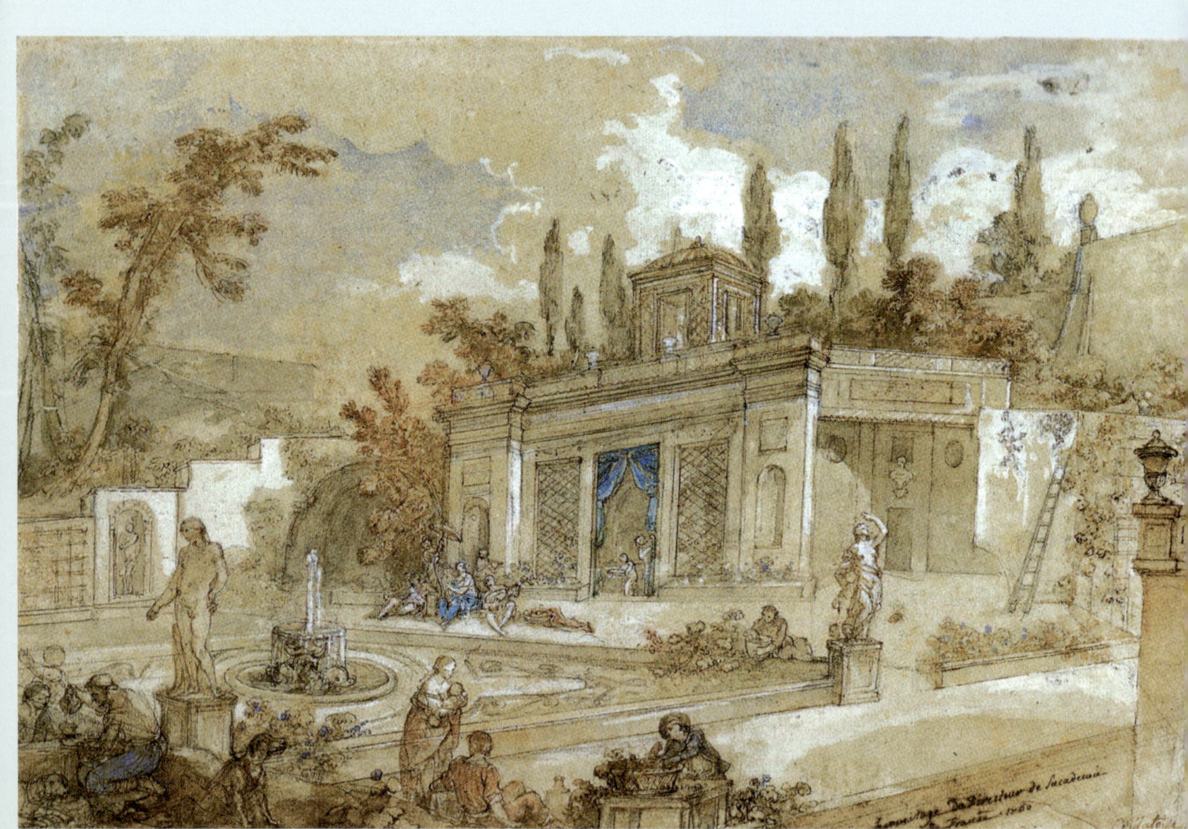

not the 17th-century ceilings in the Louvre by the Roman painter Francesco Romanelli (1610–62), and even less so the engravings that had been his introduction to the seminal works of the masters.

The beginning of his stay would turn out to be difficult and disappointing. "Overwhelmed"—according to his grandson's version of things—by the perfection of Raphael's frescoes, and "awed" by the energy Michelangelo had brought to the Sistine Chapel, Fragonard became profoundly discouraged and went into a state of depression that seems to have lasted more than a year. Natoire had introduced a new element into the residents' program, sending their drawn and painted "academic studies" to Paris so that their progress could be assessed. However, In March 1758 he was still refusing to send Marigny the studies by Fragonard and his fellow students. And we learn from Natoire's correspondence with Marigny, in which he provided regular reports on students' work, that Fragonard had taken over a year and a half to finish copying a picture by Pietro da Cortona (1596-1669) in the Capuchin church.

Little by little, however, Fragonard pulled himself together and regained his self-confidence. The letters exchanged by Natoire and Marigny are proof that his drawings were thought highly of, but his painting was seen as weakened by an excessive penchant for bright colors. Other reproaches had to do with his instability and a scattershot ardor that dispersed his energies and so prevented him from taking his studies through to perfection: "Too much passion and too little patience lead him to neglect the exactness of his copies." Nonetheless, by the summer of 1759 he had shown sufficient progress and promise for the possibility to be raised of a further year at the Academy.

And there, alas, our knowledge of his stay in Rome ends. Apart from its purely educational and professional aspects, no further information has come down to us. True, we learn that he met Jean-Baptiste Greuze (1725–1805) before the latter returned to France in the spring of 1757, and the two were sufficiently close for Fragonard, seven years younger, to nickname Greuze "the amorous cherub" a reminder that these stays in Italy were often sprinkled with romantic intrigues. Of Fragonard's own love life in Rome we know nothing, and many other questions remain unanswered. Whom did he meet? Who were his friends? How did things go with his fellow residents at the Academy? Among the latter were the painters Jean-Hugues Taraval (1729–85) and Chardin's son Jean-Pierre Chardin (1731–72), who committed suicide some years later in Venice; the sculptor Augustin Pajou (1730–1809), whose career would intersect more than once with Fragonard's; and Victor Louis (1731–1802), future architect of the Palais Royal, where Fragonard live out his last days. None of them, however, has left us any details regarding the kind of person he was or his activities in Rome.

The Right Kind of Company

While many of the Academy residents of the time have either disappeared into oblivion or are known only to specialists, one, not so far mentioned in these pages, now enjoys a fame almost equal to that of Fragonard. He was, it must be said, not a resident in the strict sense, for he had not won the royal scholarship; his place at the Palazzo Mancini was due to the French ambassador, the Comte de Stainville and future Duc de Choiseul (1719–85), the protector with whom he had arrived in Rome two years ahead of Fragonard. Hubert Robert (1733–1808) had a status all his own and a life path that could not have been more different from the latter's. Son of the Marquis de Stainville's equerry, Robert was educated at the prestigious Collège de Navarre on the Montagne Sainte-Geneviève in Paris. Cultivated, with a sound grasp of Latin, and of a naturally genial, sociable disposition, he was welcome in all the best salons and had developed his talent for drawing under the sculptor Michel-Ange Slodtz (1705–64), who sent two other students to the French Academy in Rome: André Brenet (c. 1734–c. 1792) and Pierre-François Berruer (1733–97).

Far from petrified by culture shock on his arrival in the Eternal City, Robert was immediately at his ease there. His drawings won Natoire's admiration and Marigny commissioned a picture. The director of the Academy, meanwhile, despaired of seeing the rest of his young pupils exhibit the same assurance and talent: "I should like all of them to be making the same clear progress as Mr Robert... but I mention his example in vain, there are few who do like him." Drummed into his colleagues as a paradigm, and effortlessly enjoying the privileges of his caste, Hubert Robert might easily have irritated the passionate, but timid and over-modest Fragonard. Yet the outcome was the

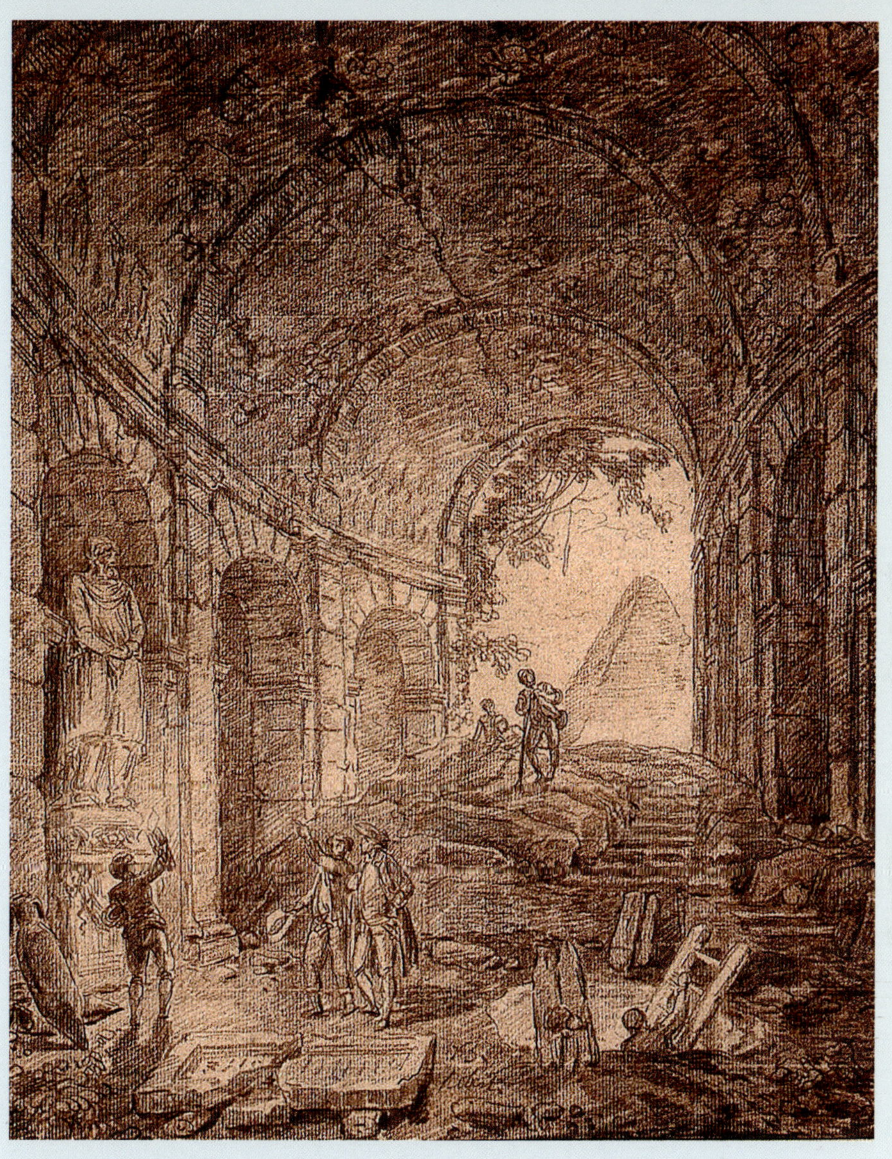

Hubert Robert
Discoverers of Antiquities,
1765, red chalk, 43 x 32.5 cm
Valence, Musée des Beaux-Arts.

Following pages
Teh Storm,
1759, oil on canvas, 73 x 97 cm
Paris, Musée du Louvre.

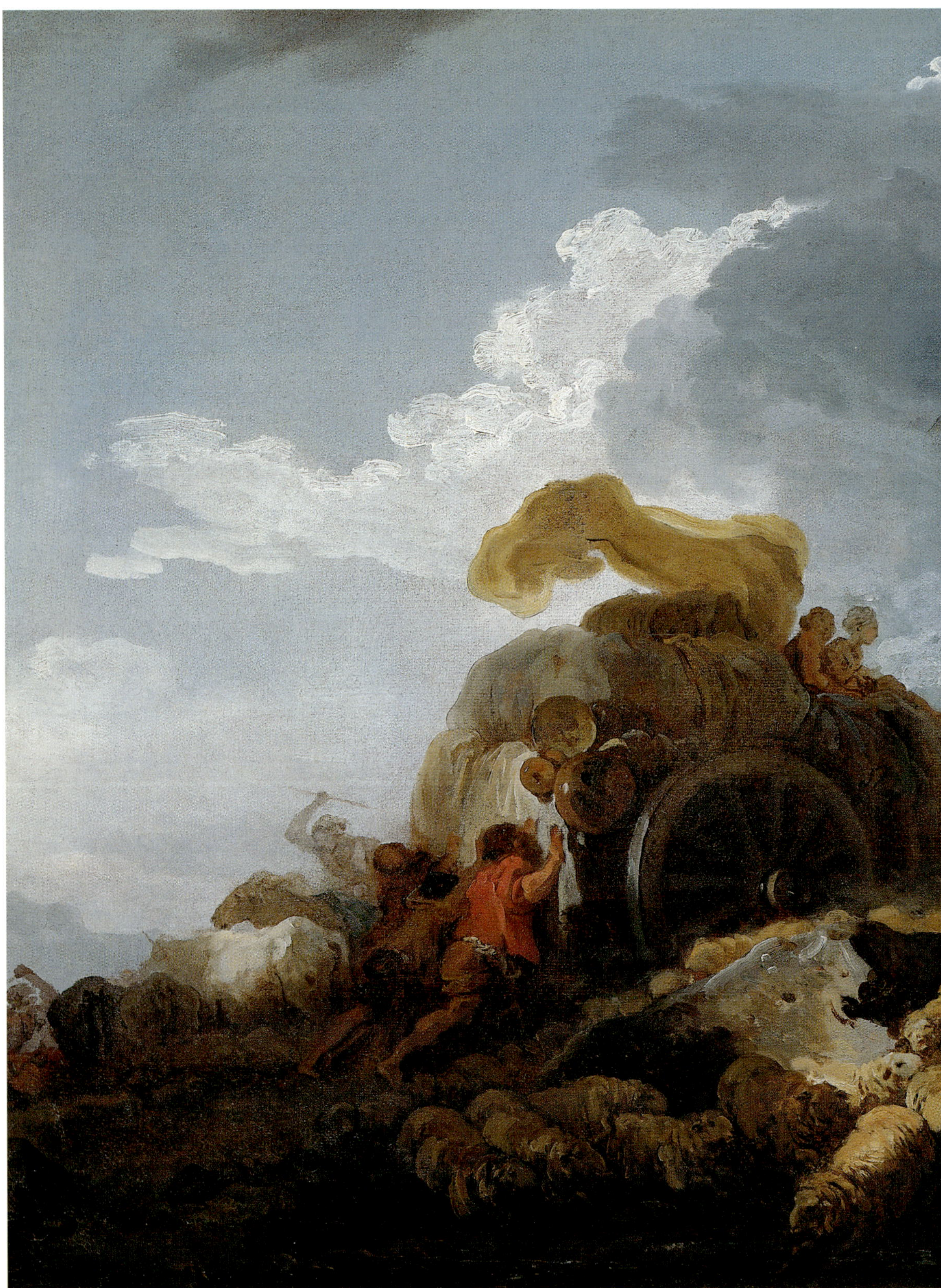

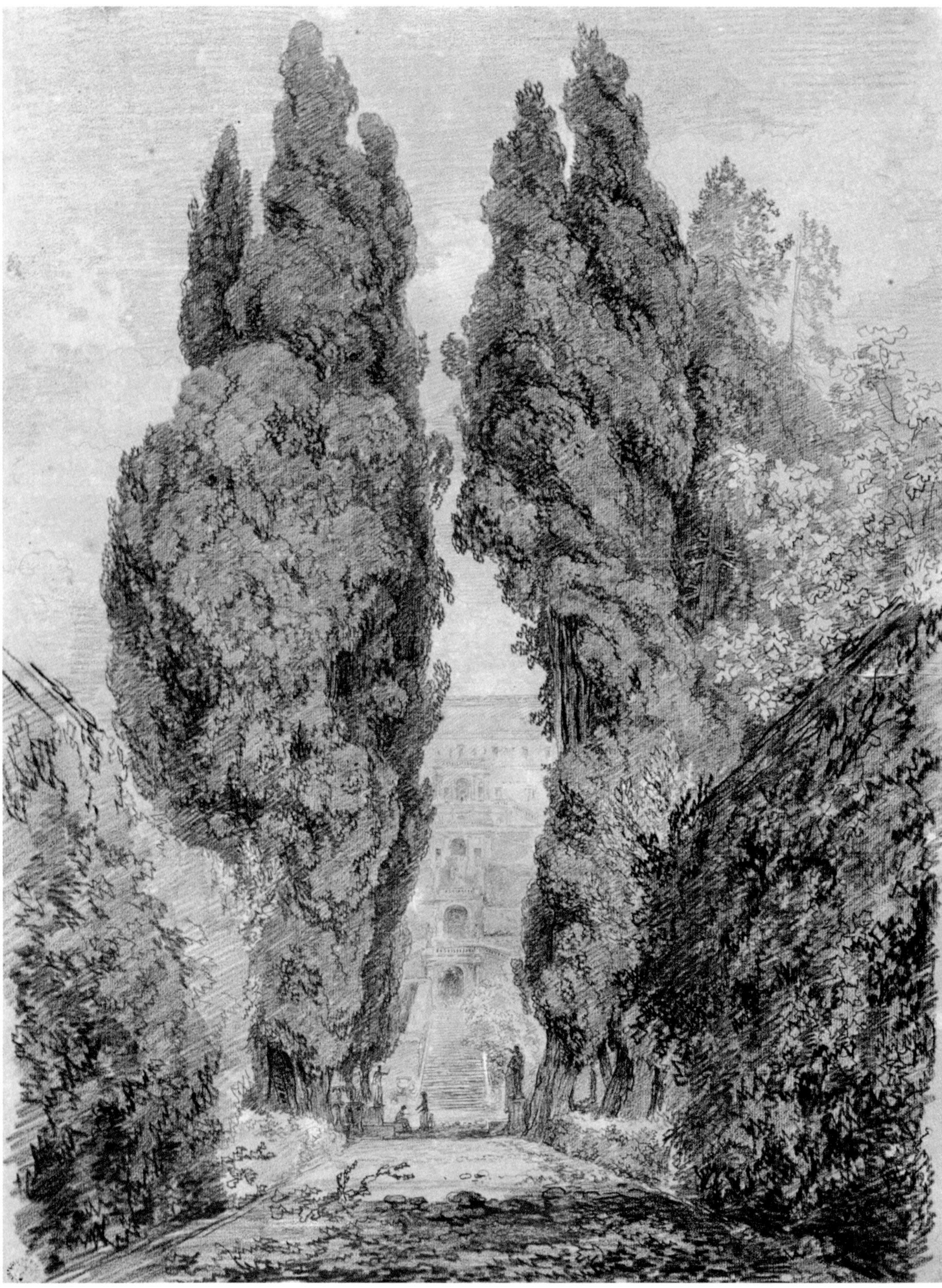

The Great Cypresses at the Villa d'Este,
1760, red chalk, 49.5 x 36.5 cm
Besançon, Musée des Beaux-Arts et d'Archéologie.

exact opposite: for the young Provençal the example could hardly have been more stimulating, and Robert played an undeniable part in enabling him, finally, to make the most of his stay in Rome.

Looking at the drawings by the two artists, we realize that there was a real process of emulation taking place. They visited the same places—sometimes together—and strove to outdo each other in their depiction of the picturesque: ruins overrun by rampant vegetation, abandoned palaces turned into stables and laundries, ramshackle huts leaning against ancient walls. Perhaps they went to the funeral together when Pope Benedict XIV died in May 1758. More certainly, they followed the building of the Trevi Fountain, completed in 1762 after more than thirty years' work. The Roman countryside and its many handsome villas provided endless material for their outdoor studies, and it is sometimes a challenge to identify the creator of a given work, the closeness of the two artists' styles reflecting the perfect understanding that united them. He who would later be known as "Robert of the ruins" revealed a marked taste for architecture, perspective, vault effects and the ancient remains he made the focus of his paintings and drawings. Fragonard seemed less interested in such matters, showing himself more receptive to the natural settings he celebrated in large red-chalk works, mostly executed at the small town of Tivoli, not far from Rome.

With its host of eye-catching locales, Tivoli offered inspiration to an endless stream of artists, and in the summer of 1760 Fragonard was able to spend several weeks there, thanks to the Abbé de Saint-Non (1727–91). Born into a family of artists, the priest had a certain gift for drawing and engraving and was also a scholar with a wide range of interests and connections on the art and intellectual scenes in Paris. His time in Rome was punctuated by two trips to Naples, the second with Hubert Robert.

The break in Tivoli gave Fragonard the chance to demonstrate his enormous skill with landscape. While his subjects are real places—the old theater of the Villa Adriana, the town's waterfalls, the gardens of the Villa d'Este—he confers on them a monumentality to be found in the work of no other artist. With resolute strokes of red chalk he builds volumes, highlights copses, shapes rocky outcrops and darkens areas to be left in shade. To convey a seething mass of windswept foliage, his touch becomes lighter and more supple, zigzagging freely in its evocation of the unchained energy of nature untamed by man. His buildings, time-worn and overshadowed by vegetation, merge discreetly with their setting, while his slightly *da sotto* points of view and his play on perspective accentuate the imposing majesty of the lofty cypresses.

It was at Tivoli that Fragonard won his artistic spurs, created his first masterpieces: Natoire would even request several of the resultant pictures, among

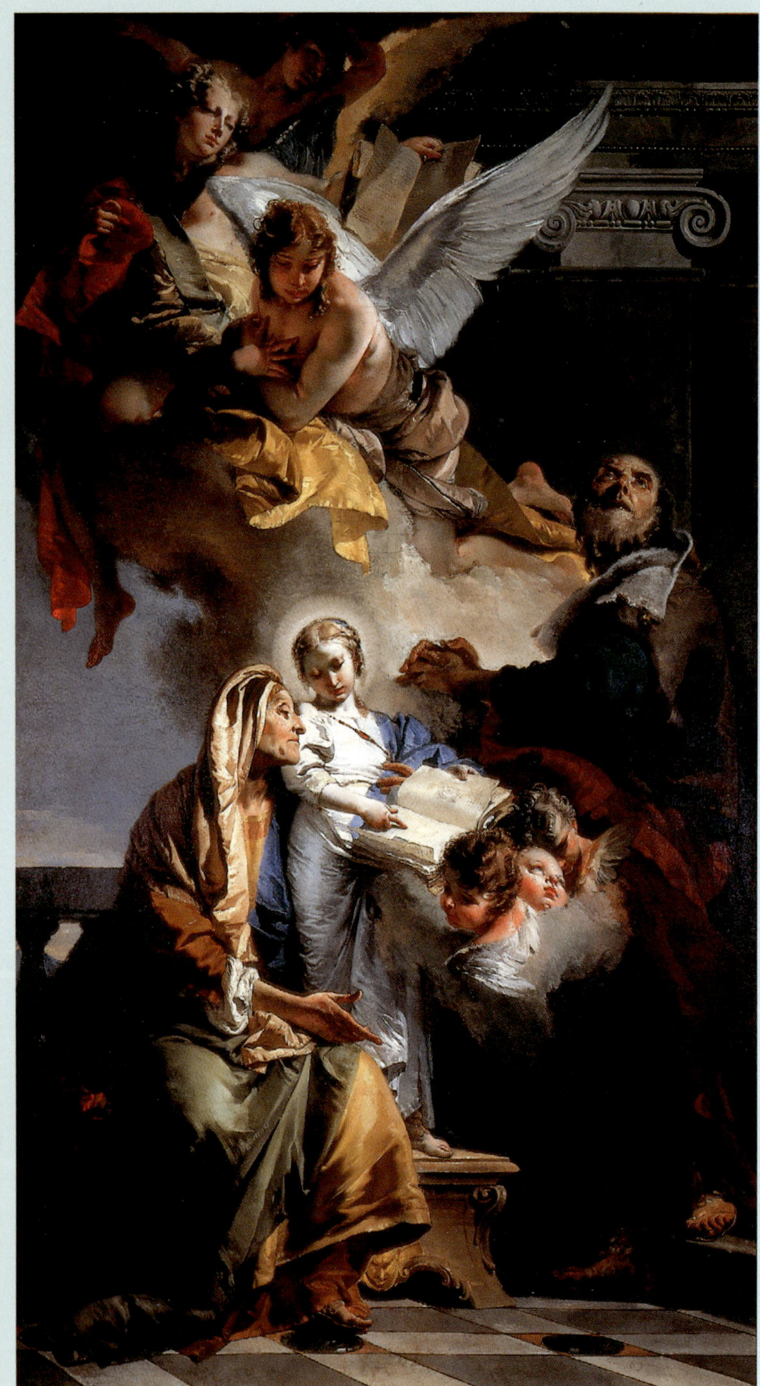

Giambattista Tiepolo,
The Education of the Virgin,
1730–32, oil on canvas, 362 x 200 cm
Venice, Santa Maria della Fava.

Following pages:
The Education of the Virgin, after Tiepolo,
1761, black chalk, 29.8 x 20 cm
Rouen, Musée des Beaux-Arts.

The Education of the Virgin,
c. 1775, oil on canvas, 92 x 73 cm
Amiens, Musée de Picardie.

them *The Grand Staircase in the Gardens of the Villa d'Este*, called l'Escalier de la Gerbe. Although the residents of the French Academy in Rome were supposed to paint solely for the king, the rules were often bent so as to allow young artists to make themselves known and build up an international clientele. It may have been through his friendship with Robert that Fragonard met Jacques-Laure Le Tonnelier, Bailli (bailiff) de Breteuil (1723–85), who came to Rome in June 1758 and officially took up his post as ambassador of the Order of Malta there the following year. The Bailli was quick to take an interest in Hubert Robert, encouraging him from the outset and providing him with accommodation when he had to leave the Palazzo Mancini.

It was for this great collector that Fragonard painted one of his first amatory scenes to cut free of Boucher's influence. *The Stolen Kiss*, shows a flaming-cheeked young man losing his hat in his haste to kiss his young neighbor. Feigning resistance, the girl is prevented by a companion holding her arms firmly down on a table. Amid all this jostling a deck of playing cards has fallen on the floor. There is nothing especially Roman about the scene, but the more assertive style and the boldness of the palette, with its chiaroscuro bringing a glow to the acid colors and heightening the white of the tablecloth and blouse, signal the acquisition of new skills. Gone are the blue-tinged pastorals and the stagy shepherds; Fragonard seems to have sloughed off an artificial language and shaped a new vocabulary of his own.

Finally, a trip to Naples—at the Abbé de Saint-Non's behest—and the young painter's stay in Rome was at an end. He left with his generous ecclesiastical patron in April 1761, but as they stopped over in every city and town where there was something worth seeing, it was more than five months before they were back in Paris. We can plot their itinerary using the daily entries in the Abbé's travel diary: after Siena and Florence came Bologna, Venice, Parma and Genoa, to name but a few of the breaks in their journey. Nor did Fragonard settle simply for inspecting the best-known paintings and decorative works—he took the time to draw them in detail.

Out of this grand tour of Italy came almost four hundred black chalk drawings in which Fragonard applied both eye and hand to the style of the masters. Capturing their spirit in a few skillful strokes, he built up an enormous repertoire of shapes, subjects and compositions which he would draw on unhesitatingly—sometimes many years after seeing the originals. One eloquent example is the handsome *Education of the Virgin*, painted in 1732 by Giambattista Tiepolo (1696-1770), which Fragonard drew in the church of Santa Maria della Fava in Venice, in the spring of 1761: the counterproof of his copy went on to become the source of a whole series of drawings and paintings on the same theme that he would make in the late 1770s.

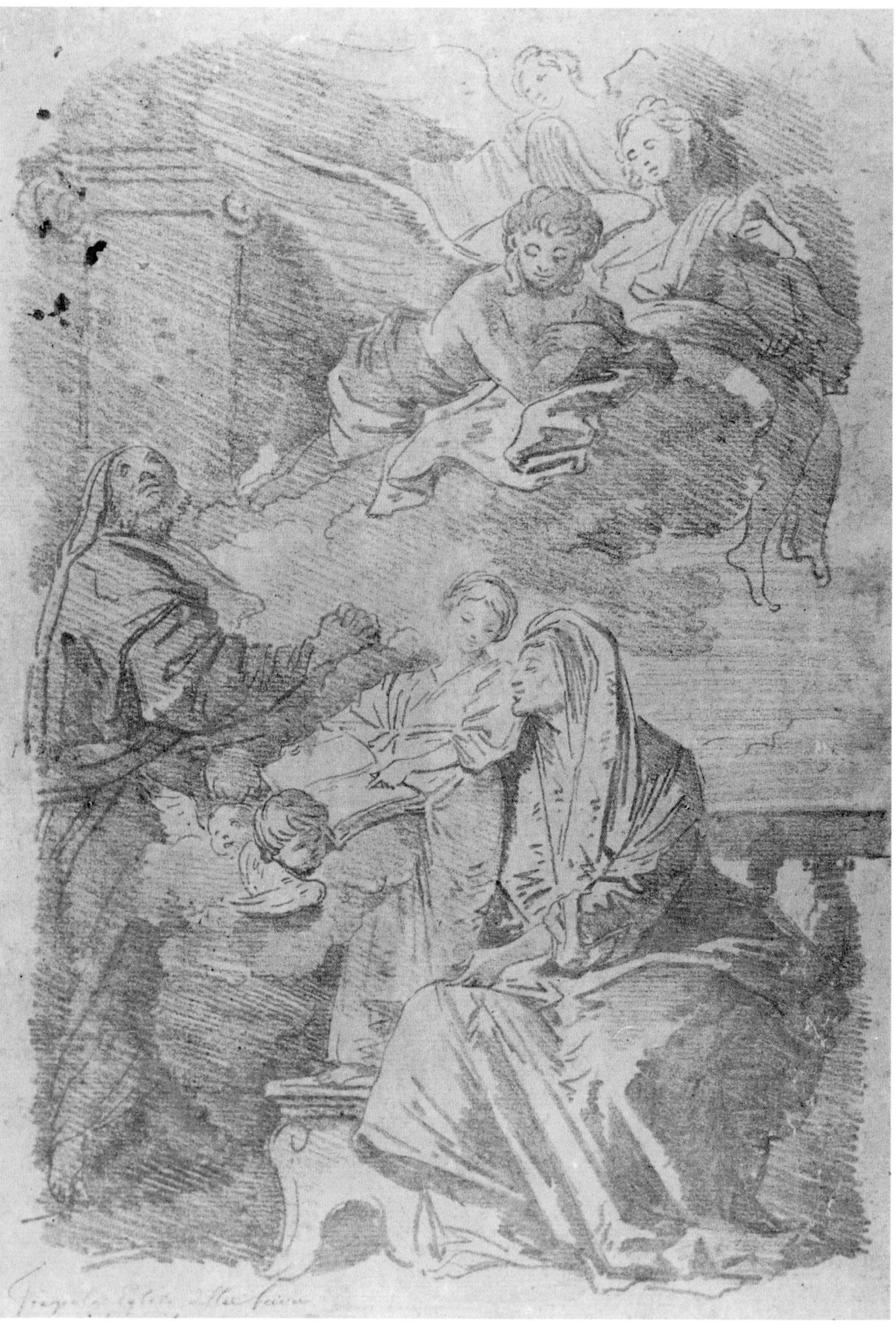

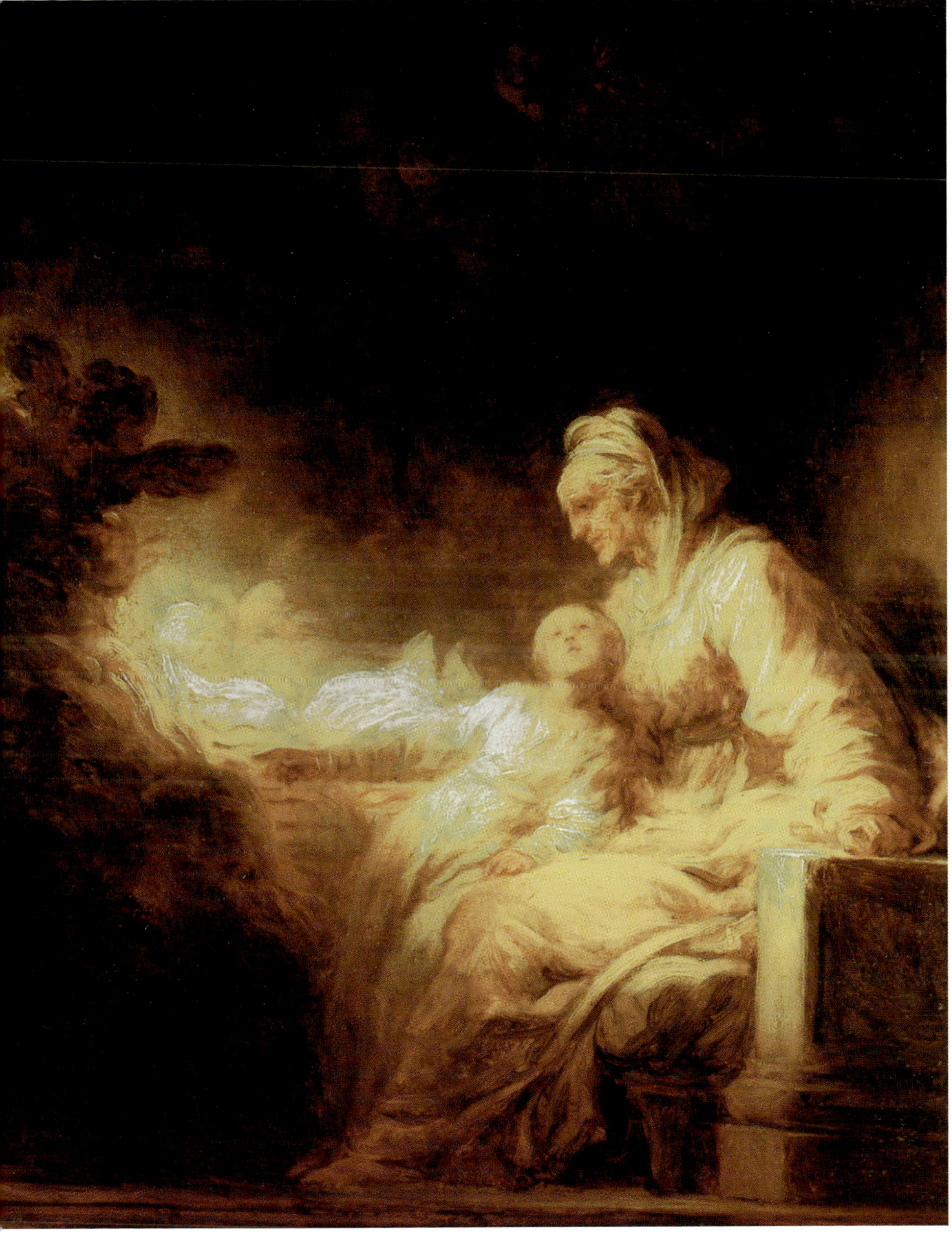

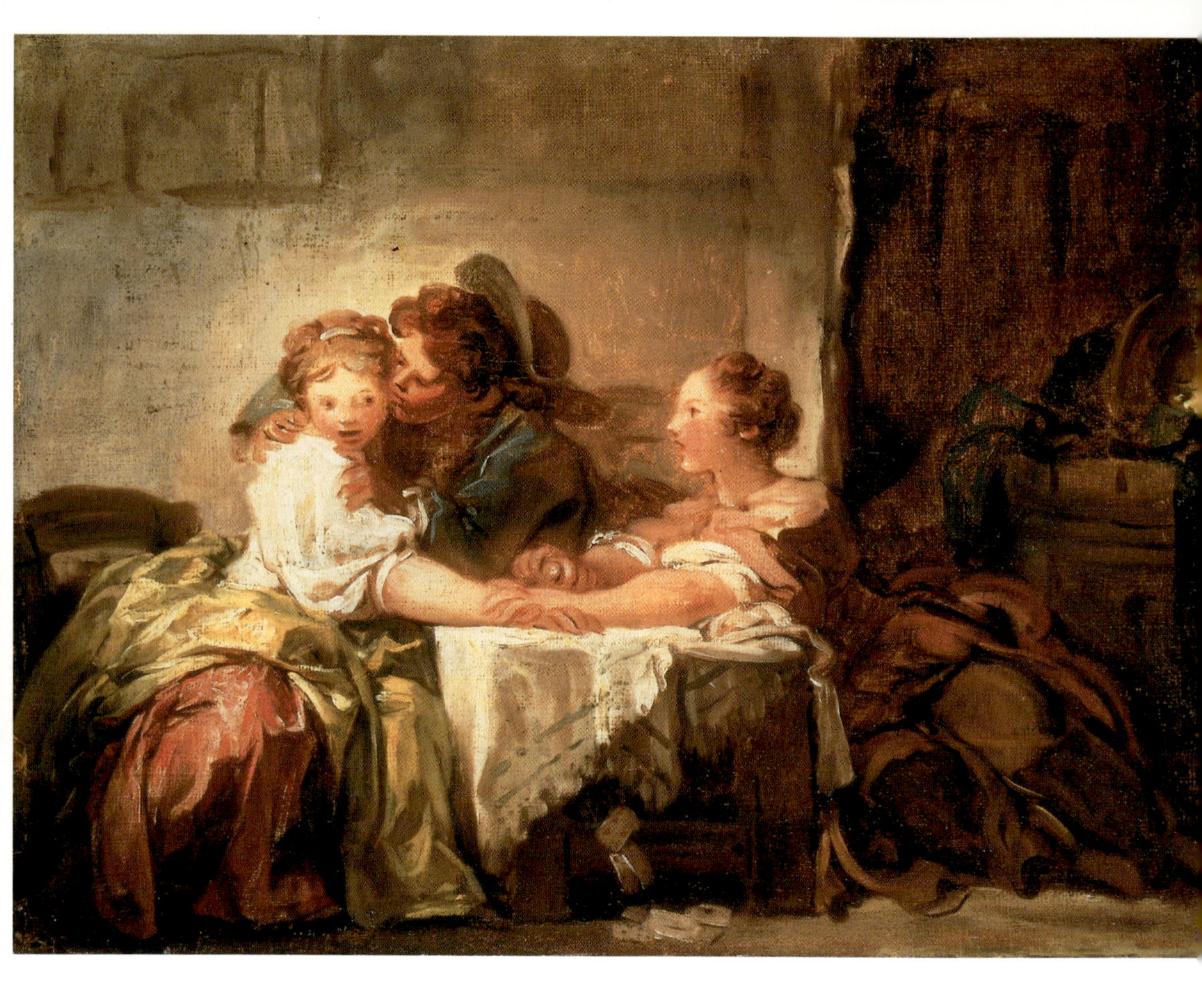

The Stolen Kiss,
c. 1759, oil on canvas, 47 x 60 cm
St Petersburg, Hermitage Museum.

The Stolen Kiss,
1759, oil on canvas, 48.3 x 63.5 cm
New York, The Metropolitan Museum of Art,
gift of Jessie Woolworth Donahue, 1956.

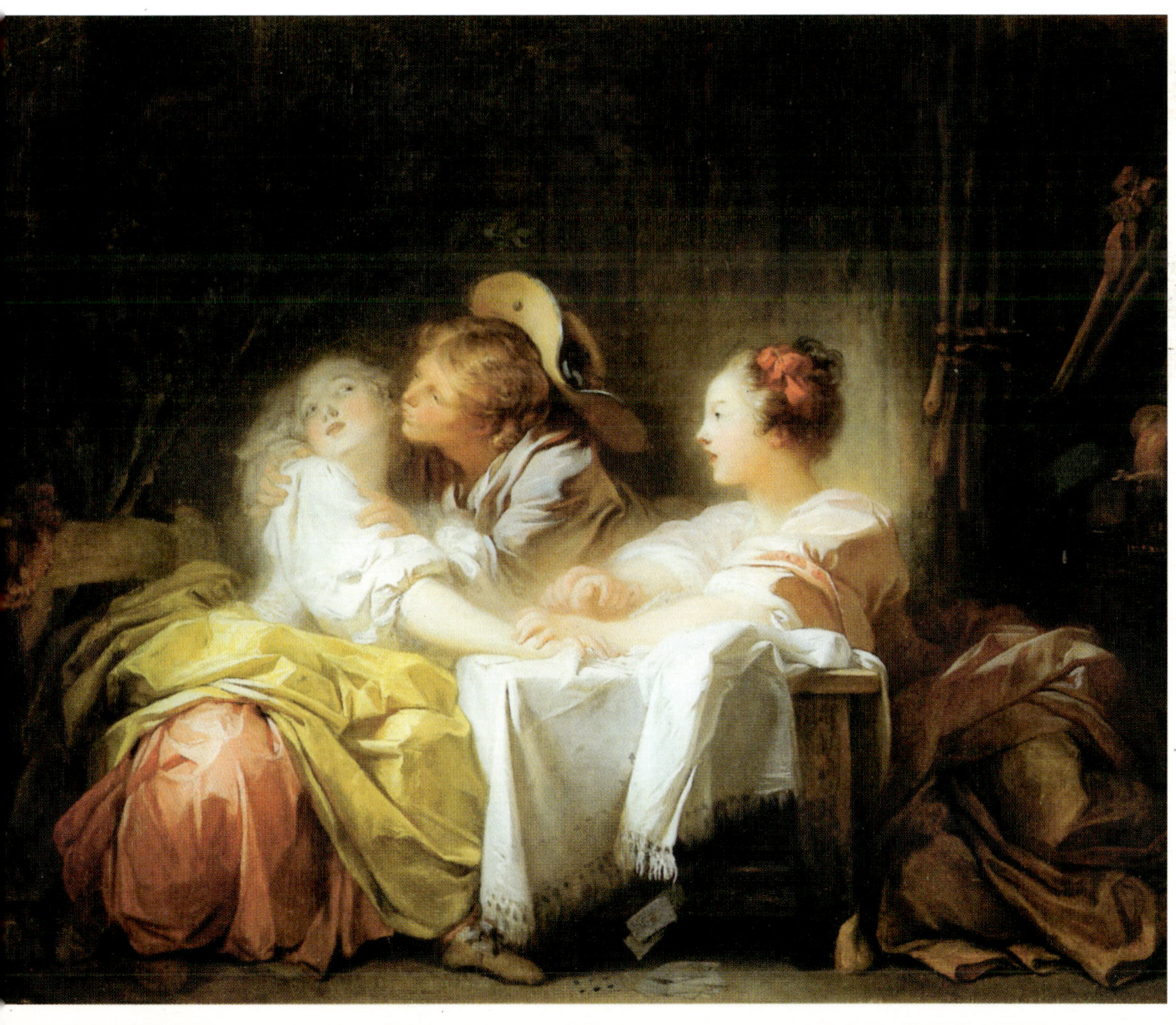

Second Stay (1773–74): No Sinecure

Twelve years after this initiatory voyage, the opportunity arose for a second trip. Another well-heeled patron, Pierre-Jacques-Onésyme Bergeret de Grancourt (1715–85), had the urge to see Italy and invited Fragonard to come with him. It was by no means uncommon at the time that travelers should be accompanied by an illustrator, whose combination of artistic discernment, historical knowledge, and experience would make for a more interesting, instructive journey. The illustrator's talents would also be used to create a visual record. A member of the body of farmers general, which managed the king's indirect taxation—duties on salt and tobacco, the *octroi* levied on goods entering cities, etc.—Bergeret was one of the wealthiest men of his time. Related by his first wife to the Abbé de Saint-Non, he was a collector of the work of Boucher and Hubert Robert and had known Fragonard for some time: among the latter's works in his possession was a scene of pink, chubby-cheeked *putti* gamboling joyously in the clouds.

The proposition was a tempting one. The timing seemed perfect, given the misunderstandings and disappointments that had plagued the artist in the preceding months. Two major commissions, for example, had fallen through: after a falling-out with the famous dancer Marie-Madeleine Guimard, Fragonard had left the decoration of her drawing-room unfinished; and there was the matter of four large canvases, commissioned by the Comtesse Du Barry and, as we shall see, purely and simply turned down. It seems likely, then, that the decision to set off with Bergeret reflected at least as much a desire to get free of legal proceedings and assorted annoyances as to see Italy again. Indeed, as the ship carrying Fragonard neared Genoa, the king's First Painter, Jean-Baptiste-Marie Pierre (1713–89), was summoning Jacques-Louis David in Paris. Then twenty-five, David was suspected of having usurped Fragonard's position as decorator of the Guimard drawing room, but Pierre seems to have been satisfied by his explanations: "David gives no impression of having anything to feel guilty about. On the contrary, he firmly believes he is helping Monsieur Fragonard by freeing him of a task his hypersensitive nature renders odious and alien to him." It would even appear that Fragonard, preferring to give up the project, had frankly encouraged David to succeed him.

Accompanying Bergeret meant Fragonard was leaving his capricious divas and financial squabbles behind, but other cares awaited him. Not the least of

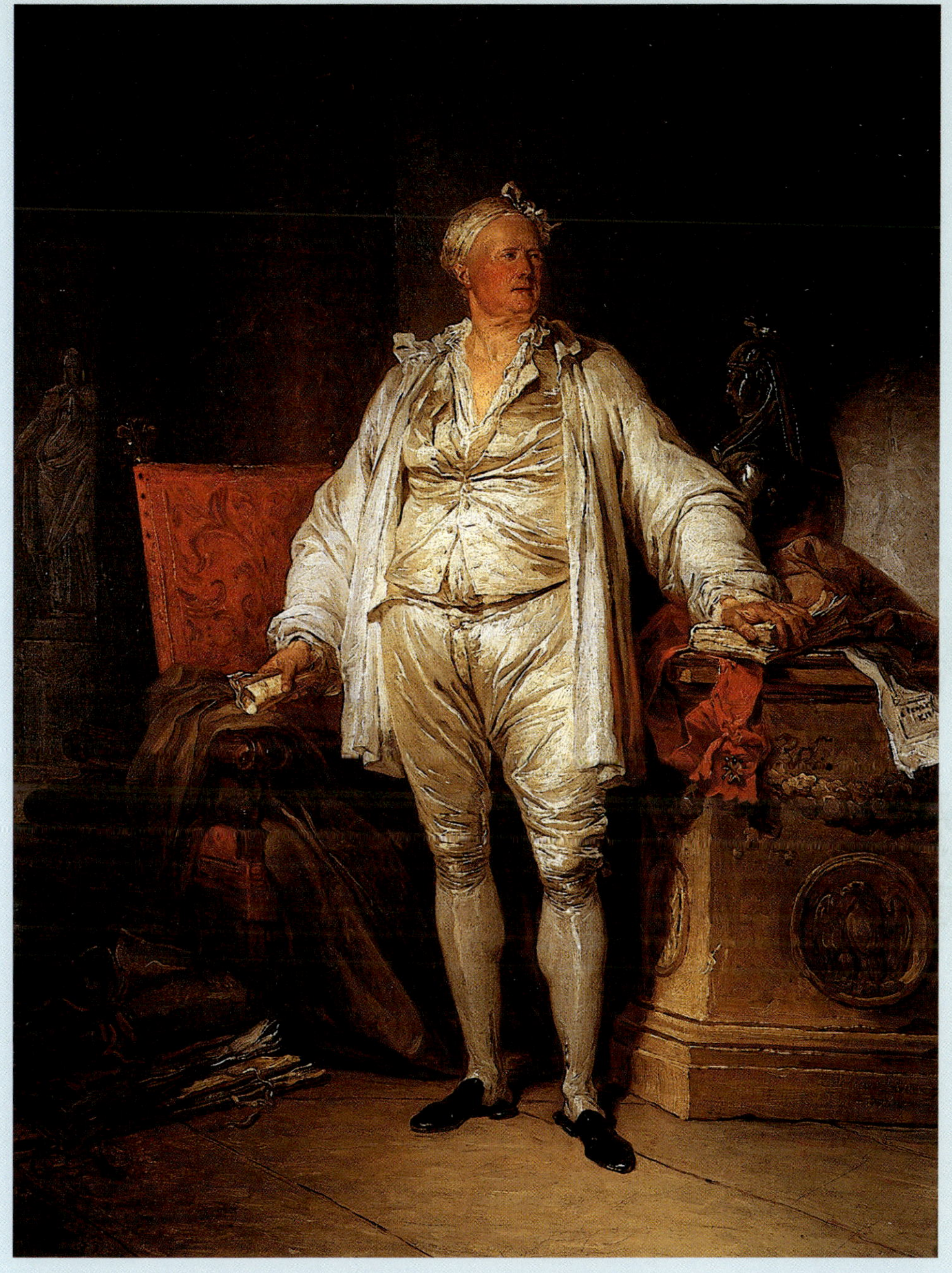

François André Vincent,
Portrait of Monsieur Bergeret,
1774, oil on canvas, 60 x 47.5 cm
Besançon, Musée des Beaux-Arts.

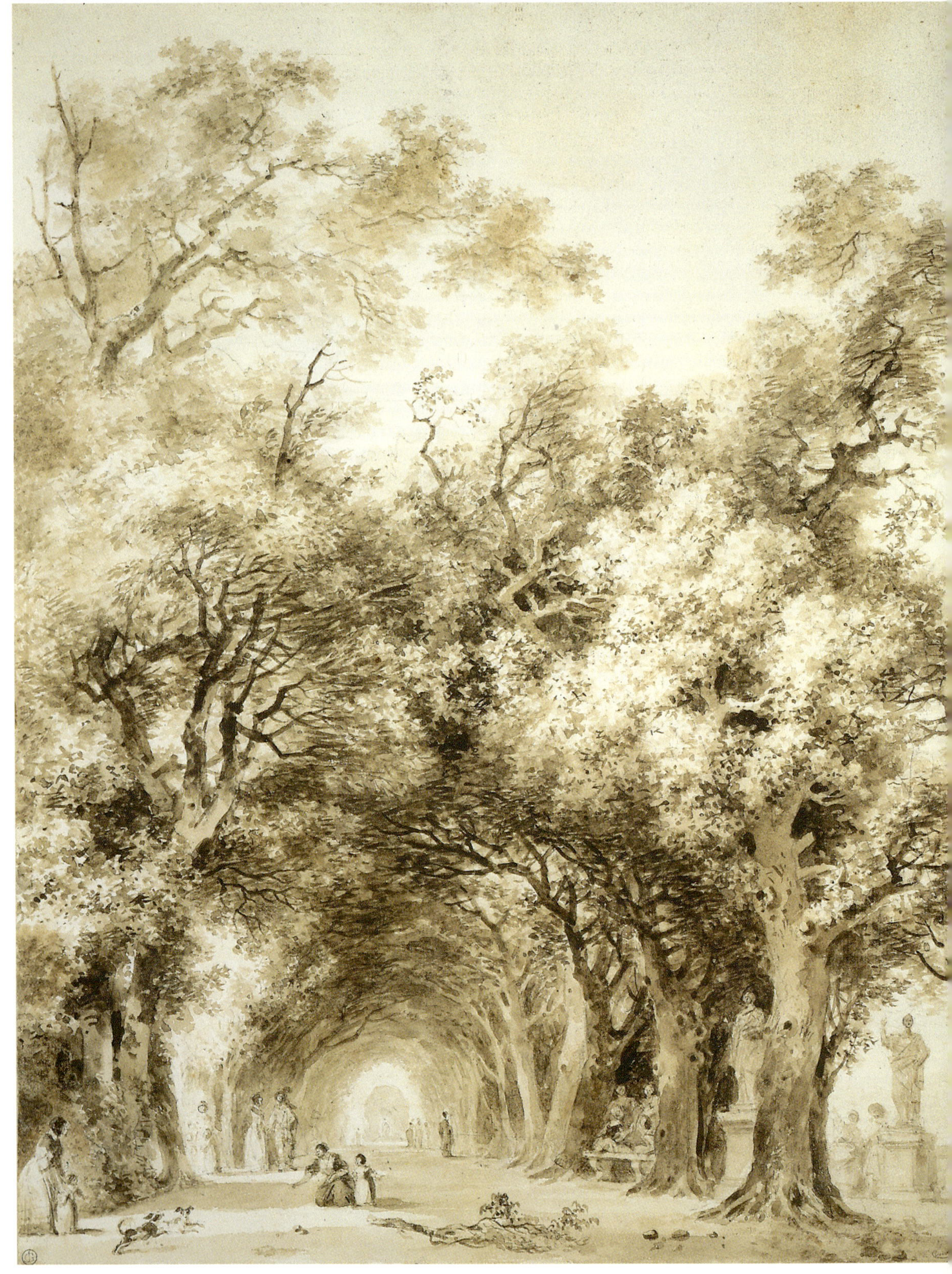

The Shaded Walk,
c. 1773–74, black chalk and wash,
45.7 x 34.7 cm
Paris, Musée du Petit Palais.

them was that in purely physical terms the planned trip was no sinecure: in barely a year the expedition would cover some four thousand miles by coach and one-horse cabriolet! In the former rode Fragonard, Bergeret, Jeanne Vignier—personal maid to the aristocrat's late spouse and later to become the third Madame Bergeret—and Fragonard's wife, with Bergeret's son Pierre-Jacques (1742-1807) and two coachmen bringing up the rear in the cabriolet. The group was rounded off by two servants.

With the exception of two weeks spent at Négrepelisse, Bergeret's fief near Montauban, in southern France, the first part of the trip was a forced march. The goal was to reach Rome as quickly as possible; they were there, Bergeret's scrupulously kept diary records, on 5 December 1773, and remained until early April 1774. Fragonard renewed his acquaintance with the Bailli de Breteuil and with Natoire, who was still in charge of the Academy. The Academy residents spotted a potential client in Bergeret and from time to time made him a gift of a drawing. The patron's drawing room saw an endless procession of the curious and of painters, sculptors, architects and even archeologists, all come to offer additions to his collection. Concerts, readings and drawing lessons helped pass the long winter nights. All this was very flattering for Bergeret, and made him feel a little like an artist himself: after all, had he not, in 1754, been elected an associate of the Academy of Painting and Sculpture in Paris? Thus the wealthy financier posed for François-André Vincent (1708–90) as the carelessly dressed "art lover", a scarf around his head and oriental slippers on his feet; an image rounded off by an Egyptian burial urn on an antique altar and portfolios of drawings lying on the floor around him.

But where was Fragonard all this time? To conduct him through Rome's churches and palaces, Bergeret seems to have preferred Pierre-Adrien Pâris (1745-1819), an Academy resident and, as the patron of the arts noted, "the best guide, knowing all the historical details... and thoroughly knowledgeable concerning all the antiquities and everything in Rome." Rather than play the lecturer for insatiable tourists, Fragonard most probably preferred delving into the city, alone or with his wife, and revisiting his favorite haunts. He must certainly have painted pictures during those four long months, but which ones? What we can identify are a number of handsome washes, dated 1774; naturally they include landscapes—or rather views inspired by the local villa gardens, notably at Tivoli, to which he made a point of returning. Here the geometrical rigor of the red chalk he used so much during his first visit has given way to the see-through interplay of different inks, but with no loss of the elegance and majesty of the earlier works. Stone pines, somber cypresses and tall firs rise in complex tiers through broad, deep vistas whose foregrounds are dotted with statues, sphinxes, fountains, and tiny, tipped-in figures.

The Dwarf Baiocco Conversing with a Young Woman,
1774, black chalk and wash, 36.6 x 28.6 cm
Frankfurt, Städelsches Kunstinstitut.

Other figures—occupying the entire sheet—point up something new in the subject matter explored during this visit. These are close-ups, people alone or with a companion in poses marked by a striking serenity. One of the finest examples from this period shows *Baiocco*, a dwarf nicknamed after the baiocchi ("pennies") he begged from customers leaving the Caffe Greco. A legendary popular figure, he was seized on as a curiosity by every artist passing through Rome, generally being shown full face so as to highlight his incongruous proportions and features only visible through his long hair and voluminous beard. Yet we sense a greater gentleness and humanity in Fragonard's side-on presentation: his subject is rendered less monstrous and his face less twisted and grimacing, and the woman who has sat on a stone bench to chat with him at his own level is looking at him in perfectly natural, simple way.

As soon as the weather became more clement, Bergeret and his little band took to the road again. The stay in Naples coincided with the death of Louis XV, yet their mourning did not exclude attendance at Niccolo Piccinni's *Olimpiade*, at the Teatro San Carlo, nor a visit to Herculaneum and Pompeii, where archeological digs had been under way since early in the century. One of the "attractions" at Pompeii was a skeleton found in the bathroom of a house and then thought to be that of a woman struck down by the eruption of Vesuvius. As Fragonard was not usually drawn to this kind of literalism, we must imagine that his version of the scene was made at Bergeret's request; a few years later the Abbé de Saint-Non would use it to illustrate his monumental *Voyage pittoresque à Naples et en Sicile* (1781–86). The engraving after Fragonard's drawing shows the skeleton lying on a heap of ashes, near a tub and a large basin, with, on the left, Bergeret and his female companion pulling back in horror from the macabre sight. The other visitors are present too: Bergeret's son, no doubt, Fragonard and his wife, and their guide, key in hand as he turns towards the group to measure the impact of a scene Bergeret did not fail to describe in his travel diary for 6 May 1774.

From there on in, things went much faster. Mid-July found our travelers in Venice, which was not really to Bergeret's taste: the charms of Italian life were lost on someone still missing Germany and the Northern countries he had visited not long before. It was now that he had the idea of a change of itinerary: instead of going directly home to France, they would return via Vienna, Prague, Frankfurt and Strasbourg. Quite a surprise for Fragonard, one imagines. For even if it meant the opportunity to see some splendid collections—the Rubens belonging to the Prince of Lichtenstein, and the Rembrandts in Dresden—his plans were in a mess. Surely, for example, the Fragonards were impatient to see their little daughter Rosalie again, after nine months separation; aged only four, she must have stayed in Paris, unless the

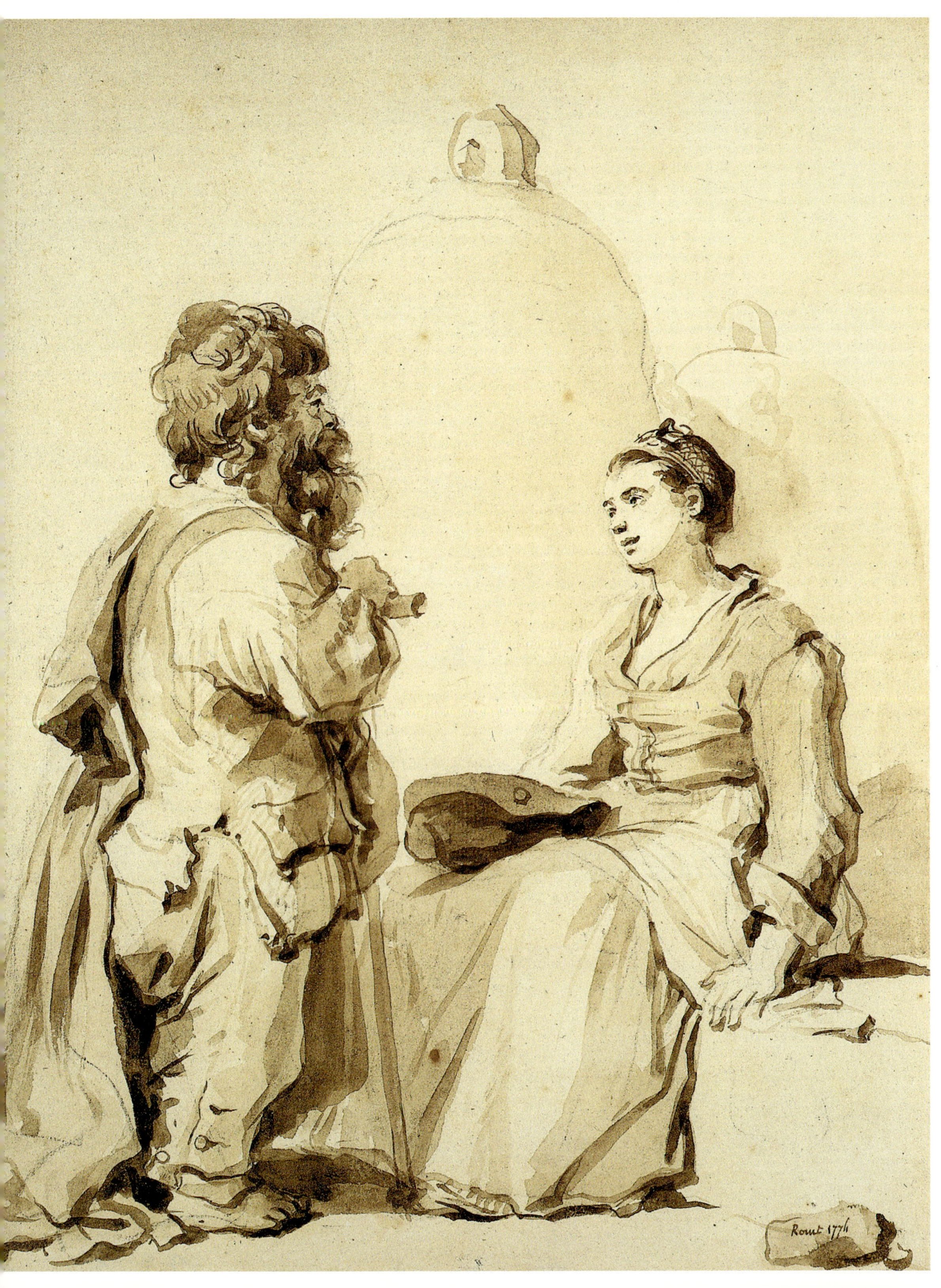
Rome 1774

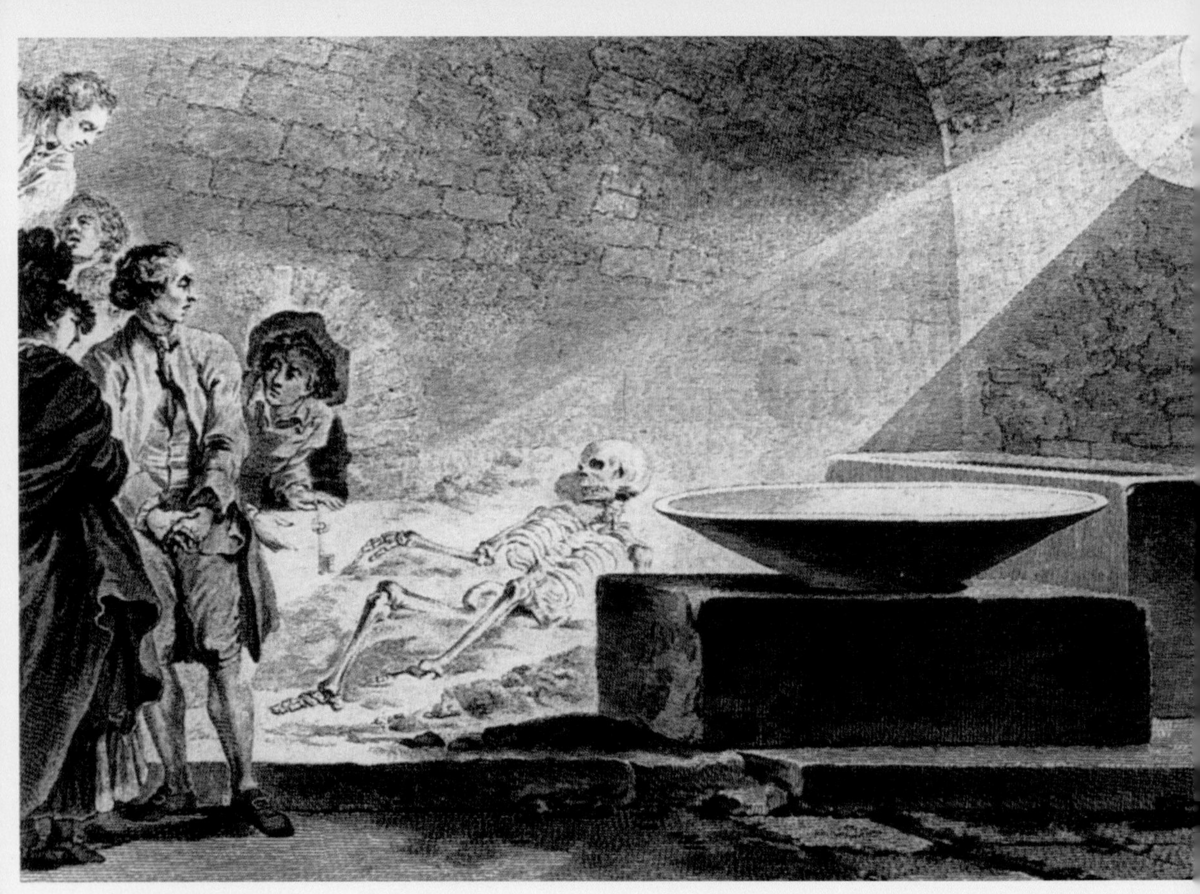

C. M. Fessard, after Fragonard
Discovery of a Skeleton in a House in Pompeii
Engraving illustrating Le Voyage pittoresque de l'abbé de Saint Non, I, *pl.* 89,
15.5 x 22.5 cm

Fragonards had sent her to relatives in Grasse, with the idea of picking her up there on the way back.

There may have been other reasons for the gradual deterioration of relations between the Fragonards and Bergeret. Bergeret's impatience—he wanted to see everything in a few minutes while at the same time harvesting as many drawings as he could from the painter and his miniaturist wife—must have been hard to put up with: the collector has left us a description of the two hard at work in the gallery in Dresden early one morning, drawing—and maybe painting—after the old masters. And after ten months of virtual cohabitation and endless hours shut up together in the coach, it is hardly surprising that tensions should begin to make themselves felt.

Things took a more dramatic turn with the return to Paris in September 1774 and a legal dispute over the travel drawings. The customary thing would have been for the artist to donate them to the sponsor of his trip; in this case Bergeret only got his pictures after a court ordered him to pay for them. Outraged by what he saw as rank ingratitude, Bergeret erased the kindly remarks that opened his travel diary and denounced the artist's "baseness" and "cowardice": as a Cicerone, he said, Fragonard had fallen well short of expectations and his erudition, "even without criticizing it to the full, was of little help to an art lover, being buried in a mass of imaginings." Disillusioned with the companion he had chosen, Bergeret went on to berate his lack of confidence and frankness. Are we to see only anger and spite in the severity of this judgment, or is there a grain of truth in it as well?

Different as they may have been in terms of length, purpose and unfolding, the two stays in Italy remain for the historian the twin pillars of Fragonard's career. Paradoxically, and in spite of the meagerness of the available data, these are—except for his last, sterile fifteen years—the two best-documented periods of his entire existence: we know where he was, we can follow his movements, and we can identify the circles he moved in, none of which information can be pinned down with any certainty for the other parts of his life. And while we have little precise information on his output during these stays, we can use his rare dated pictures and preferred subjects to divide the whole into stylistically consistent groups. The rest of his work is thus to be situated before or after the first or the second trip to Italy.

Fragonard's voyages are more, however, than just handy landmarks for the chronicling of an oeuvre. Each emerges as a crux in his artistic development and the trigger for a process of self-interrogation. That the first trip was a formative experience is clear, but the same can be said of the second. At forty as at twenty-five, doubt, self-questioning, discovery and revelation are the daily lot of anyone opting to break with a sedentary existence; here they are also the mark of an artist who never stopped learning and evolving.

III
Passing

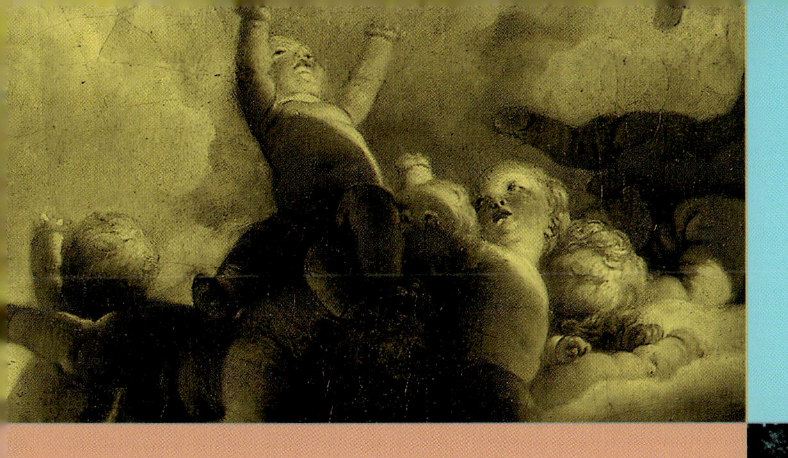

History By

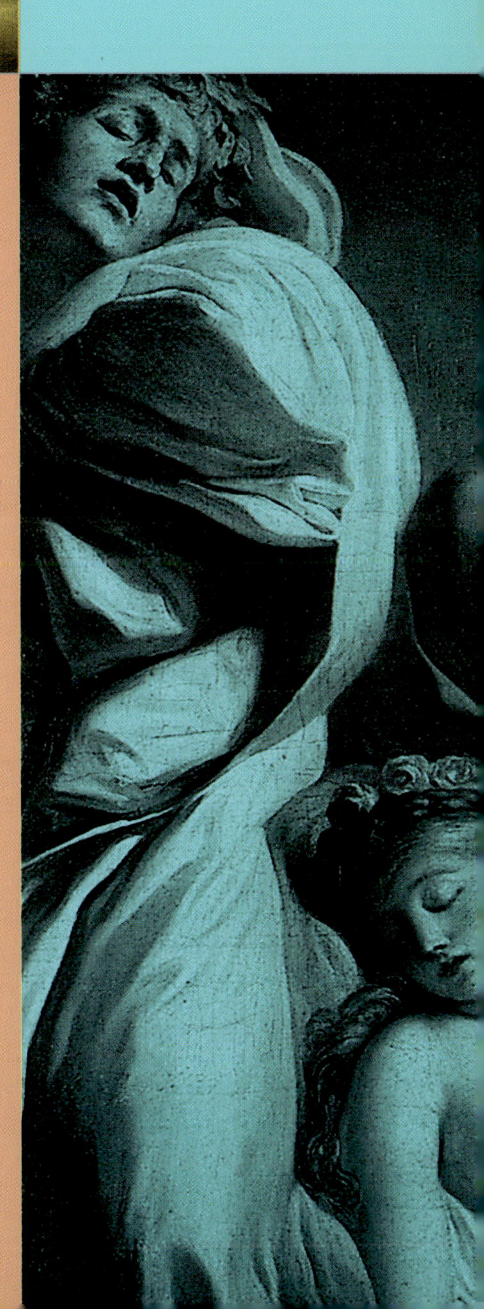

Fall 1761 marked the end of that first stay in Italy: Fragonard was back in Paris on 26 September—in the evening, as the Abbé de Saint-Non meticulously noted in his travel diary. After five years away, the artist found a country economically weakened by the conflict which, since 1756 had set France, as Austria's ally, against England and Prussia. The Seven Years' War would drag on for another two years, until, finally, the Treaty of Paris ratified England's victory and France's defeat. In Paris Greuze had the art world at his feet with *The Village Bride,* presented to the public a few days before the Salon closed. Fragonard would certainly have had time to see the exhibition, where his masters were on prominent display: Chardin, also in charge of the hanging of the works; Carle Van Loo, soon to be appointed the king's First Painter; and Boucher, the new rector of the Academy.

The Salon of 1761

For the artists of the time, venerability of age and reputation were no bulwark against the strictures of the critics, one of whom stood out in particular: the philosopher Denis Diderot (1713–84). Diderot's commentaries had begun with the previous Salon, in the form of detailed reviews in *Correspondance littéraire*, a monthly that kept German royalty up to date on the French literary and artistic scene. His irony spared no one, starting with Chardin, whose still lifes had yet to win his approval: "It's a long time since this painter actually finished anything. He can't be bothered making a real effort anymore. He works like a man of the world who has talent and fluency, but is happy just to rough out his idea with a few strokes of the brush." Diderot could not even find a kind word for a handful of pastorals and landscapes by an ageing, ailing Boucher: "This man offers everything, except the truth." Carle Van Loo, showing *Threatening Love* and *First Offering to Love*—both subjects Fragonard would later undertake—was similarly dismissed: "He lacks genius."

By contrast, one work on show captivated Diderot and the critics as one man: *The Village Bride*, commissioned from Jean-Baptiste Greuze by the Marquis de Marigny, Superintendent of the Royal Buildings. Typical of its creator's sentimental moralizing, the work is a hymn to family life: it shows an old man handing money in a purse—his daughter's dowry—to a young suitor as a token of his approval of their union. The entire family is present, along with the notary come to certify the transaction, and each individual is offering a display of emotion appropriate to his or her age and status.

A fan of the "grand genre", Diderot especially admired the way Greuze had elevated a simple, everyday scene of country life to the heights of history painting. In his view the combination of a noble, edifying subject and the distinctive expression achieved for each protagonist made the canvas worthy of the

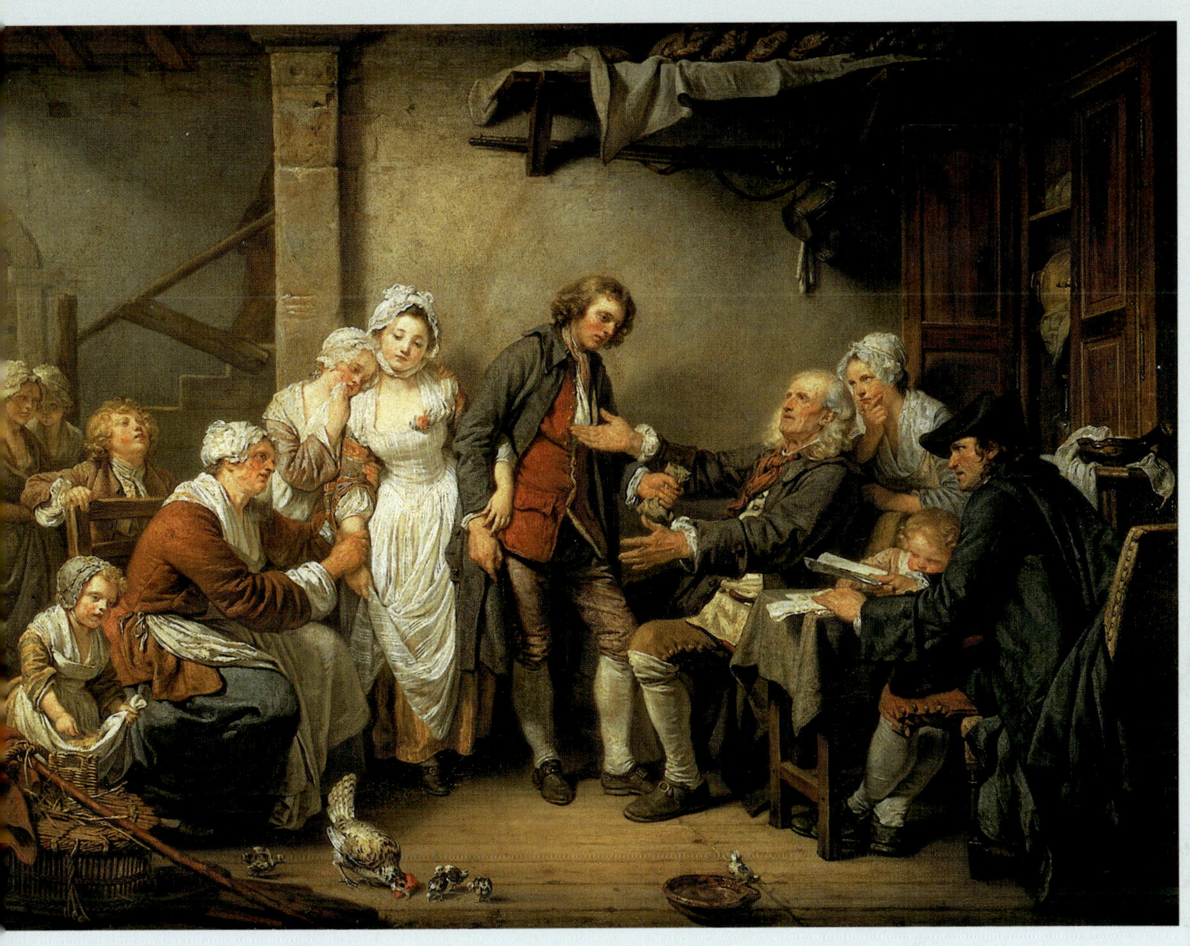

Jean-Baptiste Greuze,
The Village Bride,
1761, oil on canvas, 92 x 117 cm
Paris, Musée du Louvre.

company of the 17th-century masterpieces of history painting produced by Charles Le Brun and Nicolas Poussin: "This is unquestionably Greuze's best work so far. This picture will bring him recognition both as a skilled painter and a man of spirit and taste. His composition is shot through with delicacy of feeling and his choice of characters bears the mark of sensitivity and true moral fiber."

Thus Fragonard had barely had time to unpack when he was thrust into the hurly-burly of the Paris art scene. All this excitement and spirited debate were in total contrast with the five months he had just spent with the Abbé de Saint-Non, crisscrossing Italy as he captured on paper the endless succession of great works offered by its churches, princely palaces, and galleries, with no other concern than his own instruction and pleasure. The return to France was the beginning of a new era: he would have to present his work at the Academy if he were to be approved, then admitted, and he too would have to run the critical gauntlet. It would be simplistic to explain subsequent events and the evolution of his career solely in terms of the 1761 Salon, the reviews he got and the effect this may have had on him; yet these questions do throw light on the shifts within a career that seemed predestined to follow the academic tradition.

Approval from the Academy

Fragonard showed no great eagerness to sign up with the artistic elite of his time: it was three and a half years before he was ready to present his *Coresus Sacrifices Himself to Save Callirhoë*, but the work gained him the unanimous approval of the Academy on 30 March 1765. Taken from geographer-historian Pausanias's *Description of Greece* of 174 BC, the story is a little-known one: it inspired the composer Destouches and the librettist Roy for an opera that premiered in 1712 and played a number of times during the 18th century, but no artist before Fragonard had used the subject. The locale is the city of Calydon, dedicated to Bacchus. Wounded by the indifference of the beauteous Callirhoë, Coresus, the high priest of the temple, demands vengeance from Bacchus, who makes all the people of the city drunk. To quell the god's wrath, the oracle designates Callirhoë as a propitiatory victim, but, called upon to sacrifice her, Coresus chooses to stab himself instead. This is the moment Fragonard portrays.

The picture is unique in his oeuvre, and in several respects: firstly as the biggest picture Fragonard ever painted, and then as the only time he opted for such a dramatic subject, for so many characters, and for such a deliberately imposing architectural setting. Here we see the painter in a new light: ambitious and out to surprise and impress, but at the same time keen to please and to demonstrate the full scope of his talent in the masterful compositional balance, the dynamic of the poses, the chiaroscuro, the contrasts in the lighting, and the subtle shading of the light tones so beautifully set off by the dark red of the carpet. The jury must also have been struck by the range of emotions—surprise, stupefaction, awe, consternation—reflected in the faces of the many characters present. After all, since the famous lecture given in 1668 by Charles Le Brun—founder-member and director of the Academy—skill in the depiction of passionate feeling had become a necessary virtue of history painting. Uncritical application of the rule sometimes led to irritating exaggeration and distortion, but Fragonard's *Coresus*—the sole work in which he bowed to academic dogma—avoids this trap: a master of the allusive, he subtly settles for hints where others might have opted for heavy-handed grandiloquence.

Coresus and Callirhoë was shown to unanimous critical enthusiasm at the 1765 Salon, with Diderot, in a long article, describing the work as if recounting something seen at the theater. While alert to its faults—the overly effeminate appearance of the priest Coresus, a Callirhoë who seems more asleep than in a dead faint—he had no hesitation in acknowledging that Fragonard had already attained "all the magic, all the intelligence and all the pictorial sweep. The ideal is sublimely achieved by an artist whose precision of color and perfection of technique only time and experience can enrich... This is indeed a beautiful object, and I do not believe there is another painter in Europe capable of such imagination."

At this time Charles-Nicolas Cochin, an engraver and the Academy's secretary, seemed to want to take Fragonard under his wing, having detected in him "a modesty verging on an exaggerated self-wariness. This is why I feel he more than anyone needs the encouragement he so thoroughly deserves." And so *Coresus* was acquired for the royal collection and immediately sent to the Gobelins manufactory so a tapestry version could be made. Simultaneously a second canvas was commissioned as a pendant to the first, with Cochin insisting to Marigny that an advance should be paid—and promptly. There came, too, a further sign of the esteem in which Fragonard was held, and of the official hopes for him: he was granted accommodation at the Louvre.

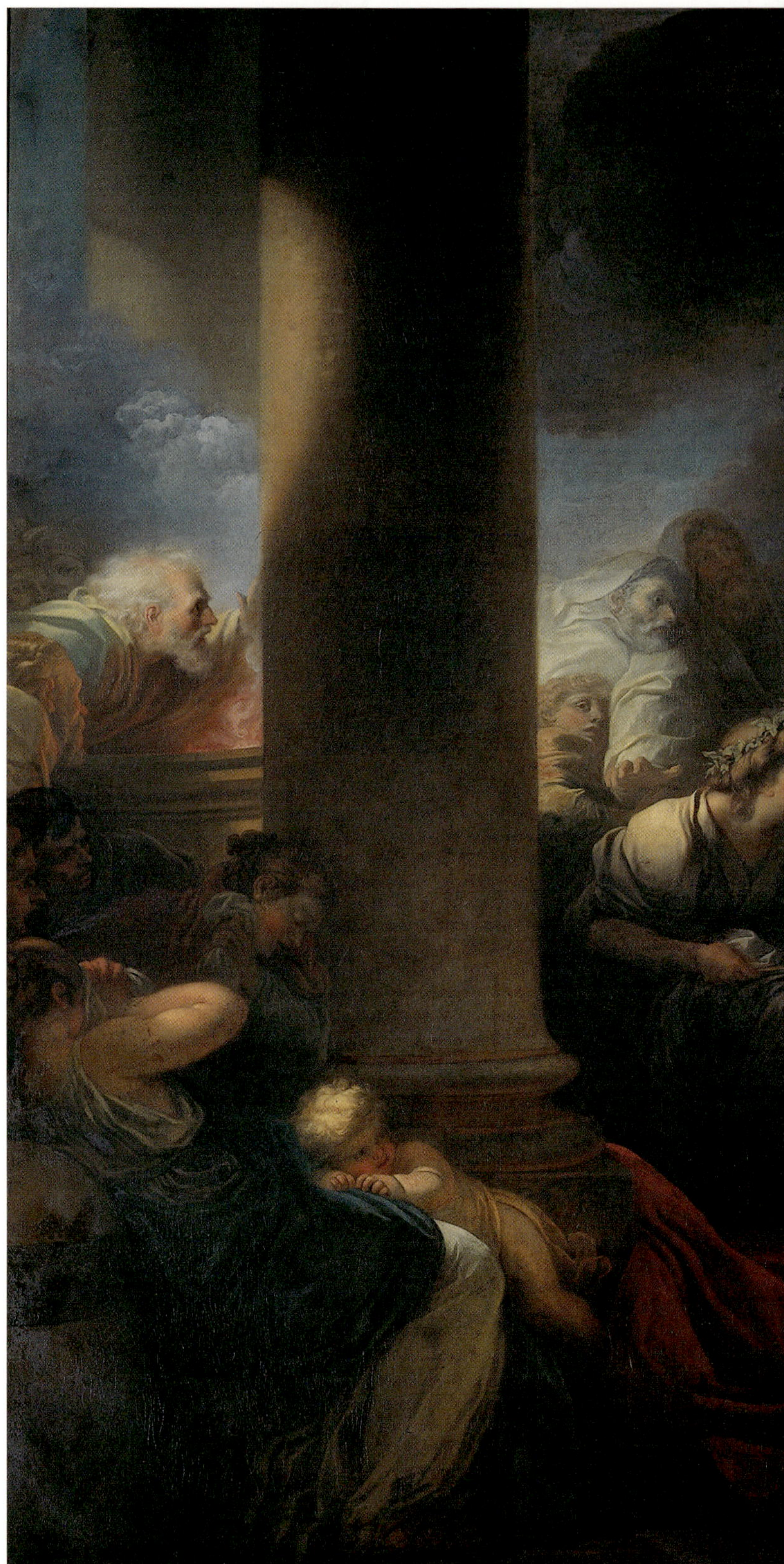

Coresus Sacrifices Himself to Save Callirhoë,
1765, oil on canvas, 311 x 400 cm
Paris, Musée du Louvre.

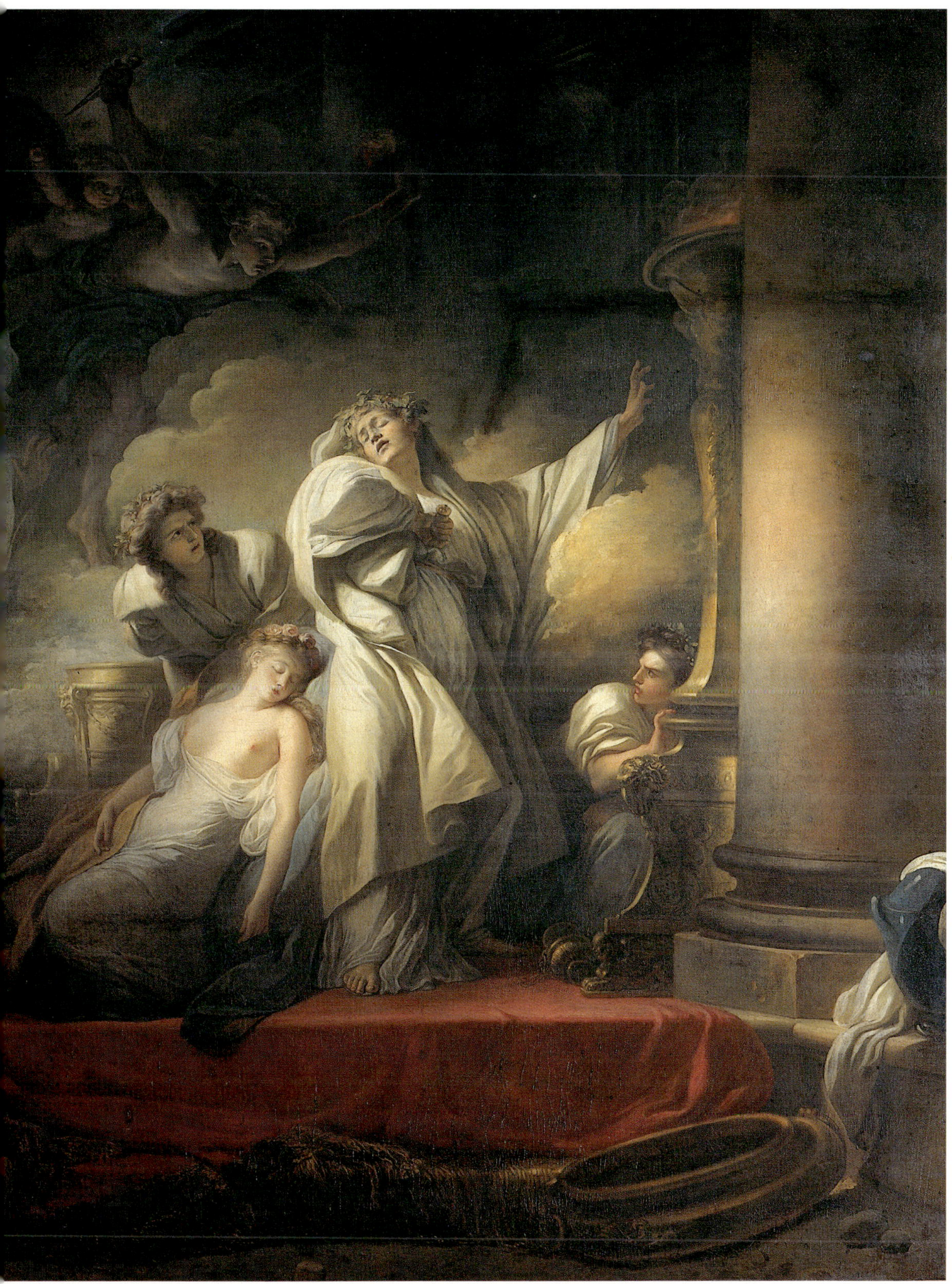

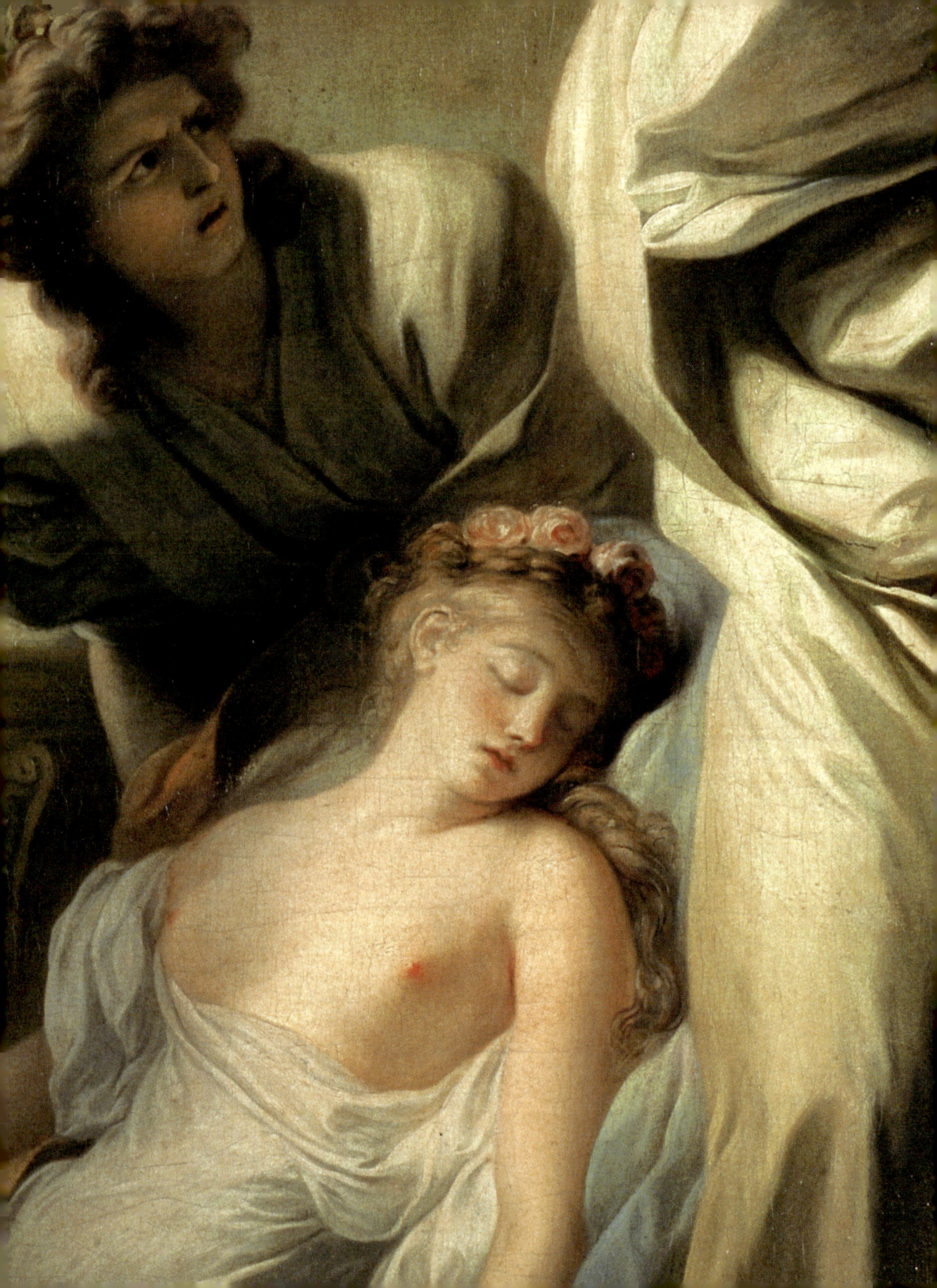

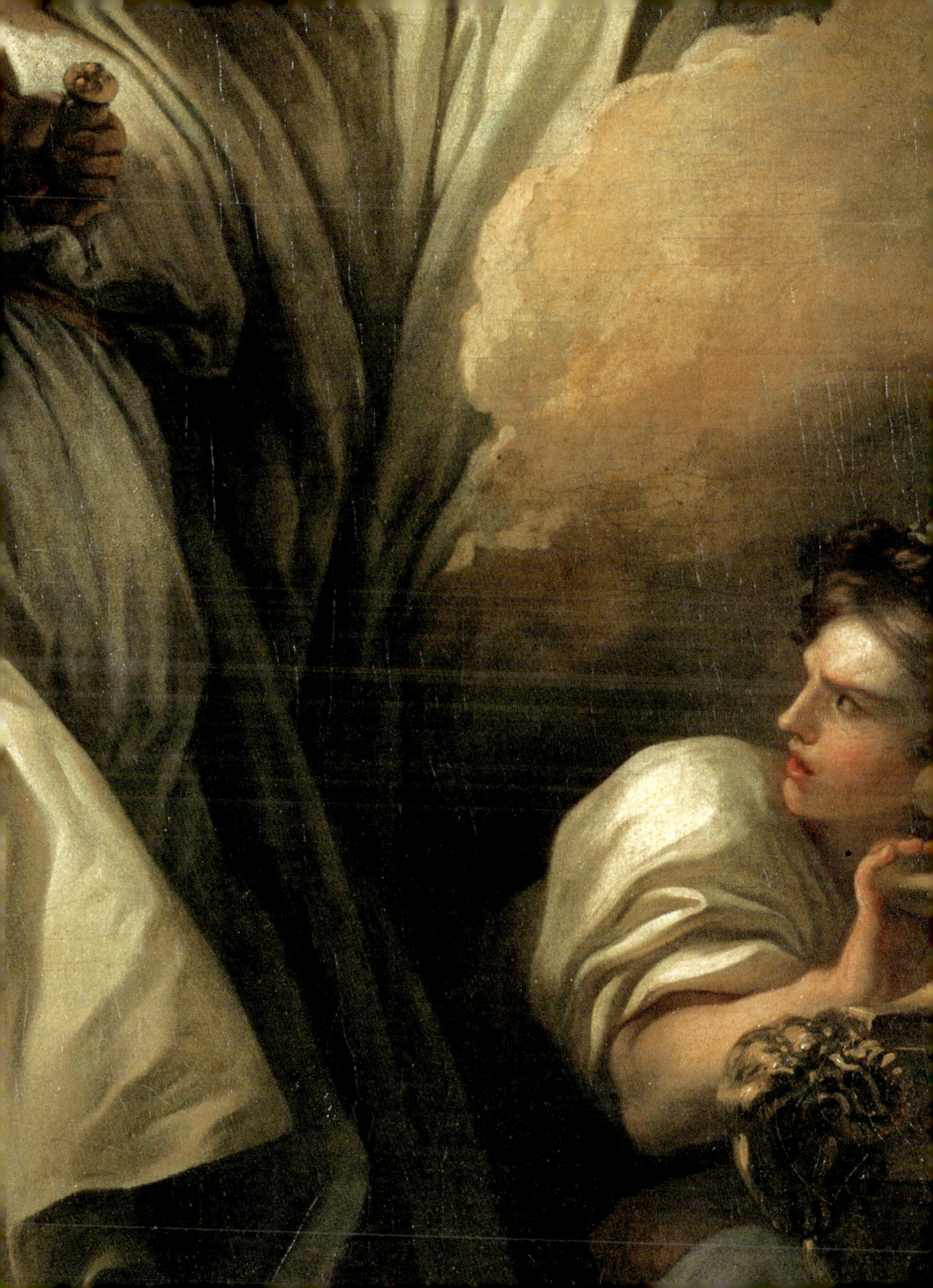

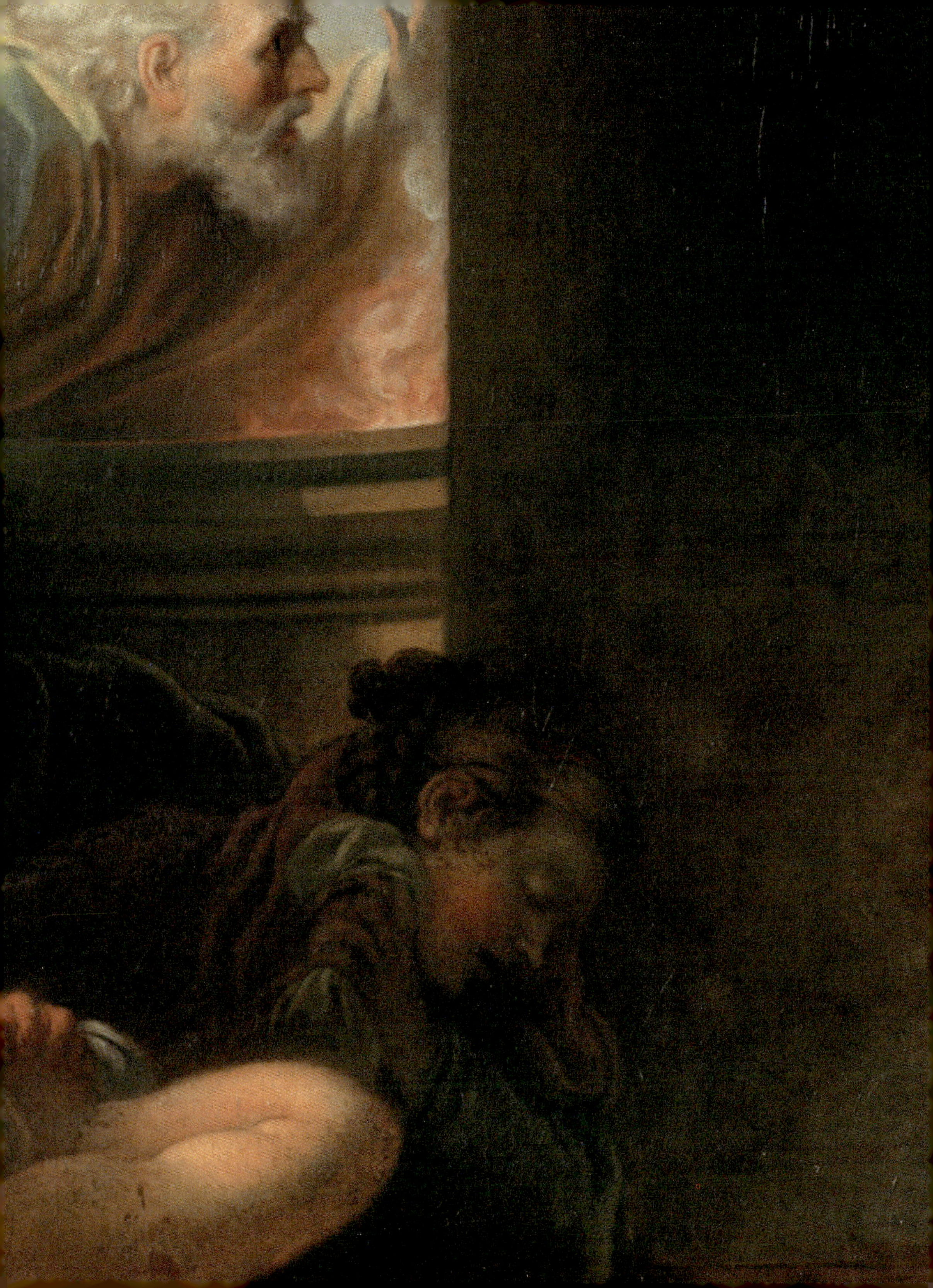

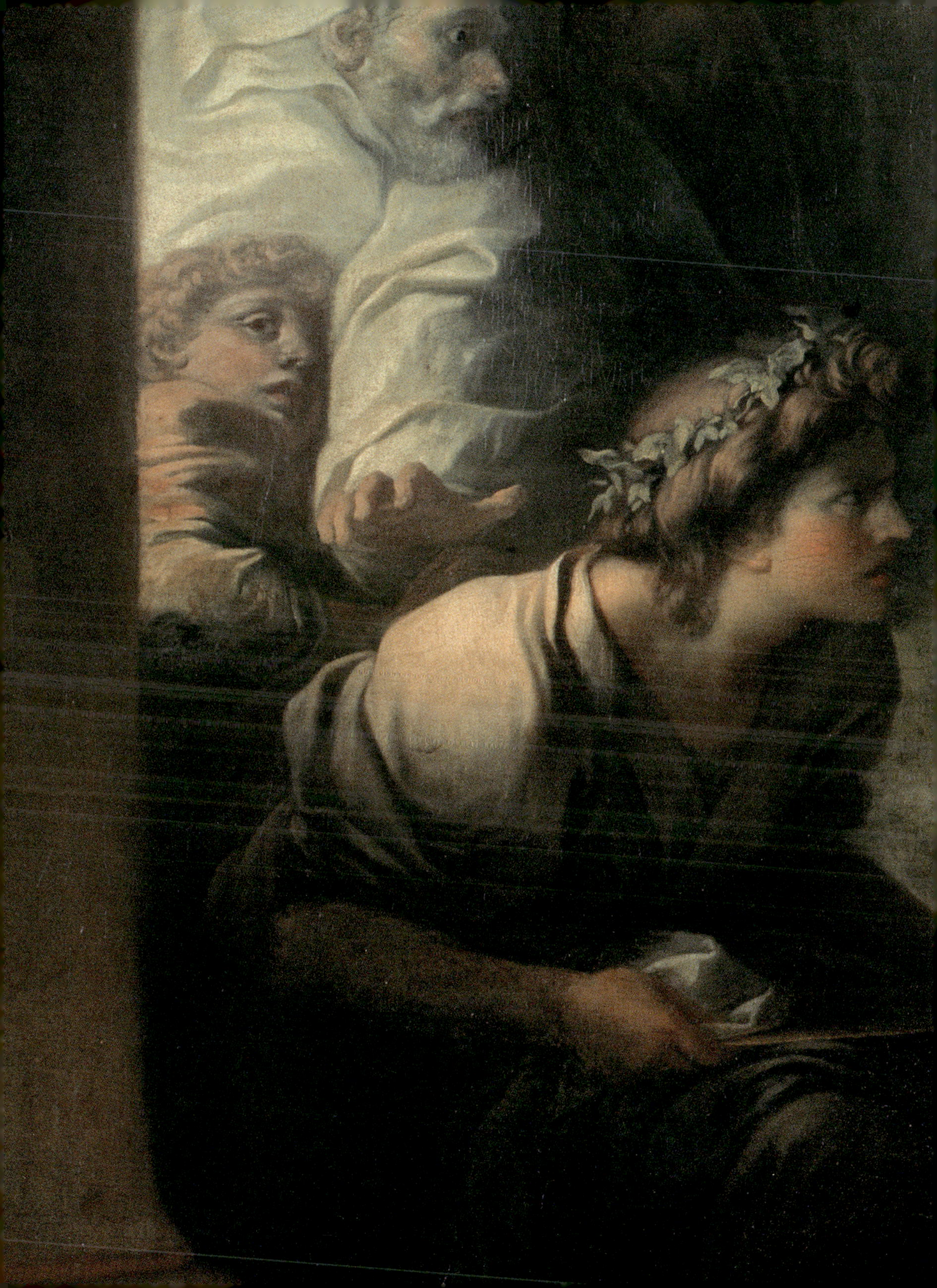

Fragonard at the Salon of 1767: the Art of Disappointing

These hopes, however, were not to be borne out at the Salon of 1767, where Fragonard showed only two paintings and a handful of drawings. "*Quantum mutatus ab illo*!" exclaimed Diderot, quoting Virgil. "How different from what he once was!" For the critic the *Swarm of Cherubs, a Group of Children in the Sky*, which then belonged to Bergeret, was a "big, beautiful omelet... without vigor, color, depth, or changes of plane... It's flat, yellowish, the same monotonous color all over and soggily painted... Mr Fragonard, this is damnably dull. A handsome omelet, succulent, yellow, and not the least bit burnt." The critic's disappointment was such that he returned several times to the "angel fricassee" in which he saw only "an aping of Boucher." The cruelest cut of all—its injustice must have deeply wounded Fragonard if it came to his ears—had to do with his training as an artist: "He has not looked enough at the great masters of the Italian school; he has brought back from Rome the Boucher-style taste, negligence and manner he went there with. A bad sign, my friend." His *Head of an Old Man* was no more kindly received: "Mr Fragonard, when one has made oneself a reputation, a little more self-respect is in order. When, after a stunning composition [*Coresus and Callirhoë*] that generated a most powerful emotion, one presents nothing but a head, I ask you—you personally—what your intention was."

While less harsh than Diderot, the other critics also expressed their disappointment. In the wake of the monumental *Coresus* they had every right to expect more than *putti* in the sky and an old man's head, however beautifully done. After the death of Carle Van Loo a few weeks before the Salon of 1765—he was not to witness the triumph of his best pupil—many had hoped to see Fragonard step into the master's shoes. But it was not to be. Despite Cochin's endless stream of encouragement, Fragonard seemed to have lost his fervor, at least for the public scene. Neither the pendant to *Coresus*—doomed to remain a mere sketch—nor the "reception piece" he owed the Academy ever saw the light of day. The same was true of two overdoors for the Château de Bellevue, and two other paintings commissioned for the dining room of the "petits appartements" at the palace at Versailles.

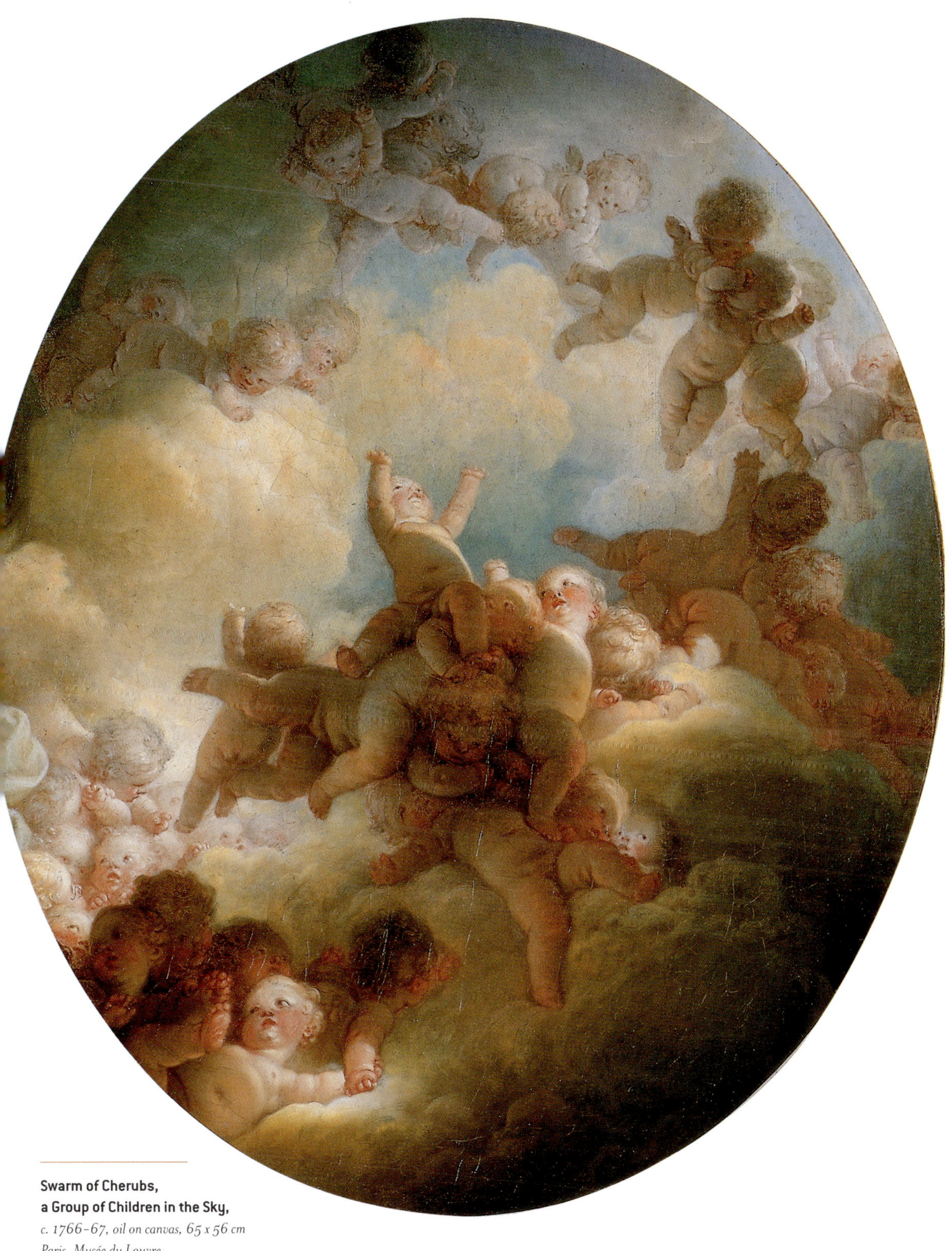

Swarm of Cherubs,
a Group of Children in the Sky,
c. 1766-67, oil on canvas, 65 x 56 cm
Paris, Musée du Louvre.

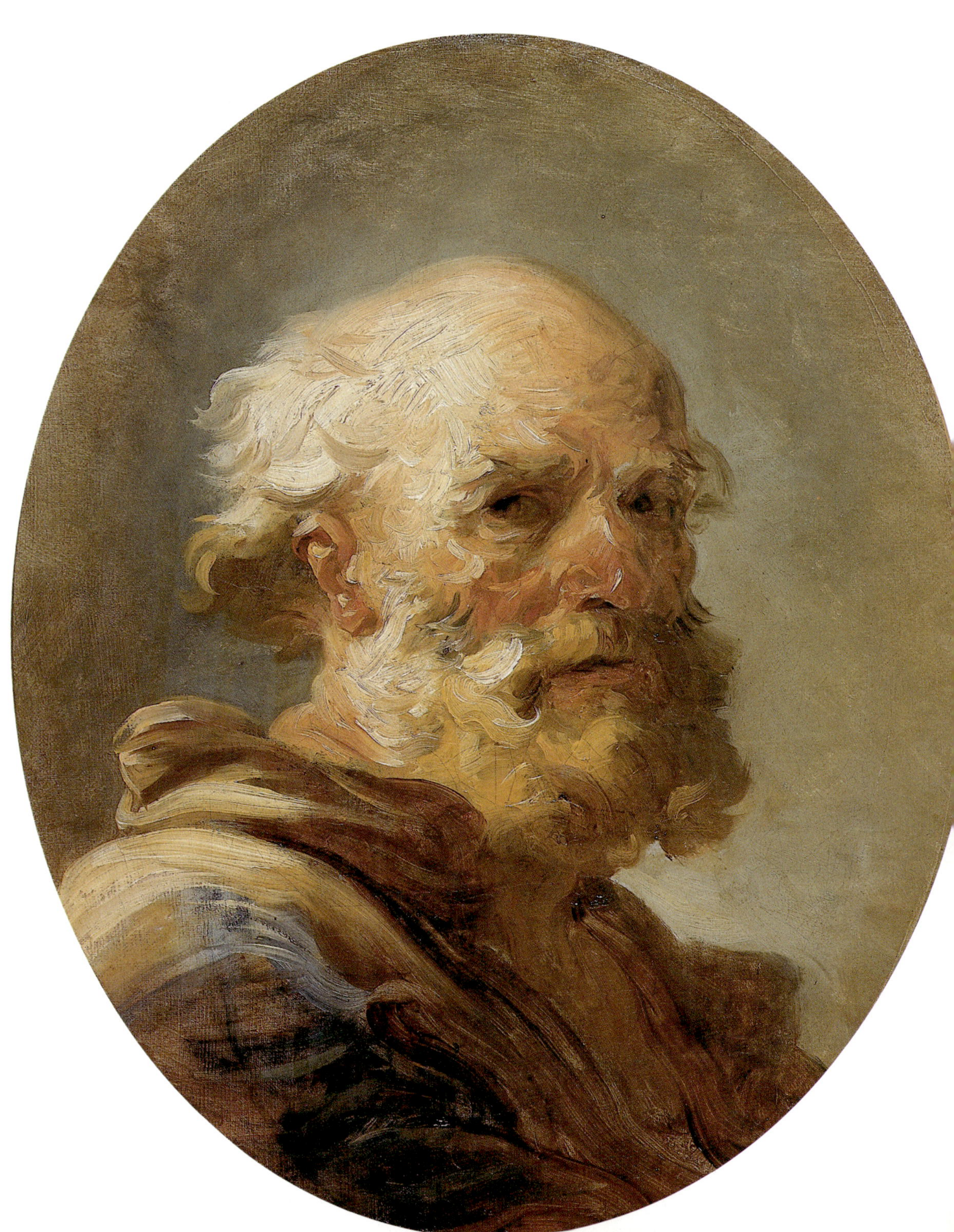

Head of an Old Man,
c. 1766–69, oil on canvas, 54 x 45 cm
Amiens, Musée de Picardie.

Education Does All,
c. 1777–80, oil on canvas, 55.5 x 66 cm
Sao Paulo, Museu de Arte.

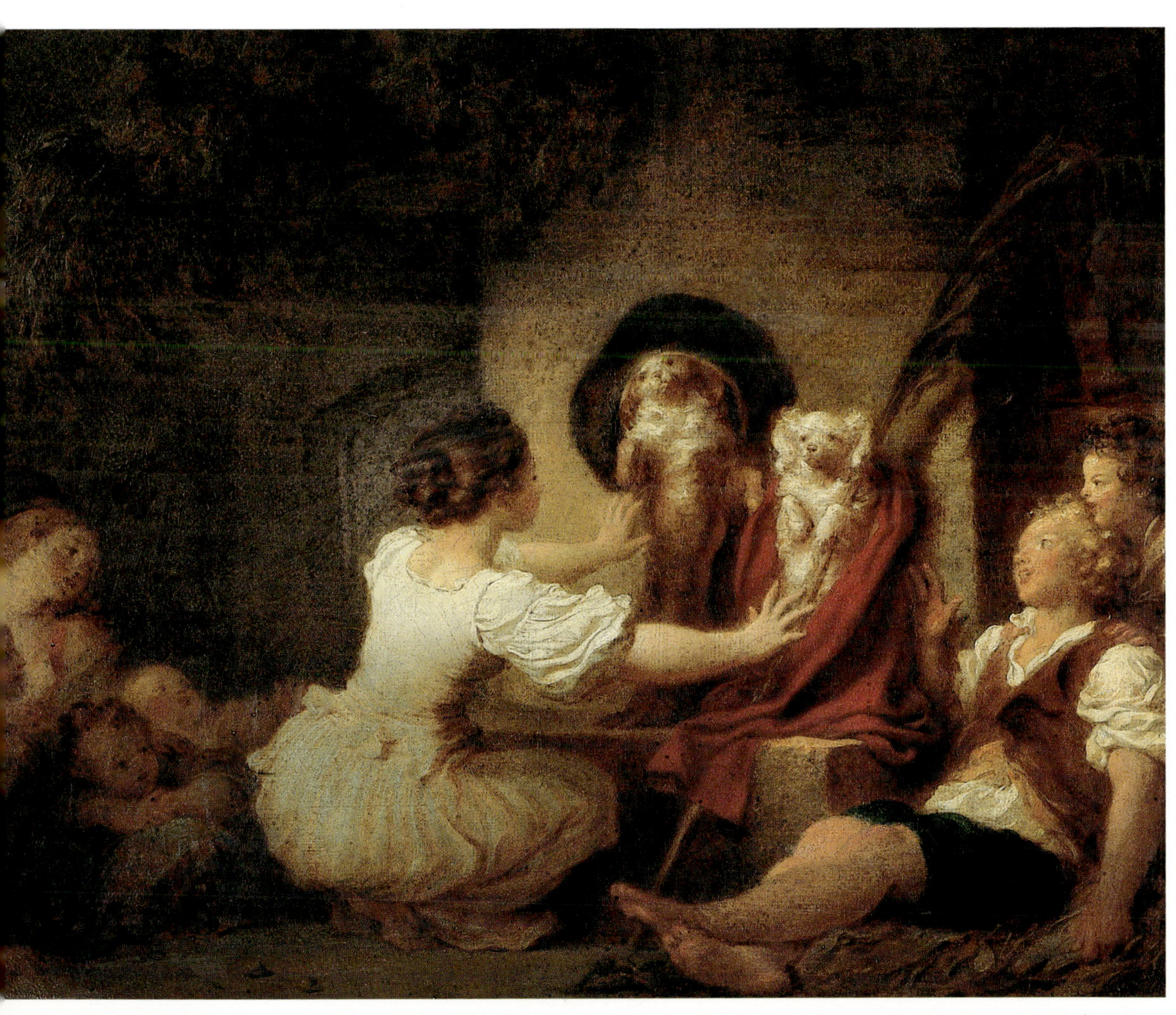

A Change of Course

In 1788 the Academy directed the handful of artists who had still not submitted their reception pieces to do so with all due speed. Some were granted extenuating circumstances: the painter-engraver Robert Strange was out of the country, a certain Portier was excused by his age—he was born in 1716!—and an even more obscure Courtois had gone blind... But in Fragonard's case the official reasons were unequivocal: his "cas ualness and irresponsibility." What lay behind this nonchalance? Was the explanation to be sought in the temperament of an artist whose contradictions Natoire had already pinpointed, and whom one of the perceptive art-lovers of his time, the great collector Pierre-Jean Mariette (1694–1774), had summed up thus: "The timidity that rules the character of this artist stays his hand and, never happy with what he has done, he effaces and reworks. This is a method harmful to talent, and one that may penalize this young painter. This would annoy me, for his efforts at getting things right deserve greater success"?

Some of his critics insinuated that "the lure of gain" and better-paid private commissions had deflected Fragonard from an official career. Even more viciously, others saw him as happy to "sparkle in boudoirs and dressing rooms" by opting for "inferior subject matter." Unlike Greuze, approved by the Academy in 1755 with his genre scene *Reading from the Bible*, and doing his utmost—unsuccessfully—to obtain definitive admission as a history painter, Fragonard seemed to attach no importance to a rank then considered superior to all others. Not only that, he was also going to prove that you could be recognized as one of the truly great without submitting to a hidebound Academy. His behavior was doubtless due more to circumstances than to any conscious decision on his part, but as such it illustrates the widening gap, in the second half of the 18th century, between official discourse and artistic reality. It was, too, symptomatic of Fragonard's character, which, doubtless emboldened by the reception given *Coresus*, was becoming more assertive: the timidity and lack of confidence so often remarked on were being offset by a will to independence which would enable him to resist official pressure—but which would also be a source of the numerous misunderstandings the future held.

Mythology and Religious History

This change of course did not mean, however, total rejection of history painting. Throughout his career Fragonard painted pictures — overdoors, sometimes in trompe-l'oeil, and series on the Hours, the Seasons and the Arts—that he often embellished with themes and personages from mythology. Here, for example, the amorous *Cephalus and Procris* find their pendant in *Jupiter and Callisto*, while Diana and Venus are recurring figures in daring compositions sometimes used to decorate ceilings. Nor should we ignore all the paintings enlivened by cupids, fluttering about or stretching their bows, sometimes in swarms and sometimes alone, sleeping peacefully or chasing after doves. Primarily decorative in intent, these scenes are not among those we most admire today, but they are the proof that even well into his career, Fragonard never completely abandoned what he had learned from Boucher—and did not ape him either, whatever Diderot might have said.

More directly bringing the history painting register into play, the pictures inspired by religious texts show us a much less known facet of the artist, even though they represent a not unimportant part of his painted and drawn oeuvre. Shunning the somber intensity of the Biblical accounts—it should be remembered that *Jeroboam Sacrificing to Idols* had been an obligatory subject—Fragonard concentrated for the most part on episodes from the life of the Virgin, the exceptions being *Christ Washing the Feet of the Apostles*, completed in 1755, a *John the Baptist* probably from the same period, and the large, recently rediscovered drawing, *Repentance of St Peter*. By thus cutting free of the established codes, he invented a new way of evoking the sacred, bringing it closer to the life of ordinary mortals with a compositional technique that was simple and unencumbered by pointless detail. The supernatural was not eliminated, however, witness the symbolic, Rembrandtesque glow emanating from the child Mary in *The Education of the Virgin*. In all these scenes, and more especially in his *Adoration of the Shepherds*, he achieves a profundity and sincerity rare in the religious painting of the time.

From History to Stories

Fragonard may have abandoned early on the idea of a career as a history painter, but he never spurned stories, fables and poetry. The opposite, in fact: looking at his oeuvre as a whole, we are struck by the place he accorded subjects from the literature of the past and of his own time. There is a tendency to consider him not especially cultivated, especially in comparison with his friend Hubert Robert, yet his paintings, black chalk drawings and washes are not mere demonstrations of the virtuosity, sensitivity and humor he could bring to portraying the misadventures of a Perrette or a Don Quixote. Here he reveals new talents: a deep, intimate grasp of narrative, an intuitive sense of plot and suspense that makes him the equal of poets and storytellers.

Two fine examples are the scenes drawn from Torquato Tasso's long poem *Jerusalem Delivered*, of 1581, whose Canto XVI was a particular source of inspiration for artists and musicians. The poem recounts the adventures of the knight Rinaldo and the enchantress Armida, whose name Lully had used for his successful opera *Armide* of 1686. Indeed, the theatricality and deliberately unnatural lighting of Fragonard's two companion pieces—*Rinaldo in the Gardens of Armida* and *Rinaldo in the Enchanted Forest*—are grounds for supposing that they were prompted by the opera, revived in Paris in 1761 and 1764. Against a backdrop of luxuriant vegetation

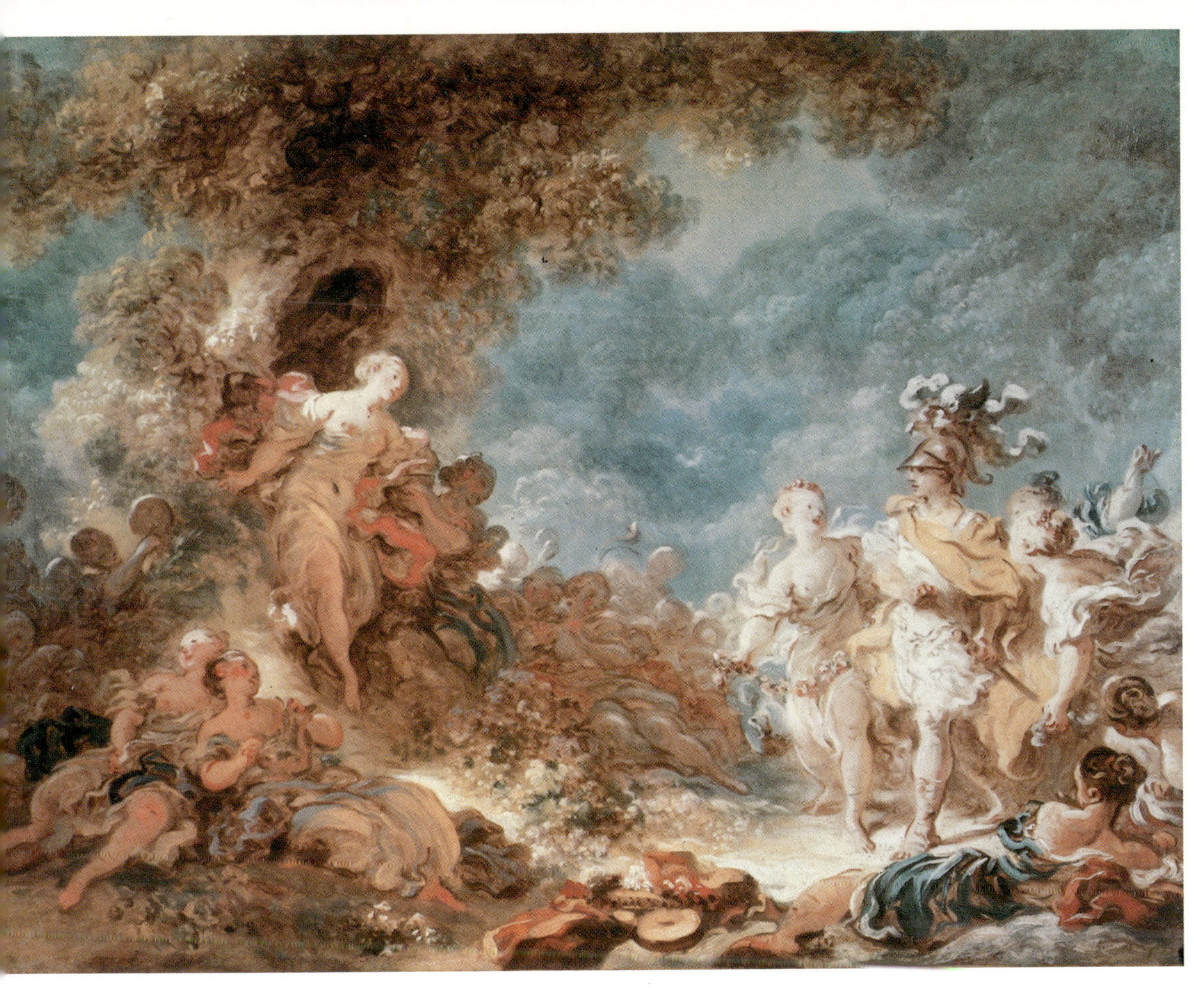

Rinaldo in the Gardens of Armida

c. 1761–64, oil on canvas, 72 x 92 cm

Paris, Musée du Louvre.

Les Petites Curieuses,
c. 1775–80, oil on panel, 16.5 x 12.5 cm
Paris, Musée du Louvre.

the protagonists meet, or confront each other, in an adroitly orchestrated ballet. But are these sketches or finished canvases? As so often with Fragonard, we cannot be sure. The power of the brushwork is all the more astonishing given that the pictures were painted while he was preparing his *Coresus* for the Academy, and that there is no stylistic similarity between them and the sketches he made for his approval piece: as he worked on the compulsory exercise, then, he was also exploring other avenues whose potential would turn out to be far richer.

We should not conclude our consideration of Fragonard as a history painter without mentioning the exchange published in *Affiches, Annonces et Avis divers* in 1784, when Maurice Blot published his engraving of Fragonard's famous *The Bolt*. The review's director, the Abbé Fontenai, while regretting the impropriety of the subject matter—"It is one of those works whose gaiety is somewhat exaggerated and which will not improve moral standards. The naked Graces of Antiquity are far more decent than this young man and this young woman, for all that they are fully dressed"—also pointed out that the engraver had neglected certain matters of detail, notably in the handling of the fabrics. This stricture drew an immediate riposte from a Monsieur de Saint-Félix, an unconditional admirer of the Fragonard painting—which he described as "striking" and the work of a true history painter—who commented that "Artists working in this genre are not obliged to vary the details of their draperies the way lesser talents do. So the engraver did not have to include something the painter had not shown." The underlying message here is that style is determined by subject. Genre painters might have to concentrate on scrupulously accurate description, but history painters were entitled to a greater freedom. Academic labeling was dismissed by Monsieur de Saint-Félix, an art lover who considered Fragonard a thoroughgoing history painter on the grounds of the quality of his work, whatever the subject matter. Such broadmindedness was not to the taste of the Abbé de Fontenai, who fired back, "The distinction between the history painter and the painter of bambocciades lies solely in their works. And since the creator of *The Bolt* was not treating a historical subject, he should have dealt with all the details essential to pictures of the inferior genre."

This independence in matters of taste on the part of true art lovers, as distinct from purely conventional official preferences, is a good pointer to the limitations of the sacrosanct hierarchy of genres and the rigidity of the system Fragonard was bucking against. Did his works not reveal a great innovator, with a creative sense equal, if not superior to that of the history painters of the time? And did he not find, in opting for more varied and accessible sources of inspiration, a more direct way of stirring the sensibility of his contemporaries and speaking to their imaginations?

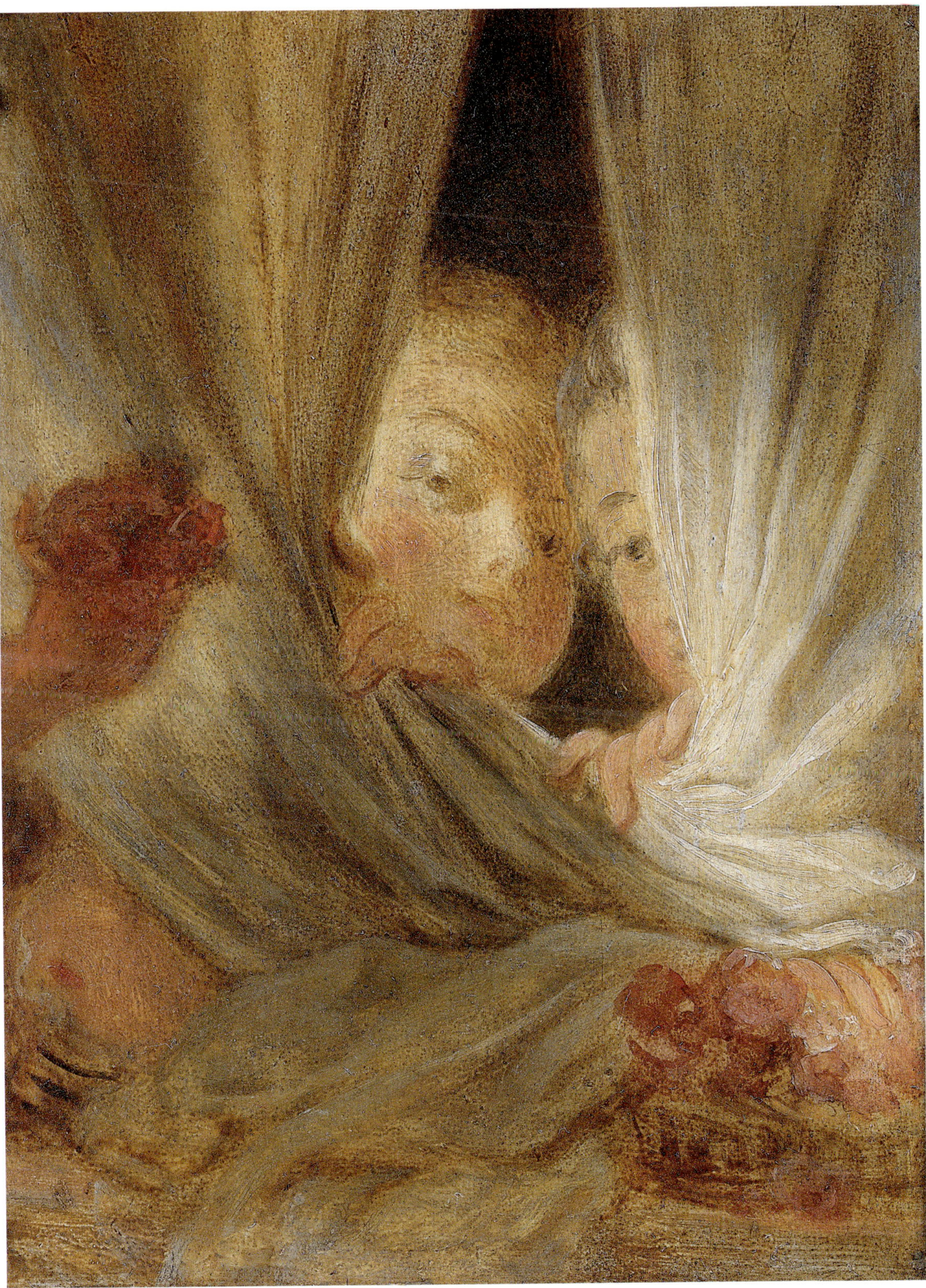

IV

Works *Appropriate* to His

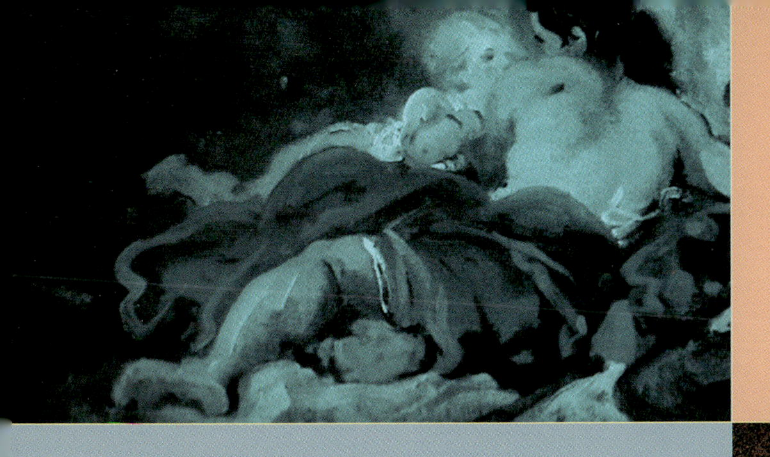

Genius

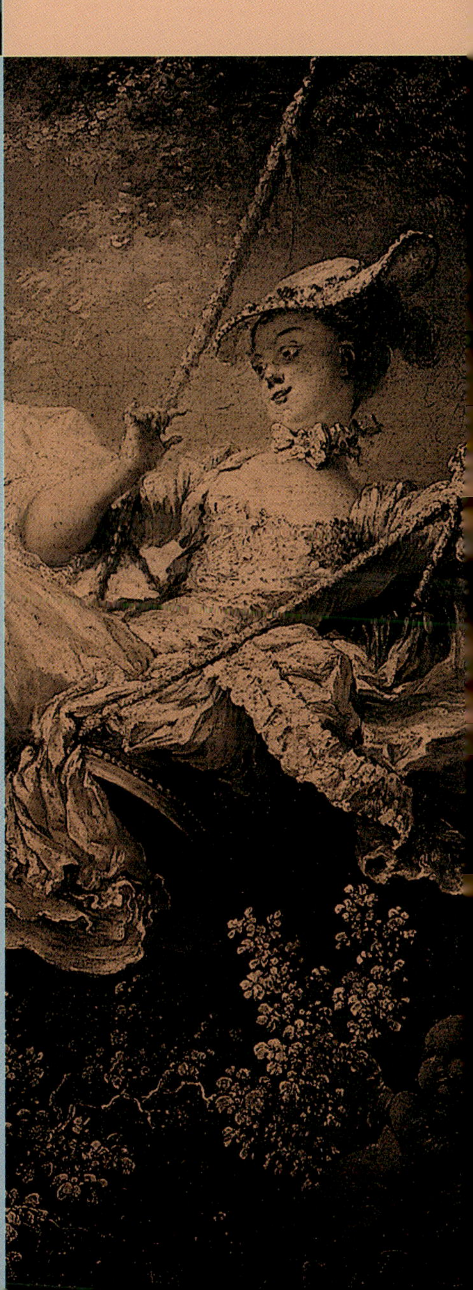

As we have already seen, Fragonard's approval by the Academy in March 1765 brought with it the purchase of his *Coresus and Callirhoë* by the king for the sum of 2400 livres. In August Cochin was interceding with Marigny with a view to getting the painter an advance: "I have long put off approaching you in Monsieur Fragonard's behalf, but his neediness leaves me no choice. Otherwise he will be forced to undertake works inappropriate to his genius and this will delay the success we may rightfully expect for him. I beg you, then, to be so kind as to grant him an advance on the painting *Coresus Sacrificing Himself* to *Save Callirhoë* that you have been so good as to reserve for the Gobelins manufactory."

An Artist's Freedom

The tone of concern mirrored the danger perfectly: imagine the artist everyone expected to breathe new life into French painting having to "undertake works inappropriate to his genius." Comparisons with the Italian school were still provoking violent debate, with the reputation of the country's institutions—and more generally its artistic eminence—in the balance. A wily politician, Cochin was attending to France's future by helping her most gifted artists move up the ladder. 1765 had seen the death not only of Carle Van Loo, but also of the promising Jean-Baptiste Deshaye (1729–65) —"the nation's premier painter" for Diderot—who had been struck down prematurely in February. Among the other artists of Fragonard's generation, there were few with convincing claims to the first rank at the Academy: Hubert Robert, back from Italy in 1765 then approved and admitted the following year, had

Genre Scenes

opted for a highly specific genre, and Greuze had not yet revealed the ambitions as a history painter that would be definitively thwarted in 1769. Great hopes rode on Jean-Hugues Taraval (1729–85), Jean-Bernard Restout (1732–97) and Nicolas-Bernard Lépicié (1735–84); like Fragonard, all three had been pupils of Van Loo, been approved in 1765 and followed the official program to the letter by presenting their "reception pieces" four years later. Fragonard would do things differently.

An initial payment of 1200 livres, followed by 600 more the following year, did not suffice to keep Fragonard on the straight and narrow. Nor would the payment of the balance—in 1773!—have been an incentive to join the ranks at the Academy. And so, in direct contradiction of Cochin's ideas on the subject, he decided to devote more time to works that can only be described, in fact, as perfectly appropriate to his genius: witness the still-enduring fame of *The Swing*, and of *The Bolt*, painted ten years later. But before looking into this aspect of the oeuvre, we should take a look at the many scenes of domestic happiness he painted—works that counterbalance the reputation for licentiousness too often attached to his name.

As early as his stay in Rome Fragonard had shown a certain fondness for genre scenes featuring children and teenagers, and would continue to explore this theme throughout his career. Rarely given an aristocratic or bourgeois setting—even if that handsome oval canvas *The Happy Family* has to be mentioned here—these domestic scenes mostly take place in modestly furnished rural interiors, with children, parents, grandparents and animals in a joyous jumble. Most of the time the action takes place at ground level, the adults squatting or sitting either on the ground or on low seats so as to be in amongst the youngsters.

One example of this kind of composition is a small, touching canvas showing the inside of a school. As is frequently the case, the spatial setting lacks depth and definition. A little daylight enters through the window set up high in the wall and an opening on the right; we can make out the spring of a vault, an imposingly hefty column and something—another column or a bulky stove?—with the slate blackboard leaning against it. A half-naked toddler stands with his back to the board: the downward look, the hand held to the chest, and the chubby legs squeezed together, with one foot on top of the other, suggest a mix of embarrassment and defiance.

Is this because he is having trouble reading the alphabet written on the blackboard—where, we note, the artist has slyly slipped in his signature after the letter F? Or because he has been scolded for not asking

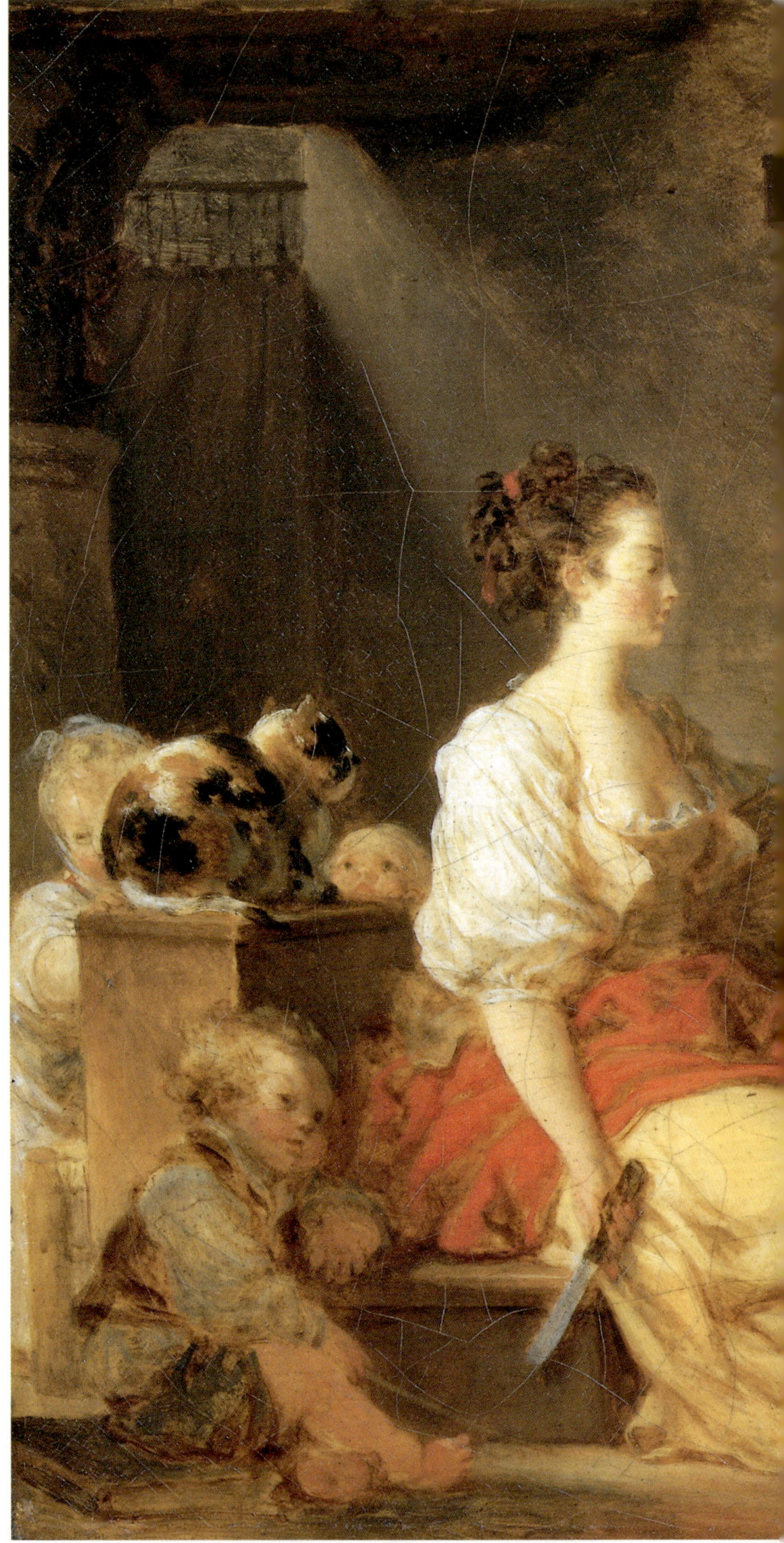

The Schoolmistress (Say "Please"),
c. 1777-80, oil on canvas,
28.9 x 37.2 cm
London, Wallace Collection.

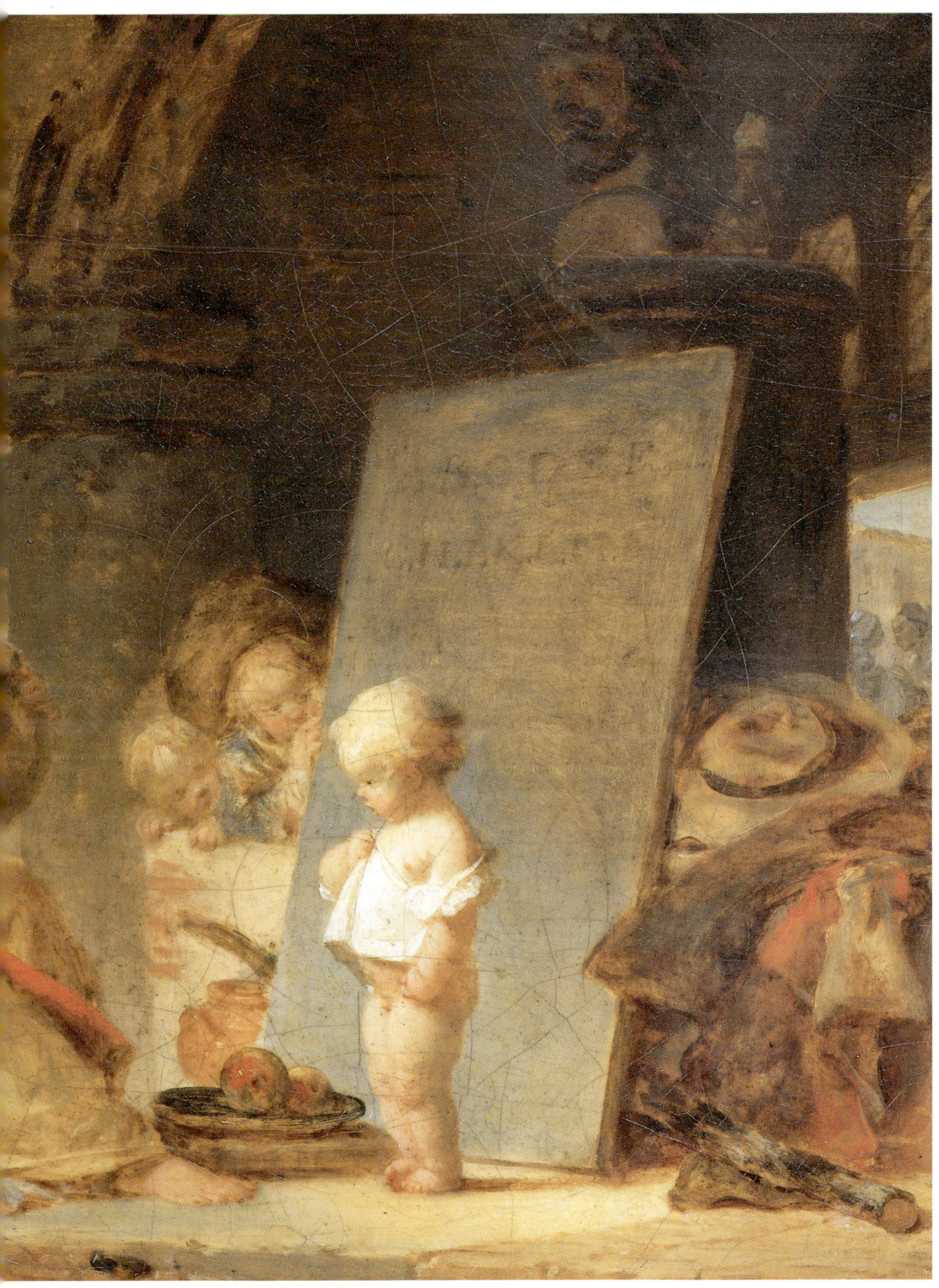

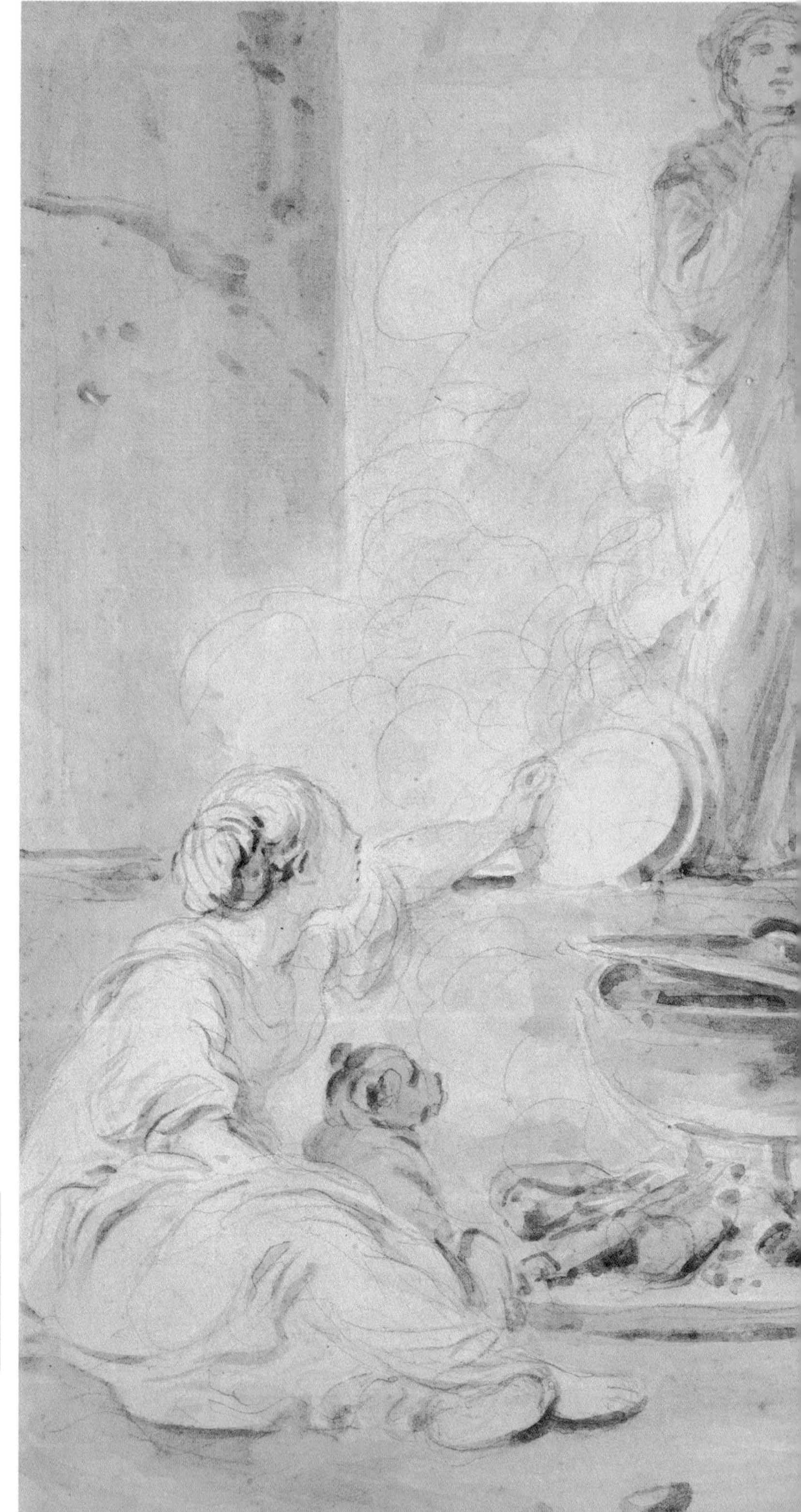

The Donkey's Dinner,
c. 1775, black chalk and wash,
34 x 49 cm
Cambridge, Mass. Fogg Art Museum,
Harvard University Art Museums,
Gift of Therese Kuhn Straus in memory of her husband, Herbert N. Straus,
Harvard Class of 1903.

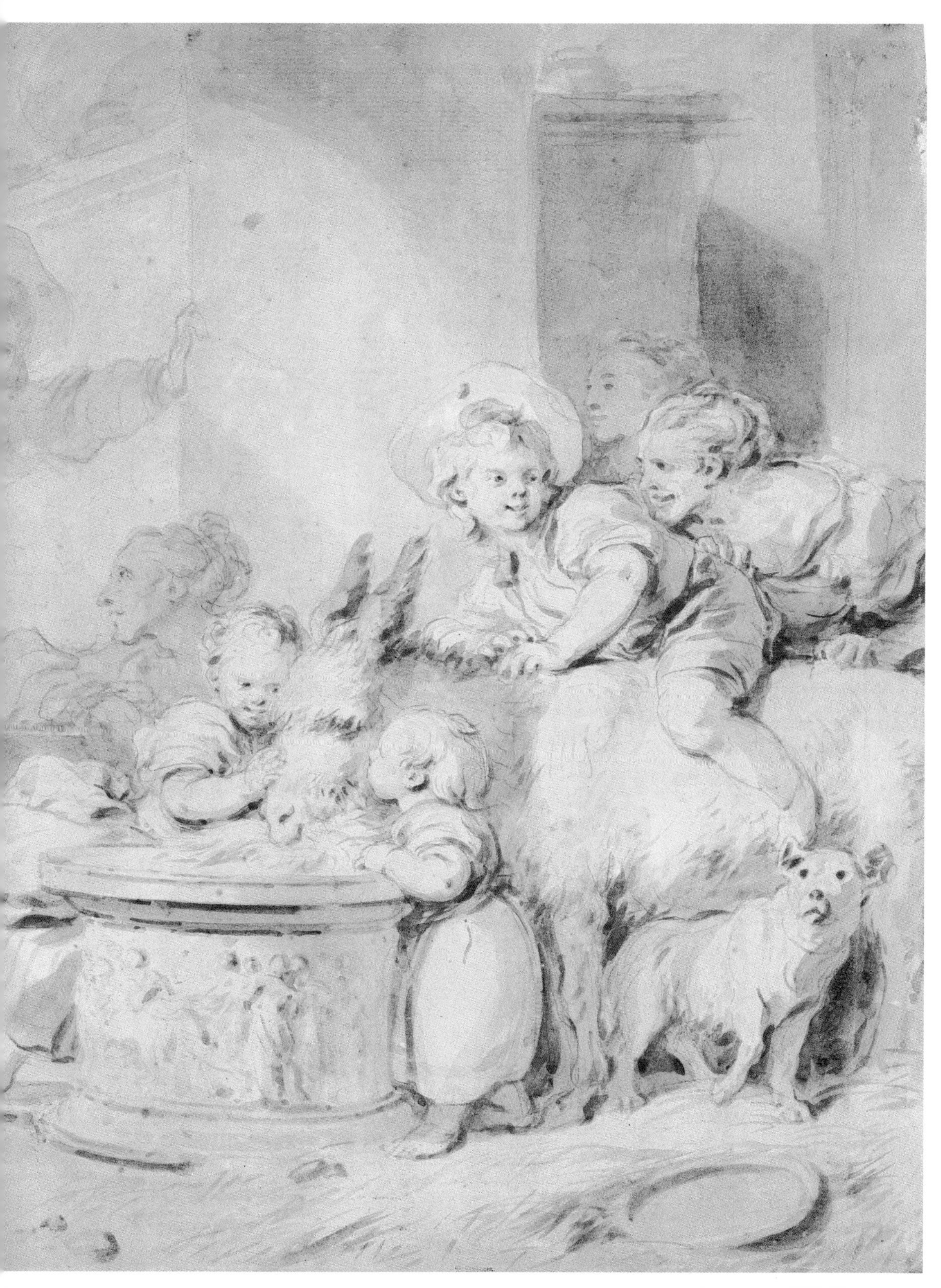

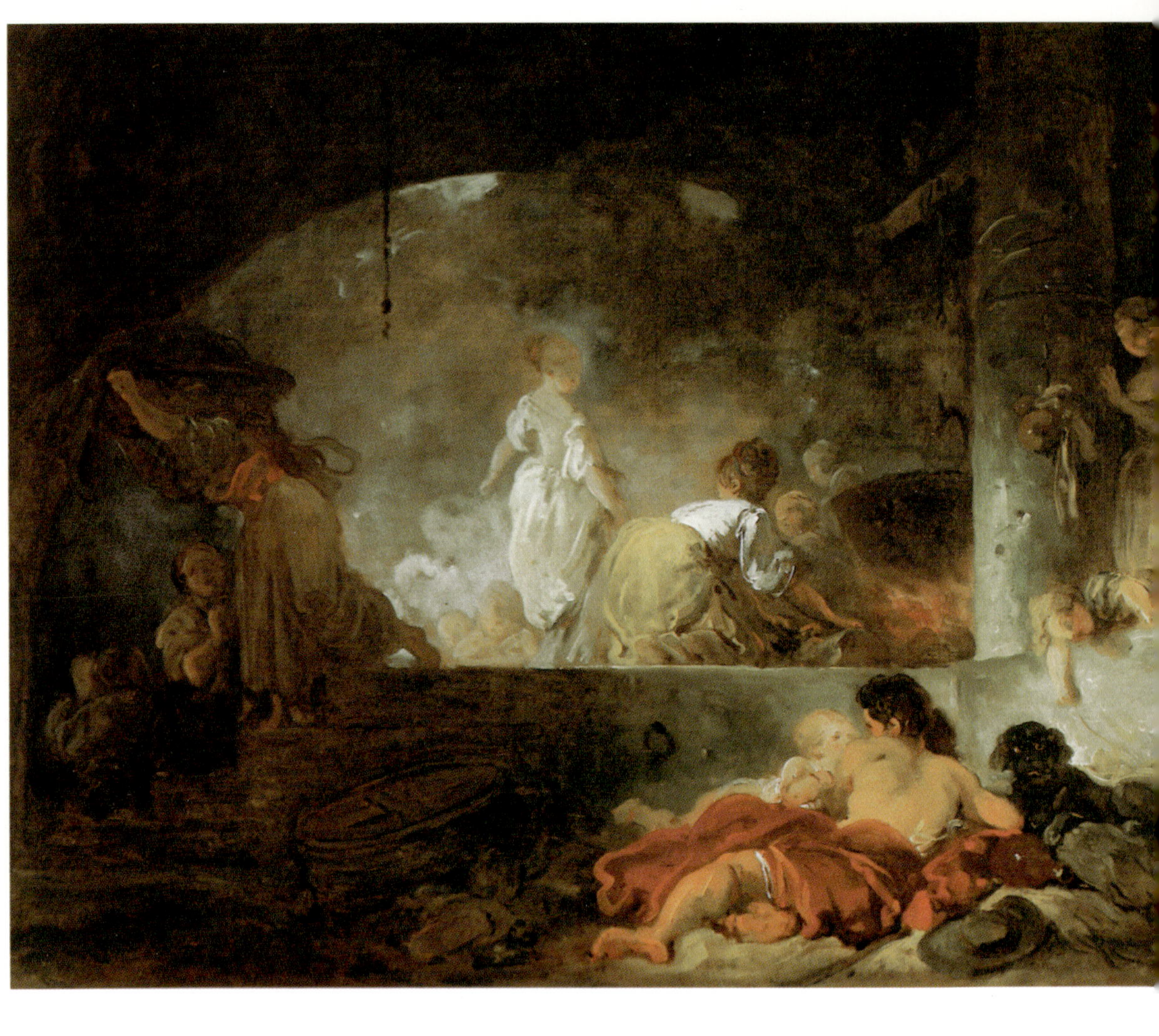

The Washerwomen ,
c. 1758-61, oil on canvas, 61.5 x 73 cm
Saint Louis, The Saint Louis Art Museum.

Bull in the Stable,
c. 1765-70, black chalk and wash, 146 x 183 cm
Paris, Musée Cognacq-Jay.

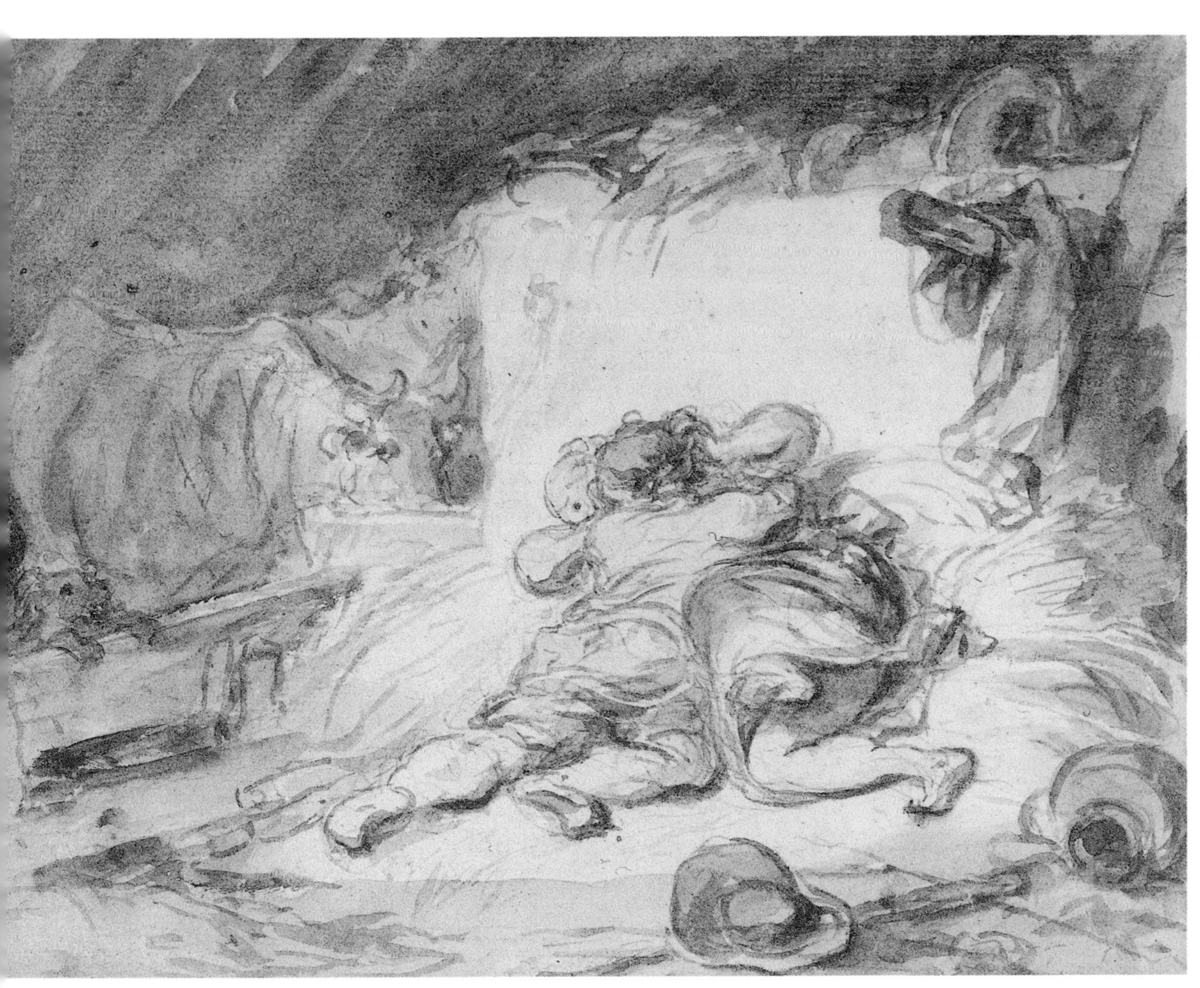

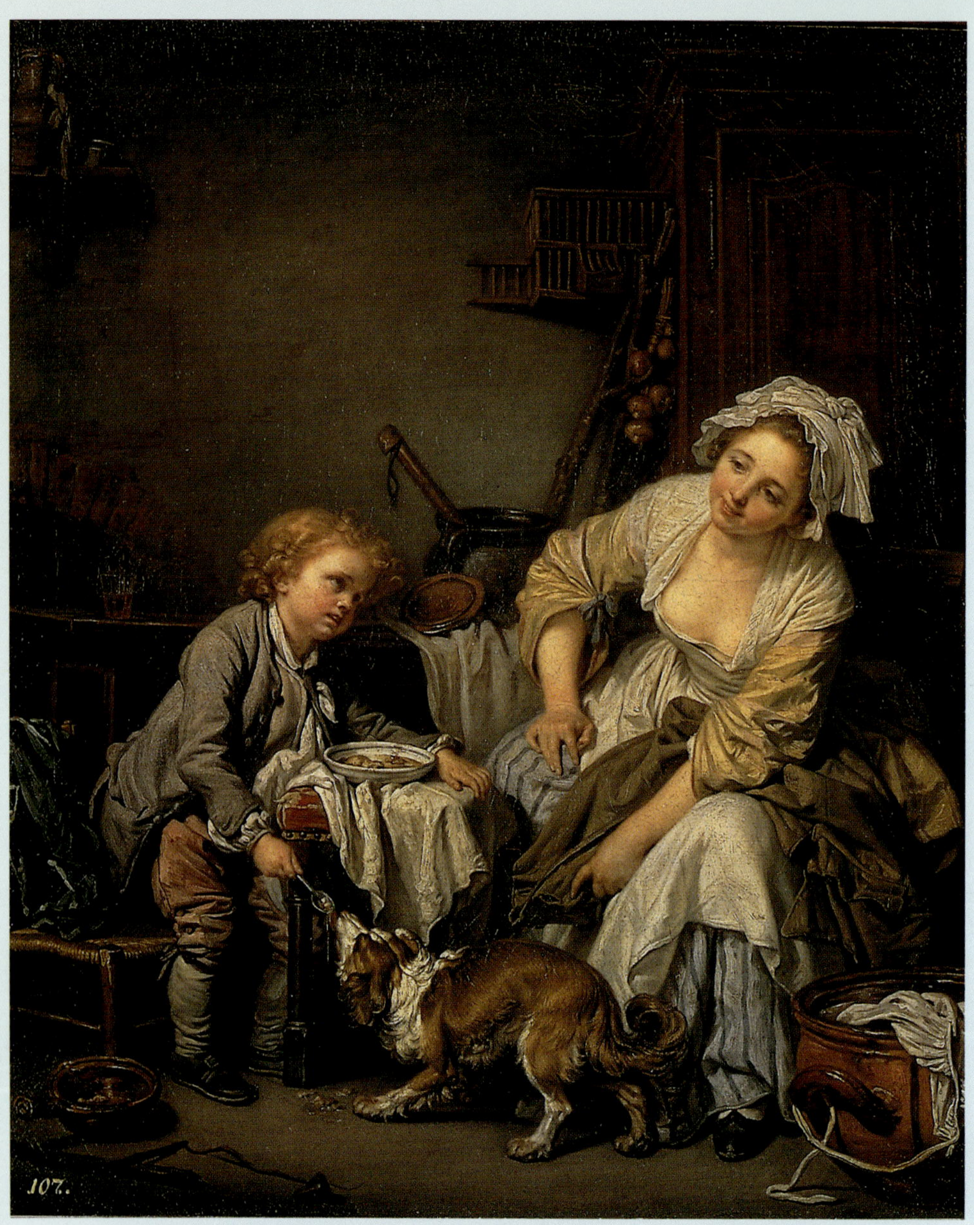

Jean-Baptiste Greuze
The Spoiled Child,
1765, oil on canvas, 66.5 x 56 cm
St Petersburg, Hermitage Museum.

politely enough for his share of the large loaf the teacher is holding? Contemporary engraver Nicolas Delaunay opted for the latter when he produced a very similar composition and called it *Say Please*. Whatever the explanation, the child's waiting is being shared by two other children sketched into the background, whose pose betrays a slightly awed curiosity. On the left, another is playing the good little pupil, looking serious and sitting just like the teacher. Two more little ones have their eyes fixed on one of the cats that sometimes make an appearance in Fragonard's pictures, this one stretched out on a chest. Successfully avoiding the trivial, the other details— the puppet head perched on the stove, the pile of clothes on the right with a big hat on top, the pretty still life of red apples at the centre—add to the work's charm: the feeling is of everyday matter-of-factness, not moralizing.

And the teacher, amid her youthful charges? There is a nobility about her pose that suggests certain antique marbles. The profile, the haughty tilt of the head, the bare neck, one leg bent and the other stretched out in front of her—all this is reminiscent of the *Minerva* in the Capitol in Rome, also known as *Rome Seated*, and there were copies at Versailles and the Tuileries. We feel Fragonard giving us a witty little nudge here, as his discreetly veiled reference invests the teacher with unchallengeable authority.

We know that in Rome, Fragonard, unlike Hubert Robert with whom he went walking, paid little attention to the vestiges that had accumulated in the city over the centuries. Far from being infected by the contemporary obsession with antiquity, he shared with Rome's inhabitants an attitude of relaxed familiarity with the past. There is a stone altar with low-relief decoration that appears quite often in his rustic interiors and, in the twilight of his career, in some allegorical scenes: the altar-stone is shown being used for preparing food, or for changing a baby, with an occasional glint of irony directed at those who consider relics of the past with religious wonderment. A drawing titled *The Donkey's Dinner* shows the eponymous animal eating its daily fare off the same altar, urged on by a group of gleeful tots; their mothers, meanwhile, are preparing their meal in a pot set under a statue of Pandora very like the one in the Capitol Museum. Plates lean against the folds of Pandora's robe, stacked on edge as if on a drying rack.

Making light of the accepted, predefined categories, Fragonard delights in mixing the genres: thus we see a pair of lovers taking advantage of a dark corner in a work devoted to a totally different subject, or infiltrating humdrum family celebration scenes. A canvas probably painted in Rome in 1756–61 shows a dark, vaulted space with a group of women busying themselves around an enormous cauldron, boiling washing which another woman then carries away in a large basket held on her head. The rapid, sketch-like technique conveys marvelously well the impression of stifling heat and of steam blurring the view as, in the foreground and a fraction lower than the main scene, a young couple lies on the ground, oblivious of the hive of activity around them. Bare to the waist, the boy is shown in back view, positioned so as to mask almost entirely the body of his companion: only her blond head can be seen. The same couple turns up again in a pleasing Fragonard wash executed some years later, embracing in a stable under the indifferent eye of a large bull.

Another picture offers a rustic interior where three boys are playing with a pair of big dogs, trying to feed fruit to the animals that have already licked the dinner plates clean. Behind them, out of the light, we see a girl trying to resist the advances of a boy scarcely older than the others—a scene that also provides the backdrop to *The Little Preacher*, probably painted some fifteen years later. The painting was shown with *Coresus* at the Salon in 1765, under the title "Children Trying to Make a Dog Eat Fruit", and rechristened by Diderot *Taking Advantage of Their Parents' Absence* —a title whose attribution to the canvas of a moral never intended by the painter points up the philosopher's view of good painting as essentially edifying. At the same Salon Greuze presented a similar subject which, as was his habit, he turned into an instructive little scene: in portrait format, *The Spoiled Child shows* a curly-headed child watched by an indulgent mother as he gives his spoon to a dog to lick. A drawing showing a girl doing the same—but being scolded by her mother—suggests that Greuze was thinking in terms of a contrasting pendant that would further highlight his didactic intent.

There exist a number of works by the two artists in which their different visions are brought to bear on the same subject. The example given above illustrates both the closeness of their worlds and the gulf that separated them, not so much in terms of form as of content. Both were astute observers of childhood, but their individual messages differ in the compositional approach and their underlying intentions. Greuze is more detached from his models, seeking to turn each painting into a trigger for moral reflection and commentary. Fragonard, on the other hand, brings a tender eye to the world around him: we sense him smiling as he paints, holding the narrative aspect in check as he instills fresh life into the banality of the everyday with touches of whimsy or humor. Unlike Greuze, who forces his point of view on us and dictates what would we should see and think, Fragonard simply asks us to look: it is up to us to divine what is going on in the darkness, to find understanding through the still, silent contemplation that is the only means of letting the telling detail rise to the surface, and so of penetrating to the heart of the artist's feelings.

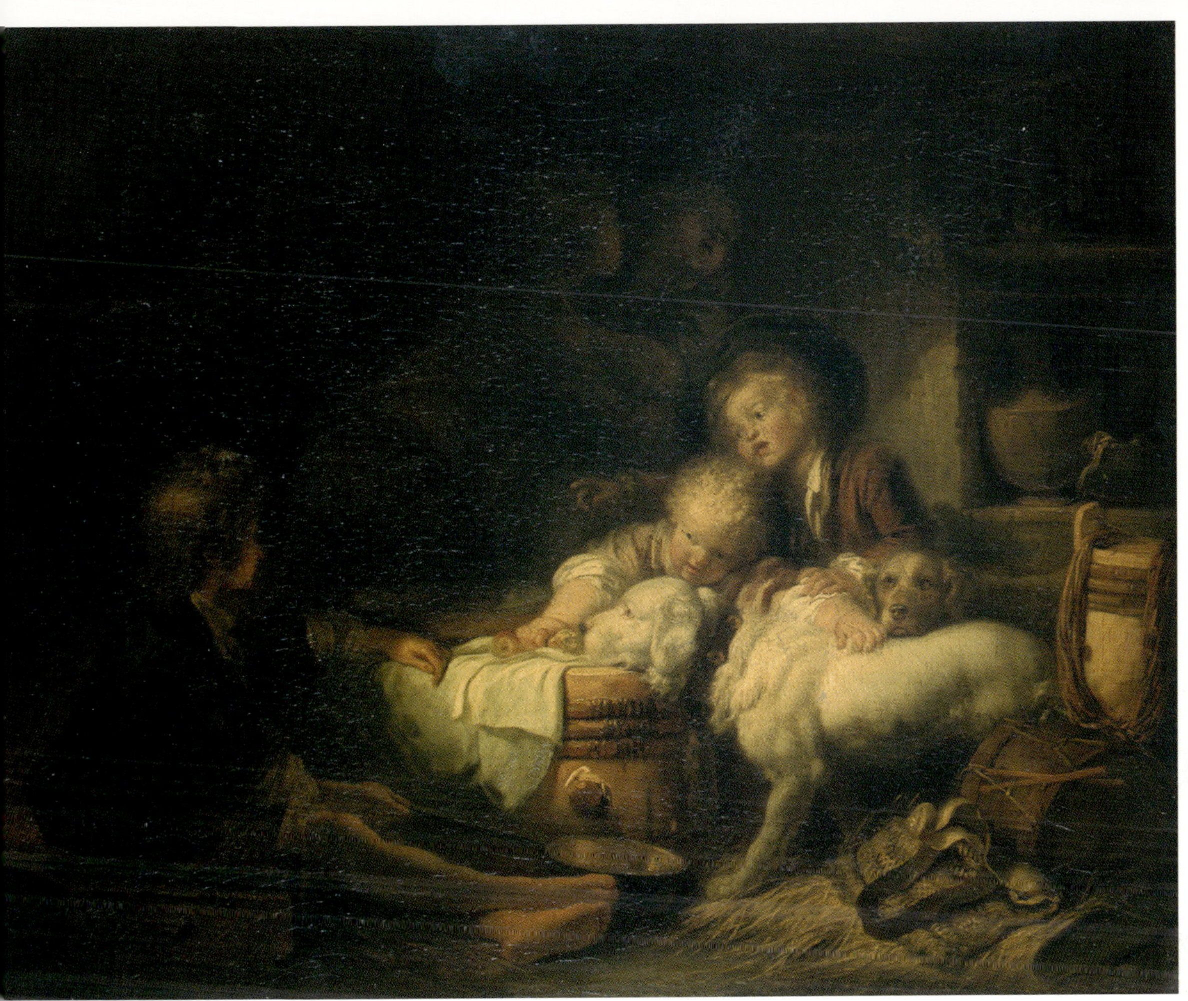

Taking Advantage of Their Parents' Absence,
1765, oil on canvas, 50 x 60.5 cm
St Petersburg, Hermitage Museum.

Lovers and Libertines

As we know, Fragonard did not restrict his gallant scenes to the half-light of the kitchen or the discreet nook. But what exactly is meant by "gallant" here? Once again, Fragonard eludes any strict definition, plumbing every nuance—boudoir eroticism, lyrical pledgings, naughty goings-on, fevered sensuality—of the impulses of the body and the mind. He doubtless began to specialize in this field early on, as Cochin's misgivings, mentioned above, indicate. But if he had learnt from Boucher the art of dressing up the risqué in the garb of the innocently pastoral, he did not confine himself to this genre and its mind-numbing repetition.

Le feu aux poudres may have been painted before Fragonard received Academy approval. Verging on the bawdy, it nonetheless skirts vulgarity with brushwork whose skimming caress of the flesh areas enlivens the whole scene. For all that he draws on the ubiquitous literary libertinism of the time, Fragonard is not to be identified with its specialist illustrators and engravers. No mythological alibis here, and no false modesty: breasts are bared, and nightgowns raised as Fragonard—eschewing the mass of ribald detail and the overcharged narrative of popular prints and the gouaches of the masters—opts for the essentials, for the abandon of the naked body and the sensuality of embraces given such freshness and spontaneity by the youth of his models. His *Beginning as a Model* has been compared with *The Honest Model*, by Boucher's son-in-law Pierre-Antoine Baudouin (1723-69), a specialist in softcore boudoir scenes. Where Baudouin stresses narrative with exaggerated poses and an accumulation of scrupulously brushed detail, Fragonard, combining sweetness of color with a style that is fluent, unfussy, and bordering on the allusive, turns works like *The Kiss* and *The Happy Lovers* into examples of pure poetry.

Humor can set the tone too, as in the famous *Girl Making a Dog Dance on Her Bed*, sometimes wrongly titled *La Gimblette* ("The Ring-Biscuit"). So innocent do the pleasures portrayed seem—a pink-cheeked child is shown playing with her white King Charles spaniel—that the register is mischievous rather than suggestive. The intimacy between the pair is illustrated by the bright blue ribbon to be seen both around the dog's neck and in the bonnet that has fallen onto the pillow in all the excitement. Another picture shows three girls cavorting with their puppies amid the bolsters and curtains of a big bed, and there are several drawings of roomfuls of impish girls at play. Here we have another Fragonard, the indiscreet chronicler of youthful female goings-on.

It may well be in this special realm of the risqué that Fragonard shows himself at his most inventive, turning the hackneyed into the unexpected in works whose reputed scandalousness has overshadowed their artistic virtues and their charm. One paradoxical outcome has been that *The Swing* is Fragonard's most famous painting, but not his most respected: endlessly reproduced in all sorts of pointless contexts—calendars, chocolate boxes, kitsch knick-knacks—it now earns only a condescending smile; endlessly referred to, it is valued less for its artistic qualities than as the emblem of an 18th century supposedly ruled by the superficial and the bawdy. One can only do artistic justice to the original by going to see it in the Wallace Collection in London: the Collection's rules forbid all loans and the picture has not left the precincts since 1784. Surrounded by seven other canvases by the master, it stands out here as the remarkable work it is, with its background, colors, lighting and, of course, its subject, combining to form a scene as strange as it is fascinating.

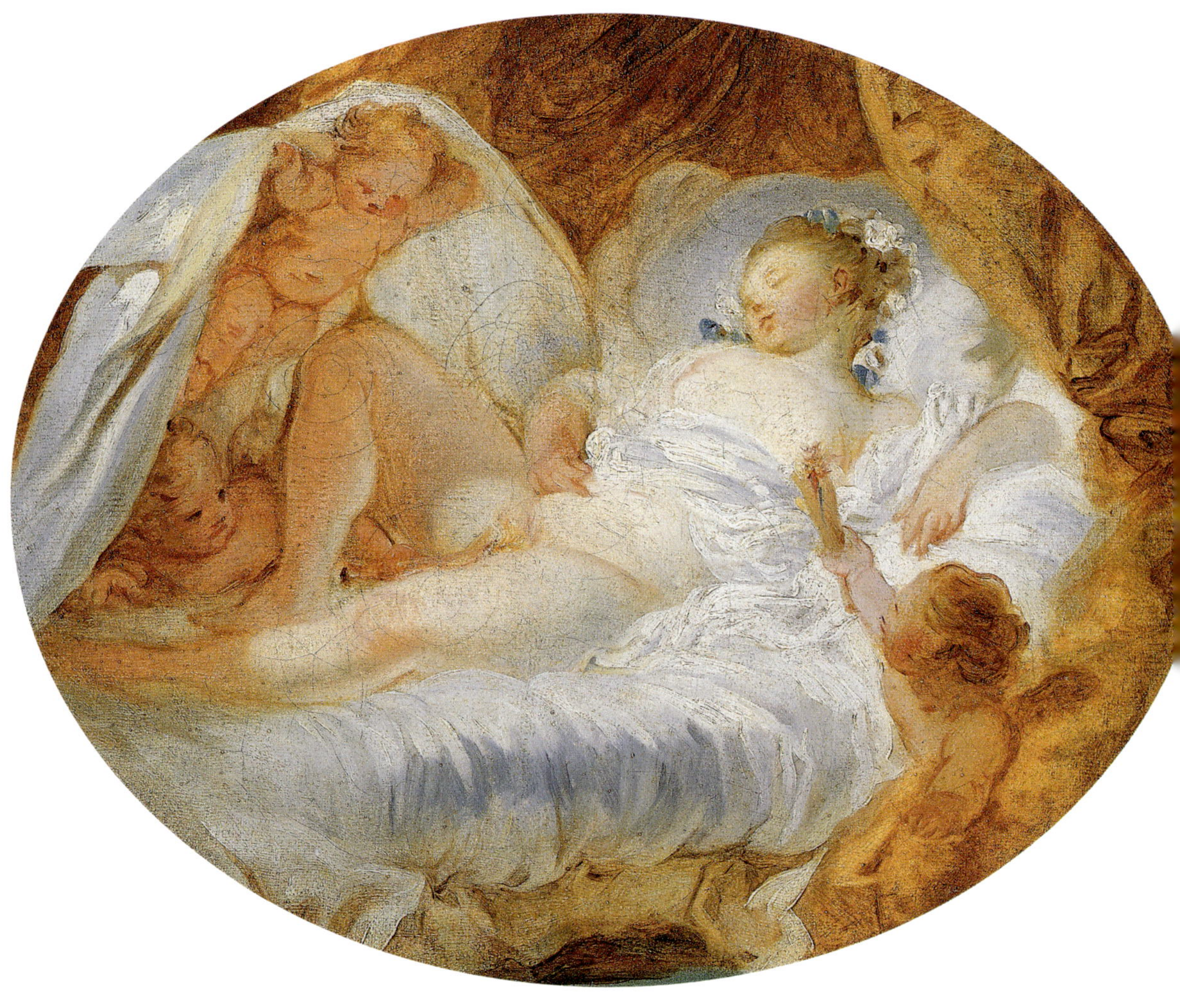

Le Feu aux Poudres,
c. 1763-64, oil on canvas, 37 x 45 cm
Paris, Musée du Louvre.

Le Feu aux Poudres,
c. 1770, black chalk and sepia wash, 24.4 x 37.1 cm
Paris, Musée du Louvre.

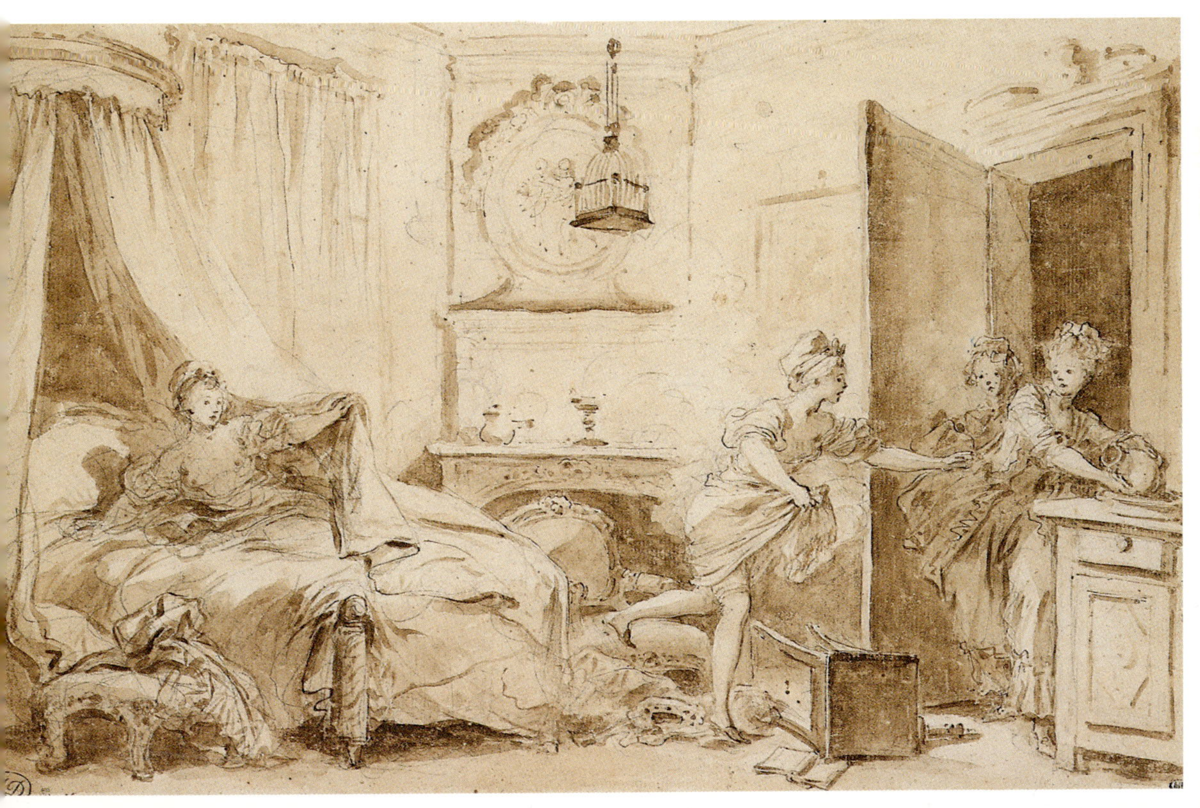

Pierre-Antoine Baudoin,
The Honest Model,
1769, gouache on vellum, 40.6 x 35.7 cm
Washington, National Gallery of Art.

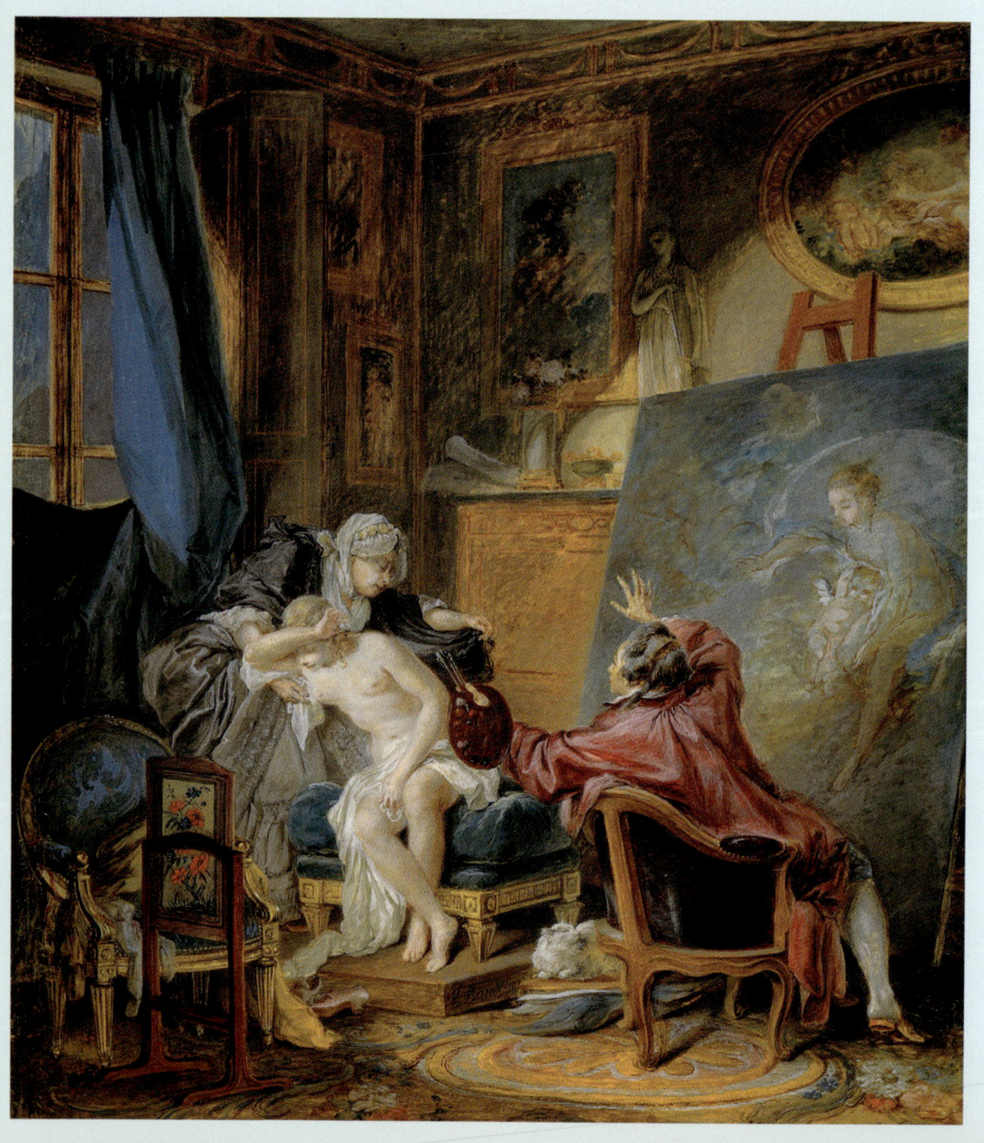

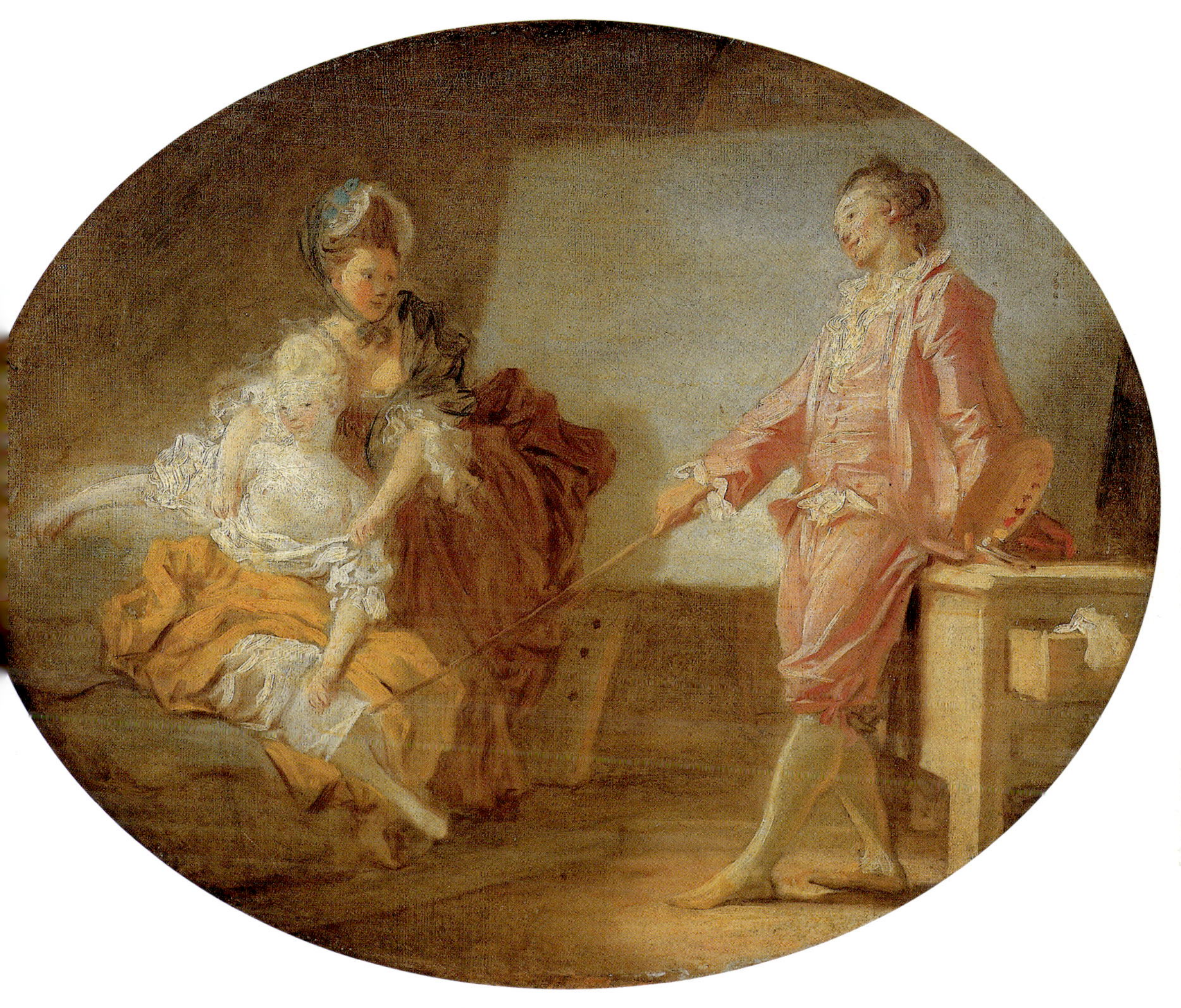

Beginning as a Model,
c. 1770, oil on canvas, 54 x 65 cm
Paris, Musée Jacquemart-André.

Girl Making a Dog Dance on Her Bed,
c. 1770, oil on canvas, 89 x 70 cm
Munich, Alte Pinakothek.

If we can believe the *chansonnier*-playwright Charles Collé (1709–83), the work was initially commissioned from Gabriel-François Doyen (1726-1806) in 1767. "A gentleman of the Court" whose identity remains unknown is said to have called on the painter with the following request: "I should like you to paint Madame (pointing to his mistress) on a swing set in motion by a bishop. You will place me in such a way as to view the legs of this beauteous child—and even more, if you wish to enliven your picture." Although somewhat taken aback, Doyen, freshly acclaimed at the Salon for his austere *Miracle des ardents* ("Miracle of St Genevieve"), now in the church of St Roch in Paris, came up with some extra suggestions of his own: "Ah, monsieur, in addition to the central idea for the picture, we should have madame's shoes flying through the air, with cupids catching them." However—and still according to Collé—Doyen eventually turned the commission down, suggesting Fragonard as his replacement. But is this account, now as famous as the picture to whose fame it has substantially contributed, to be taken as gospel? Would Fragonard have been ready simply to espouse his colleague's flying slipper idea? Are we not looking here at a typically Fragonard detail, further proof of his mischievously inventive turn of mind?

The scene itself is full of surprises. Firstly there is the artificiality of the setting: that oppressive vegetation, its shades of blue and green gleaming with touches of silver and gold, its gnarled trunks and twisted branches. And materializing as if out of another world, the elegant swing, with its red velvet seat and its delectable, pink-clad rider. All eyes converge on this apparition: those of the lover in the foreground, reclining amid a cluster of flowering shrubs; of the Cupid sitting in silence on his pedestal; of the *putto* lolling, with his companion, on a sculpted dolphin; and of the man whose face reveals all the pleasure he is taking in keeping the swing in motion. There is nothing of the bishop about him: he looks more like one of those complacent or blind husbands so frequent in the salacious novels then in fashion. This is a frankly risqué subject, and without skirting its scabrous, racy side, Fragonard has succeeded perfectly in capturing the lover's desire—or rather fantasy. The latter's ecstatic expression and pose are those of someone waking from a dream and delightfully startled to find that dream become reality. That this young woman displaying her charms is no mere illusion is attested by a detail whose realism is thoroughly at odds with the romanticized setting: the ropes of the swing are worn in places, with loose shreds visible here and there. No dream-swing would ever suffer from such a flaw...

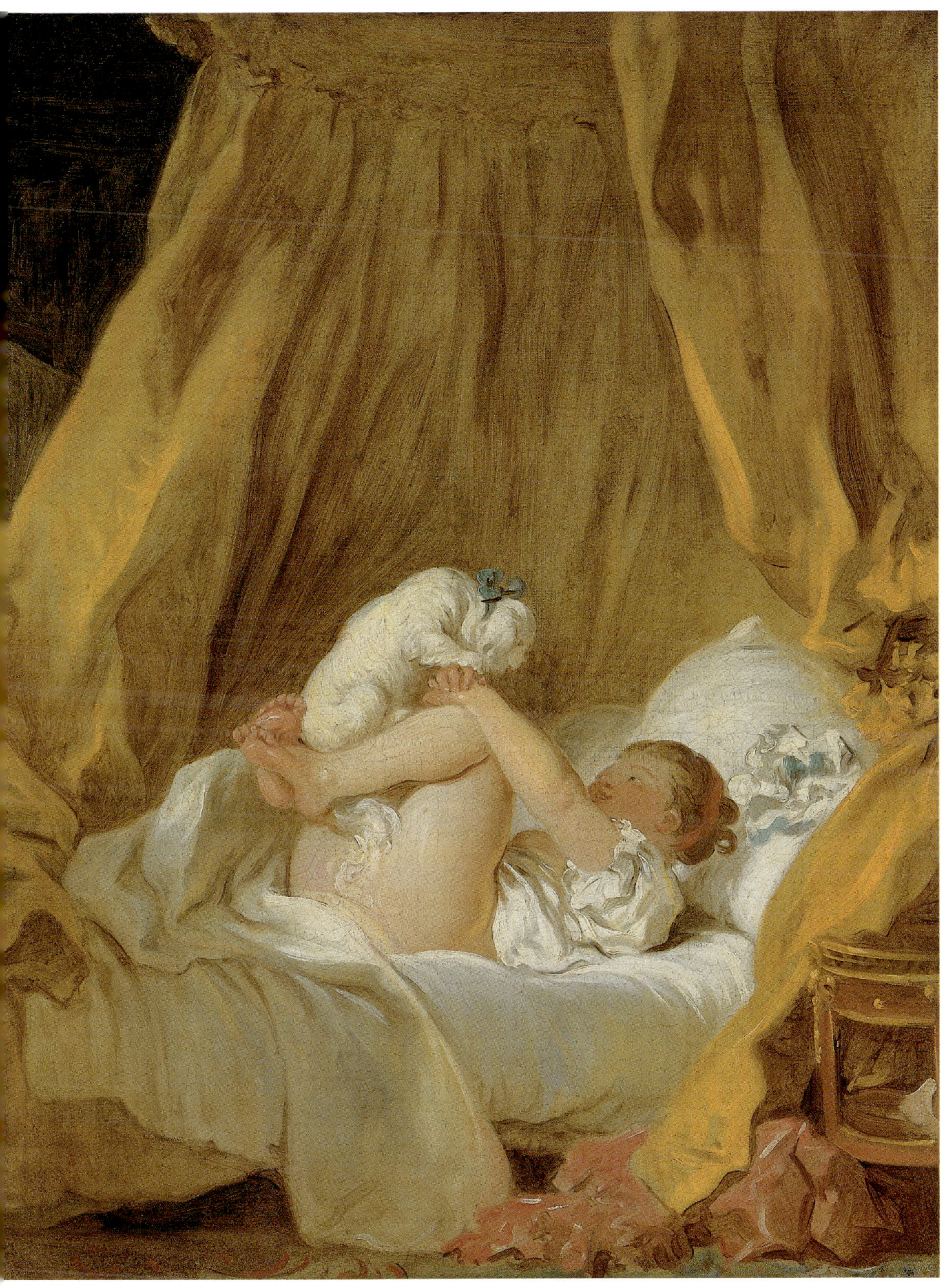

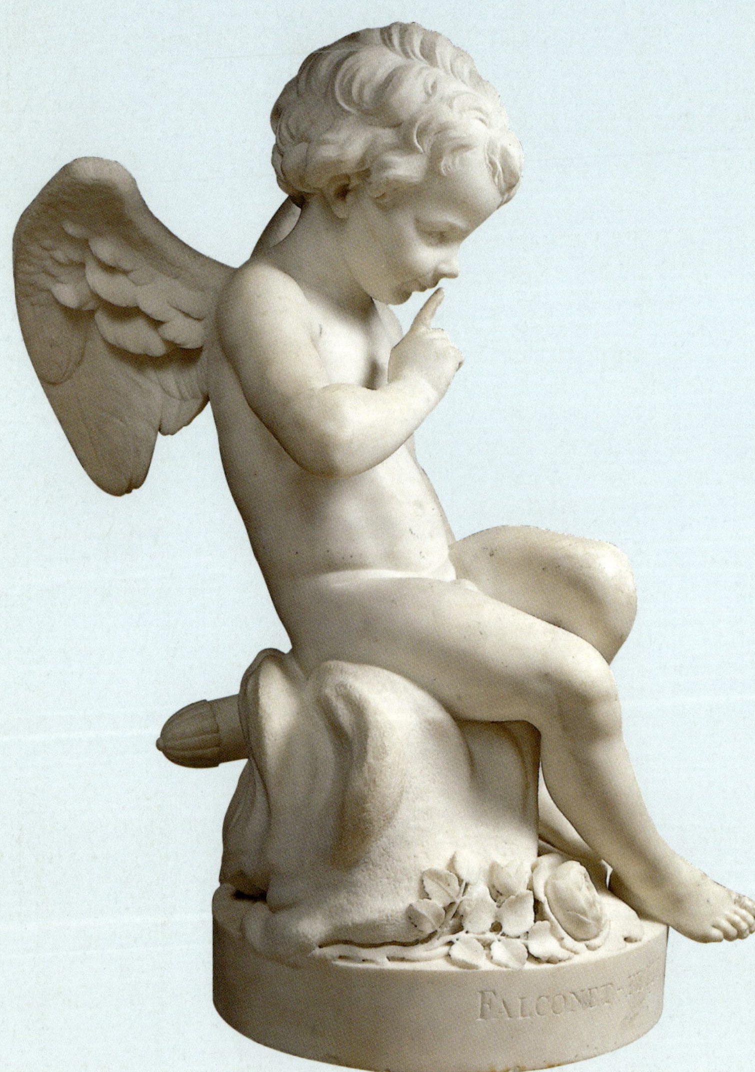

Etienne-Maurice Falconet,
Threatening Love,
1755, marble, 91.5 x 50x 62 cm
Paris, Musée du Louvre.

The Swing,
1767, oil on canvas, 81 x 64.2 cm
London, Wallace Collection.

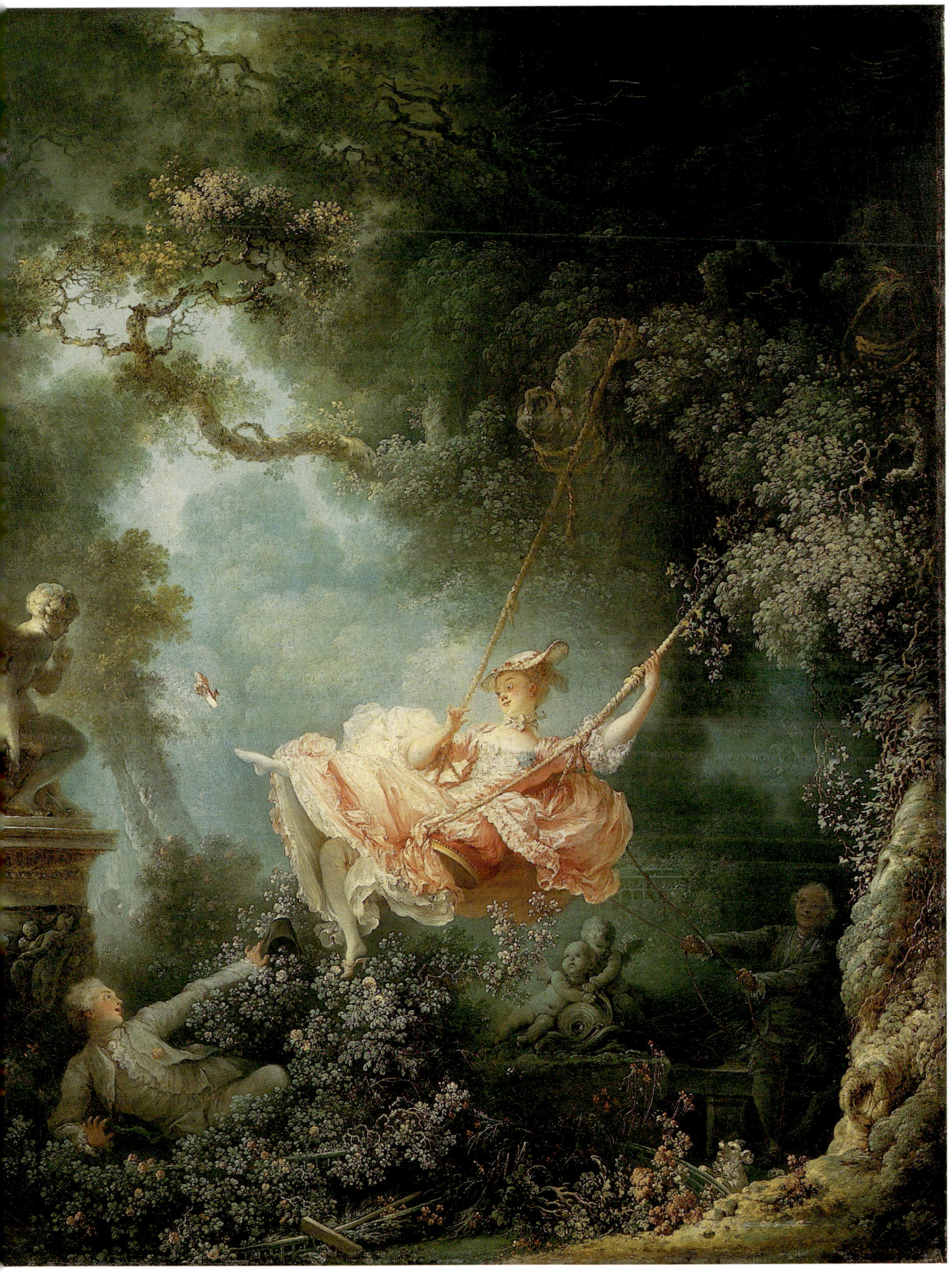

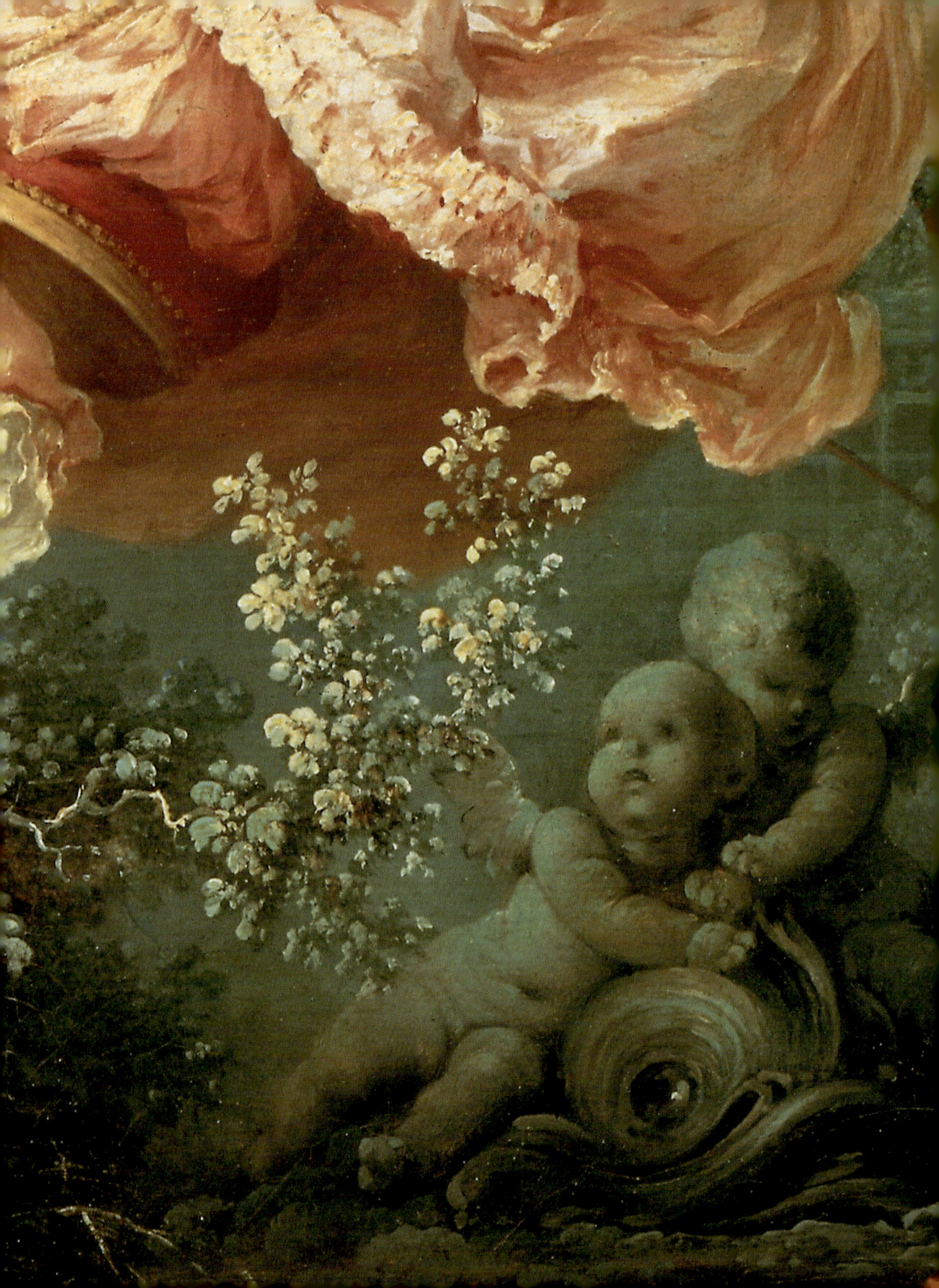

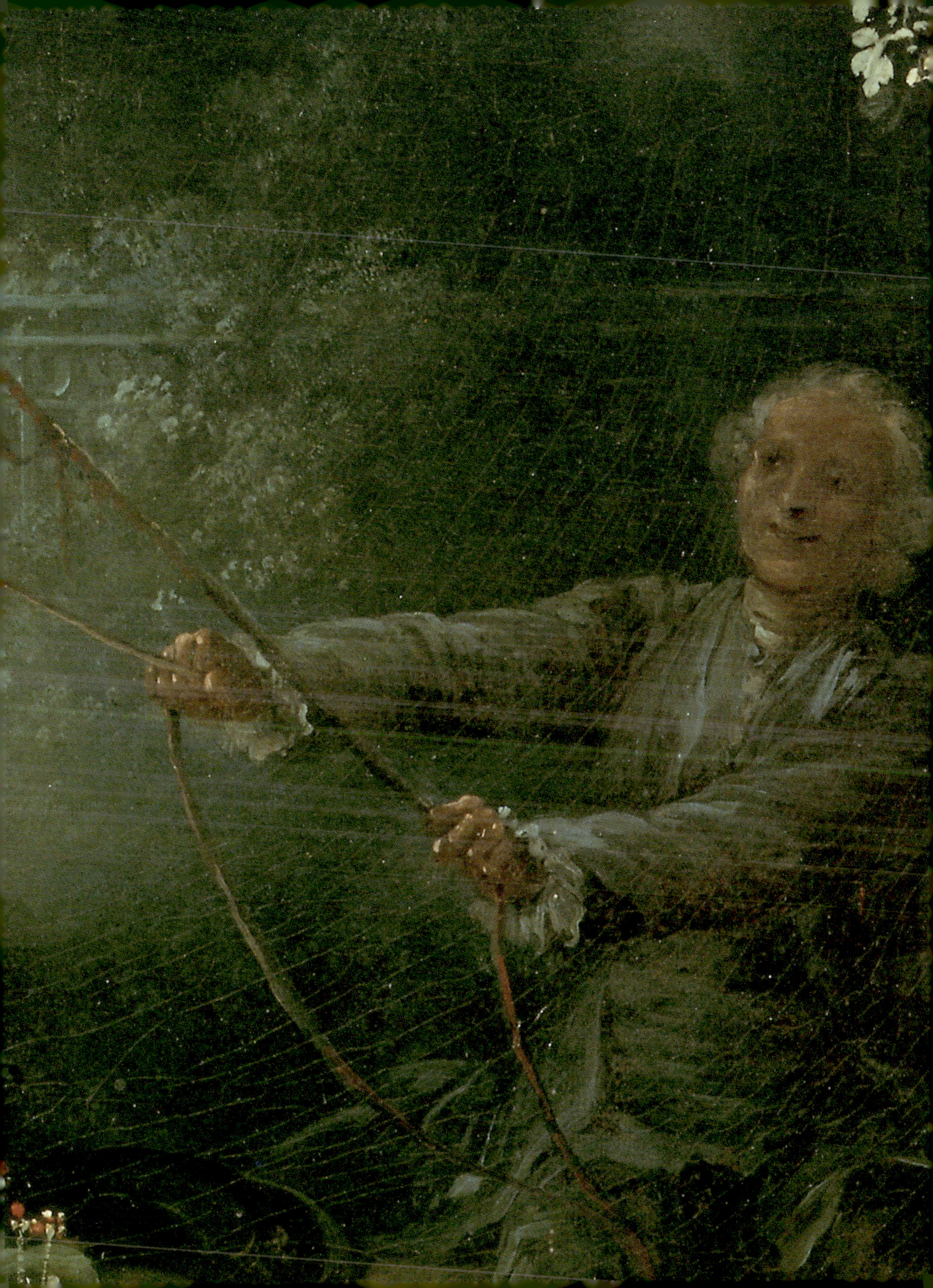

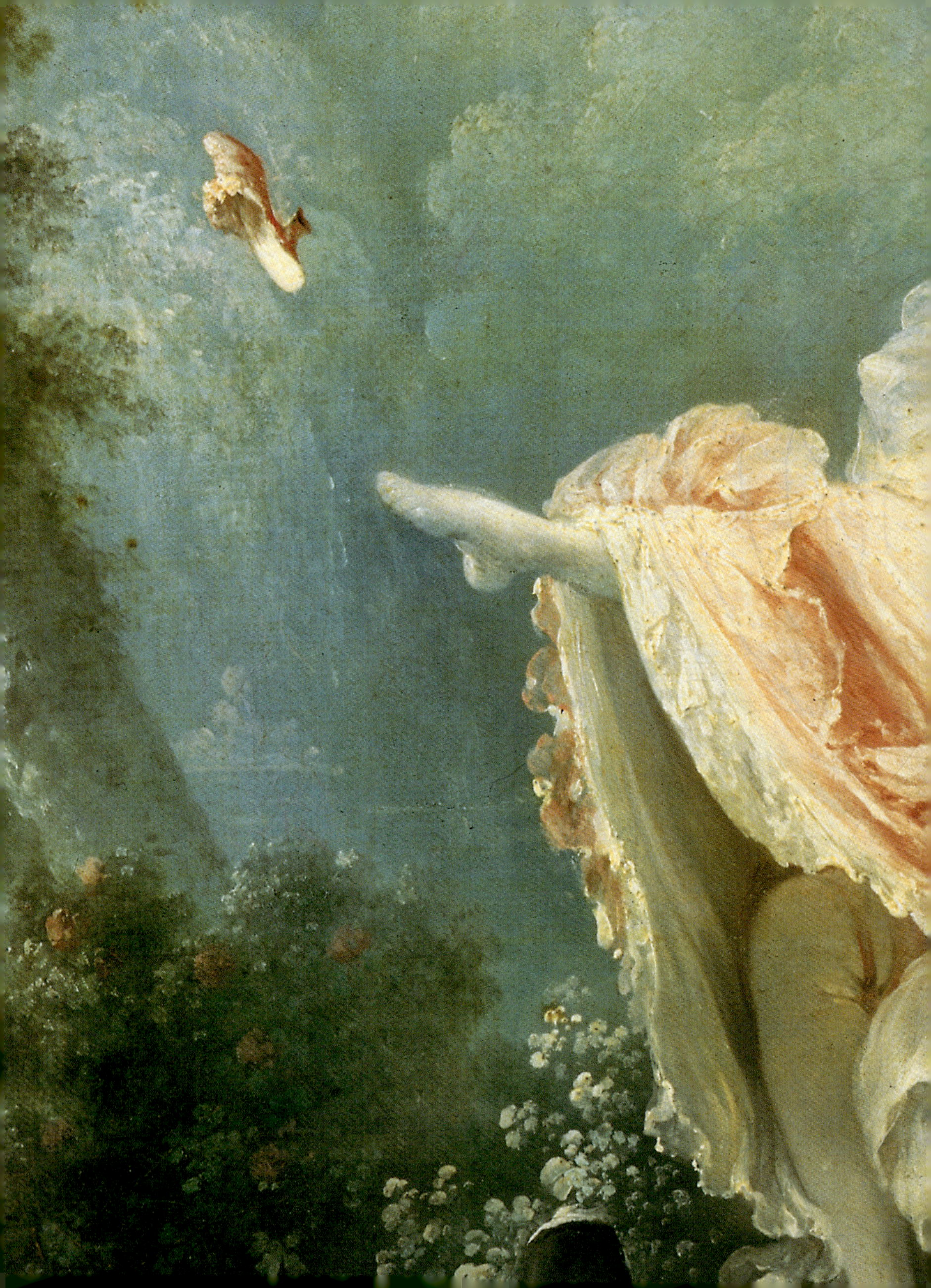

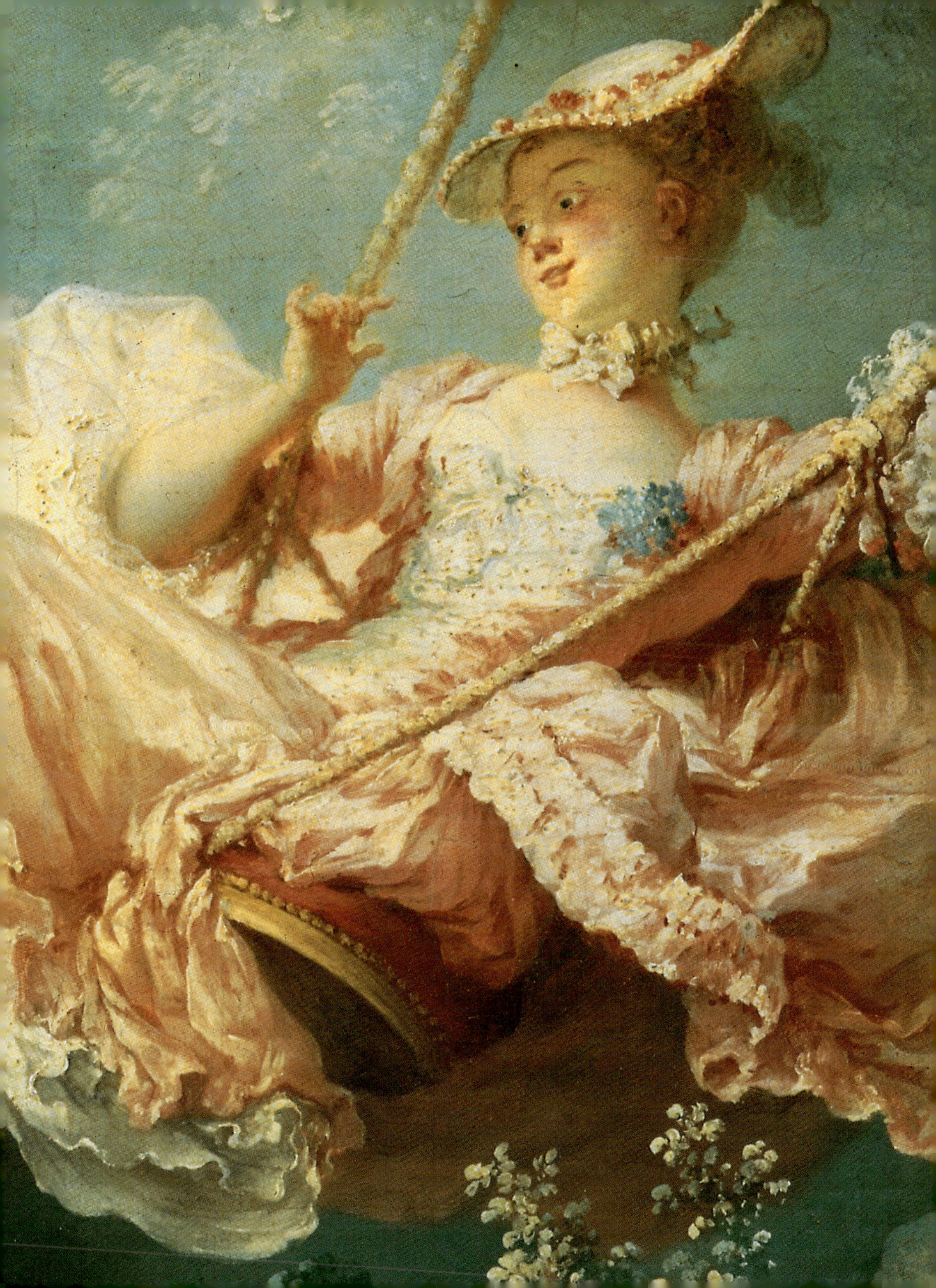

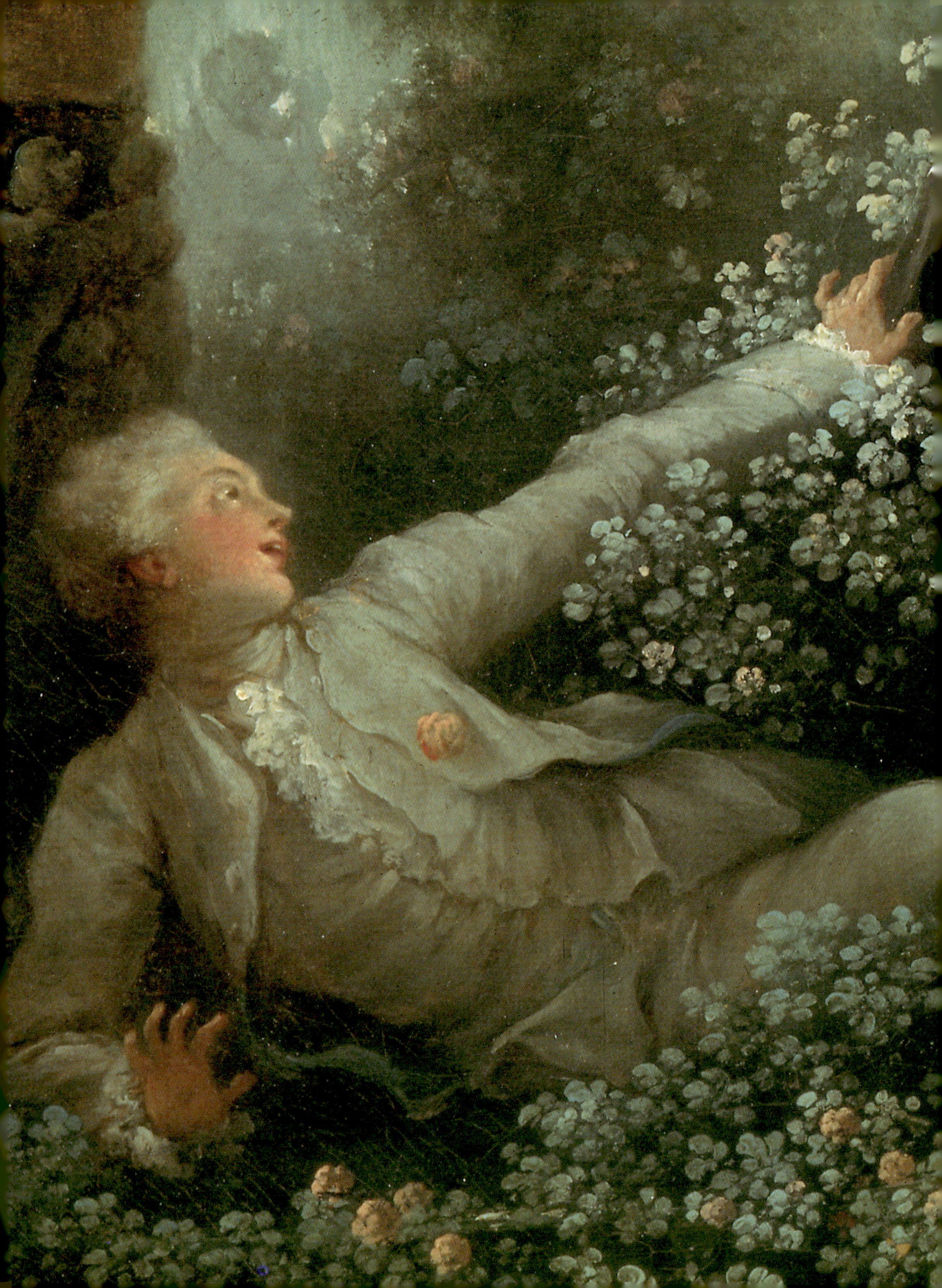

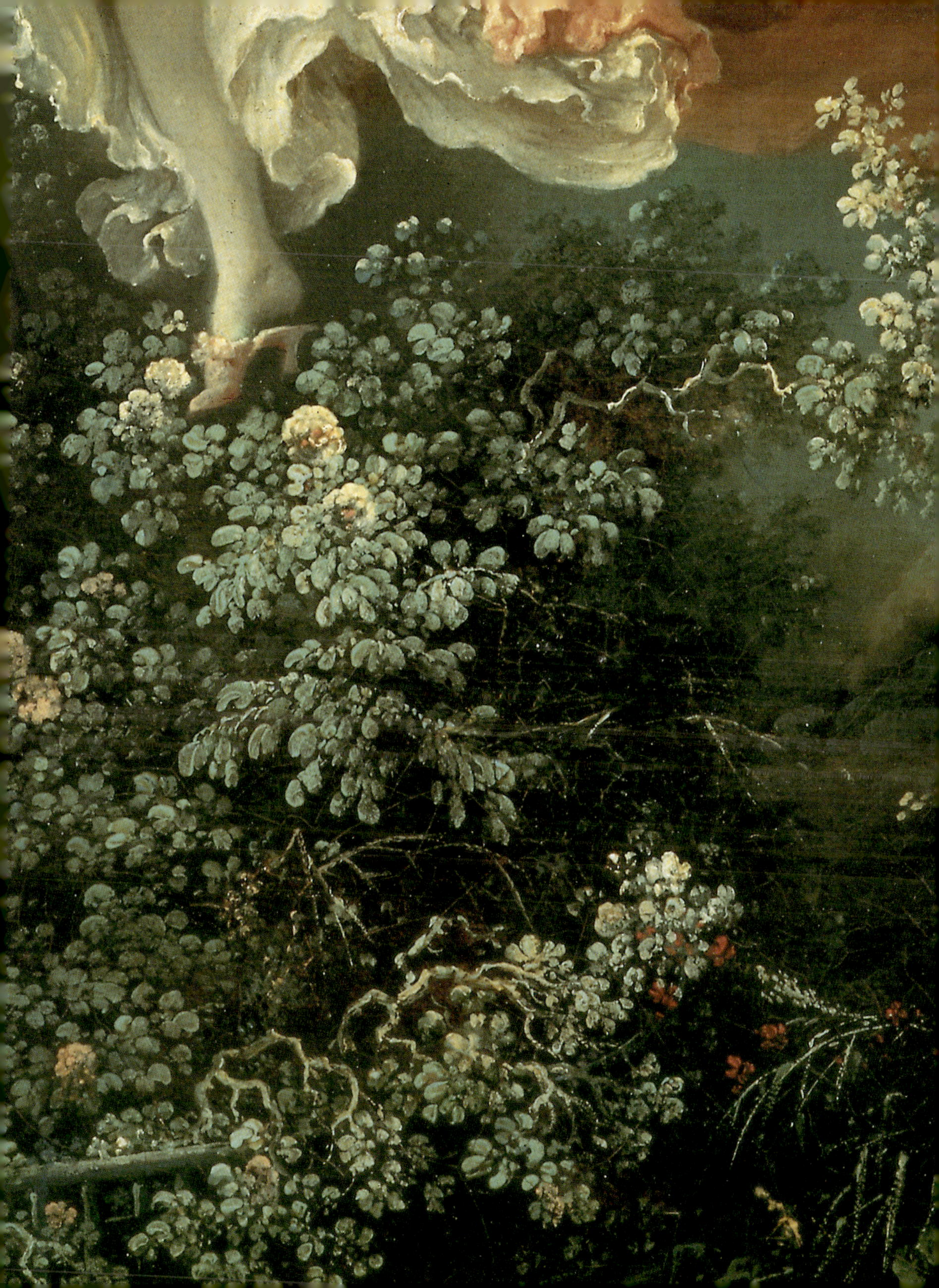

The Du Barry Pavilion at Louveciennes

Commissioned from Fragonard by Louis XV's mistress Madame Du Barry (1743–93) at an unknown date, these four large canvases take us into a world of finer feeling and authentic sensitivity.

In 1770 Madame Du Barry had already acquired four allegorical Fragonard overdoors in the Boucher manner—*Love Setting the World Aflame*, *Day*, and *Night*—for the château at Louveciennes, near Paris, given to her by her royal lover a year before. It may have been after this purchase that she asked Fragonard to decorate the cul-de-four drawing room in the delightful pavilion built deep in the grounds of the château by Claude-Nicolas Ledoux (1736–1806) in 1771. Ledoux, who would go on to design the saltworks at Arc-et-Senans, had already attracted attention with some notably innovative buildings. Like Fragonard, he had opted for a career that remained marginal in official terms, and was only admitted to the Academy in 1773

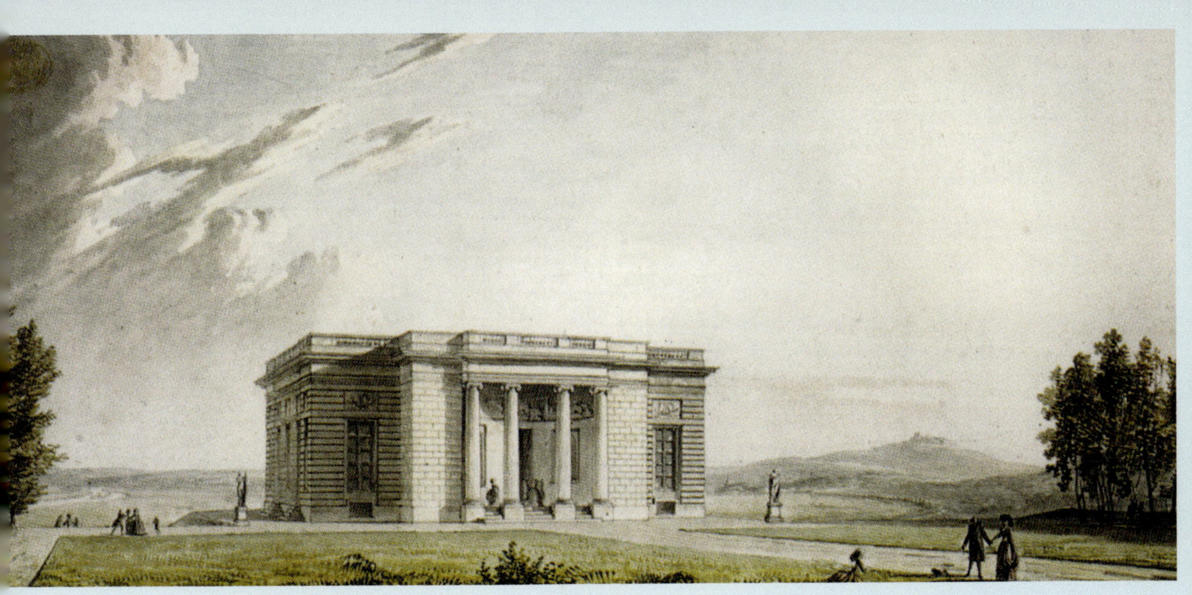

French school, 18th century,
View of the Pavilion built by Ledoux at Louveciennes,
watercolor
London, The British Library

The Pursuit,
1771-72, oil on canvas, 318 x 215.5 cm
New York, The Frick Collection.

through the influence of Madame Du Barry herself. The pavilion he built for her overlooking the Seine Valley underwent successive modifications before being rebuilt, almost identically, after the Second World War; the sober, thoroughly Neoclassical elegance of its facade has remained intact.

Known in the 18th century as *Love's Progress*, Fragonard's four new paintings drew considerable comment from the very first, yet no fully satisfactory explanation has been advanced of their content, or of what led Madame Du Barry to change her mind: after their installation in the pavilion at Louveciennes, Fragonard was obliged to remove them. Were they painted in response to a brief worked out with their intended recipient? Do they constitute a narrative and, if so, in what order are they to be considered? Or are they simply a rendering of the different stages of any love affair? The mystery surrounding what many consider Fragonard's masterpiece adds to the fascination they hold for the viewer, and sharpens the desire to seize their creator's intentions, to penetrate the secrets of his imagination.

In each of them a different, stunningly exuberant setting of flowers and foliage frames a new form of pastoral. From splendid trees luxuriant branches sway against clear skies as hop plants send their twining creepers up the lofty trunks; rose bushes, orange trees in boxes, and hollyhocks emerge in lively contrast with bright harmonies of greens and blues. And in each composition a statue counterpoints the scene being played out in the foreground. In *The Pursuit*, just as in *The Swing*, two *putti* are perched on a dolphin with water gushing from its mouth, their childish play mirroring that of the young people—not much more than children—at the edge of the stone pond: the lad holds out a rose to his surprised lass, who pretends to take flight as her two companions hold her back. And the apple on the bench to the right, next to the plump bunches of grapes: are we to give it the meaning attributed by some to the apple in *The Bolt*? Are we, indeed, in the Garden of Eden, before the loss of innocence?

The figures in the other pictures, while very young, are not teenagers. We note that in the work as a whole, the costumes—especially in the case of the men—are akin to those of the "fantasy portraits" of the time. In *The Meeting*, while the young lady is wearing a dress not unlike that of the heroine of *The Pursuit*, her suitor is sporting a red satin jacket with a frilled collar and a blue bow. Using a ladder to reach the somewhat overgrown garden, he is shown stepping over the low wall to join his beloved, who has a letter in her hand: but a letter written by this elegant young man or by someone else? Their meeting seems to have been disturbed—we guess this from their poses and the way they are both looking in the same direction—by, probably, the noise of someone approaching. He looks transfixed, and she resembles a doe at bay. The game of love is sometimes fraught with danger: such seems to be the message of

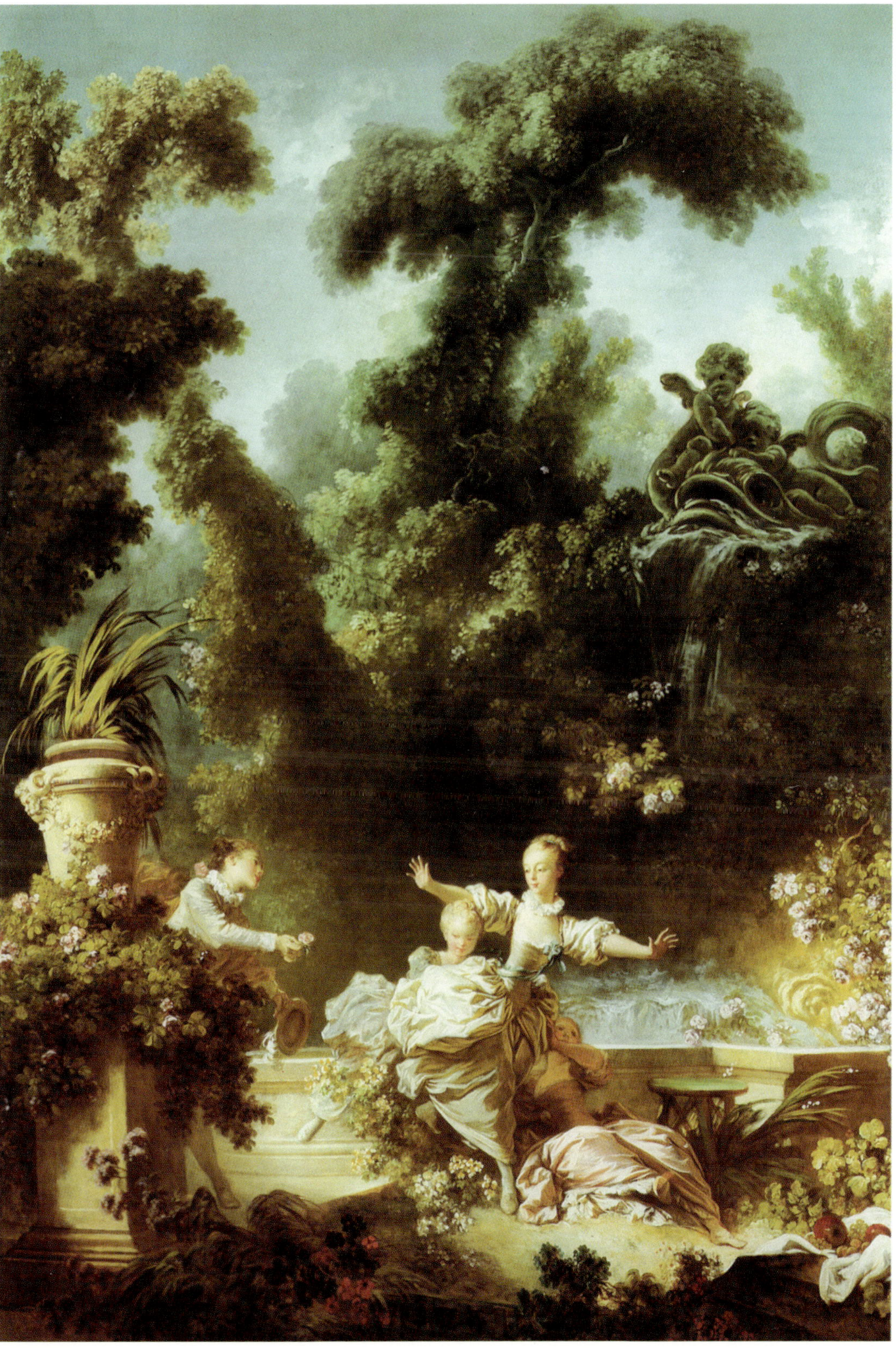

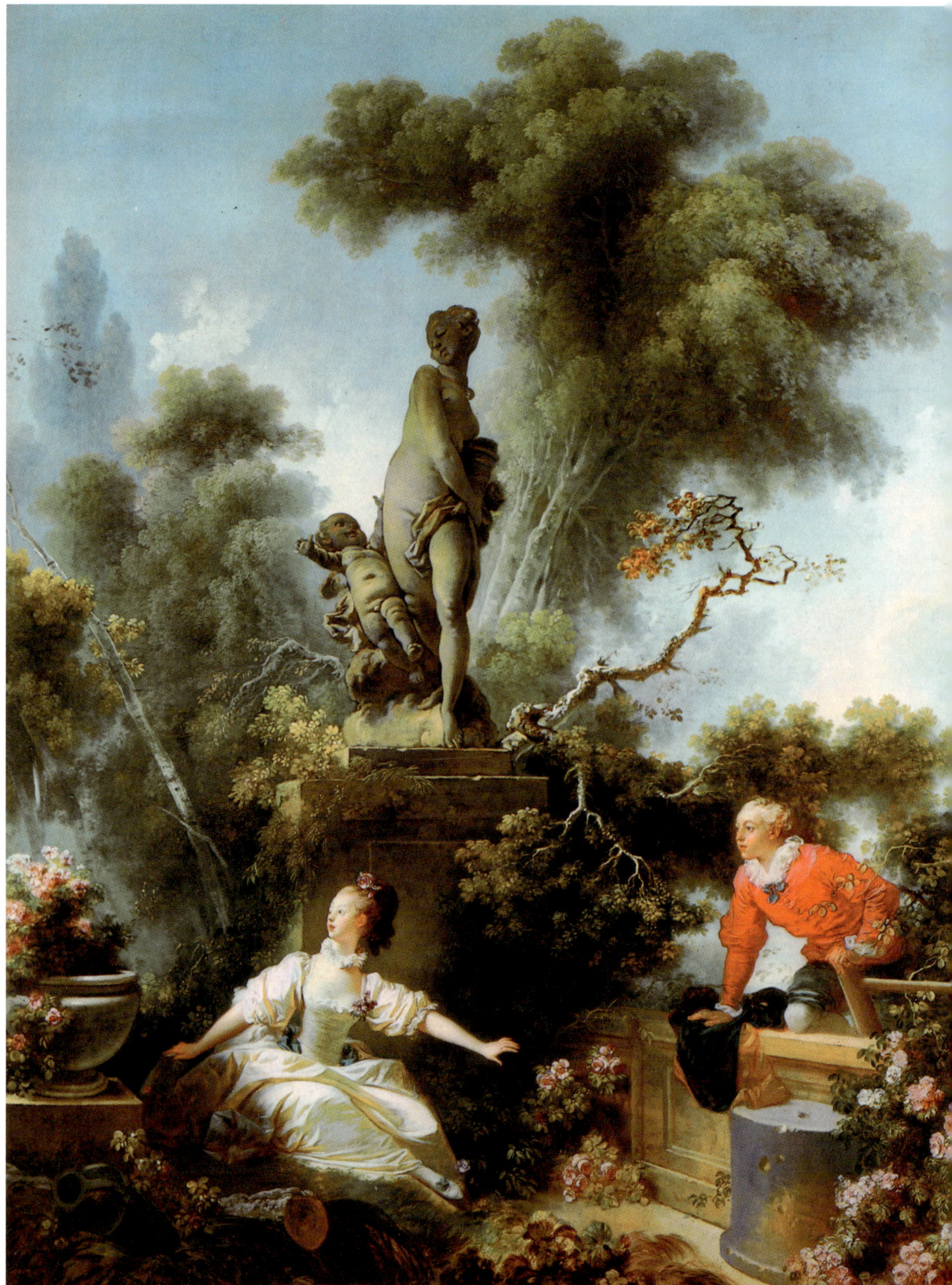

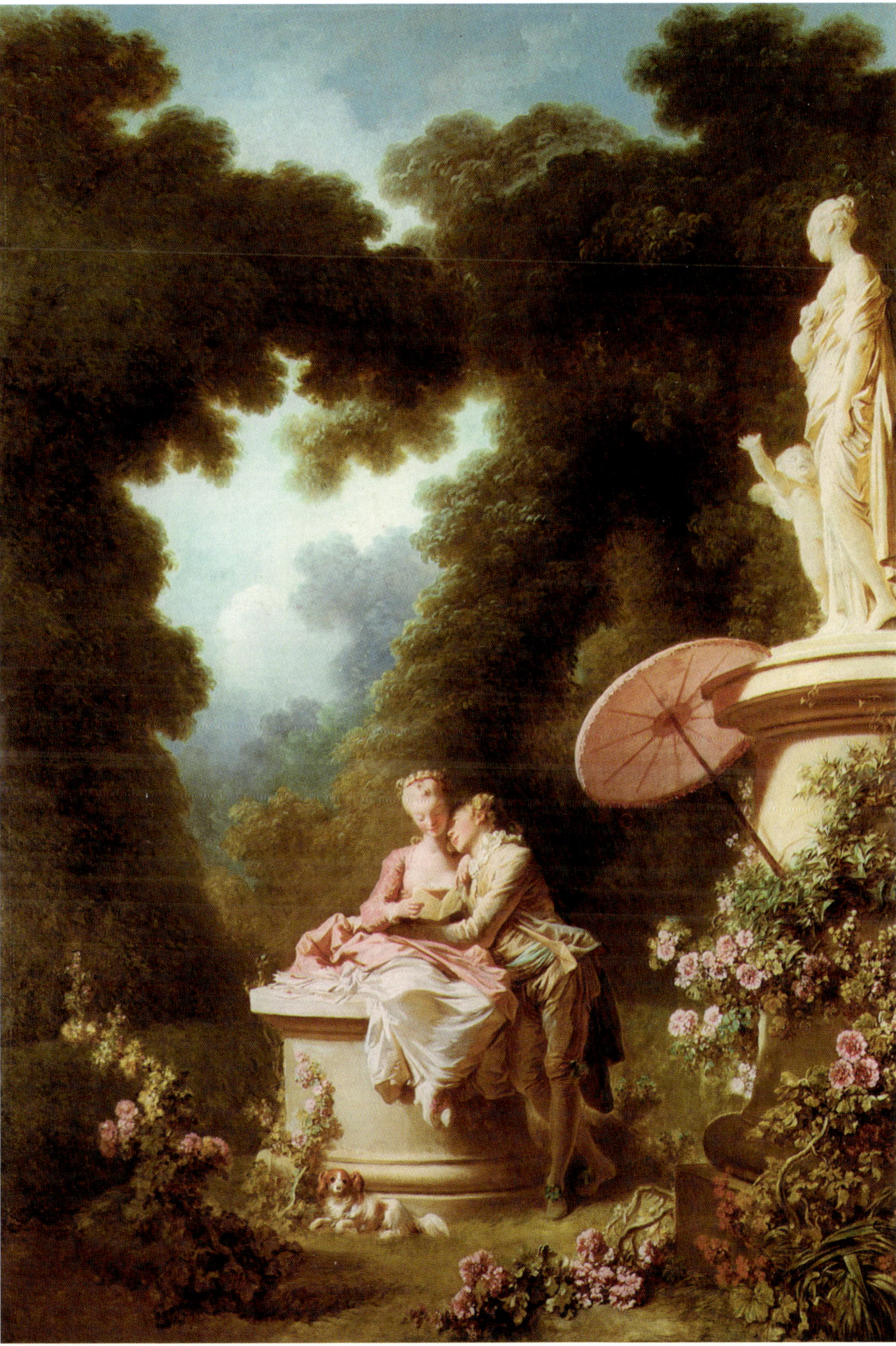

Previous pages:
left page,
The Meeting,
1771–72, oil on canvas, 318 x 243 cm
New York, The Frick Collection.
right page,
Love Letters,
1771–72, oil on canvas, 317 x 217 cm,
New York, The Frick Collection.

The Lover Crowned,
1771–72, oil on canvas, 318 x 243 cm
New York, The Frick Collection.

the beauteous nymph—Venus or Diana—set above them on a pedestal and holding her quiver out of reach of a covetous little cupid.

The following scene takes place under the sign of friendship. Set this time to the right, the statue in *Love Letters* embodies the traditional personification as laid down in the treatises on the visual repertoire: a woman in a simple white robe, throat and left shoulder uncovered, barefoot, and holding a heart in her right hand. By adding an amatory element to the sculpture, the presence of a winged *putto* begging for the heart sharpens the focus on the scene of a young woman seated on a stone plinth in the tender embrace of her beloved. Has the young man not come, too, to plead for a little more than friendship? Will she resist him? Has love been supplanted in her heart by friendship? The letters she has been rereading—she has a bundle of them beside her—have brought a delicate pink flush of emotion to her cheeks. And the King Charles spaniel sitting at her feat: to what pledges of fidelity is his presence an allusion? Love, friendship? Nothing is certain here and emotional confusion reigns in the hearts of the young people, just like the hollyhocks in this improbable garden.

The fourth canvas, *The Lover Crowned*, takes blatant artifice even further in a complex superposition of steps partly overrun by a grassy slope, low walls, a wooden fence, orange trees in boxes and rose bushes. A cupid sleeps in the cast shadow of tall poplars, resting on a rock against which his quiver of arrows is also leaning. If love is slumbering, what are the feelings of the couple posing for a drawing? Is the presence of the sketcher, like that of the musical score and two instruments—a tambourine and a mandolin—a reference to Madame Du Barry's role as a patron of the arts? Certain details in the other paintings could likewise be interpreted as relating to the king's mistress: the young suitor's face and ruffed jacket in *The Meeting* are reminiscent of the 1765 *Portrait de la Du Barry* by François-Hubert Drouais (1727–75), in which the subject is shown disguised as a pageboy. Similarly the statue of Friendship surveying the couple in *Love Letters* offers major resemblances with *Fidelity Embodied by Madame Du Barry Holding the King's Heart*, a sculpture long attributed to Augustin Pajou. Could these be mere coincidences?

The remarks of one of the few visitors to have seen the paintings before their removal from the pavilion tend to indicate the opposite, with their description of "four large pictures by Monsieur Fragonard, whose subjects are pastoral love and which appear to be allegories of the loves of the mistress of the house." If this were indeed the case, the reasons for the rejection of the commissioned works would be plain. Born Jeanne Bécu, "the bastard daughter of a monk and a cook", La Du Barry had been the mistress of Jean Du Barry, known as "The Rake", before marrying his brother Guillaume and succeeding in having herself

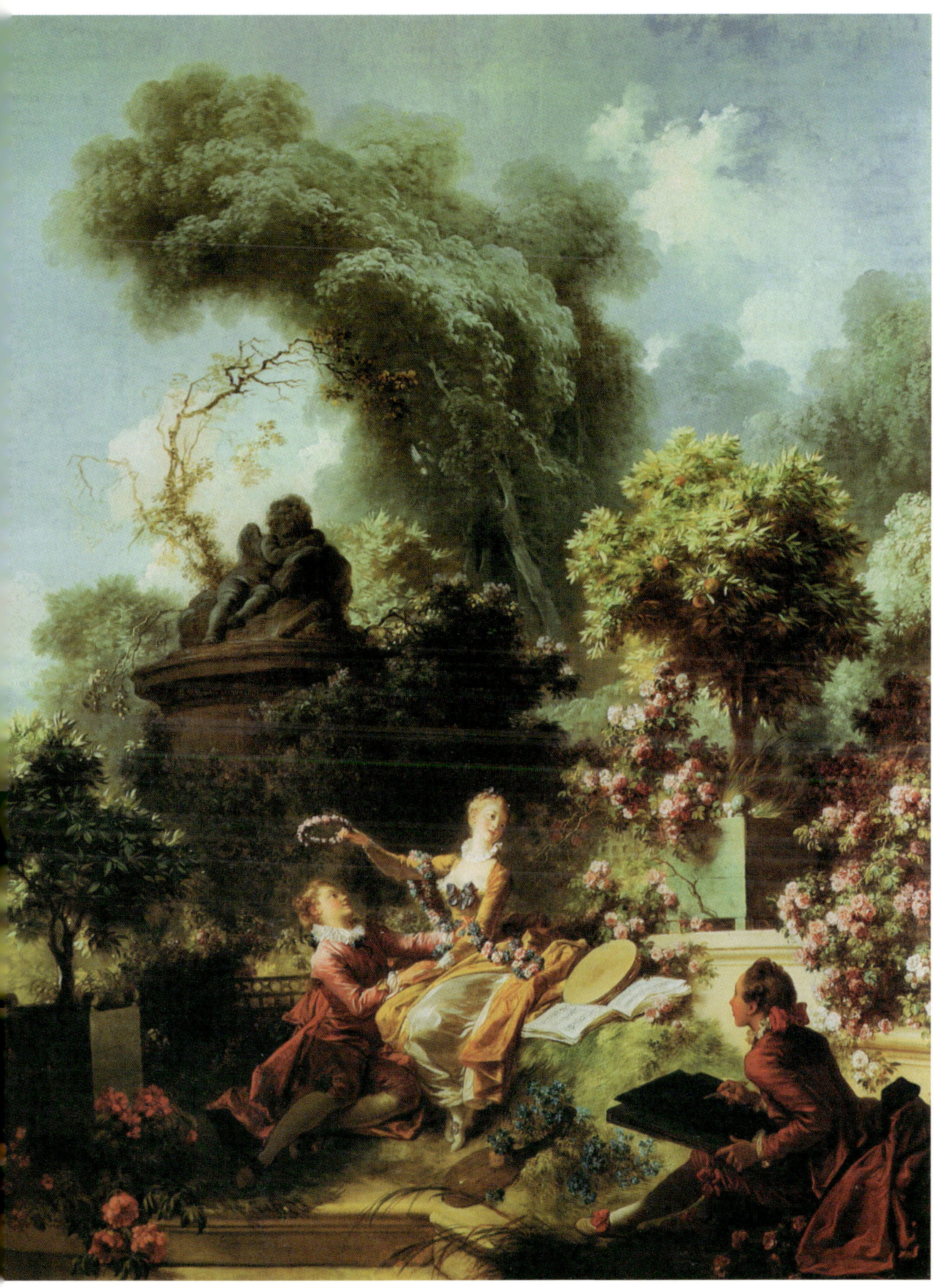

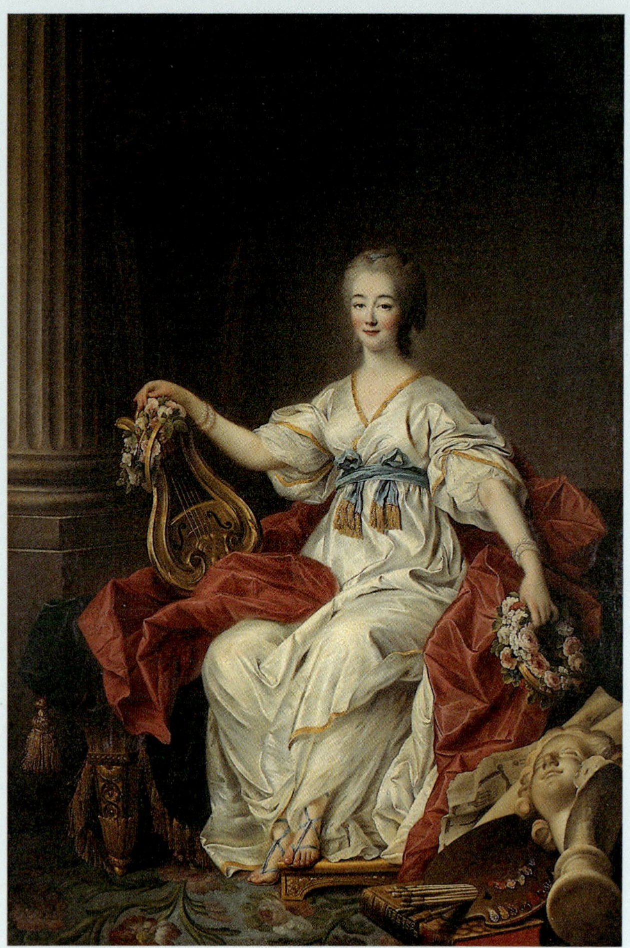

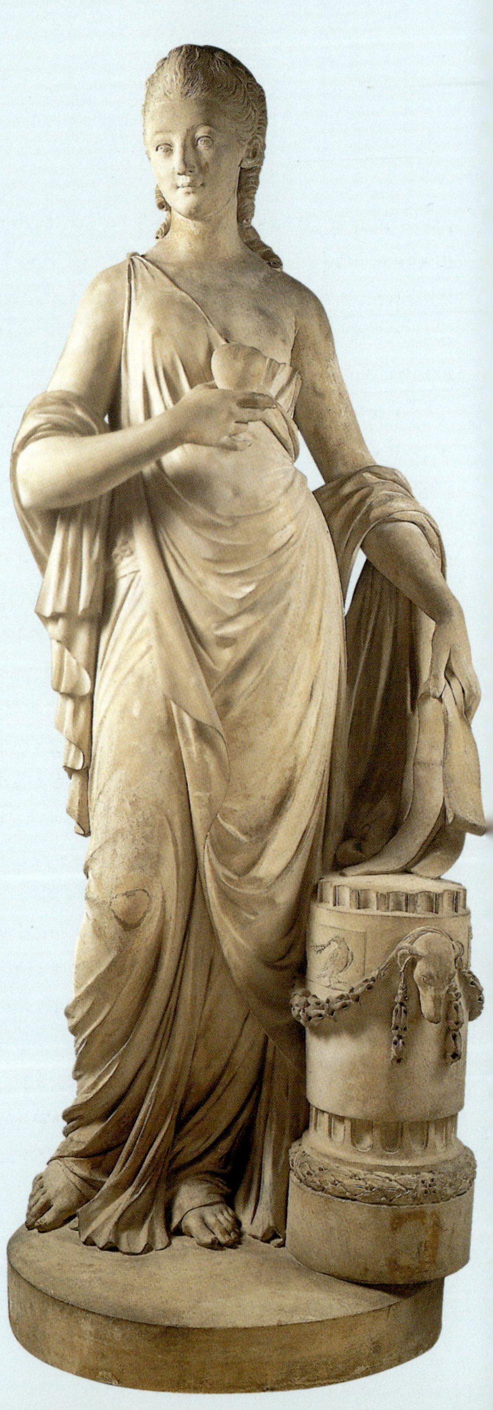

François-Hubert Drouais,
Madame Du Barry as a Muse,
1771, oil on canvas, 198 x 141 cm,
Versailles, Chambre de Commerce et d'Industrie.

French School, 18th century,
(formerly attributed to Augustin Pajou)
Fidelity Embodied by Madame Du Barry Holding the King's Heart,
stone, 190 x 67 cm
Marly-le-Roi/Louveciennes, Musée-Promenade (on loan from the Musée du Louvre).

presented at Court in April 1769. But can we really imagine Fragonard being so inept? Can we really imagine him using these pictures even to hint at the "career" of the illustrious figure who had commissioned them?

To replace the Fragonards, Madame Du Barry turned to Joseph-Marie Vien (1716–1809), and this suggests a more likely explanation for her refusal. Like Fragonard, Vien had studied with Natoire and used his stay in Rome (1744–50) to look closely at the recent excavations at Herculaneum. Convinced that the painting of antiquity was superior to that of his own time, he became its ardent advocate, to the point of making a case for a return to encaustic. His *La marchande d'amours* ("Vendor of Cupids"), adapted from a Roman painting, met with enormous success at the Salon of 1763, two years before Fragonard's *Coresus*. This work launched the icily pared down "Greek style", a forerunner of Neoclassicism, which Vien proceeded to use for the pavilion at Louveciennes. The critics agreed among themselves to call the work as a whole "Love's Progress in the Hearts of Young Women". Two of the canvases were completed in 1773—*Two Greek Maidens Swear Never to Love* and *Young Greek Maidens Deck Sleeping Cupid with Flowers*—and the series was soon rounded off with *Lover Crowning His Mistress* and *The Temple of Hymen*.

While the overall theme can be related to the (still hypothetical) one chosen by Fragonard, the Vien series is totally different in its "antique" treatment of the figures and setting: costumes, colonnades, sacrificial altar, etc. A further difference lies in the unambiguously traditional use of living—as opposed to sculpted—cupids, and the personification of time as a bearded old man with wings and a scythe. The four scenes knit readily into a simple story: a couple swearing fidelity before the altar of Hymen. Everything here—the austere composition, the soberness of the palette, the smoothness of surface and the stiffness of the poses—is in striking contrast with liveliness and vividness of the Fragonard work. In a true sign of the times, classical rhetoric has taken over from light-hearted banter. Doubtless, however, the four Vien paintings fitted better with Ledoux's architecture and the new fashion Madame Du Barry would herself follow when she sat for the portraitist Drouais wearing a simple Greek-style tunic tied beneath the bust.

The first two of Vien's series for Louveciennes were shown at the Salon in 1773, receiving an ambivalent reception. We can well imagine Fragonard's reaction as not especially positive, but he did not dwell on the subject for long: in October of the same year he left Paris for Italy in the company of his wife and a patron who would remain loyal to him, Bergeret de Grancourt.

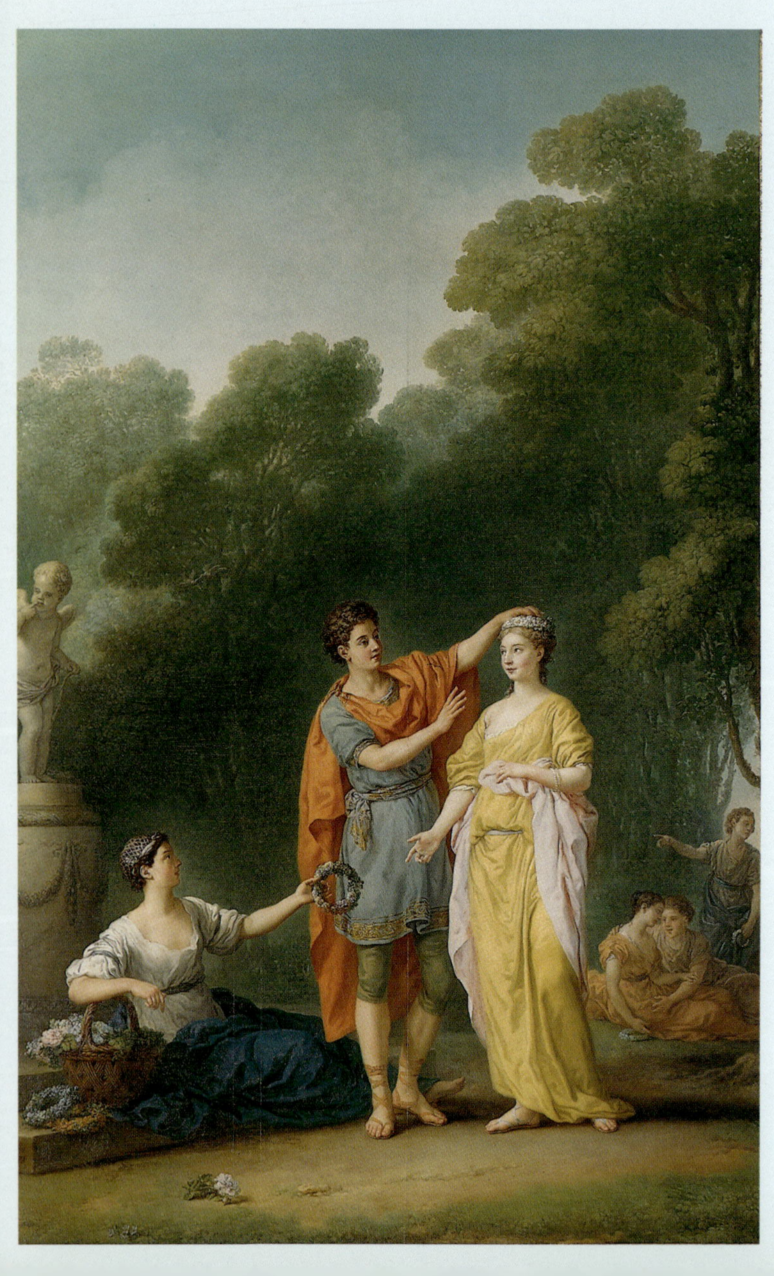

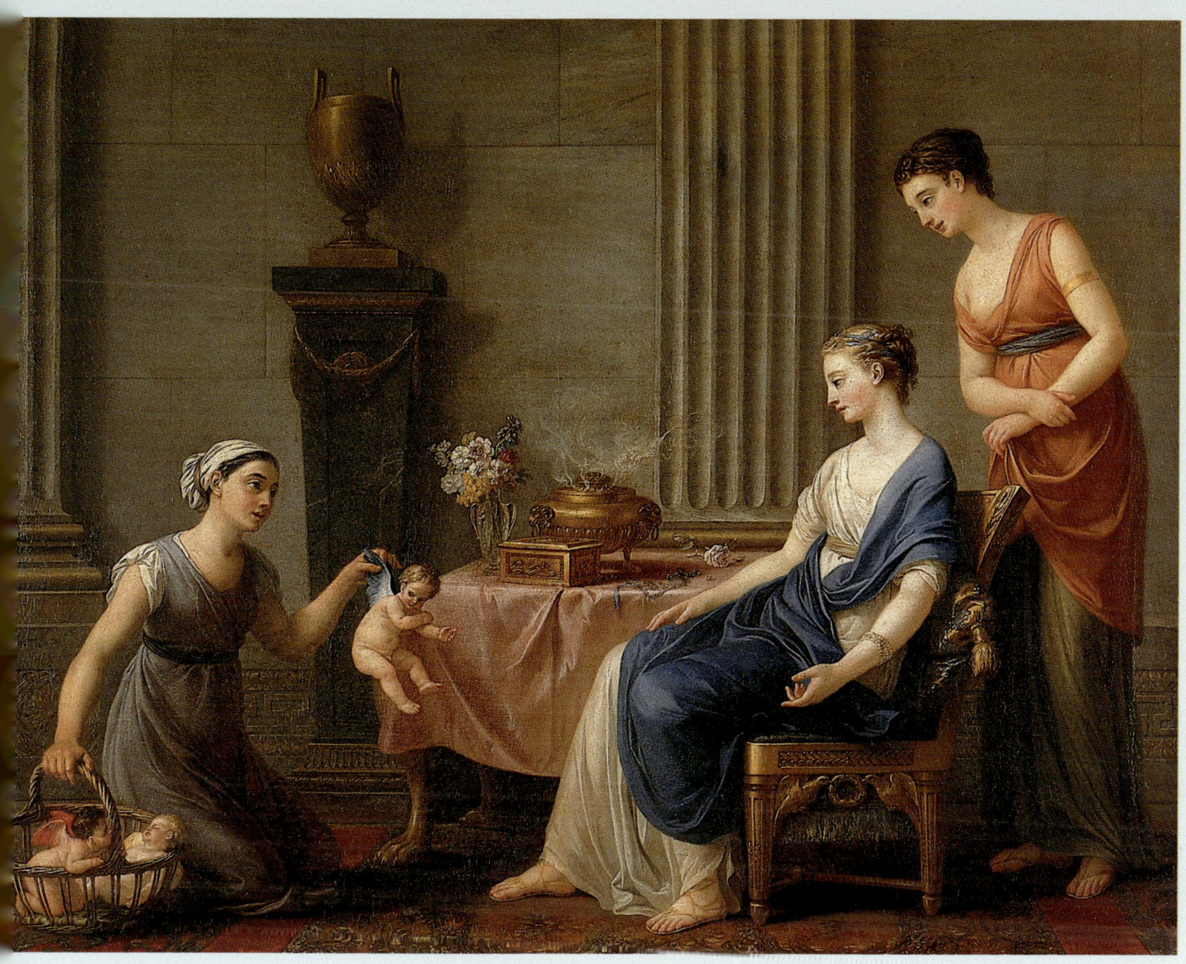

Joseph-Marie Vien,
The Cupid Seller
1763, oil on canvas, 98x122 cm
Fontainebleau, Château.

Joseph-Marie Vien,
Lover Crowning His Mistress,
1773, oil on canvas, 335 x 202 cm
Paris, Musée du Louvre.

V

Cypresses,
Hornbeam
and

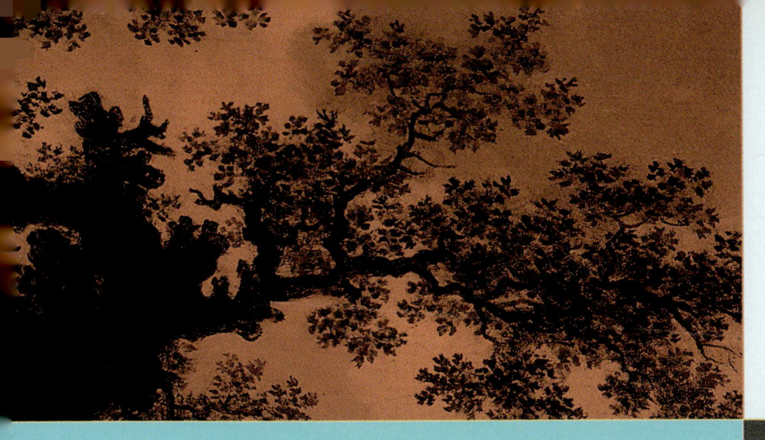

Hollyhocks

From Pastoral to Italian Landscape

Every phase in Fragonard's career was marked in one way or another by his use of nature, a field in which his considerable range points up yet again the variety of his sources of inspiration and the extent of his talents. He first ventured onto this terrain during his time with Boucher, that master of Rococo extravagance. His teacher unfailingly chose just the right natural surroundings for his mythological scenes, in the form of the deliciously artificial environments that notably characterized his stage sets, and to which Fragonard very probably contributed. This was nature rich, concentrated and spirited: the perfect setting for the frolicking of naiads and other nymphs, and, with its minglings of blue-greens, shadings of gray and golden glows, for scenes of pastoral love.

Fragonard's canvases from this period show just how skillfully he had transformed his master's approach into his own. Steps in the foreground, a glimpse of a distant dovecote, stone balustrades and benches here and there: thus did he structure the picture space, establish views, and create happy surprises. He brought a greater spatial openness to his compositions, made play with resonant chromatic harmonies: the red of hollyhocks complementing the scarlet apron of a shepherdess, the flicker of light on foliage echoing the yellow satin dress of a girl high on a swing.

The first stay in Italy, as we have seen, was a revelation. Yet at least as crucial as Michelangelo, Raphael, Domenichino and Caravaggio, were the walks he took with Hubert Robert and the Abbé de Saint-Non. Boucher may have inculcated in his pupil the art of balance in landscape composition, and provided him with a repertoire of readymade forms, but with this immersion in the Roman countryside all the lessons went out the window. Nature has its own laws, to which repetition is alien and which do not always—if ever—sit well with the constraints of two-dimensional representation. Out of the long al fresco drawing sessions Fragonard now undertook, came compositions whose simplicity was founded in myriad nuances; the time had not yet come when painters would set their easels up outdoors and record their impressions directly, but those large red chalk drawings, for all that they are mere monochromes,

Italian Landscape with Two Strollers,
1760, red chalk, 36 x 45.8 cm
Angers, Musée des Beaux-Arts.

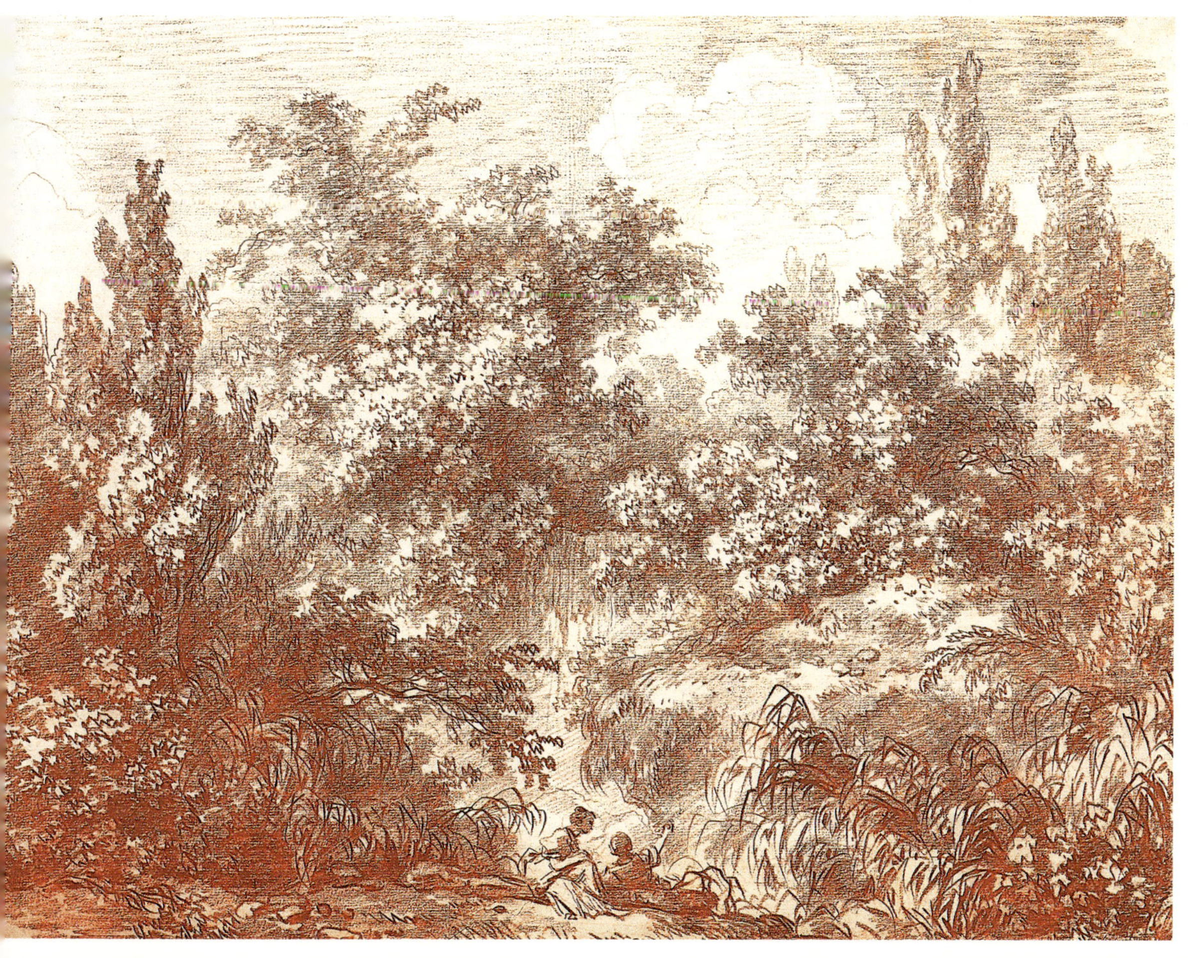

speak to us with a subtlety and sensitivity not to be found in his studio landscapes of the same period.

The best-known of these drawings were done at Tivoli. Built in the 16th century for Hippolyte d'Este, the Villa d'Este was in a state of advanced dilapidation by Fragonard's time. The holm-oak hedges were unpruned, the paths overgrown, and the fountains in a sorry state. The trees had spread every which way and the cypresses had reached alarming heights. Yet in spite of this picturesque jumble, we cannot help noticing how the artist has homed in unerringly on the underlying classical order, choosing angles that stress the views, the symmetry and the orchestration of the garden as it originally was. Nor did he restrict himself to the established beauty spots: in drawings as visually gratifying as they are impressively monumental and geometrically meticulous, he set out to capture all nature's wildness, both in the grounds of the villa and beyond, in less-frequented places no buildings had ever embellished. Space engulfed by dense foliage, terraces overrun by teeming plant life, rocky outcrops battered by torrents: nothing is immobile here, but neither is there any muddle in these virtuoso pages.

Looking North

Unlike Hubert Robert, Fragonard did not go on to use the grounds and gardens of his Italian scenes as leitmotifs for later works. He needed to make fresh discoveries, to try out other ways of describing nature. The Northern approach, for instance. The work of the 17th-century Dutch masters was especially prized at the time: not just the genre scenes, but also the landscapes that were especially sought after by collectors. Boucher had a substantial personal collection of works from this school: eighty-two paintings and more than a thousand drawings from which he sometimes drew material for his picturesque landscapes. His post-mortem catalogue of 1771 included, among others, works attributed to Rembrandt, Bril, Van Ostade, Berchem, Jordaens and Van Goyen, and at the sale Fragonard himself managed to acquire a portrait of a burgomaster attributed to Van Dyck. His interest in the Northern School began very early, but one or more trips to Flanders and Holland—it now seems certain that he was at Malines in the summer of 1773—enabled him to deepen both his knowledge and his love of its practitioners.

Even without these contacts, there were enough pictures by Ruisdael, Hobbema and Berchem in private collections in Paris and on the art market there for Fragonard to get to know these artists well and to soak himself in their style. We know, for example, that he borrowed a "view of a woodland path" by the Dutchman Jacob Ruisdael (1628/29–82) from the art dealer and expert Jean-Baptiste-Pierre Lebrun—husband of Madame Vigée-Lebrun—to use as a model for one of his own landscapes. His skill in imitating the work of his illustrious predecessors was much admired and his own painting regarded as worthy of comparison with theirs. On one occasion the Chevalier de Clesle, finding a Ruisdael in his collection too sparsely populated, sought counsel from Fragonard, who deftly added in human figures and animals. In the home of a certain Monsieur de Boynes, another lover of the Northern painters, a Fragonard—a small hill leading down to a pond, with washerwomen and sheep—was hung as a pendant to a work by Dutchman Jan Wynants (1620/25–84). This latter gambit, an occasional feature of the private art scene in Paris, was a diverting way of testing visitors' ability to distinguish the original from the imitation.

Yet Fragonard's landscapes speak more eloquently than any anecdote. We know of some twenty pictures by him—mostly on canvas, but some on wood—which offer a striking resemblance to the Northern models. In them we find not only the picnics and rustic scenes the masters were so fond of, but also their technique, with its glazes and generous impasto. Like them, Fragonard composed his landscapes with a marked emphasis on skies traversed by clouds running the entire gamut of the grays. Below, a little promontory, a picturesque rocky outcrop or a watering place would bring the colors of autumn into the picture. Fragonard also caught weather and atmosphere with the same subtlety as Ruisdael, using patches of sunlight to highlight the tips of bushes and the coats of animals.

He seems to have continued with this kind of landscape until late in his career. They were much sought after, and the prices they fetched may have been an incentive, but he never opted for facility or repetition. Working within austerely narrow limits, he varied his scenes and brought them to life with a few tellingly picturesque details: a mill, a hut, a shepherd couple. It was doubtless from the Northern masters that he also borrowed the idea of the tree, reaching skyward with bare, lightning-shattered branches that we will later come upon in a totally different context.

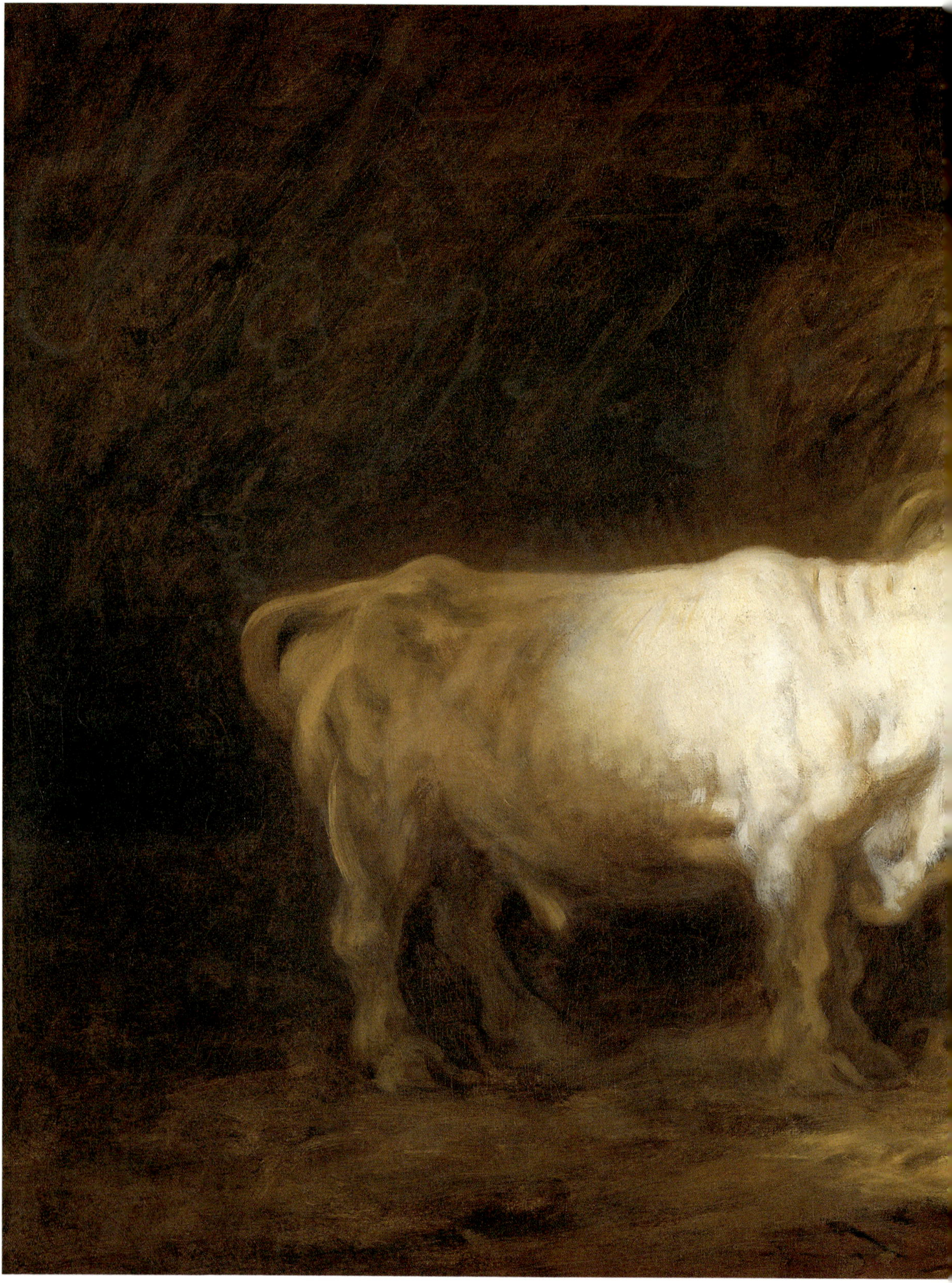

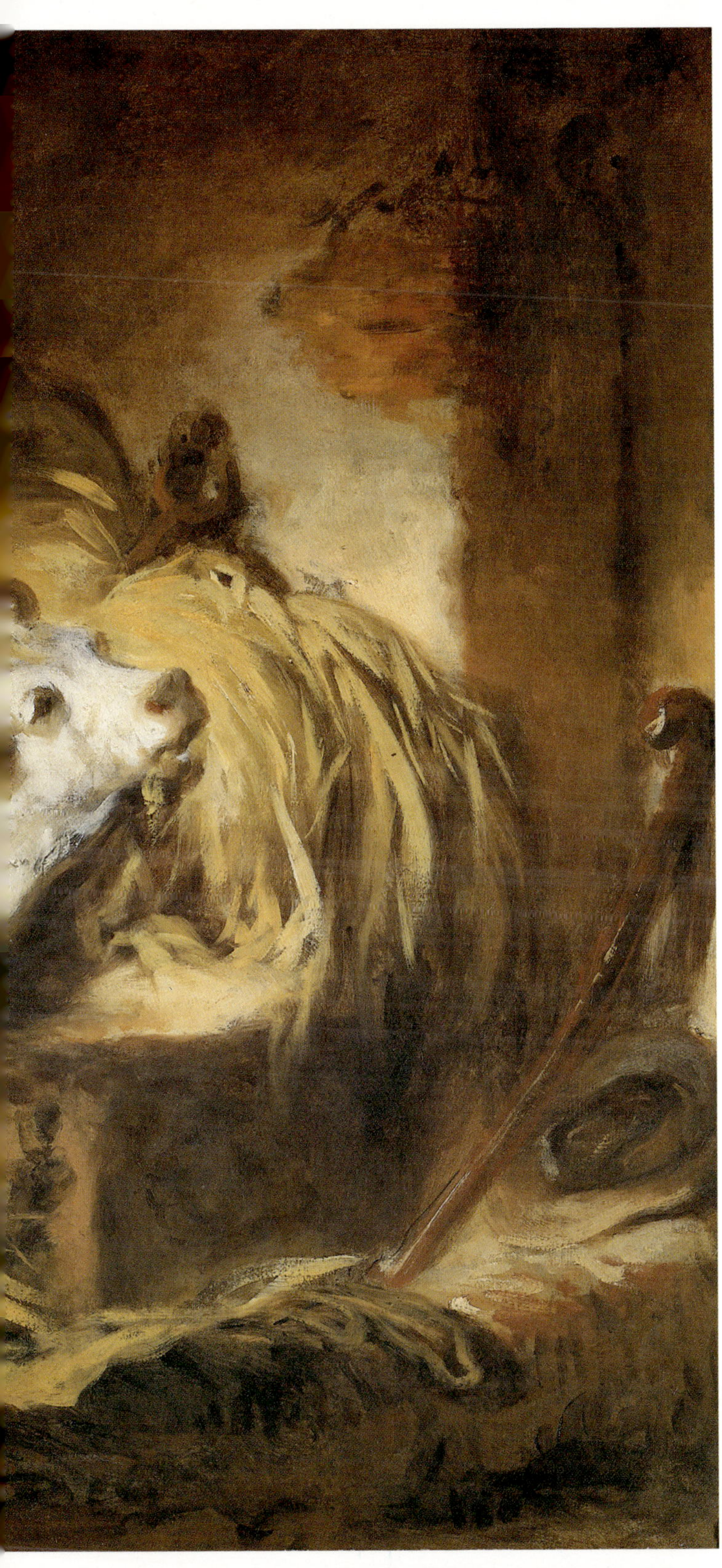

The White Bull in the Stable,
c. 1765, oil on canvas, 72.5 x 91 cm
Paris, Musée du Louvre.

Mercury and Argus,
after Karel Fabritius ,
c. 1762, oil on canvas, 59 x 73 cm
Paris, Musée du Louvre.

Karel Fabritius,
Mercury and Argus ,
1645-47, oil on canvas, 73.5 x 104 cm
Los Angeles, Los Angeles County Museum of Art.

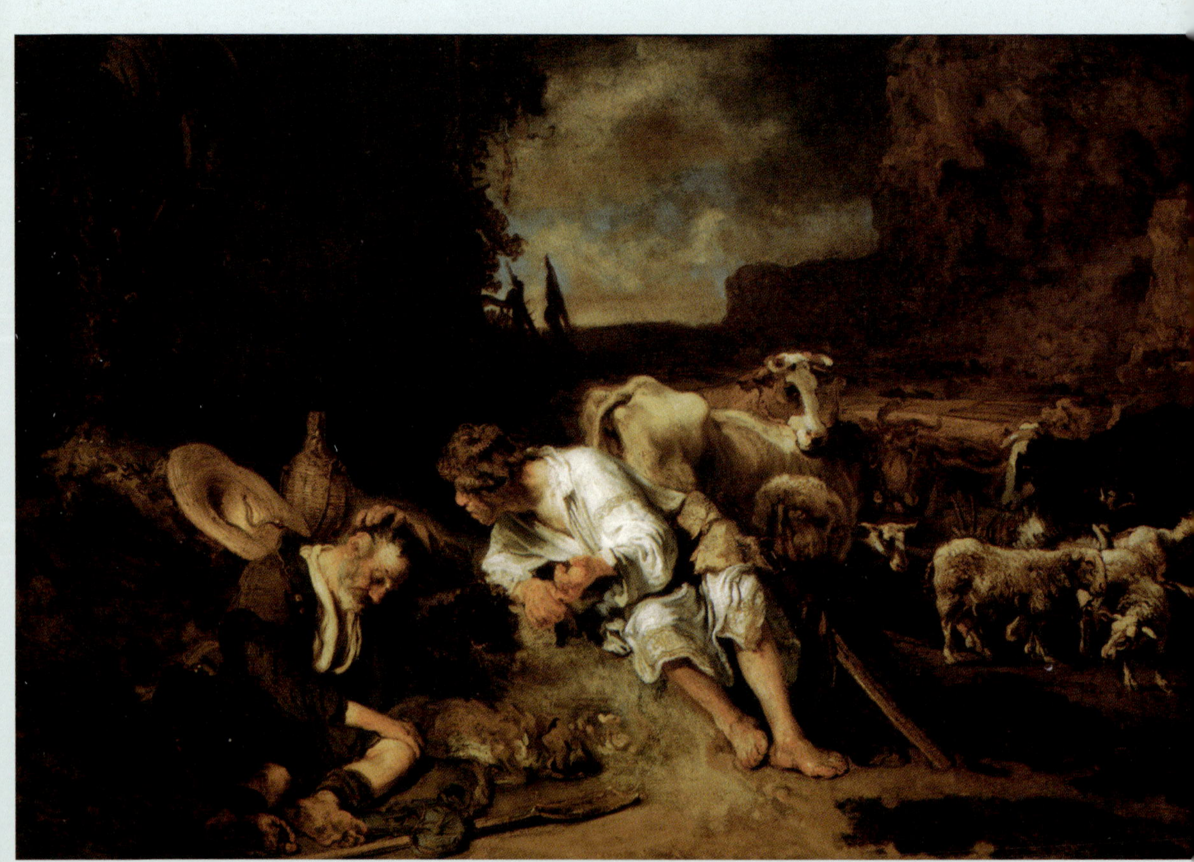

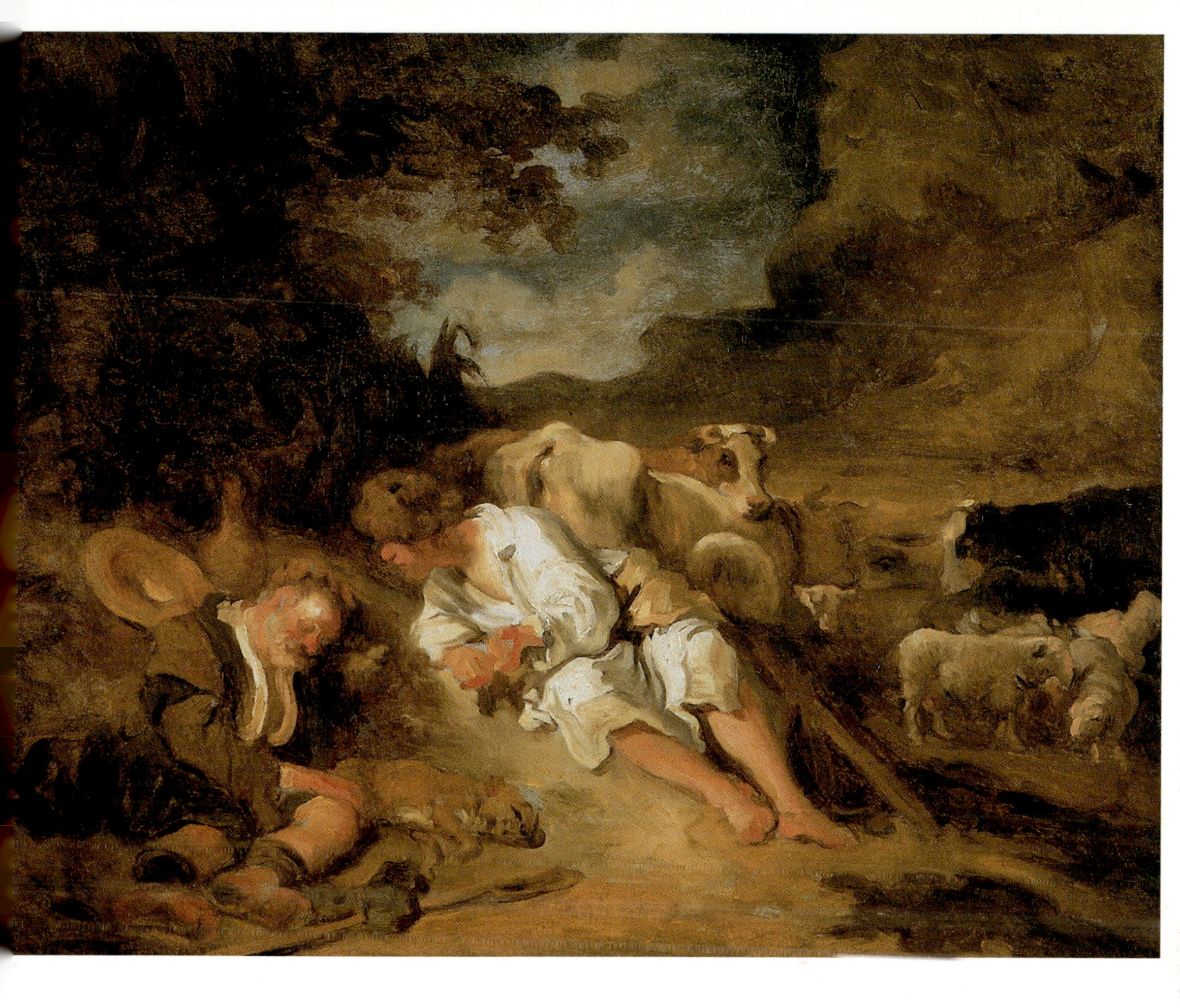

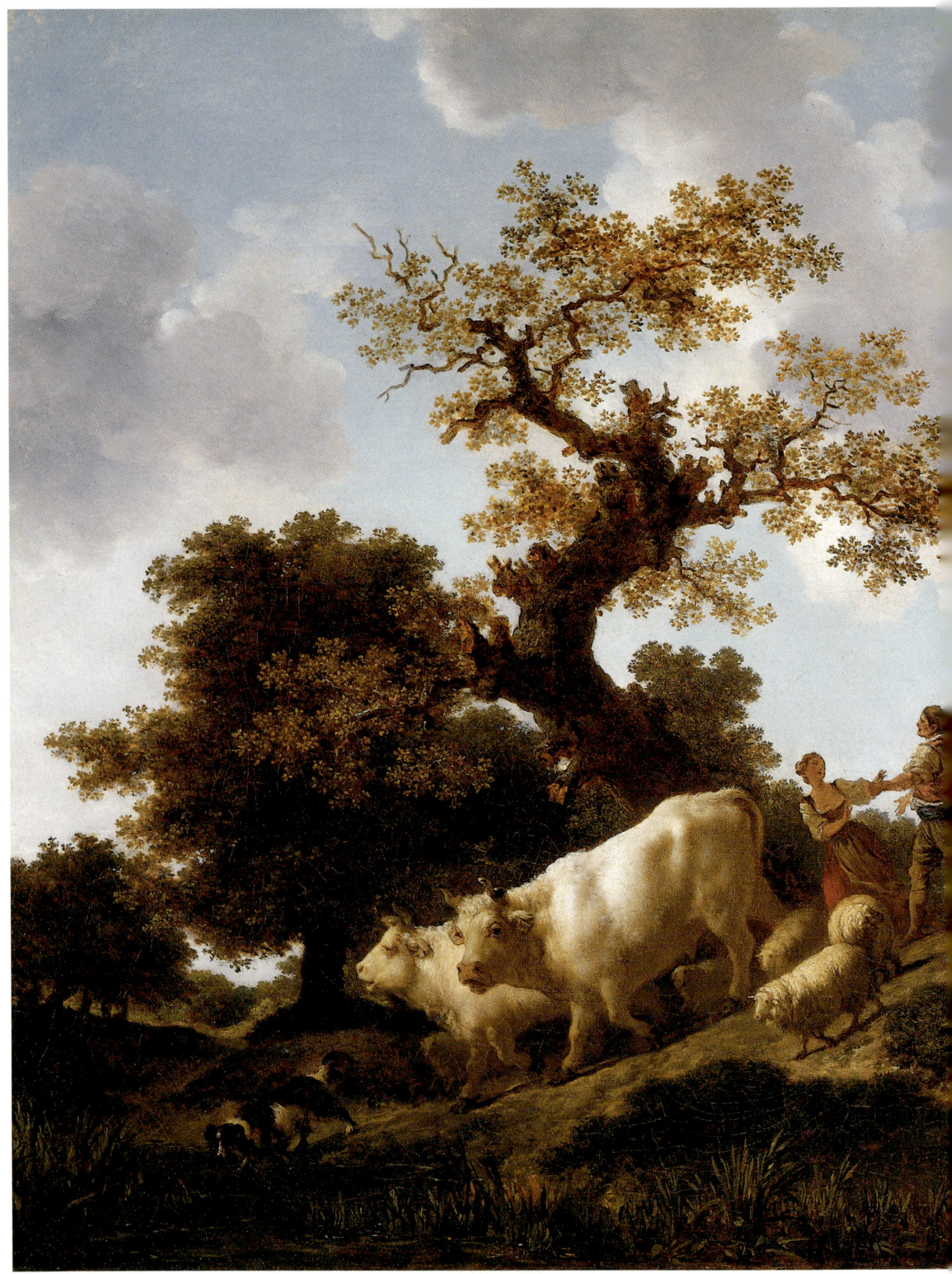

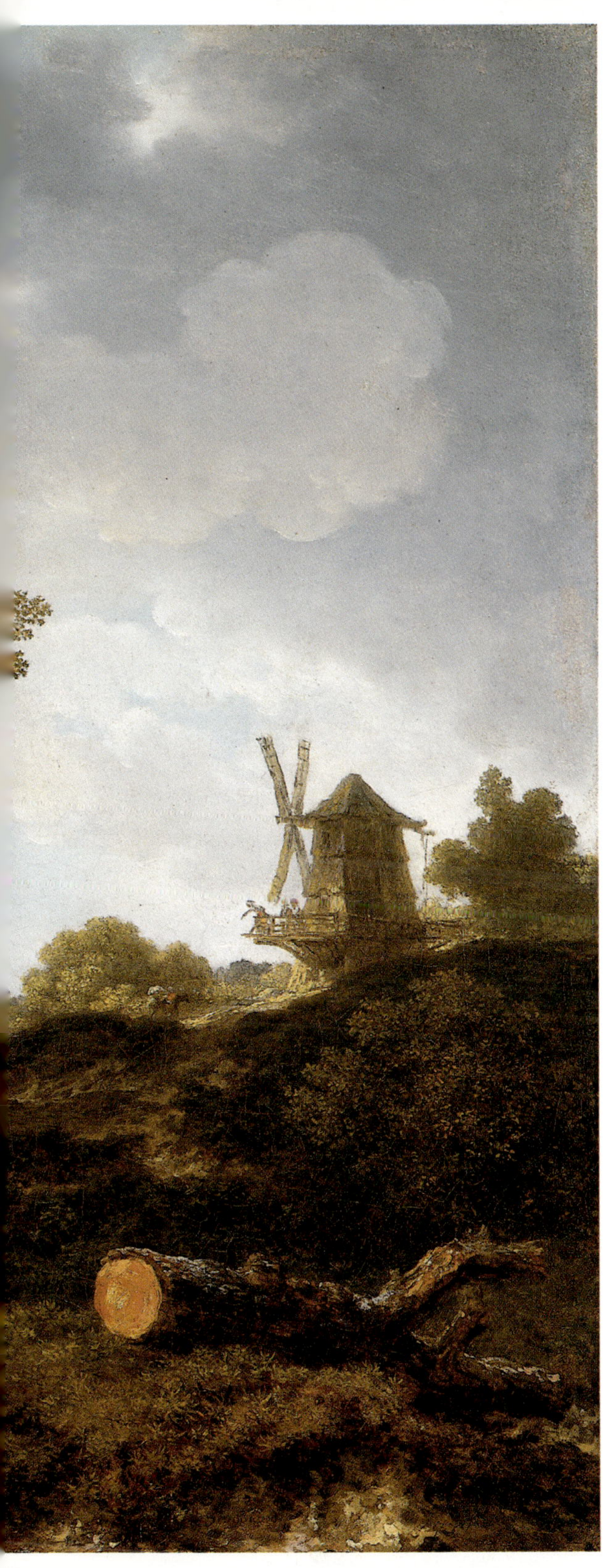

Return of the Drove,
c. 1768–70, oil on canvas, 64 x 80 cm
Worcester, The Worcester Art Museum.

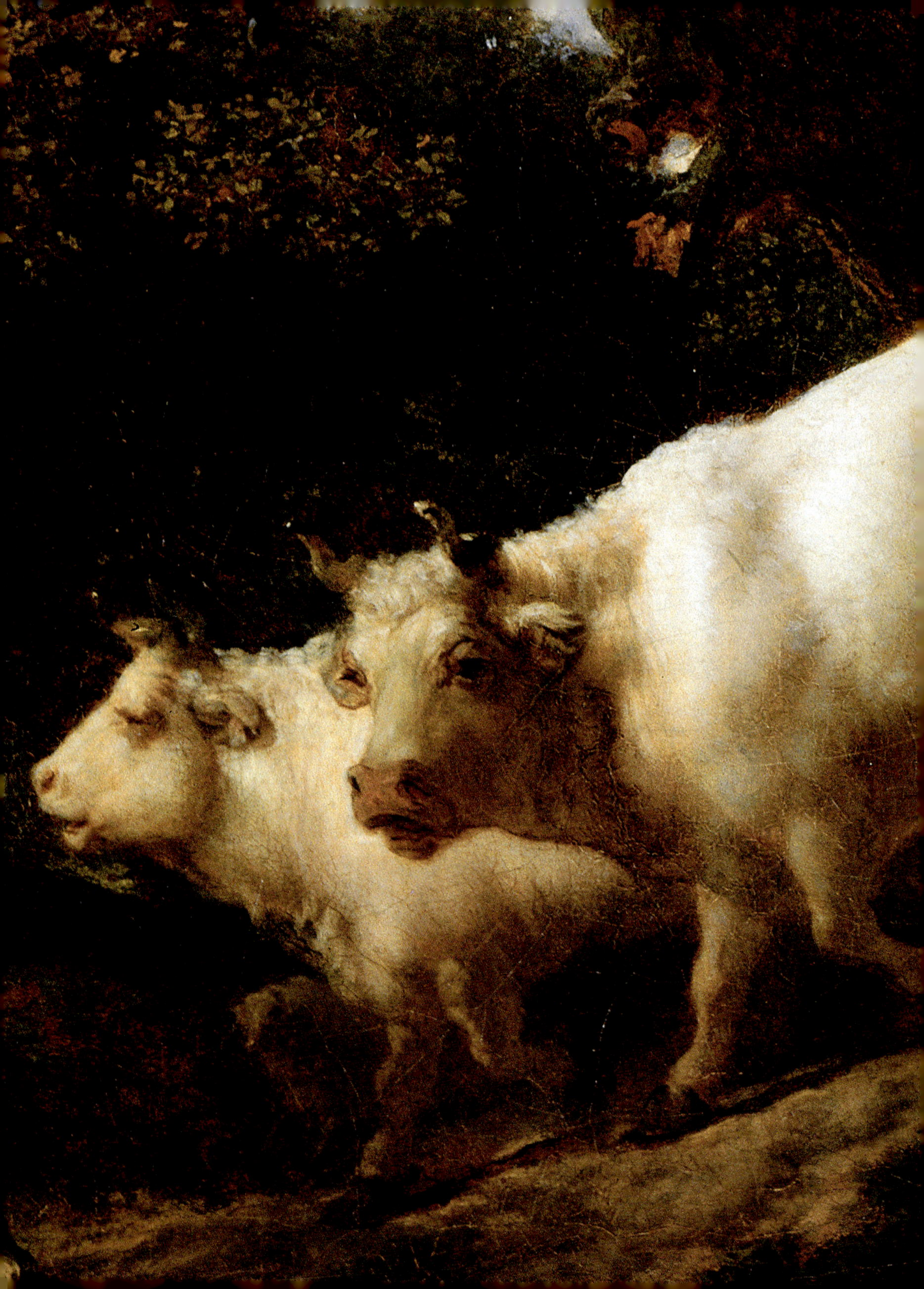

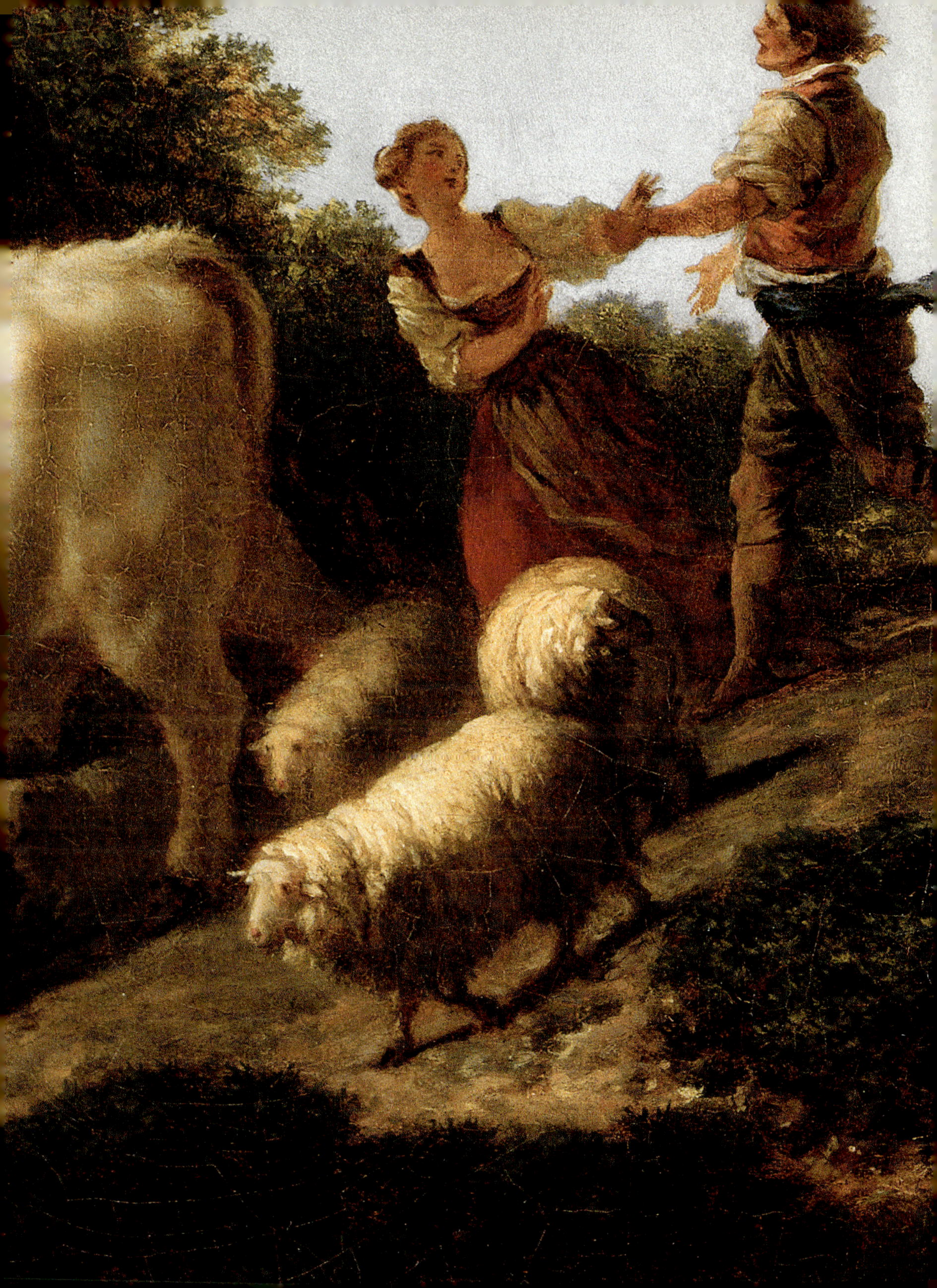

Reverie or Reality?

Initiated into the art of landscape under Mediterranean skies, then immersed in the study of the Dutch masters, Fragonard would go on to develop a personal vision preserved in a host of (mostly wash) drawings, some paintings and a large-scale decorative piece. None of these works can be dated with any real accuracy and with very few exceptions their locations have not yet been identified. Once again, then, we are plunged into an uncertainty that summons us to approach his landscapes as moments of the purest delectation. Even so, certain questions still need to be asked. Are these landscapes, like his portraits, the product of fantasy? Was Fragonard's "gardening" a way of creating a world of his own? Or is the opposite the case, the masterpieces using the then fashionable parks and gardens motif being simply a reflection of the current trend?

In the 18th century the model garden created by André Le Nôtre for Nicolas Fouquet, then for Louis XIV, still held sway, as attested by the republication in 1747 of *The Theory and Practise of Gardening* by Antoine-Joseph Dezallier d'Argenville (1680–1765). A lawyer at the Parliament of Paris as well as a great art lover and

The Isle of Love,
c. 1773-76, oil on canvas, 71 x 90 cm
Lisbon, Museu Calouste Gulbenkian.

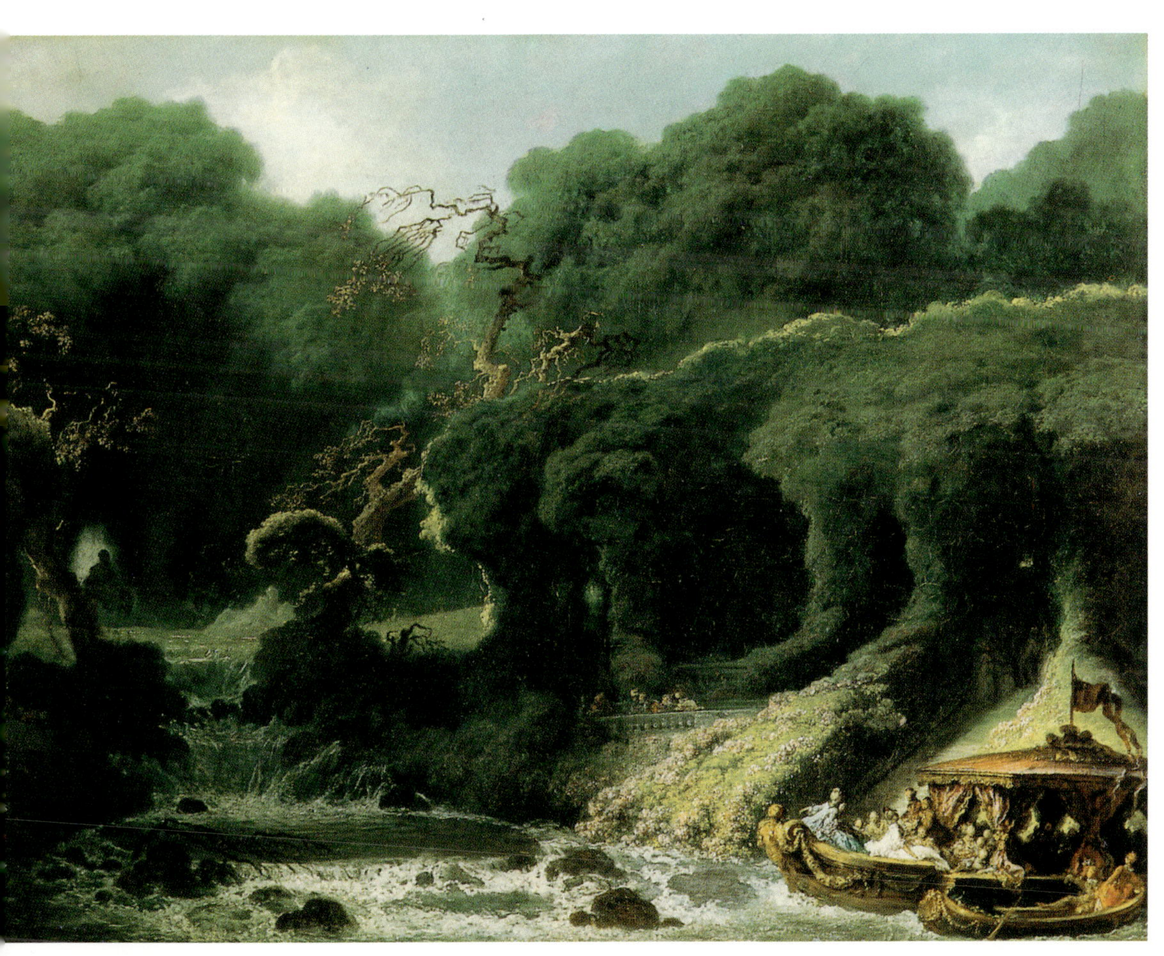

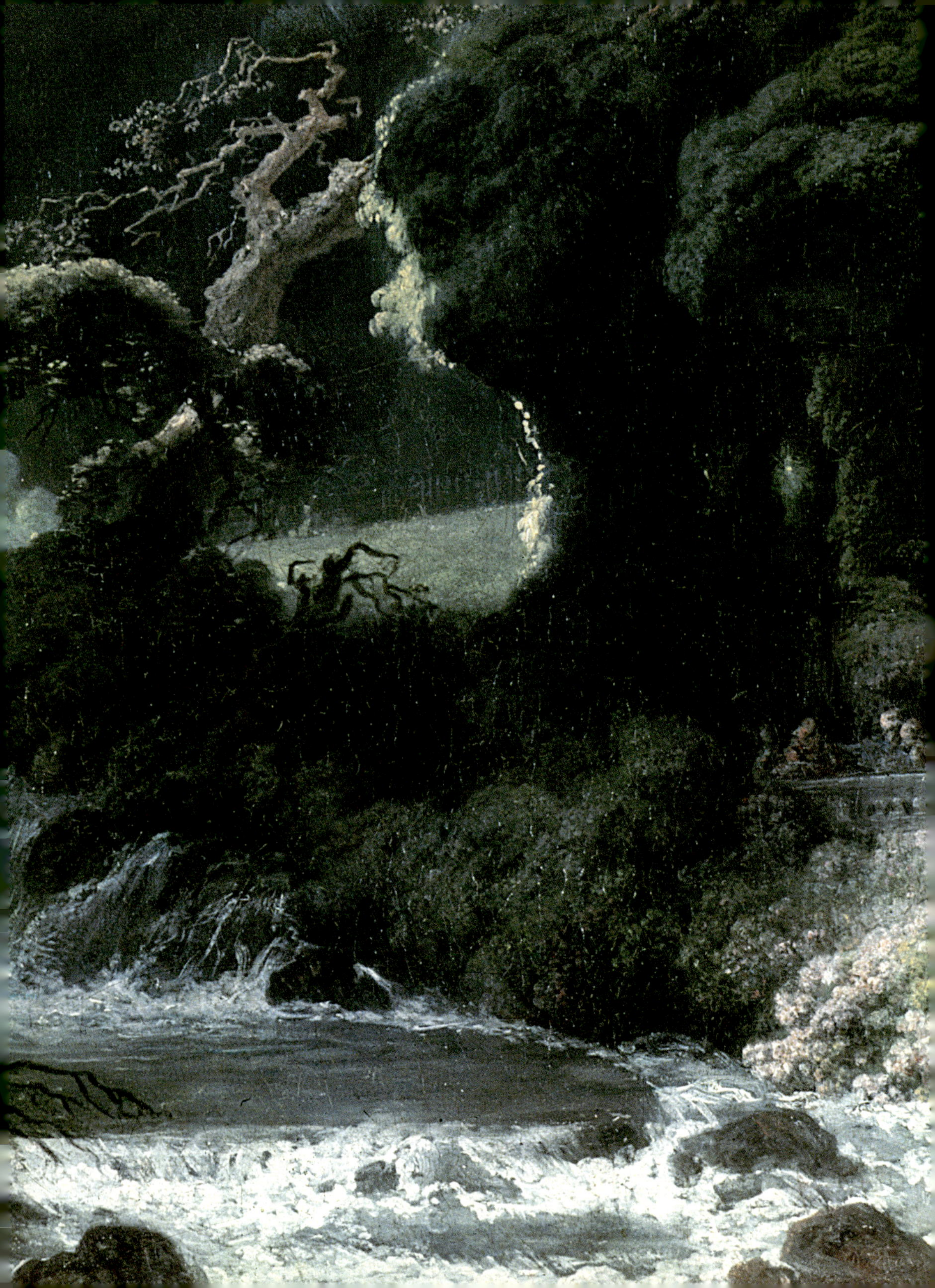

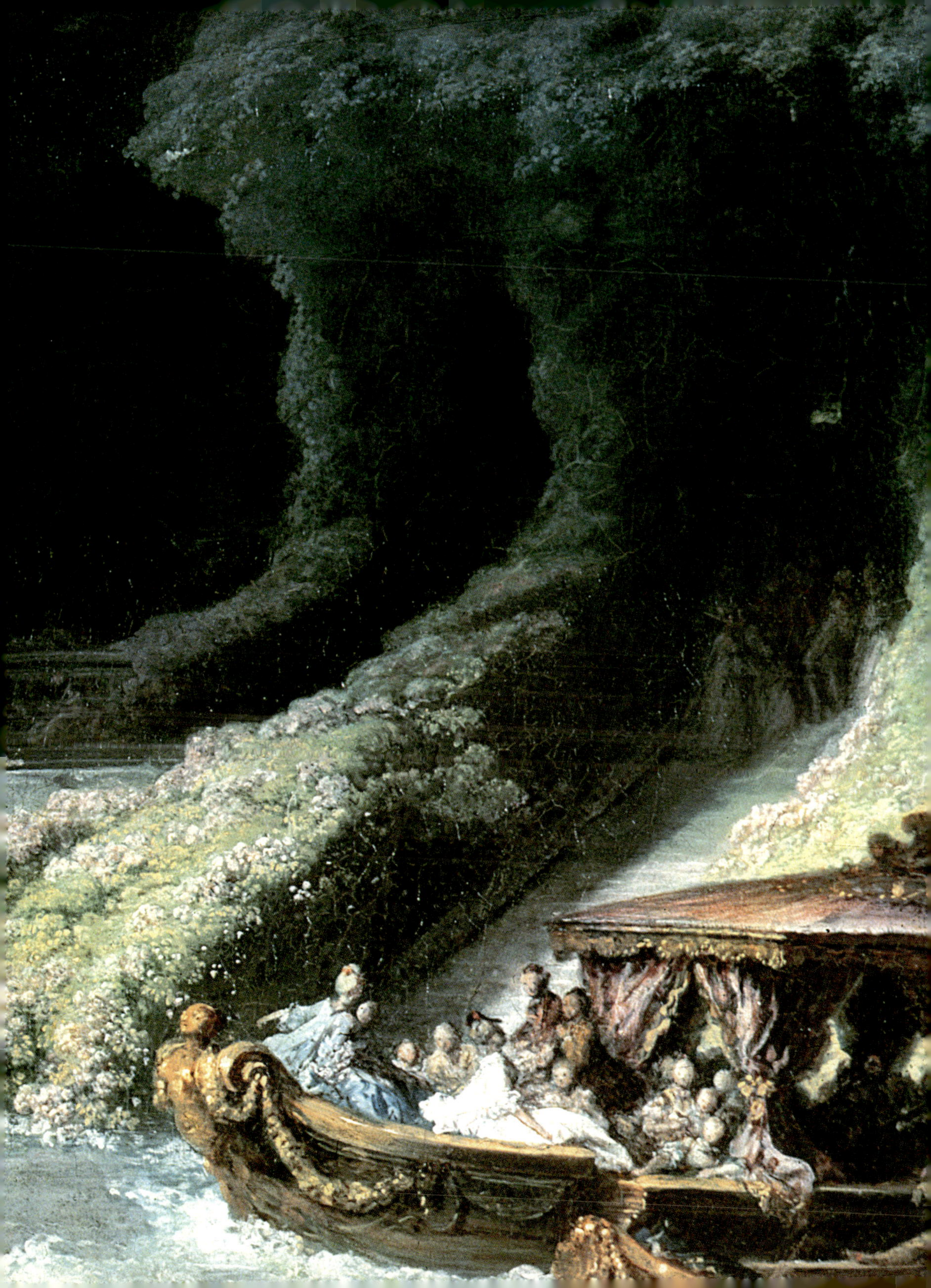

collector, Dezallier d'Argenville had published the first edition of his book in 1709; and given the extent of his knowledge in the field, Diderot and d'Alembert had asked him to contribute some six hundred entries on gardening and hydraulics to their *Encyclopédie*. Generously illustrated with engravings, his book was almost exclusively devoted to the creation of private grounds; as such it was a kind of manual for the wealthy as well as for gardeners, those "goldsmiths of the earth" whose talents were urged on the reader as indispensable. *The Theory and Practise of Gardening* was in fact a vehicle for the ideas of Le Nôtre, who had left no treatise of his own: organized down to the last detail, landscape was to be constructed as a series of terraces linked by sets of steps. Unswerving paths would run between flowerbeds hedged with box clipped straight as a die, with fences structuring the space and ensuring the rule of symmetry. Views would converge on a fountain, a group sculpture or a copse transformed by topiary into an outdoor sitting room. Yet even as he advocated proportion and balance, Dezallier d'Argenville introduced a new principle that would challenge the orderliness of the classical French garden: "Art must yield to Nature."

With the exception of the vedutists, and of topographers ordered to make literal portraits of gardens, painters seem to have stuck with this maxim, preferring the picturesqueness of neglect to pure, manmade domestication. In the years 1740–50 nature began to reassert itself in many such long-established gardens as that of the Prince de Guise at Arcueil, near Paris. Among the artists who went there to draw were Boucher, Natoire, Pierre and the animal painter Jean-Baptiste Oudry (1686–1755), whose hundred or so views were unique testimony to a garden that was to be destroyed some years later.

Fragonard too seems to have been a visitor to a beauty spot whose charm was increased by the fading of its original glory: rampant vegetation softened the garden's rigid linearity and rounded off its corners; the high, openwork fences were swallowed up by spreading arbors; rose bushes spilled over the trellises intended to contain them; and mighty trees stood high above the surrounding woodland, their roots threatening the flights of steps. This elegant disorder fit perfectly with the rules of Rococo taste, equally well illustrated by skilled siting of fountains and statues. A pool fed by stone dolphins, or a clearing surrounded by hedges pruned to form arcades and steps provided venues for the distractions of the idle rich: amorous conversations, games of blind man's buff, and rides on swings.

This impression of an outdoor theater was even more striking in a work christened *The Isle of Love* when it went on sale in 1795. The title is a reference to Watteau's *Embarkation for Cythera*, whose poetry the Fragonard at least equals. On the edge of a pool fed by a waterfall, terraces have been taken over by mossy hornbeams that form, as it were, cavities or grottoes full of dense, mysterious shadow. Rose bushes tumble down towards the water. To the right is a handsome boat with its dinghy and we descry, on a staircase, silhouettes advancing to meet the boat's passengers. There are other people on the terraces, too, some of them contemplating nature's beauties from a balustrade, as if on a balcony. A touch of sunlight skims the tops of the arbor, gilding for a brief moment the crooked trunk of a tree and its gnarled, unruly branches.

At the time when Fragonard was bequeathing us these last portraits of now-vanished gardens, another approach to the presentation of nature had arrived from across the English Channel. In contrast with the purism of the French style, it proposed the relative simplicity and naturalness heralded by Dezallier d'Argenville, and took as its models the paintings of Claude Lorrain, Nicolas Poussin and Salvator Rosa. The idea was no longer the planning-out of an enclosed space, but the opening-up of that space and its integration into the larger setting. Thus the "English" or "landscaped" garden came to supplant a local equivalent rendered too costly by the veritable army of gardeners it required and too ephemeral by its fragile wooden trellises. At the same time Jean-Jacques Rousseau's *The New Eloise* (1761) was singing the praises of rural life and pointing up the subtle links between the soul and landscape. Architects painted pictures showing verdant spaces dotted with mills and ruins, while painters were commissioned to portray these new parks with their winding paths and grassy hills and valleys.

Claude-Henri Watelet (1718–86) testified to this change in his *Essay on Gardens* of 1774. A high-ranking tax official, Watelet was also a collector, engraver and illustrator, and had come to know Fragonard and Hubert Robert during a stay in Rome. Robert's paintings played a major part in the spread of the new style, which in practise was at quite a remove from the English ideal: supposedly "natural", it in fact called for considerable manipulation of nature. With an eye to the future, Robert was already painting mature gardens that mingled memories of Italy with the picturesque buildings dictated by the latest fashion. He also helped plan numerous parks in the Paris environs: Ermenonville, Méréville, Mortefontaine, Jeurre, Rambouillet and, of course, Versailles, where he was appointed Designer of the Royal Gardens in 1778.

A succession of stays in the country—at Carrières, near Saint-Germain-en-Laye (not far from Watelet's Moulin-Joli residence); then at Charenton; and finally, during the Revolution, at Evry-Petit-Bourg, east of Paris—meant Fragonard could not but know of the changes taking place in approaches to landscape. *The Isle of Love*, with its water splashing over rocks rather than merely filling pools, could be seen as a pointer to the transitional gardens in which nature was begin-

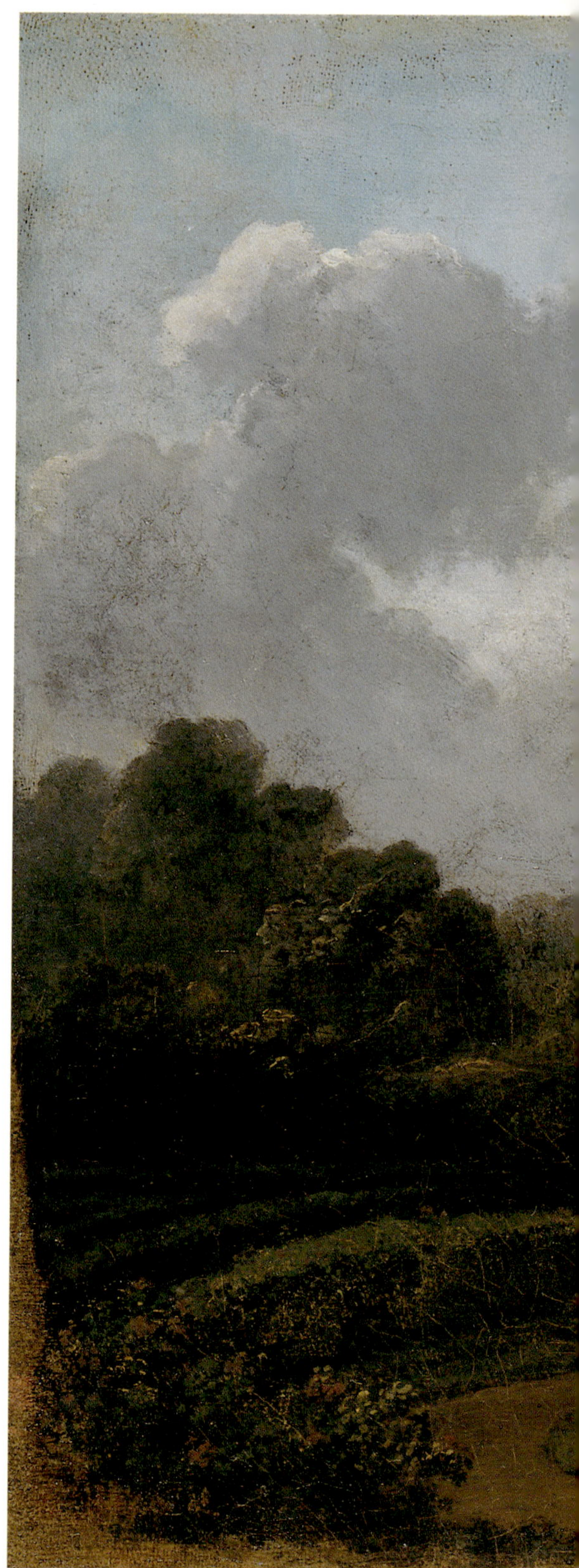

Blindman's Buff,

c. 1770, oil on canvas, 38 x 45 cm
Paris, Musée du Louvre.

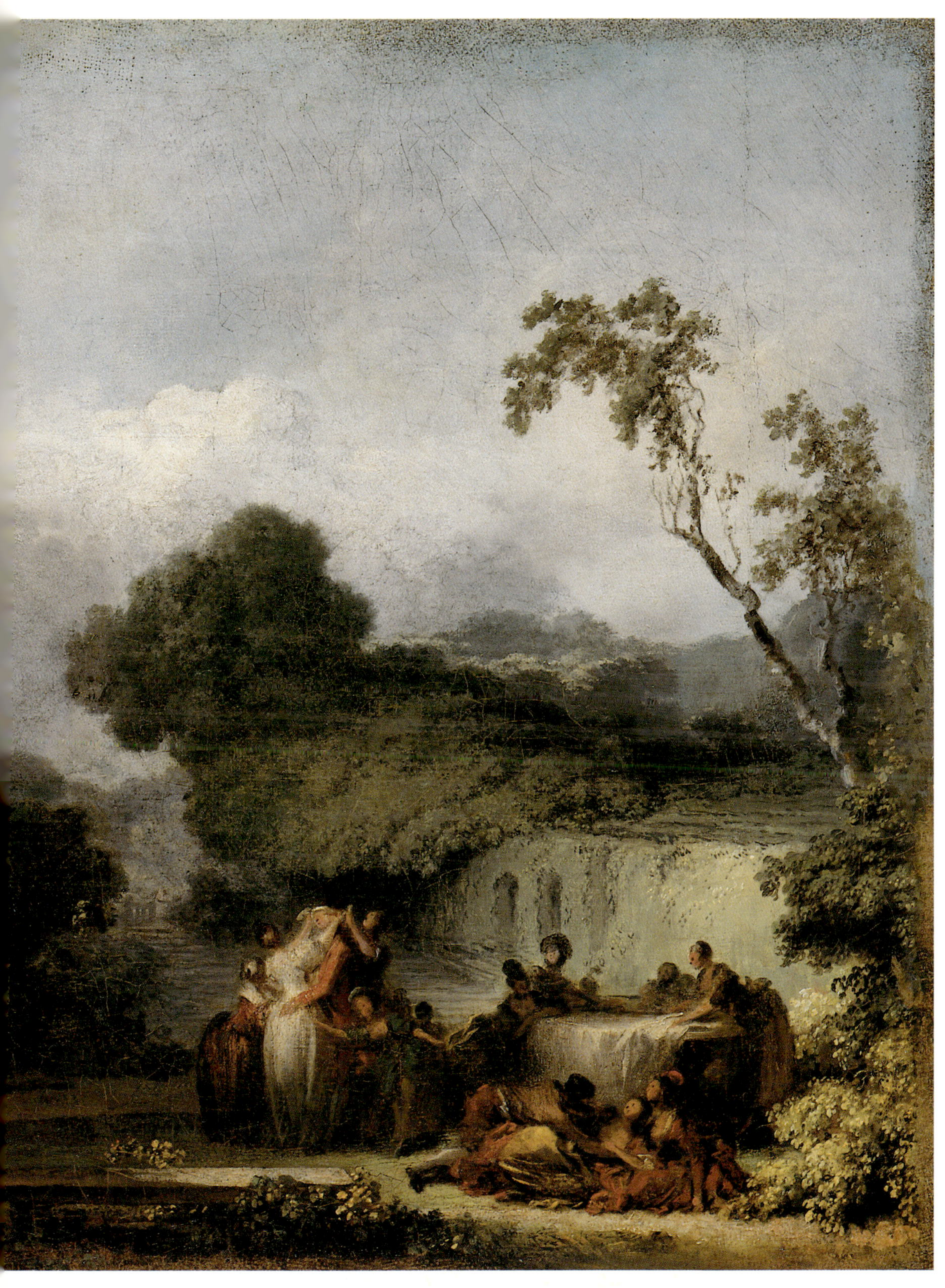

ning to have its say at the expense of the classical model. In the circles Fragonard moved in the art of gardening had many enthusiasts, who kept up to date on new varieties of plants and regularly visited specialists in search of the latest arrivals. The Duc d'Harcourt, whose portrait Fragonard painted, was the author of a *Treatise on the Decoration of Outdoors, Gardens and Parks,* applying its principles to his own property in Normandy. The architect Pierre-Adrien Pâris—Bergeret's erstwhile guide in Rome—drew up a number of projects for Bergeret, with whose family Fragonard had finally managed to patch things up. The Bergerets had several properties and parks in and around L'Isle-Adam and Nointel; for their estate at Cassan Bergeret's son commissioned an Anglo-Chinese garden, of which only the Chinese pavilion has survived.

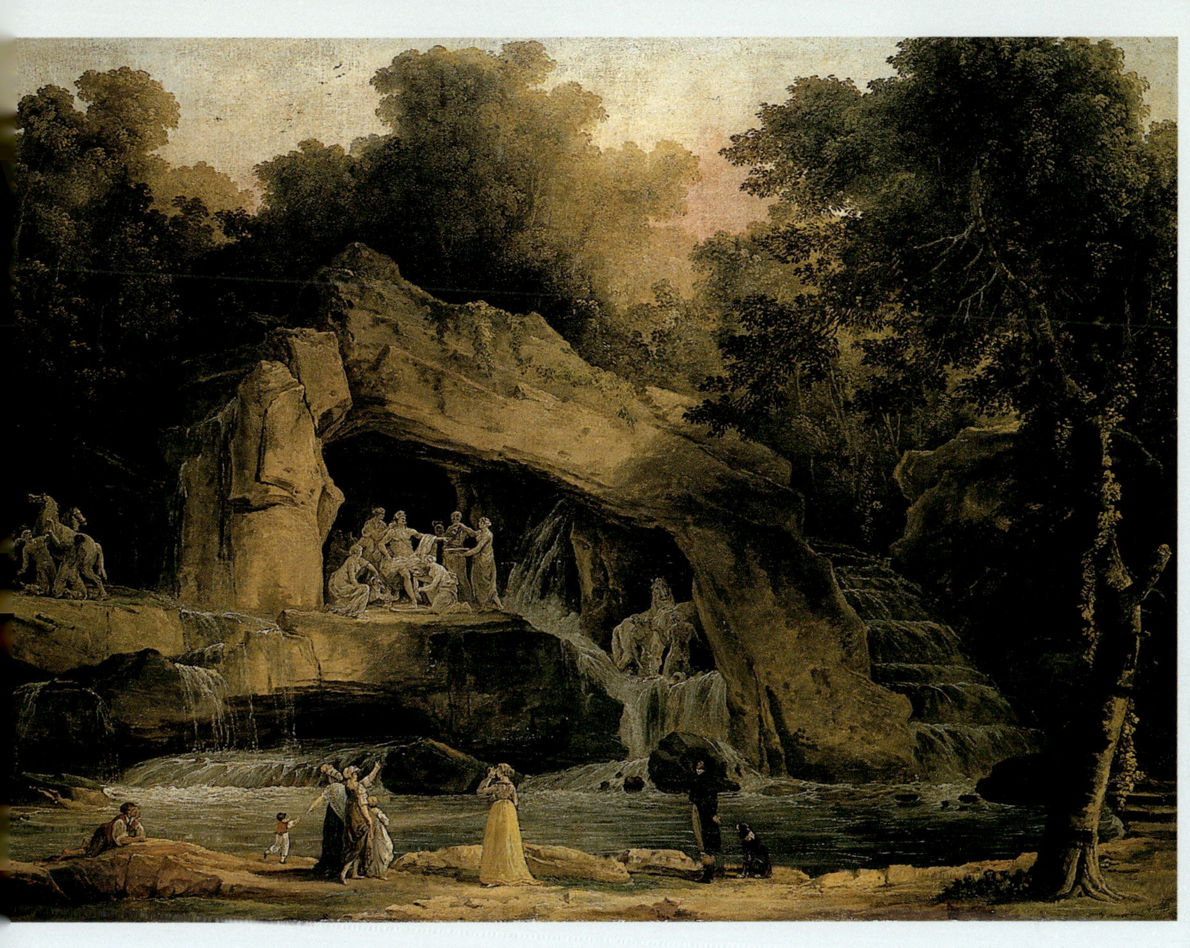

Hubert Robert,
The Apollo Baths at Versailles,
1803, oil on canvas, 99 x 130 cm
Paris, Musée Carnavalet.

Landscaped Drawing Rooms

In 1775 Fragonard painted for Louis-Pierre-Sébastien Marchal de Sainscy, the king's steward and governor of Abbeville, five large canvases hung in the latter's Paris townhouse, on the Rue des Fossés (now the Rue d'Aboukir). In the 19th century the largest of the five was given the title *The Fair at Saint-Cloud*. Every year on the last three Sundays of September, the grounds of the Château de Saint-Cloud were home to a busy fair that drew many artists; but even though a rising mass of white water forms the composition's focal point just right of center, we cannot be sure that this was, in fact, Saint-Cloud—whose fountain, according to Dezallier d'Argenville, enjoyed "an unrivaled reputation." Fragonard shows us various attractions under the spreading branches, among the junipers, on a pedestal and in shady arbors. Simply dressed strollers form small, bright-colored groups listening to the barker, watching the puppeteer or visiting the covered stands where toys and trinkets are on sale. The curiosity of the children is being sparked by a lottery in the foreground and a doughnut vendor in front of the balustrade.

The four other canvases making up the group use the portrait format and must originally have been the same height as *The Fair at Saint-Cloud*. Two of them seem to have been cropped at an unknown date, but the group has retained a chromatic harmony based on a mix of different bluish-greens and a range of yellows extending from very bright to burnished gold. The sweep of the picture of the fair is complemented by four variations on the theme of outdoor fun: *The Swing, Blindman's Buff, A Game of Horse and Rider,* and *A Game of Hot Cockles*. In the first two, details like the balustrades marking out the boundaries of the garden or a pool, and the fountain harmonizing with the waterfall, establish a link with *The Fair at Saint-Cloud*, but the ambience could not be more different: these are more private get-togethers. The rendering of the setting is different, too: in each case the eye is led well beyond the foreground, in the first painting to a wooded valley overlooked by a whitish mountain, and in the second to a treed, sloping meadow where a group of people

Following pages,
The Fair at Saint-Cloud,
c. 1775-1780, oil on canvas, 216 x 335 cm
Paris, Banque de France.

are chatting. Do not these vistas point to the new esthetic, which seeks to extend the limits of the park by concealing or lowering the fences, creating those famous English ha-has and thus significantly opening up the view?

The last two canvases provide an even more obvious illustration of this interpenetration of garden and landscape, this time closer to the English models than to French adaptations in the Hubert Robert manner. The game of hot cockles—the kneeling man, whose head-covering is being removed, has to guess who has smacked his hand—is taking place on the fringe of a fairly classically designed garden. We see boxed shrubs set around a marble statue, a flowerbed dotted with red and blue and framed with discreet latticework, and to the right, on a pedestal decorated in the antique style, *Threatening Love* by Etienne-Maurice Falconet (1716–91). Originally made for Madame de Pompadour, this statue had found many admirers at the Salon in 1755. Fragonard had already used it in *The Swing*; interestingly, Bergeret was the owner of a plaster copy. In the midground of Fragonard's scene two steps and a low metal balustrade give access to a narrow, hedged path leading into the woods. In *A Game of Horse and Rider*, the setting is the untouched outdoors, with tall birches and a lightning-struck tree standing on the bank of a canal. The wildness of the place is underscored by the presence of a band of ragged, barefoot kids playing horse and rider, with one of them running forward to leap onto the horse formed by the others and make it collapse. Nonetheless this is the spot chosen by a couple, shown sitting on the ground. In the background rise Lombardy poplars, their silhouettes reminiscent of those of cypresses, as a small boat draws up to the bank of the canal.

Long since scattered—one at the Banque de France, the others in the National Gallery in Washington—the set of pictures can be taken as a run-through of the theme of rural entertainment, somewhere between arcadian landscape and *fête galante*. Here we are at a far remove from Boucher's pastorals with their invented trees and shrubs. The tipped orange-tree box in the foreground of *The Fair at Saint-Cloud* is probably no more than a whim on the part of the artist, who does not hesitate to inject a note of humor, either: in *Blindman's Buff* the three vestal virgins forming the base of the fountain seem to be afraid of being splashed. Fragonard doubtless chose the trees and colors appropriate to the atmosphere he was after, but was surely drawing on real places rather than delving into his stock of memories. In the series destined for the pavilion at Louveciennes, trees, plants and flowers were used to create a setting that would enhance the amorous scenes portrayed. Here the principal actor is nature: true, nature welcoming and partly tamed, but uncorrupted by art and ready to display its disorder and the marks left by the elements and the passage of time.

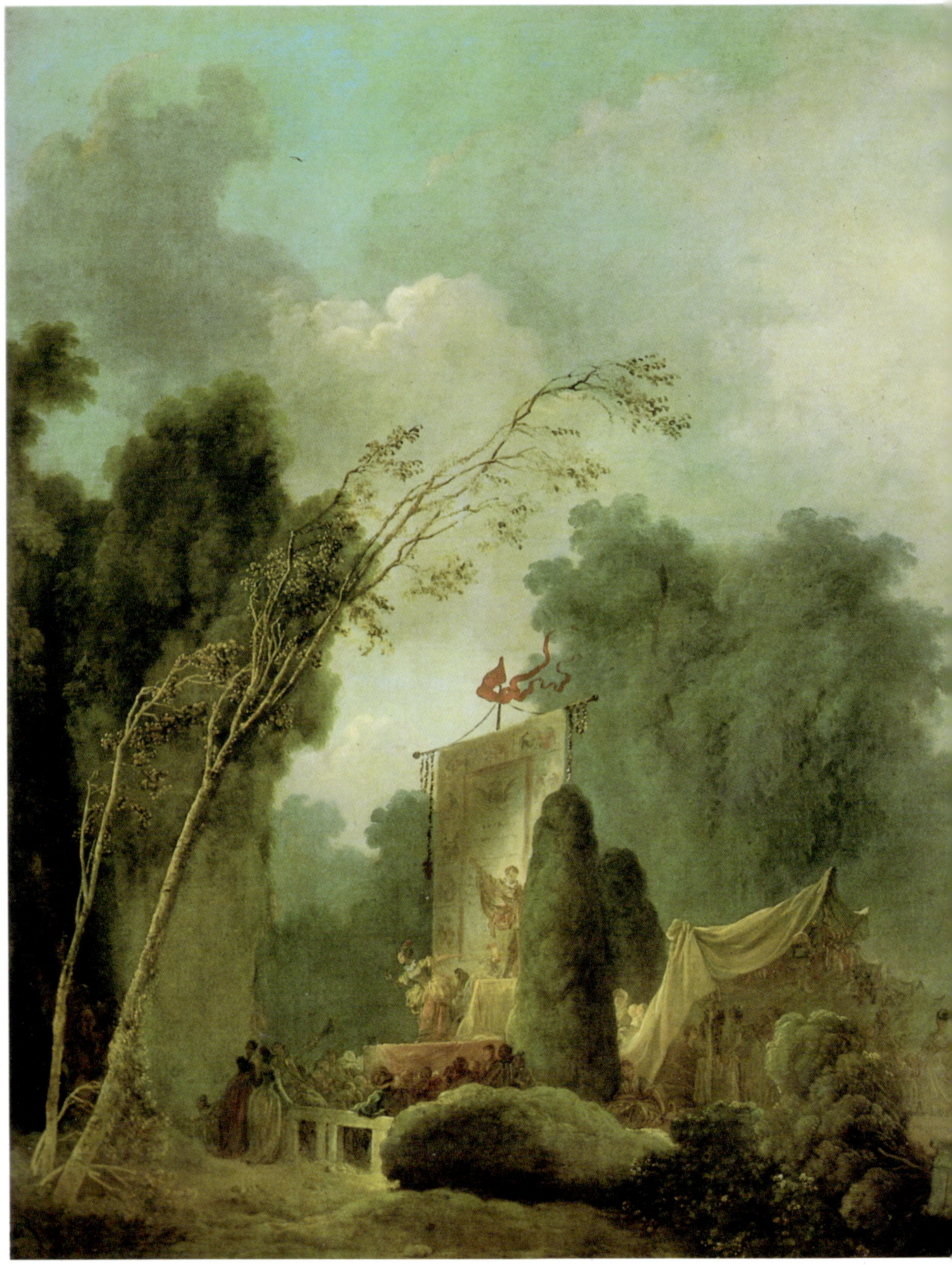

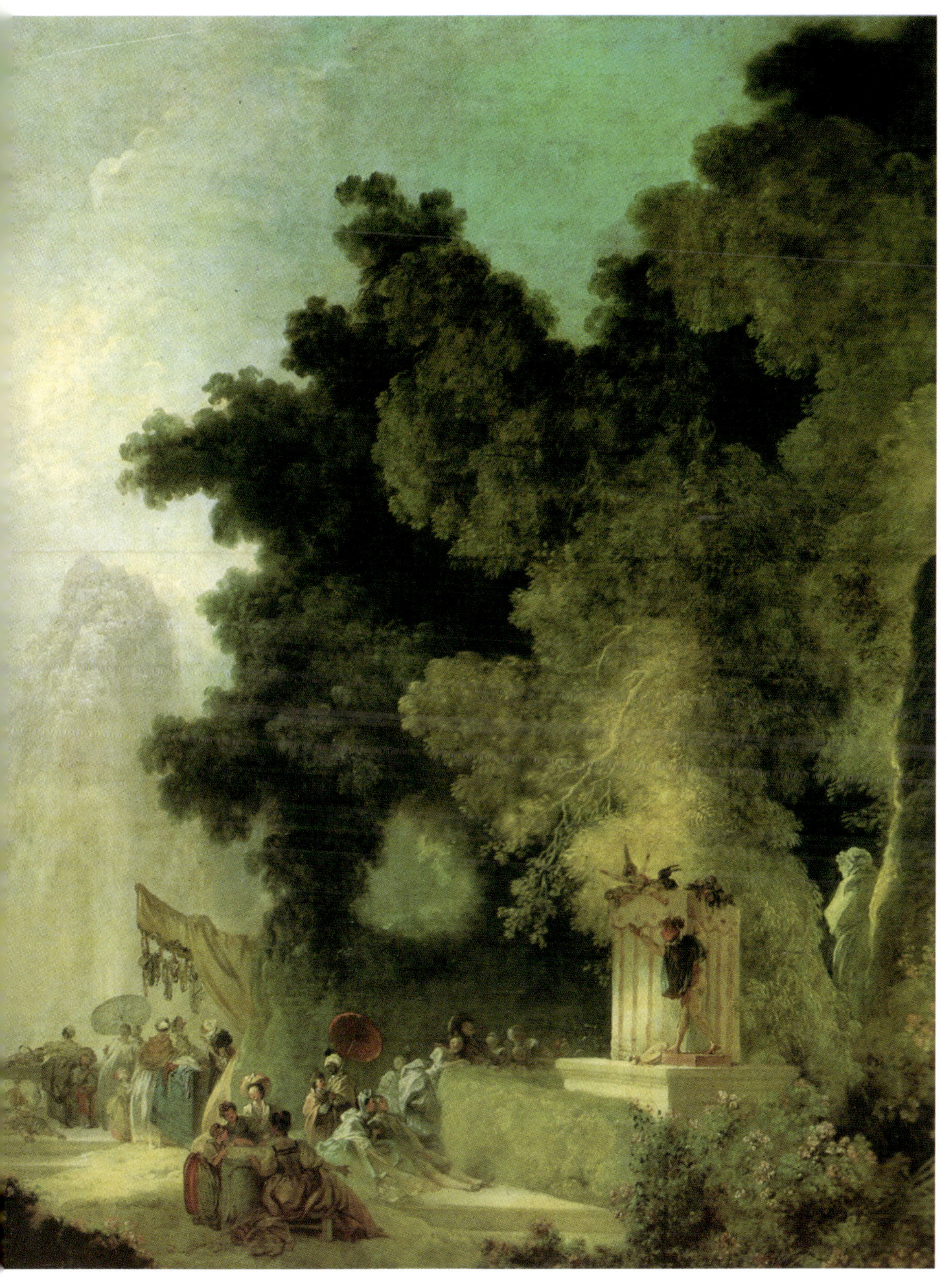

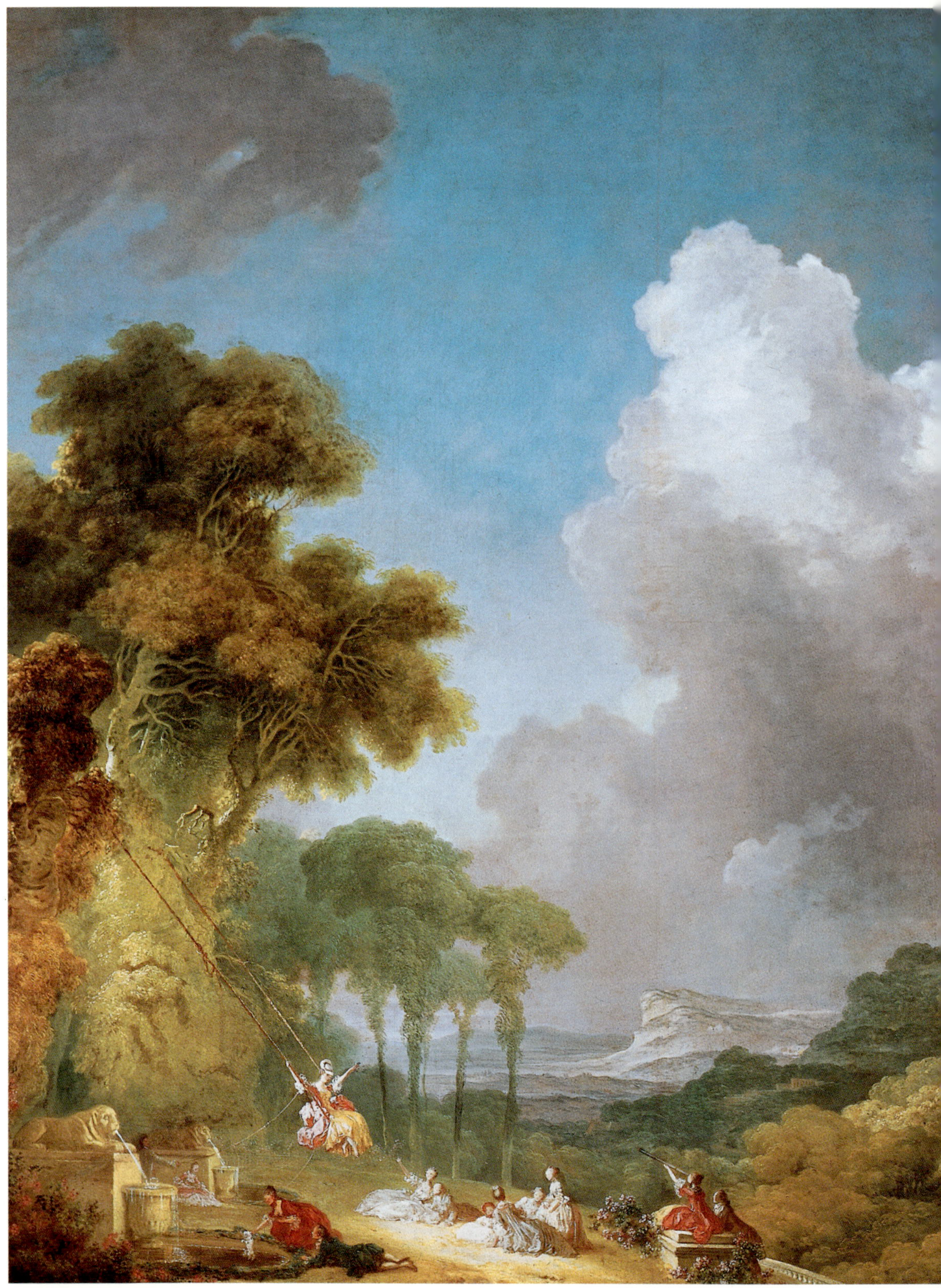

The Swing,
c. 1775–80, oil on canvas, 216 x 185.5 cm
Washington, National Gallery of Art.

Blindman's Buff ,
c. 1775–80, oil on canvas, 216 x 198 cm
Washington, National Gallery of Art.

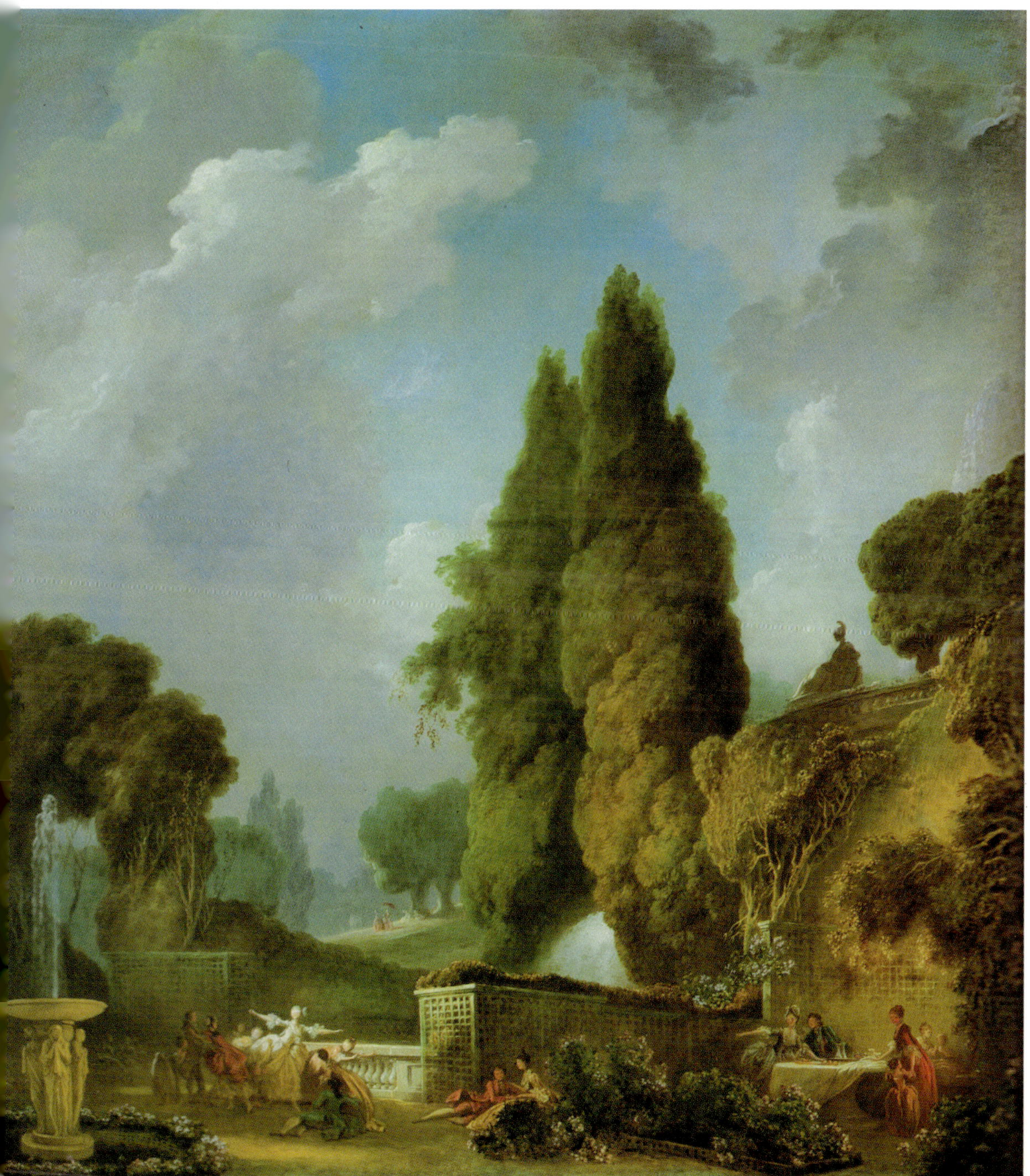

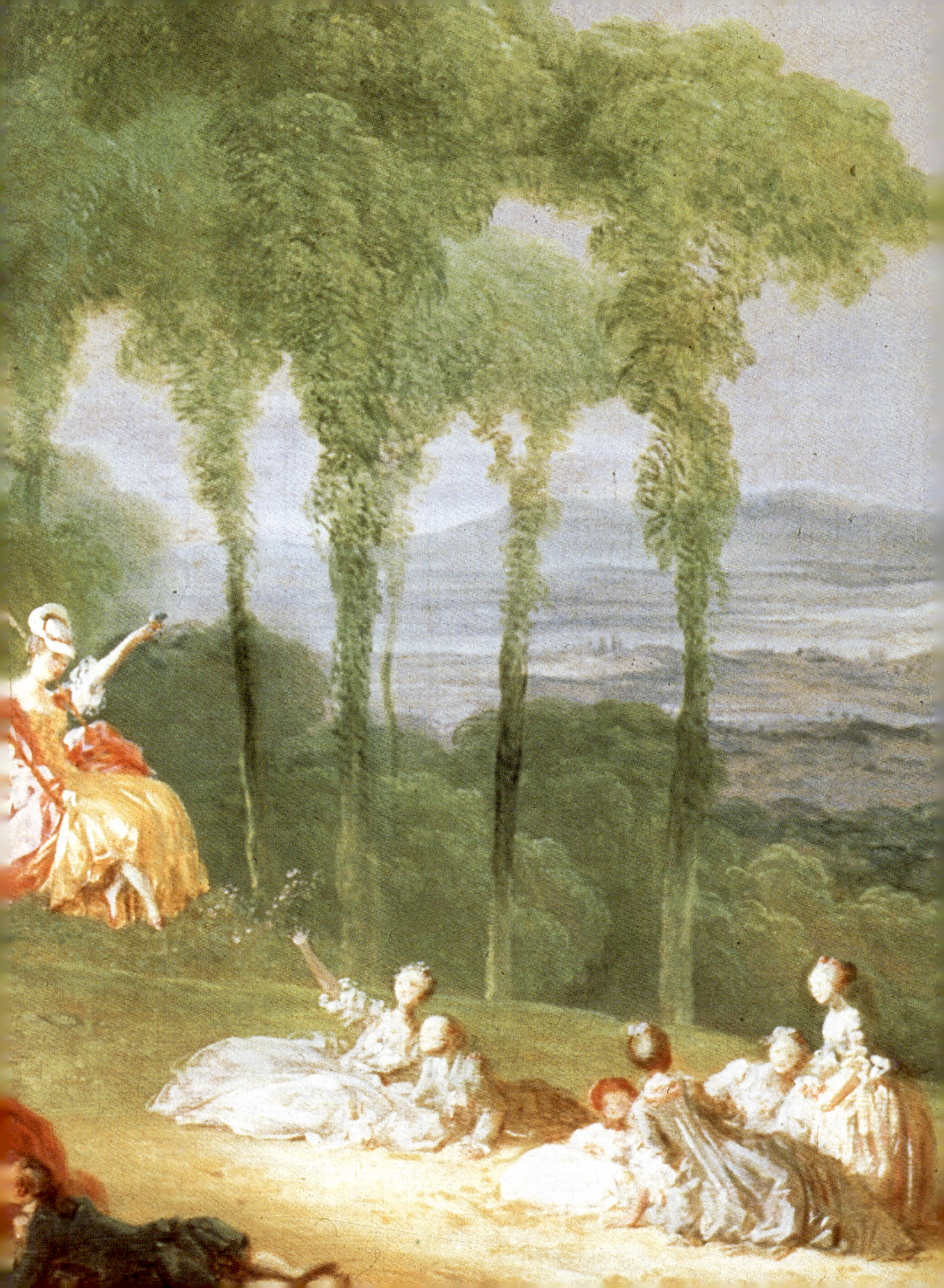

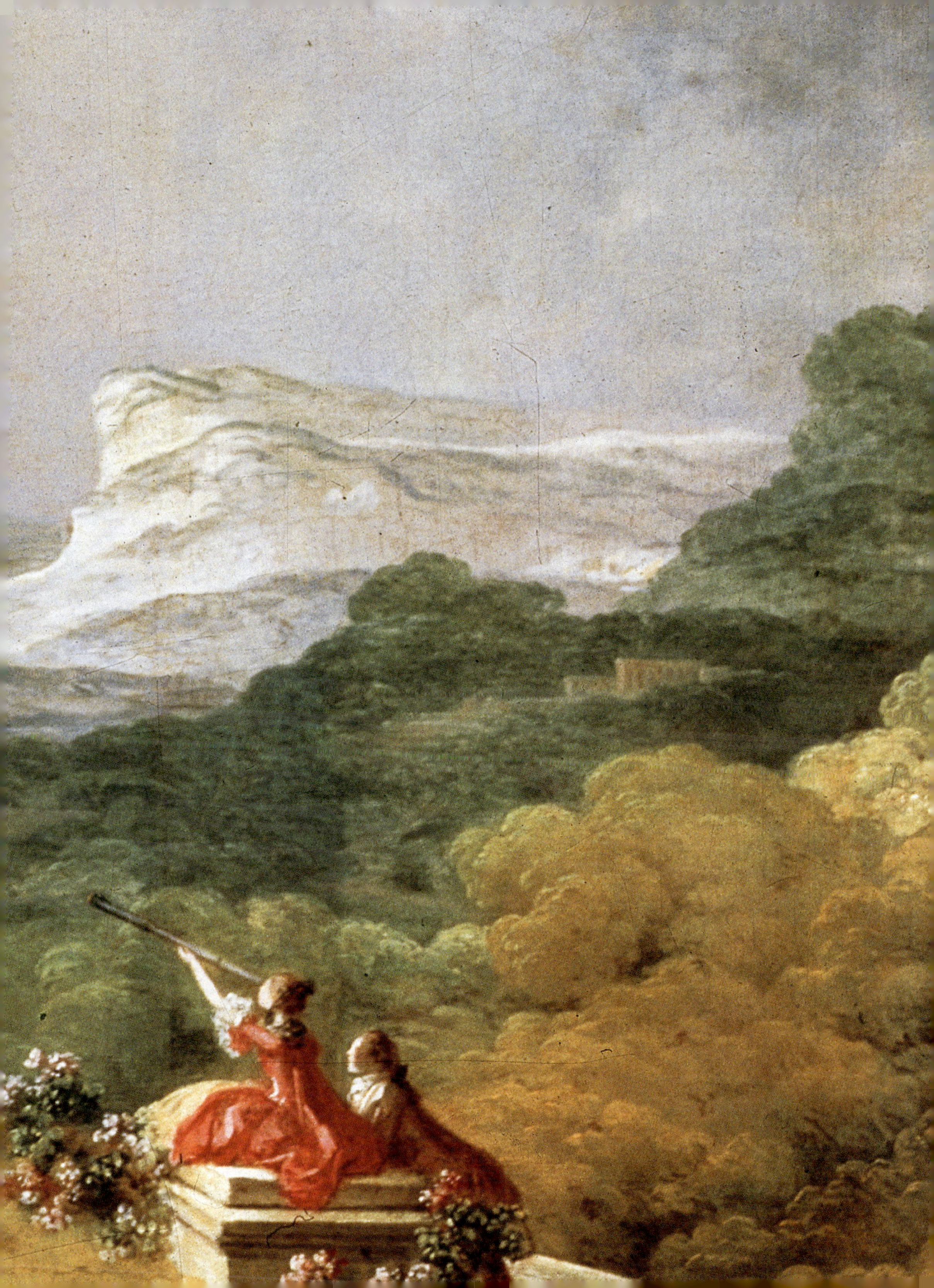

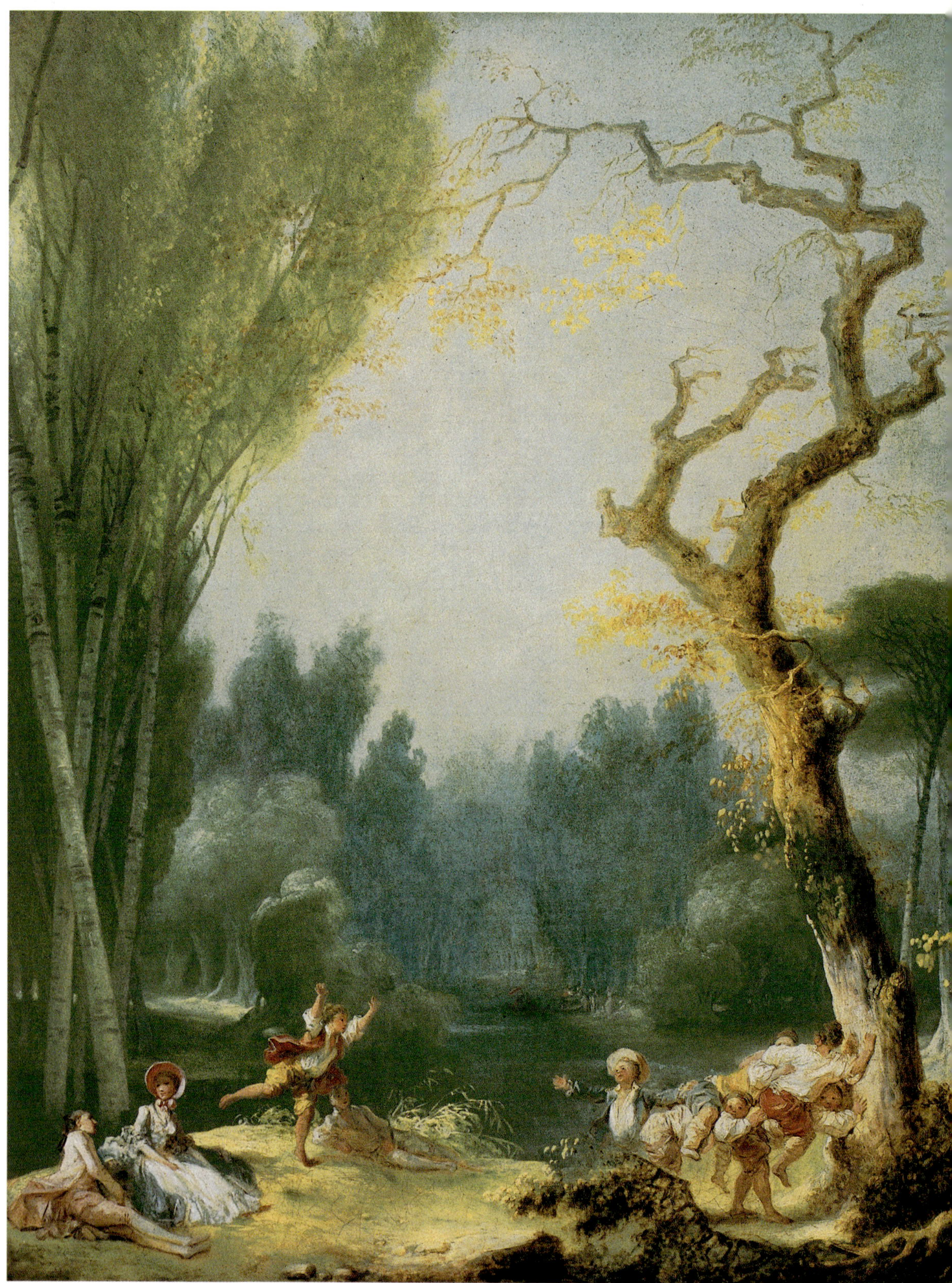

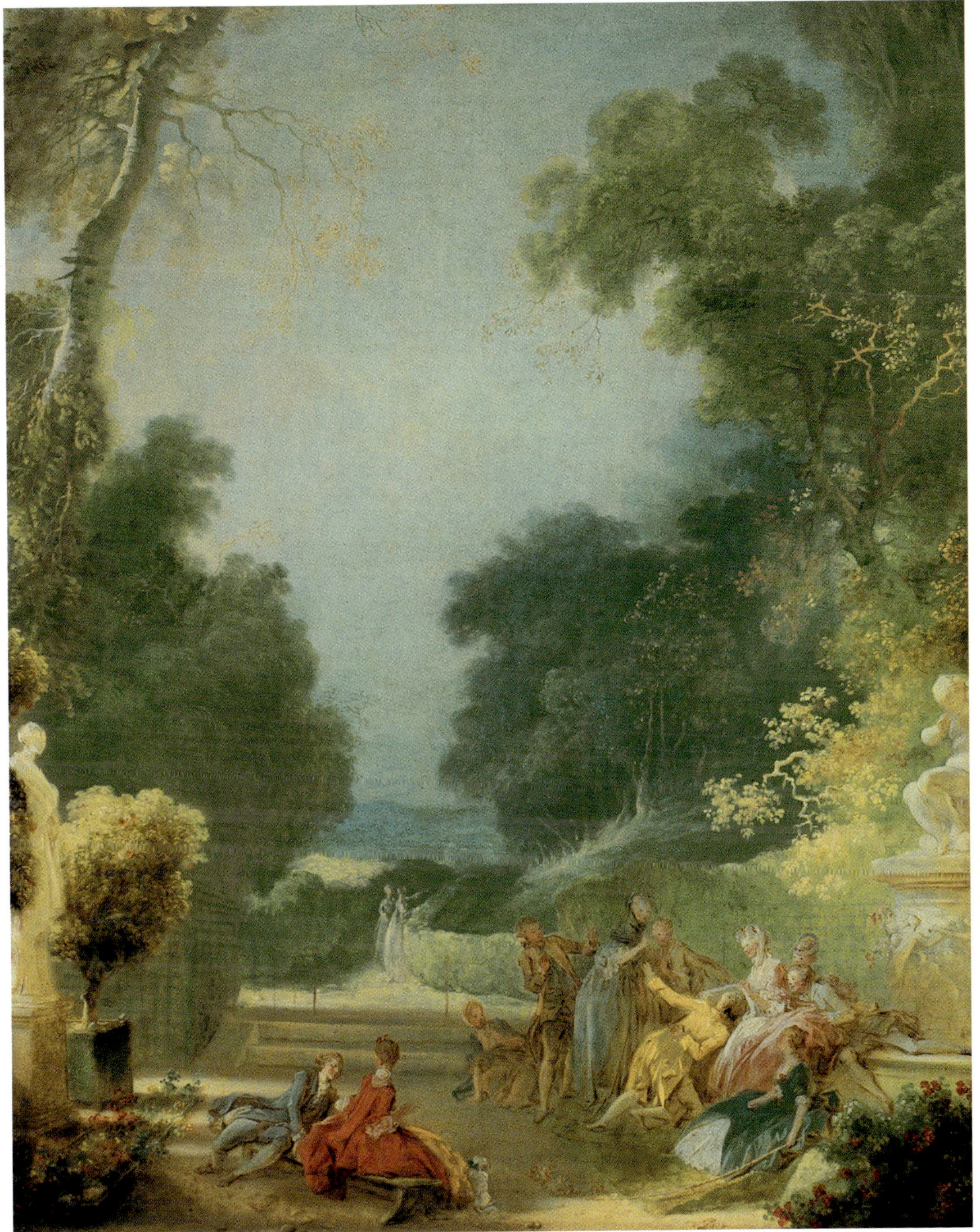

A Game of Horse and Rider,
c. 1775–80, oil on canvas, 115 x 87.5 cm
Washington, National Gallery of Art.

A Game of Hot Cockles,
c. 1775–80, oil on canvas, 115.6 x 91.5 cm
Washington, National Gallery of Art.

VI
"In Just Hour"

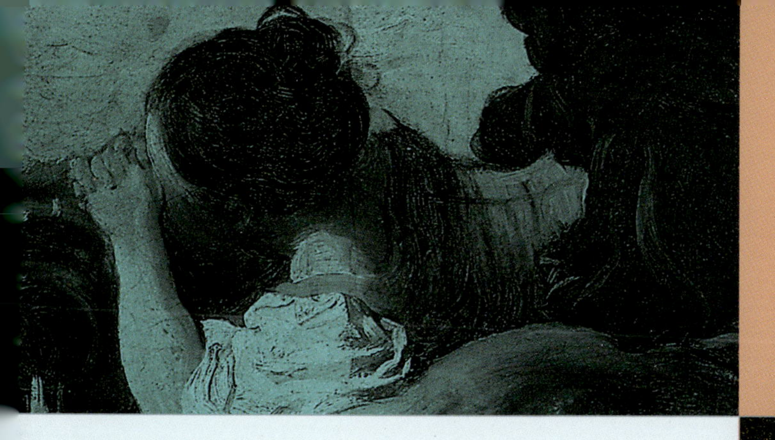

One

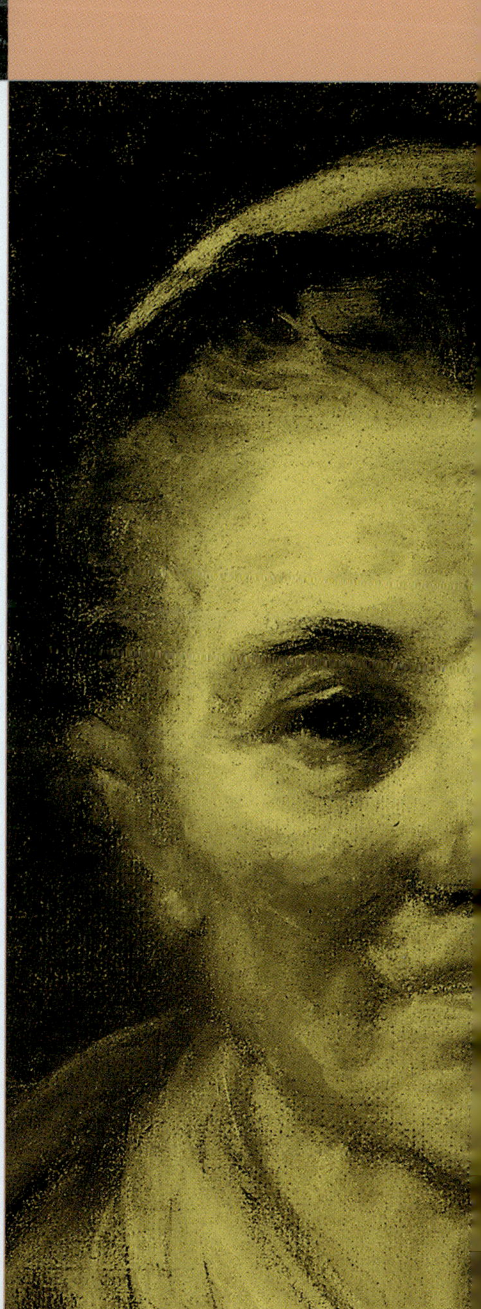

On the back of a certain Fragonard is a label bearing the words "Portrait of Mr De La Bretêche, painted by Fragonard in 1769 in just one hour." Likewise on the back of another canvas is a label reading, "Portrait of Mr L'abbé de St. Non, painted by Fragonard in 1769 in just one hour." These cases are worth mentioning, given how rarely we can identify with any confidence the people in Fragonard's paintings. We already know of the ties between the Abbé Saint-Non and the artist: the two had stayed at Tivoli in the summer of 1760 before returning to France together, with stopovers at all the places of interest along the way. The Abbé's loyalty and generosity were never found wanting. He commissioned Fragonard to create the frontispieces for his luxury five-volume *Voyage pittoresque à Naples et en Sicile*, and used some of his drawings to accompany the descriptions of the art treasures of the Italian south. When he died in 1791, his will proved that he had not forgotten his painter friend, who appeared on the list of those to whom he had left works from his collection. So it was natural that Fragonard should paint his patron's portrait and that of the Abbé's beloved older brother, Louis de La Bretèche.

In addition to the names of their subjects, the labels on the portraits specify that each was painted "in just one hour"—a revelation that continues to astonish even today and which, given that speed of execution is considered a proof of virtuosity, doubtless drew the admiration of the artist's contemporaries. Whether or not the claim is to be taken literally is less important, however, than Fragonard's way of doing what he did: his "style" in other words. It should be pointed out in passing that in the case of Fragonard it is not completely accurate to speak of "style" in the singular: throughout his career he showed just how capable he was of adapting both technique and approach to fit the subject matter or the purpose of the drawing or painting in hand. Yet there remains a common denominator to his oeuvre: rather than sheer rapidity, we are looking at energy, spontaneity and endurance, virtues particularly evident in the series of portraits that includes those of the Abbé de Saint-Non and his brother La Bretèche.

Portrait of the Abbé de Saint-Non,
1769, oil on canvas, 80 x 65 cm
Paris, Musée du Louvre.

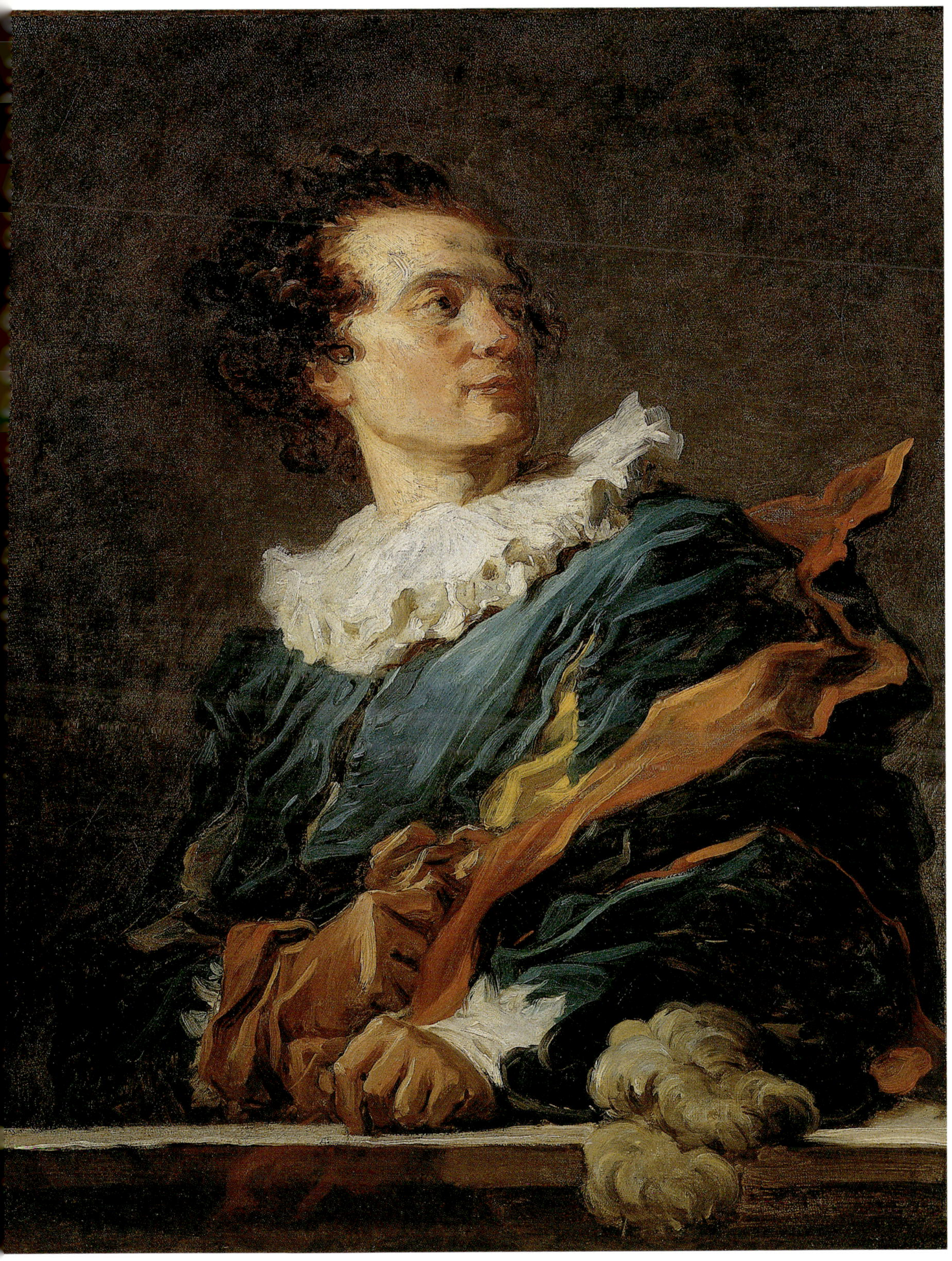

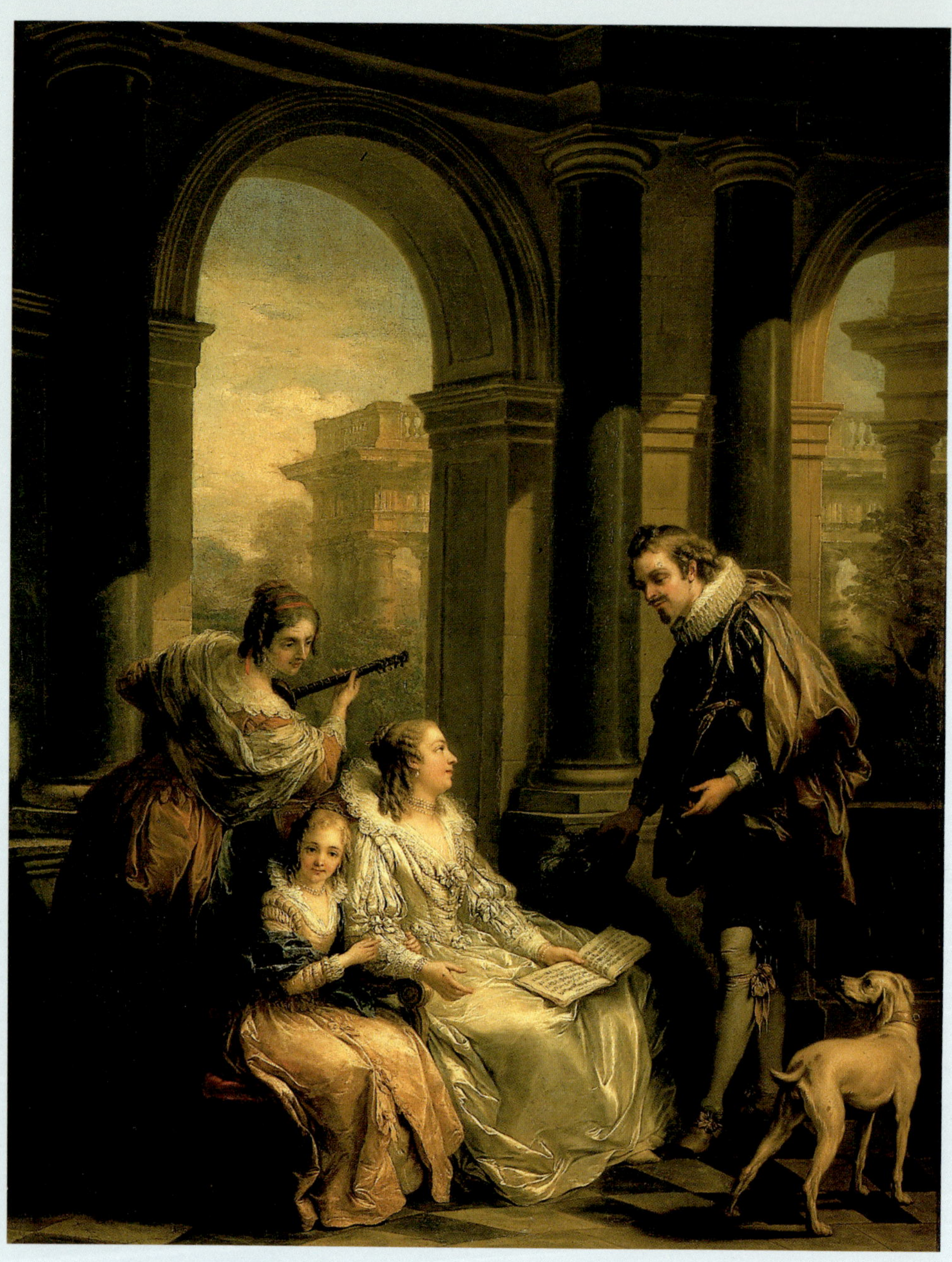

Carle Van Loo,
The Spanish Conversation,
1754, oil on canvas, 164 x 129 cm
St Petersburg, Hermitage Museum.

Figures de Fantaisie

We know of sixteen canvases by Fragonard—but can reasonably presume that there were many others—of pretty much the same size (around 80 centimeters high by 65 wide), offering half-length portraits of men and women. In the foreground the model leans on a stone parapet or a table, clad in rich 17th-century robes of the kind to be seen, for example, in portraits by Rubens. This kind of dress was described at the time as "the Spanish style"—although the name was the only Spanish thing about it—and one of the artists responsible for launching the fashion was Fragonard's former teacher Carle Van Loo. Painted in this vein, Van Loo's *Spanish Conversation* and *Spanish Reading* had met with great success at the Salons of 1755 and 1761.

This same type of dress was used by Fragonard for his series of portraits: doublet and slashed sleeves for the men, low-necked bodice descending in a V onto the skirt for the women. Then there were the accessories: goffered ruff, high starched collarette or wide white collar, white lace cuffs, gold chain, pearl necklace, feathered hat or toque, sword, and more. From one canvas to the next some of the costumes reappear almost like two peas in a pod; only a few details and color shadings—most often with the accent on flamboyant

Portrait of Madame Fragonard,
c. 1777, black chalk and wash, 19.5 x 15.7 cm
Besançon, Musée des Beaux-Arts.

yellows—allow us to tell them apart. It seems that in his studio Fragonard, like Rembrandt, had an entire wardrobe for his models to draw on. Could this have been a ploy on his part? By having his models dress themselves as if for a stage part, could he lead them to reveal, beneath the blatant artificiality of the costume, hidden aspects of their personality? Whatever the case, these figures radiate a force and presence that few portraits of the period can rival.

But who were Fragonard's models? The paintings in this series are usually classified together as "fantasy portraits", an eighteenth-century term indicating that the painter, instead of portraying a specific person, has drawn on his memory or his imagination. However, the fact that two of the portraits—Saint-Non and his brother—are specifically labeled, has led to questions about the identity of the other picturesquely got-up models. Family tradition has it that two other pictures show François-Henri, Duc d'Harcourt (1726–1802) and his younger brother Anne-François, Duc de Beuvron (1727–97). Documentary material from the period also permits the supposition that the man shown with his hand resting on a globe of the world could be the astronomer Jérôme de Lalande (1732–1807). Another figure is said to be Diderot, whose connections with Fragonard are well known: the painter had provided three academic studies of male figures for the "Drawing" chapter in the *Encyclopédie*, and after the success of *Coresus* and the enthusiastic reception given the picture by Diderot, it is quite possible that he wanted to paint the philosopher. On the other hand it seems surprising that Diderot, never loath to comment on portraits of himself, nowhere alludes to this "fantasy portrait."

With the Saint-Non and La Bretèche pictures of 1769—the date is even tipped in on the bottom of the latter—we have a point of reference allowing for reliable siting of the series within the artist's career. Given this date we might have expected Fragonard to have brushed the portrait of Marie-Anne Gérard (1745–1823), who he married the same year. Also a native of Grasse, Marie-Anne was a not untalented miniaturist, even if given to pastiche of her husband's work. However, nothing allows us to see her in the handsome figure of *A Young Girl Reading*, the singer leafing through a score or yet another singer holding a sheet of music. As it happens, only one of the five female portraits in the series has been identified with any certainty.

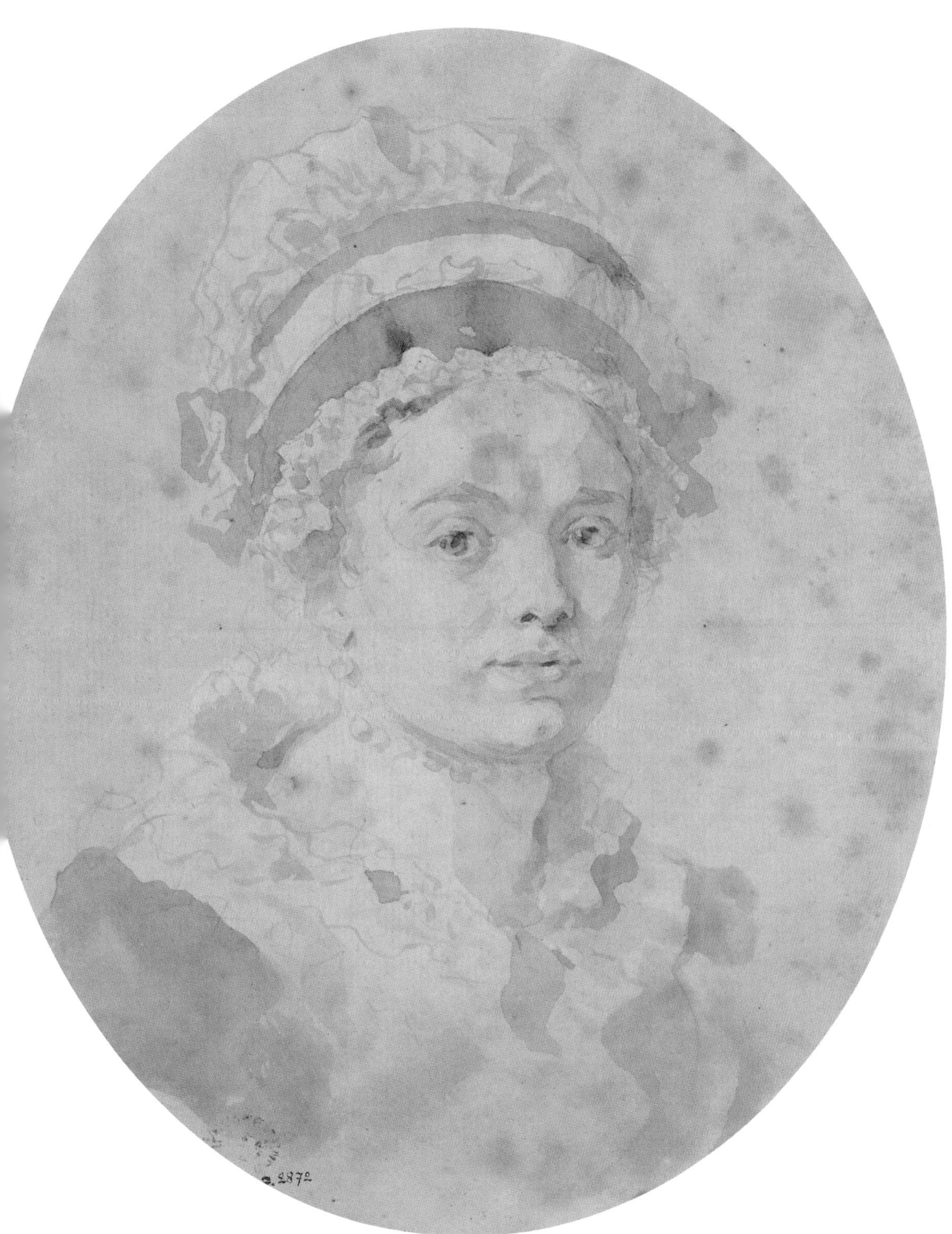

Mademoiselle Guimard

In all probability the young woman with the powdered hair, the fine blue ribbon round her neck and the wasp waist, is the famous Marie-Madeleine Guimard, known as La Guimard (1743–1816). First Dancer at the Comédie Française in 1756, she premiered at the Opera six years later, enjoying a reputation based as much on her acting ability as on the status of her lovers, among whom was the Prince de Soubise and, according to an unconfirmed tradition, Fragonard himself. The portrait must surely predate the quarrel between them concerning the decoration of the Rue d'Antin townhouse she had dedicated to Terpsichore, goddess of the dance. Built by Claude-Nicolas Ledoux, this was quite as elegant a piece of design as the Du Barry pavilion built at Louveciennes at the same period: in addition to the living quarters, Ledoux had included a greenhouse with latticework,

Portrait of Mademoiselle Guimard,
c. 1770, oil on canvas, 81.5 x 65 cm
Paris, Musée du Louvre.

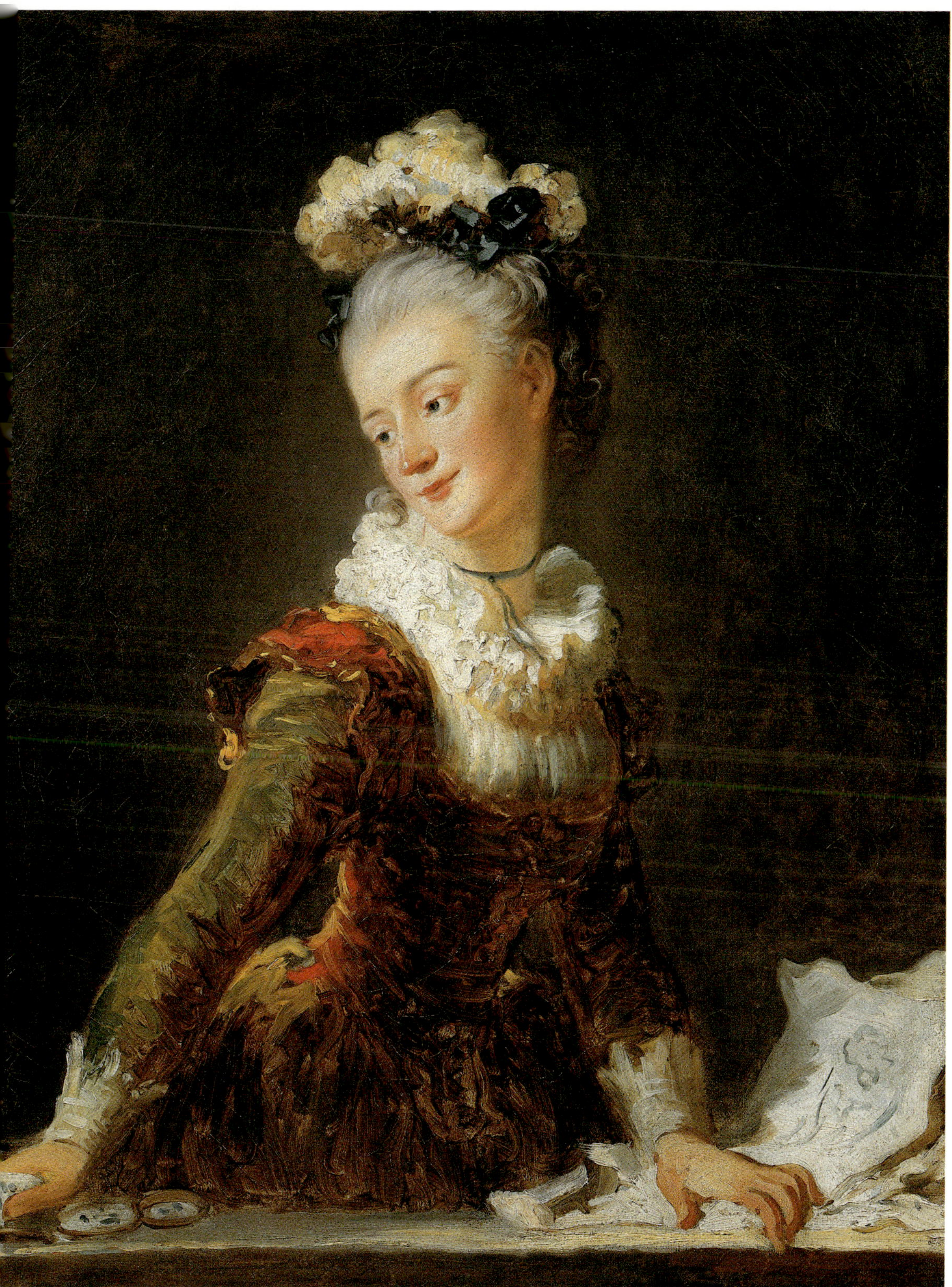

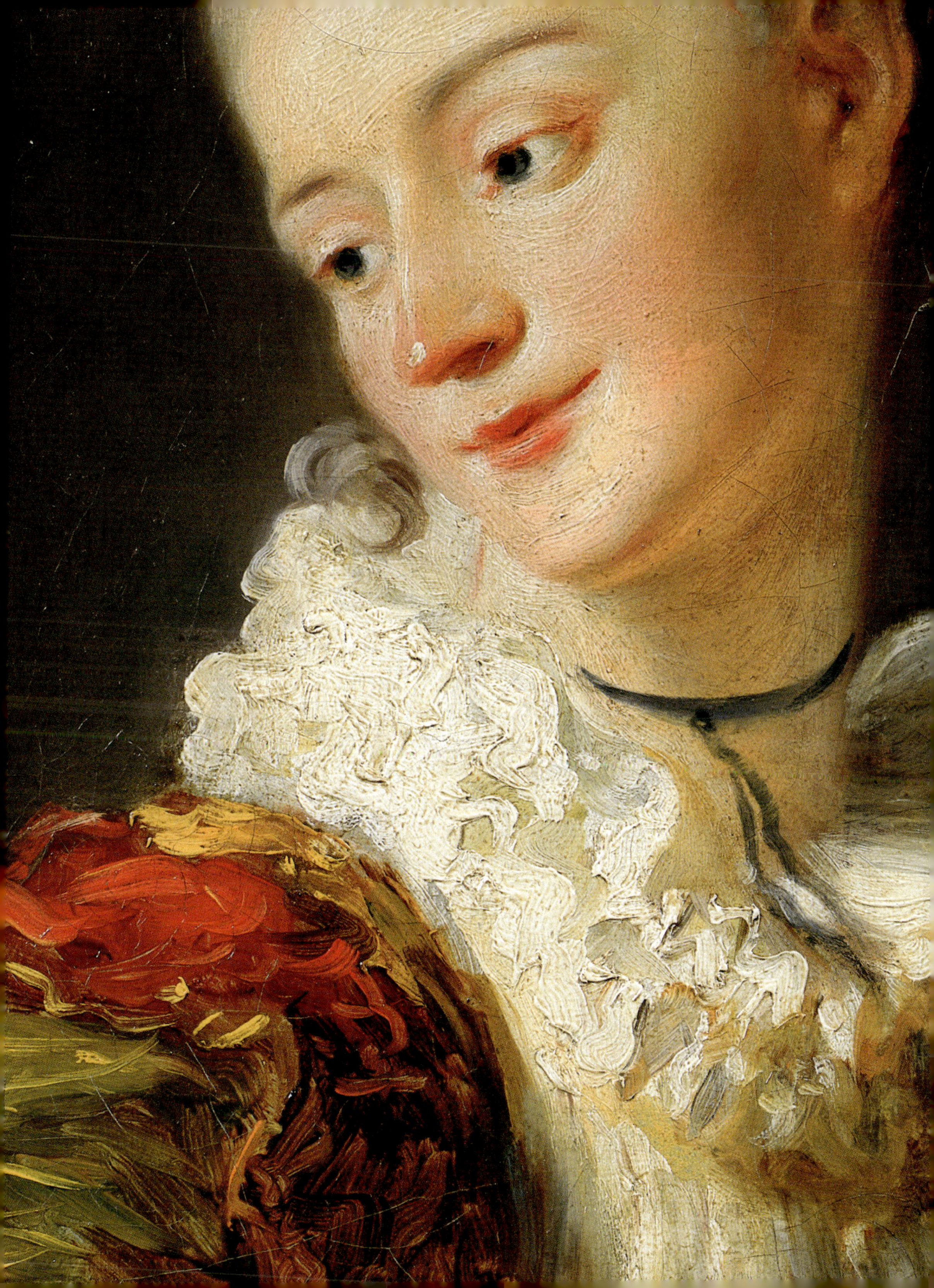

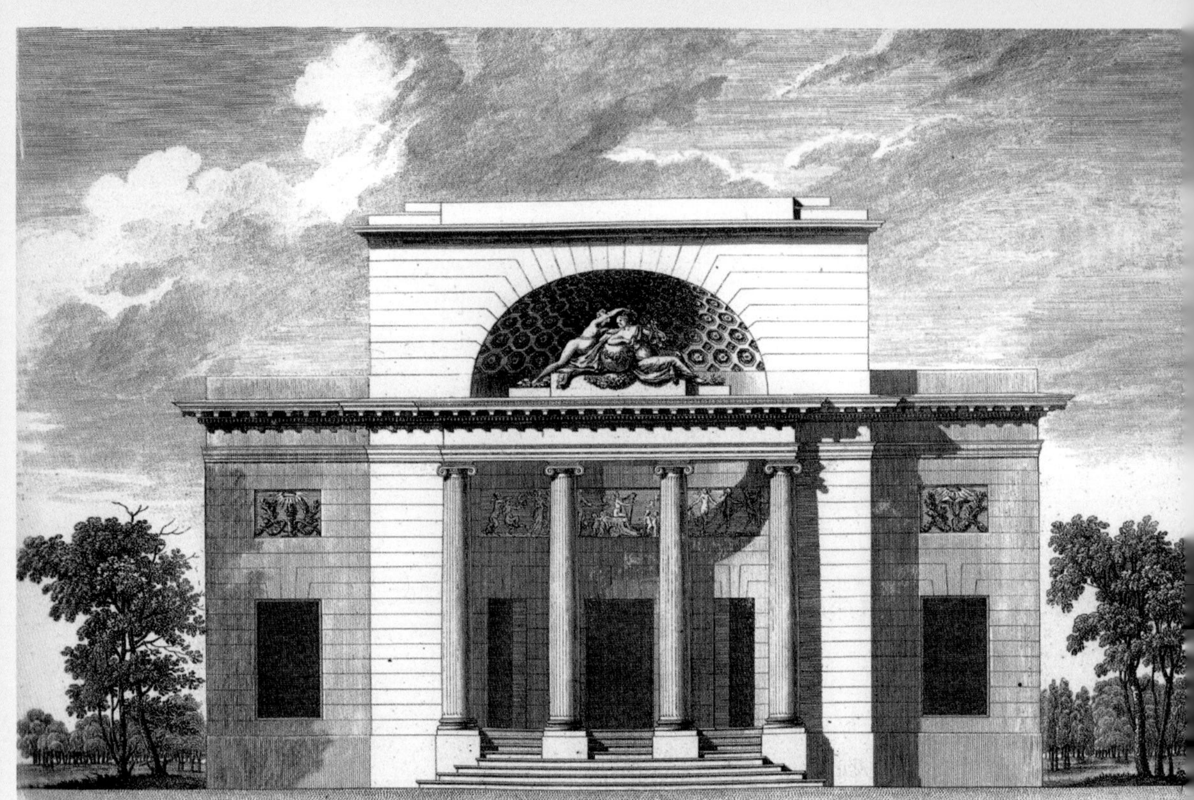

Delagardette,
Mademoiselle Guimard's House on the Chaussée d'Antin
engraving reprinted in Ledoux, Architecture... Paris, 1847, pl. 176.
Paris, Bibliothèque des Arts Décoratifs.

Jacques-Louis David,
The Harmony of Poetry and Music,
1773, black chalk, 19.3 x 15.9 cm
Paris, Ecole Nationale Supérieure des Beaux-Arts.

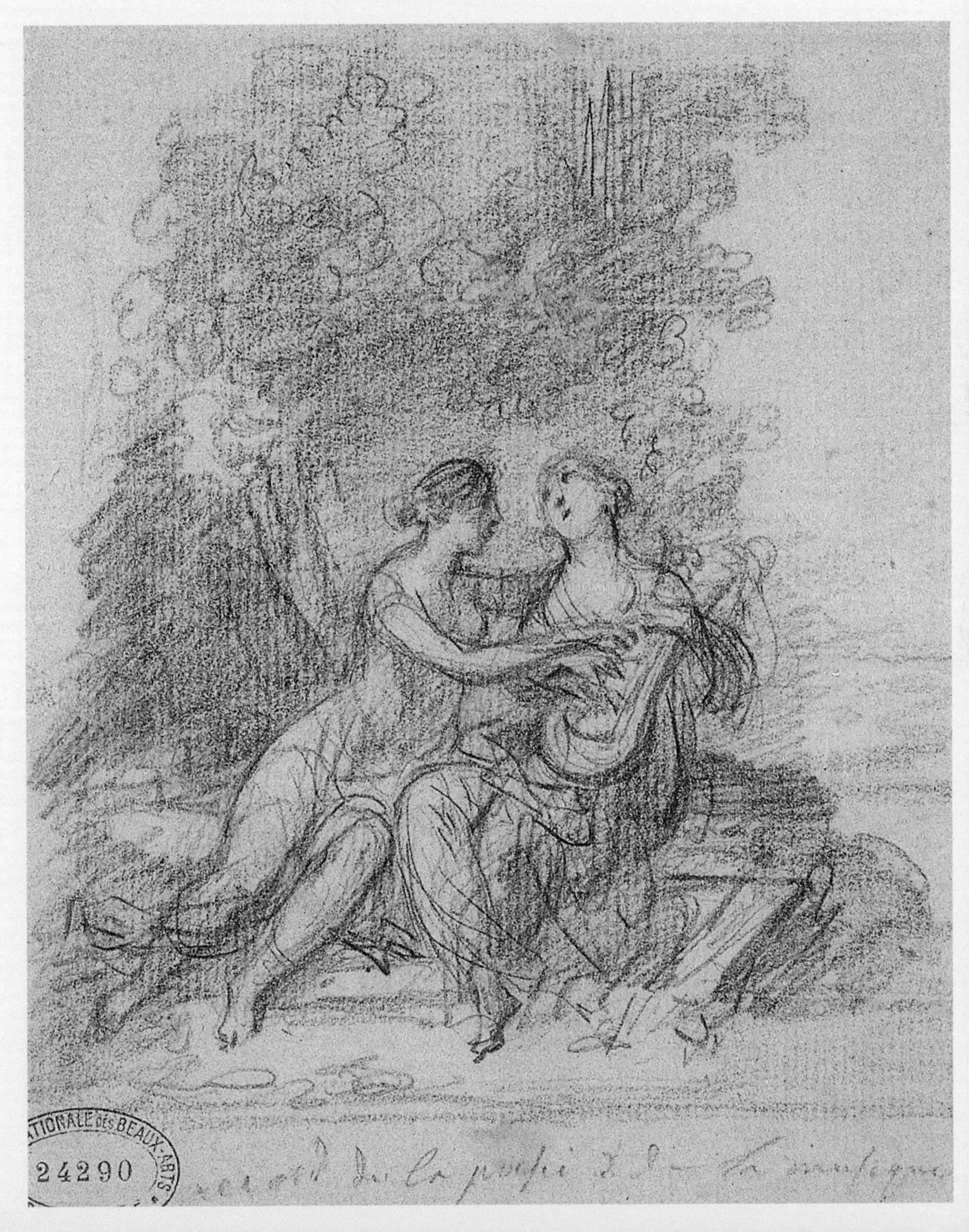
ATIONALE des BEAUX-ARTS
24290

a bath house and a "portable" theater that could be assembled and dismantled as needed. The inaugural performance took place in it on 8 September 1772.

It was in the course of the following year that a falling-out took place between the lady of the house and the painter in charge of decorating the drawing room. The root of the problem would seem to have been Fragonard's fee: while 6000 livres had been agreed on for the commission, Fragonard, once the work had been roughed out, upped his price to 20,000 livres and demanded a much longer completion period. The dancer, however, was in a hurry and handed over Fragonard's project to Jacques-Louis David (1748–1825), an as yet unknown painter with a succession of failures in the Prix de Rome scholarship behind him. As mentioned in an earlier chapter, David was summoned to explain himself, by which time Fragonard had already left for Italy. Much was written about the affair: according to the gossip columnists, shortly after David took over, Fragonard slipped into the house to see how his young rival was making out and took his revenge on La Guimard by transforming her portrait into that of a Fury. Unfortunately the building was demolished in the 19th century; and apart from some handsome red chalk drawings of the Muses, which may preserve their memory, all trace of the four mythological compositions sold as Fragonards in 1844 has been lost. Nor do we have any idea of the fate of the portrait mutilated by Fragonard—if indeed it ever existed. Whatever the case, it could not be the "fantasy portrait" showing La Guimard looking just a shade affected, head lightly tilted towards her shoulder like a diva posing in front of her fans. And the crumpled papers her left hand is resting on: could they be Fragonard's sketches for the decoration of her townhouse?

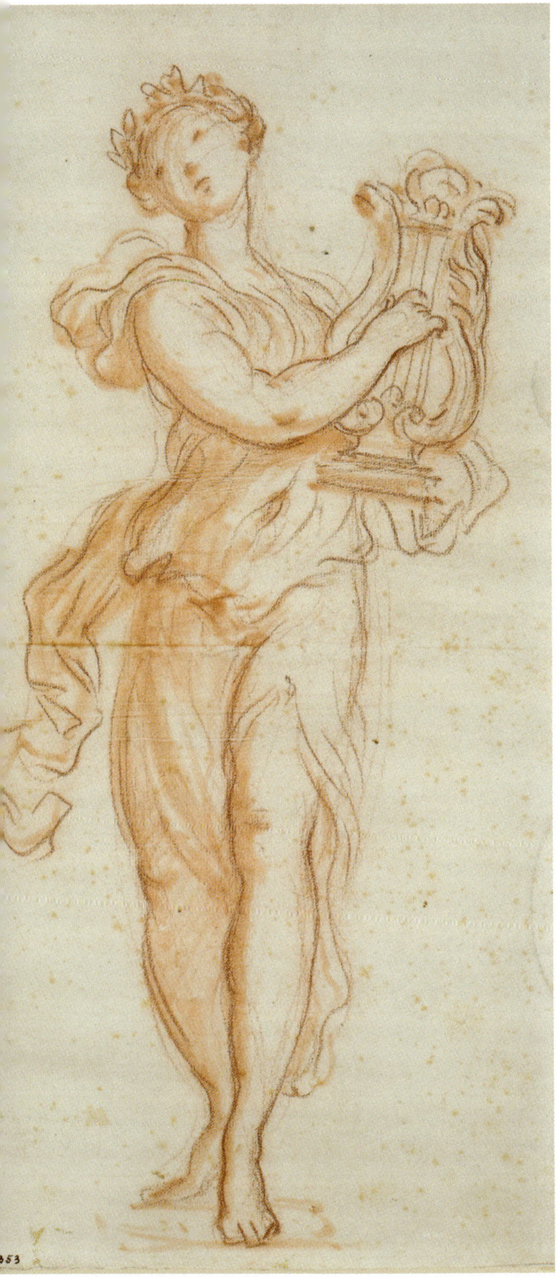

A Muse ("Erato")
c. 1770, red chalk, 41.6 x 19.7 cm
Besançon, Musée des Beaux-Arts.

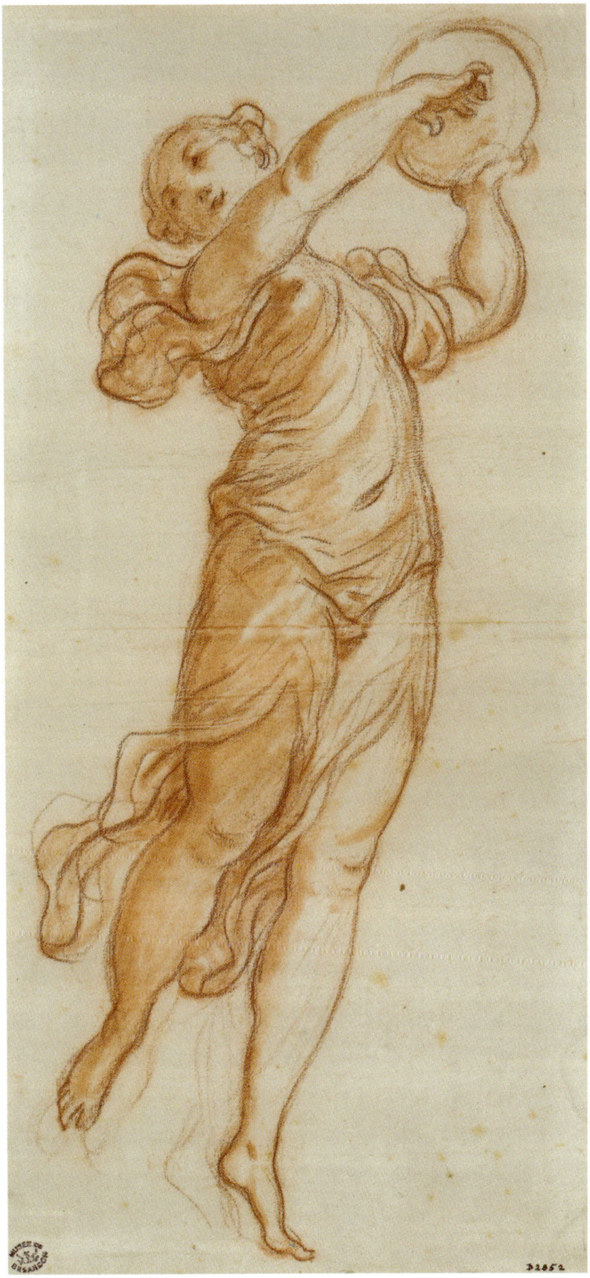

A Muse ("Terpsichore")
c. 1770, red chalk, 41.6 x 19.7 cm
Besançon, Musée des Beaux-Arts.

The Art of the Sketch

The La Guimard episode, a further reminder of Fragonard's difficulty in fulfilling commissions and meeting deadlines, is in sharp contrast with the spectacular rapidity he brought to the "figures de fantaisie." How can someone capable of knocking out a brilliant, striking portrait "in just one hour" struggle to finish a painting or a decoration project? The problem here is surely that same mix of passion and hesitancy that characterized Fragonard and so disconcerted his teachers. Such inner conflict could have totally paralyzed him, yet its effect was to set him to work using, simultaneously, different media and separate stylistic registers. The "figures de fantaisie" are a masterly demonstration of his touch, with no attempt made to conceal the back-and-forth movement of the brush. He even used the marks left in the fresh paint, sometimes reworking them with the handle of the brush, sculpting volume and intensifying color effects he then rounded off with gobbets of white impasto that caught the light and heightened the modeling of his ruffs.

While the pictures in this uninhibited style earned the admiration of Fragonard's contemporaries, they were most often deemed sketches rather than finished works. The modern eye has long since been instructed by the unabashed brushwork of the Impressionists, and we now accord these rugged, lusty Fragonards the same respect as other more delicate, more meticulously polished examples of his painting. This was, of course, not the case in the 18th century, and the artist seems to have deliberately cultivated a certain ambiguity concerning his ranking of his own works—which may also explain why we often encounter several versions of the same subject, each treated differently. This tendency was evident early in his career, beginning with *The Stolen Kiss*, painted, as we recall for the Bailli de Breteuil and of which there also exists a "sketched" version of the same dimensions. Plenty of other works offer similar stylistic variants, as in the two or three known renderings of *Visit to the Wet Nurse, Sultana on an Ottoman* and *The Visitation*. The use of the same format excludes the likelihood of one being a study for the other, preliminary sketches usually being markedly smaller than the final work.

We find, too, canvases on which the artist has rapidly jotted down elements of larger compositions: an example is the stallholders' tents that would appear in *The Fair at Saint-Cloud*, or the young man's head later found bent over the cradle in the tender family scene of *The Return Home*. In the case of the Du Barry series, there exist two rough drafts setting out the composition of two of the four panels. This type of sketch is rare, however: the "Frago" method was all spontaneity, with no underdrawing and few preliminary studies, whether drawn or painted.

The most recent catalogue of Fragonard's drawings, dating from 1970, lists some three thousand in all. But since then dozens more have surfaced: he was a tireless, superbly gifted maker of drawings, whether the medium was black chalk, red chalk or wash. The works that have come down to us indicate that, unlike his teacher Boucher or his contemporary Greuze, with the multiple studies of details—facial expressions, hand positions, folds of draperies—that preceded each new canvas, Fragonard rarely bothered with any major preparations. It may be, of course, that his rough drafts and studies have simply been lost, as might be deduced from the few compositional bits and pieces surviving from broken-up sketchbooks.

Only two of the artist's notebooks have lived to tell the tale. One, in Amsterdam, contains small black chalk landscapes, clearly taken from the life. The second, belonging to the Fogg Art Museum in Cambridge, Massachusetts, offers a handful of zigzag trees, but what really catches the eye is a dozen studies as fascinating as they are mysterious: page after page of amazing, scribbled drawings in crayon or sepia ink, vertical or horizontal in format, and totally unfathomable. Clearly they are working towards the same subject—a painting? an illustration for a future engraving?—but no known work by the artist can be linked to them. Their lines twist like wire as the same near-indecipherable silhouettes recur from one page to the next. Is this a reclining body in the foreground, or a cradle? A religious scene, or a family celebration? We sense, behind the rapidity of stroke and the quasi-obsessional repetition of the same structure, the feverishness of an artist impatient to find the form that matches his idea; and we realize just how wide is the gap between the rough draft and the final result, how much work must go into achieving that ultimate appearance of effortlessness.

Apart from providing these all too rare insights into the practical side of his creative process, Fragonard's graphic work reveals that he practiced drawing for its own sake, and not merely as a necessary stage in the preparation of his paintings. All the main themes of his painted oeuvre are there: landscape, family genre scenes, amorous situations. Interestingly, it is in the last of these that he allows himself even greater freedom and daring, as we note in his work on the fables of La Fontaine, one of the authors he took pleasure in illustrating.

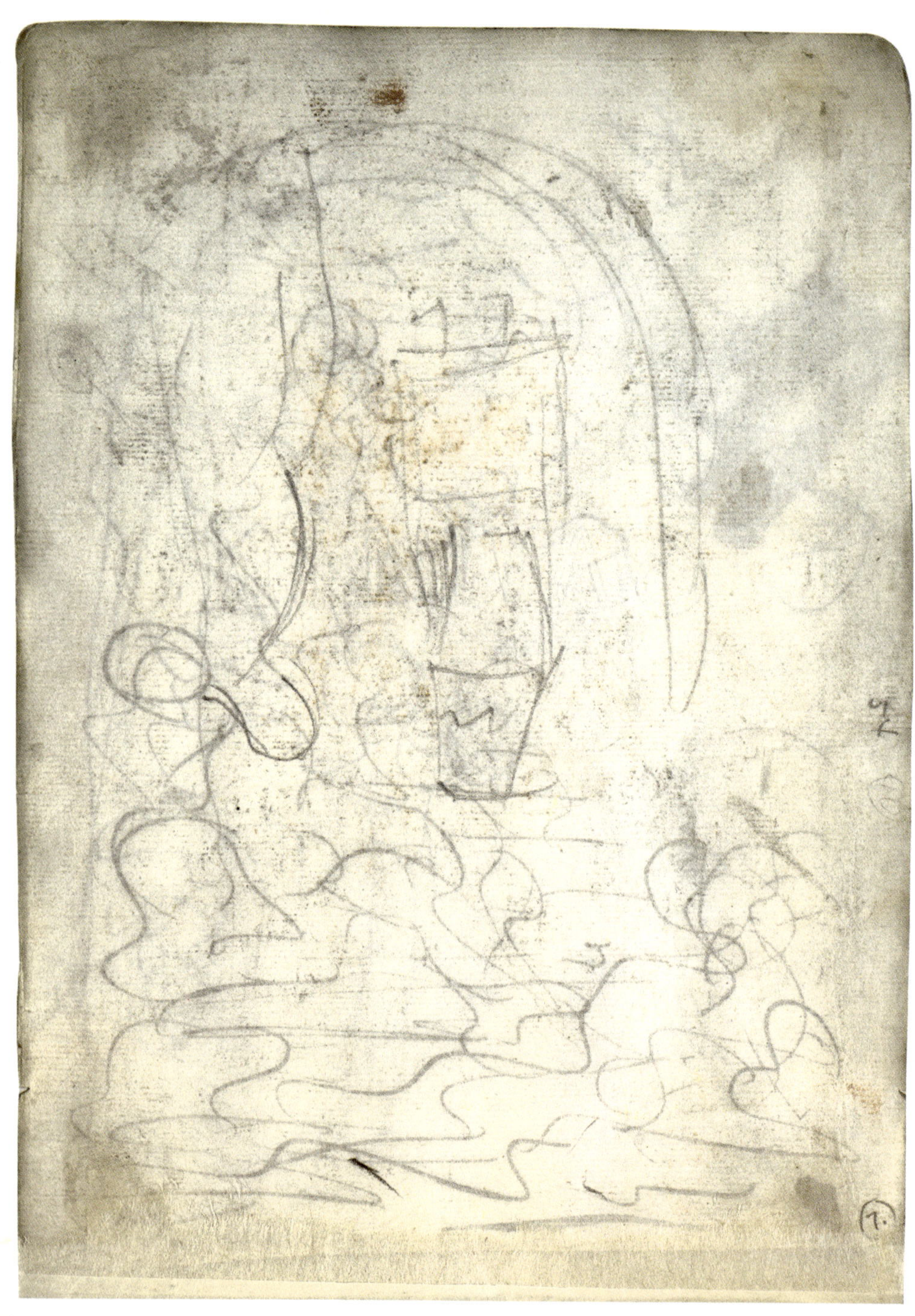

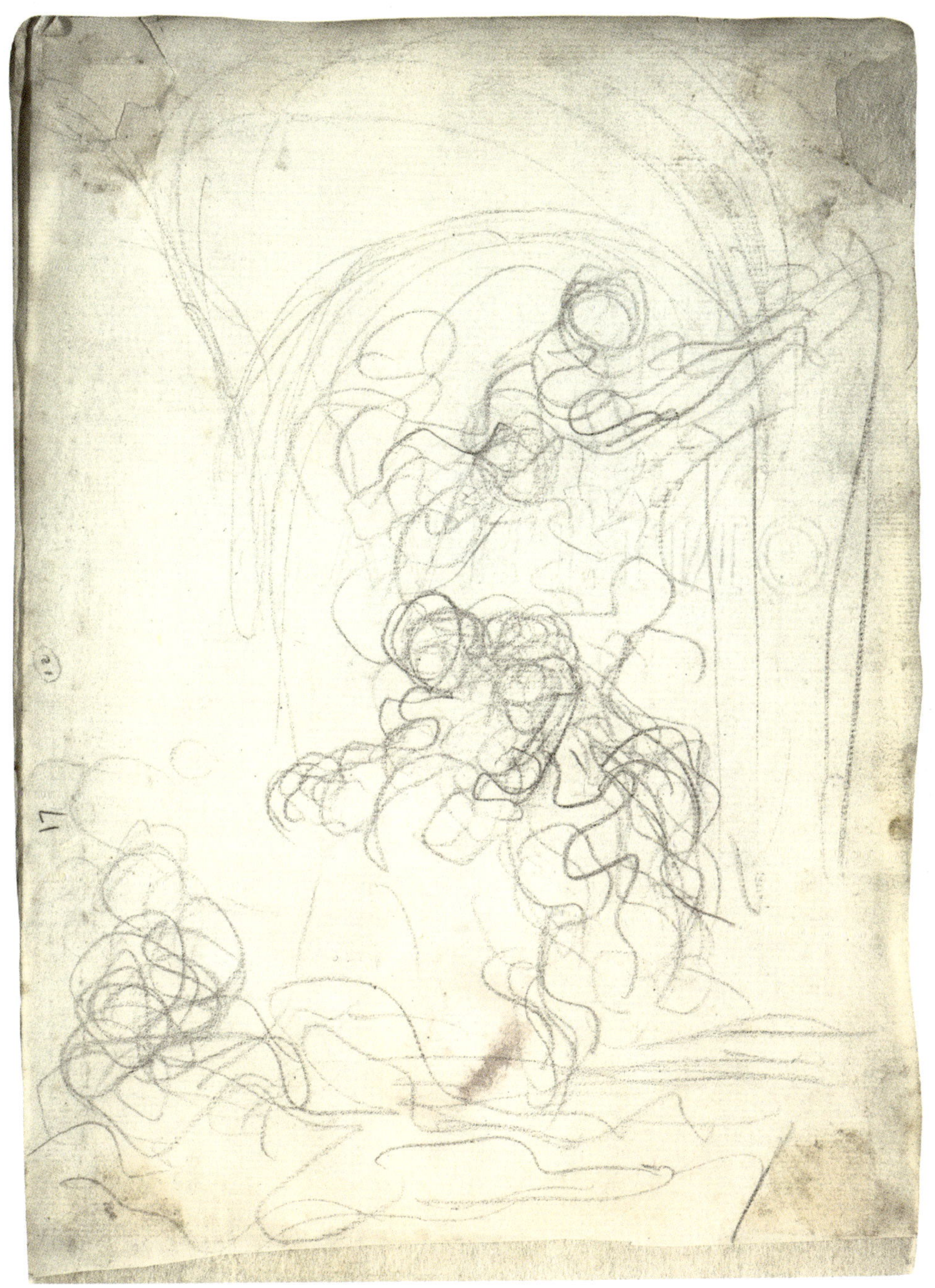

Study for a Composition with Figures,
c. 1758-65 ?, black chalk, 24.3 x 16.5 cm
Cambridge, Fogg Art Museum,
Harvard University Art Museums,
Louise Haskell Daly Fund.

Study for a Composition with Figures,
c. 1758-65 ?, pen and sepia ink, 16.5 x 24.3 cm
Cambridge, Fogg Art Museum,
Harvard University Art Museums,
Louise Haskell Daly Fund

A Passionate Reader

So few examples do we have of Fragonard's handwriting that he has been too readily suspected of an ignorance verging on illiteracy. Yet this is to ignore the fact that he was a voracious reader and a subtle, inspired interpreter of the writers both of the past and of his own time, using them as sources for a host of drawings and some of his paintings. Thus he drew on Jean de La Fontaine's celebrated fable "Perrette and the Pail of Milk" for a brilliantly spirited oval canvas that ignores the moral content of the tale in favor of its witty, comical side. Daringly he covers a large part of the picture area with a swirling cloud of white: the dreams of the milkmaid going up in smoke as two passers-by guffaw heartily. Their mocking laughter, however, has less to do with the girl's clumsiness than with the spectacle offered by her disarranged skirt...

Another work by La Fontaine, *Tales and Novels in Verse*, was the trigger for several series of drawings. Since their appearance in 1664–82, these licentious little stories had inspired a number of artists, notably those of Boucher's generation. In the course of the 1760s Fragonard produced some fifty black chalk compositions putting the work into pictures in a risqué

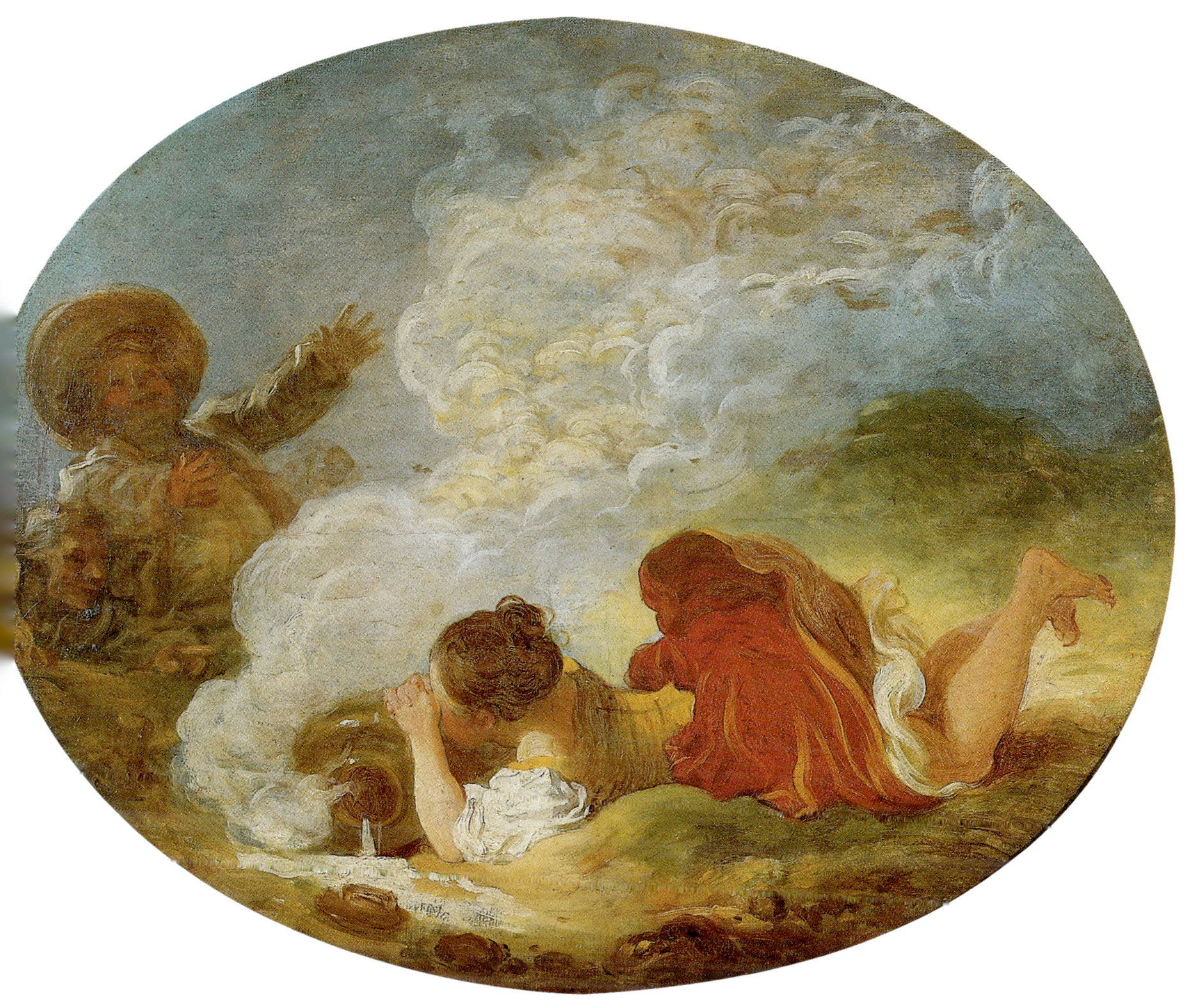

Perrette and the Pail of Milk,
c. 1768–70, oil on canvas, 53 x 63 cm
Paris, Musée Cognacq-Jay.

Following pages:
left page,
The Devil of Papefiguière,
illustration for La fontaine's *Tales*
c. 1770, bistre wash on black chalk, 20.10 x 14 cm
Paris, Musée du Petit Palais.
right page,
St Michael Explaining to Silence
the Mission He Must Accomplish,
illustration for Ariosto's *Orlando Furioso*
c. 1780, black chalk and sepia wash, 38.3 x 25.6 cm
Frankfurt, Städelsches Kunstinstitut.

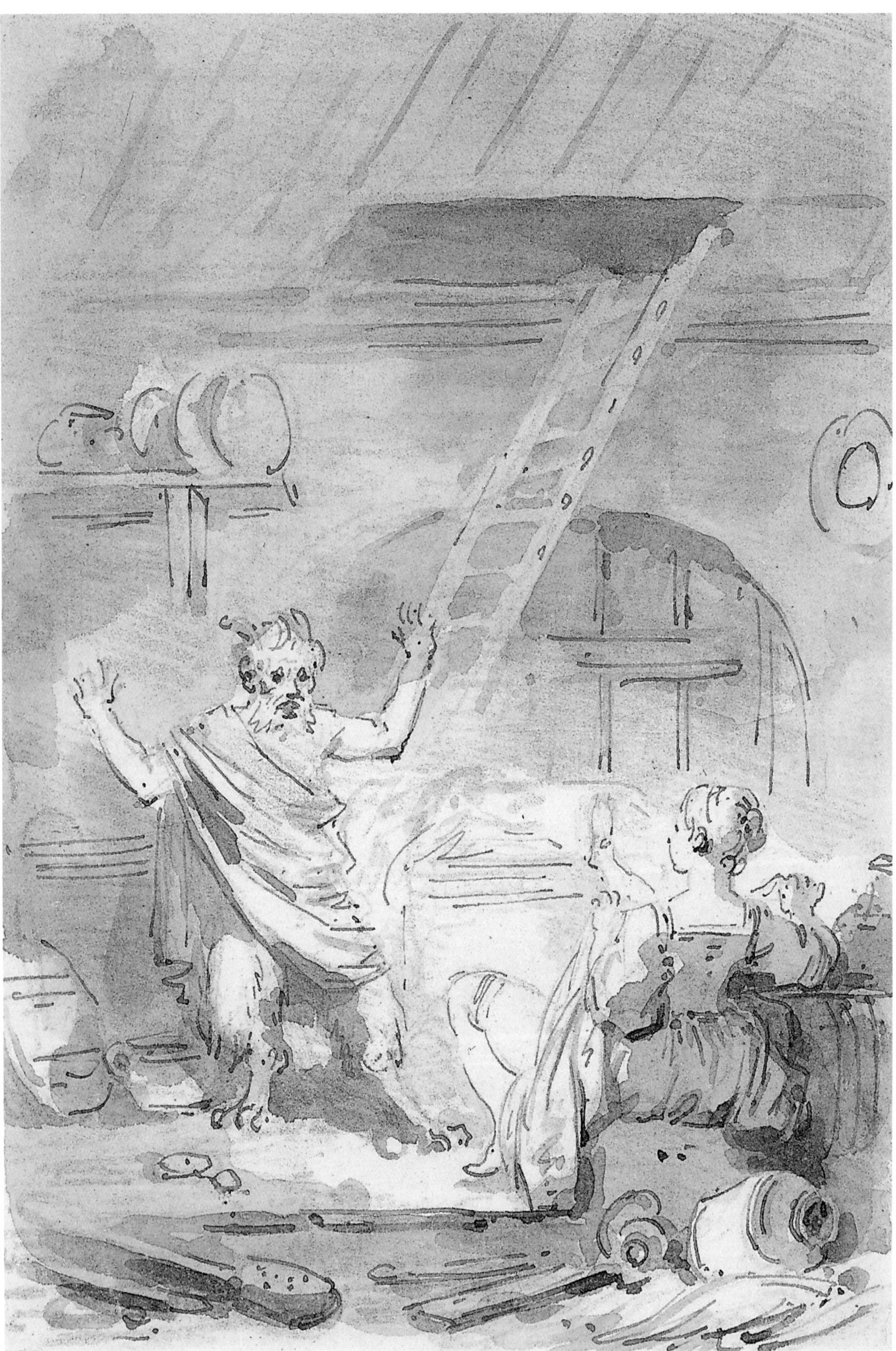

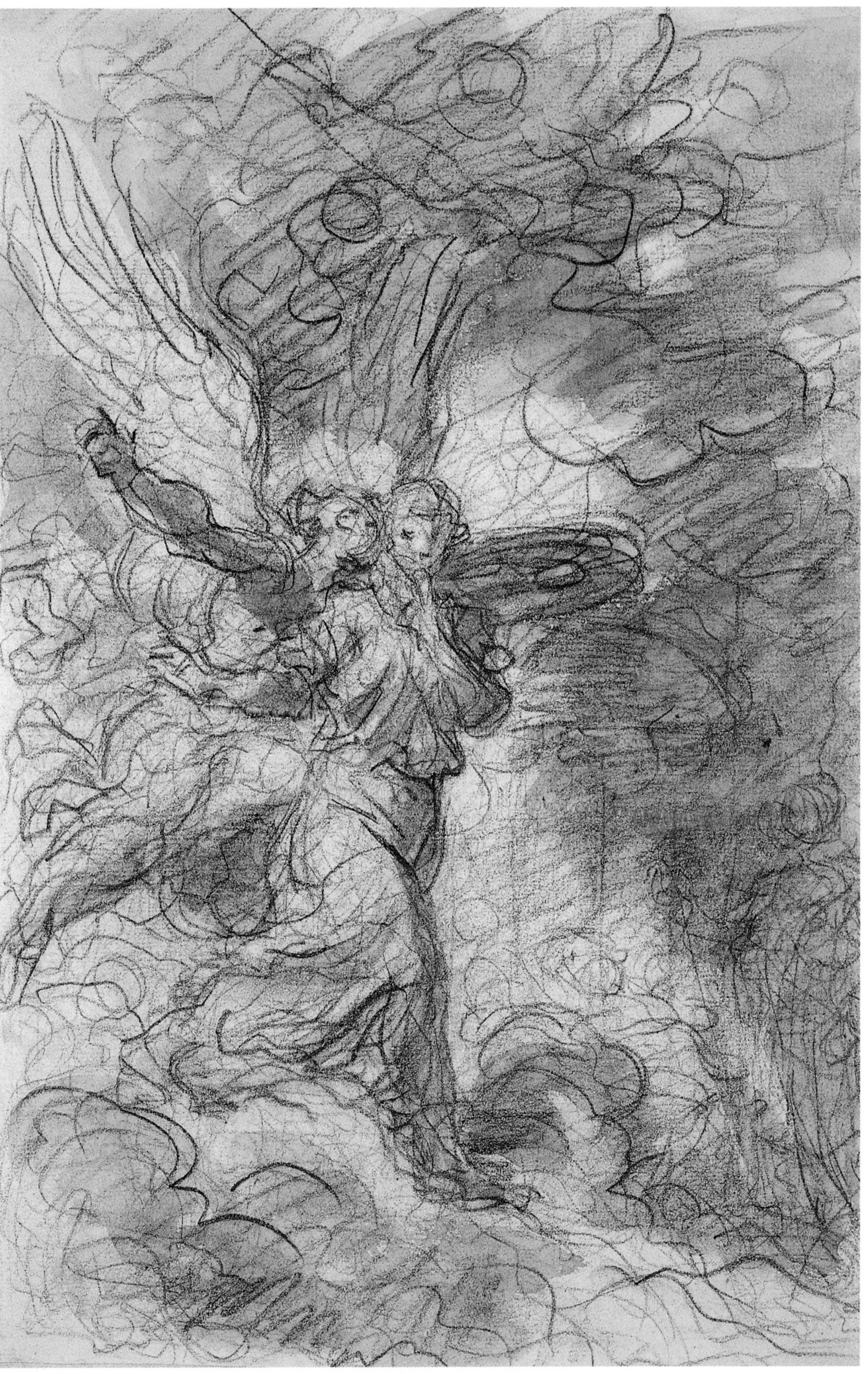

and sometimes even bawdy way. Heightened with wash, this series, according to a prospectus of 1789, was to be engraved for an illustrated edition of the *Tales*; ultimately only a few plates were ever made, publication probably having been interrupted by the French Revolution.

Contemporary authors like Marmontel, Saint-Lambert and the Chevalier de Boufflers also provided Fragonard with subject matter for paintings and drawings, but the one who enthused him most was the Renaissance Italian Ludovico Ariosto (1474–1533). *Orlando Furioso*, a vast epic poem recounting the adventures of sundry heroes against a backdrop of war between pagans and Christians, inspired a kind of comic strip before its time, close to one hundred and eighty drawings—black chalk with wash highlights—that succeed each other as breathlessly as the deeds of the knights, princesses, maguses, witches, giants, hippogriffs and demons that make up the cast. As in his paintings, Fragonard injects intensity and movement with a touch whose supple edginess seems an attempt to equal the writer in all his expressively poetic force. Nonetheless, after sixteen cantos of the work's forty-six, the series came to a halt; it remained unfinished and no illustrated edition using these dazzlingly energetic virtuoso works would ever be published. The same fate awaited his *Don Quixote*, and as with the Ariosto, we have no idea why or for whom the project was undertaken. The scale was more modest—fewer than thirty illustrations for the Cervantes are known today—but the venture highlights Fragonard's taste for chivalry, the epic and the fantastic. And comparison with professional illustrators of his time, such as Cochin and Jean-Michel Moreau, shows us just how profoundly original and innovative he was in this field.

Powder, gouache and copper

To round off our survey of Fragonard's exploration of the graphic arts field, we should look at the various other media he used—only occasionally, it is true, but always aptly. The few pastel portraits that have come down to us are proof of how magnificently well he could use powdery texture to capture the subtlest nuances of a child's face or the lined features of an old family retainer. He also sometimes highlighted his genre scenes with a few touches of watercolor wash, thus preparing the palette he needed for a coming painting. Gouache, on the other hand, was used to create small-format versions of finished works in oils; this may have been, for him, a way a preserving the memory of pictures he was particularly fond of. Such is the case with *The Little Park*, a work on vellum also known as *The Gardens of the Villa d'Este*, and *The Isle of Love*, whose graying clouds, in the version on paper at the Gulbenkian Foundation in Lisbon, embody a more somber vision of that idyllic landscape.

Nor should we forget the engravings, even if the oeuvre includes only some twenty in all. It was probably in Boucher's atelier that Fragonard learnt etching, his earliest known venture into the field being a reproduction of a drawing by the master. Most of the prints he made were in fact based on works by other artists; some of them date from his return from Italy late in 1761 or early the following year, and were transcriptions of his own drawings of works he had seen and admired during the journey with the Abbé de Saint-Non. It would be another fifteen years before he worked on copper plates again. How are we to explain this abrupt, very brief return—maybe a half-dozen etchings—to a medium in which he had never shown any special interest or any marked ability, except by the need to teach the technique to his young sister-in-law Marguerite Gérard? His wife's sister did in fact sign one of these etchings, based on a delicious Fragonard composition showing children playing with a cat wrapped up like a baby: "The first plate by Mademoiselle Gérard, aged 16 years in 1778." Fragonard was doubtless the principal creator of the work, given the sureness of its execution, but the teacher-pupil relationship did not end there. It would even be a core feature of the last years of the artist's career.

Portrait of Sophie
c. 1780, pastel, 60 x 40 cm
Besançon, Musée des Beaux-Arts.

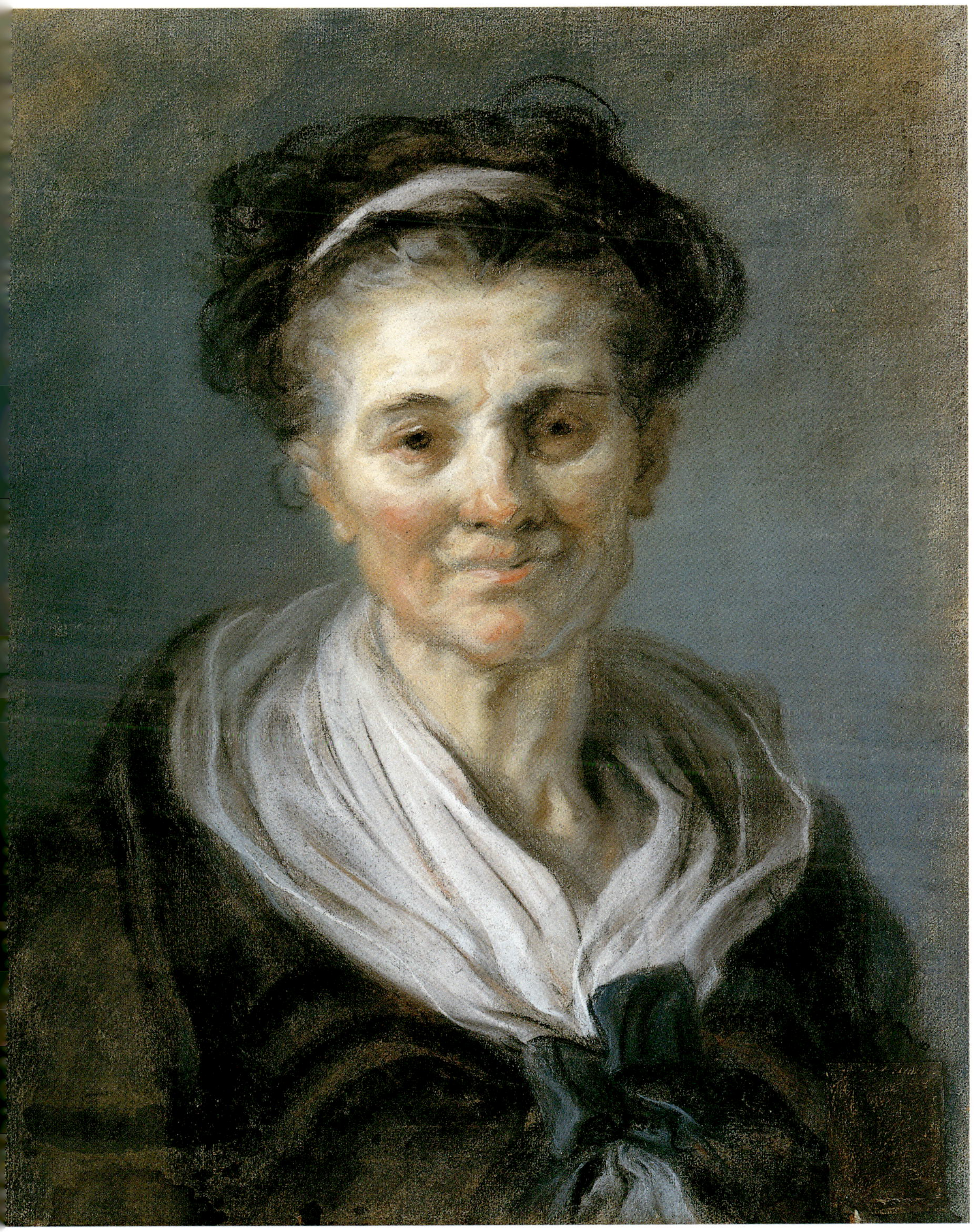

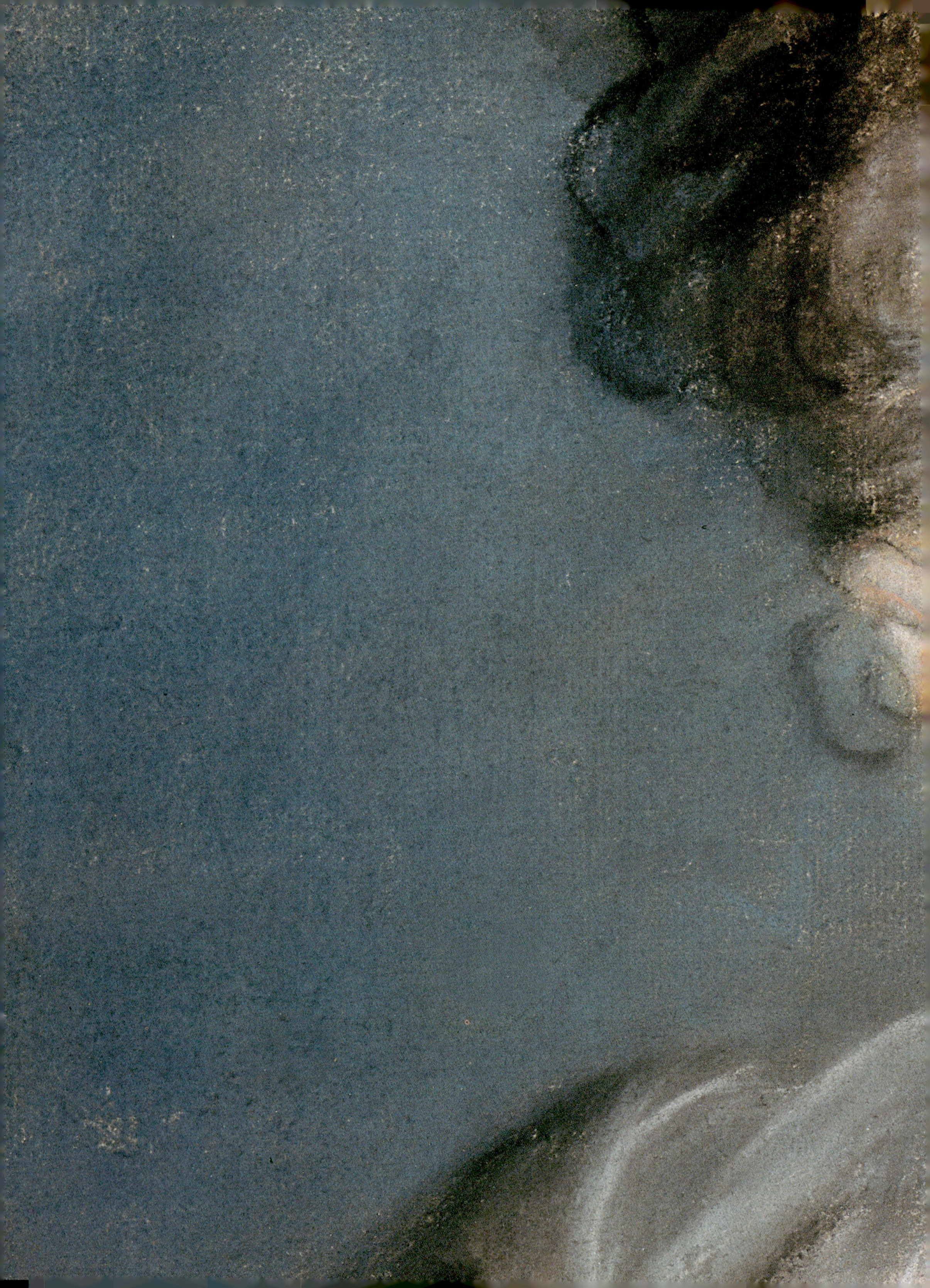

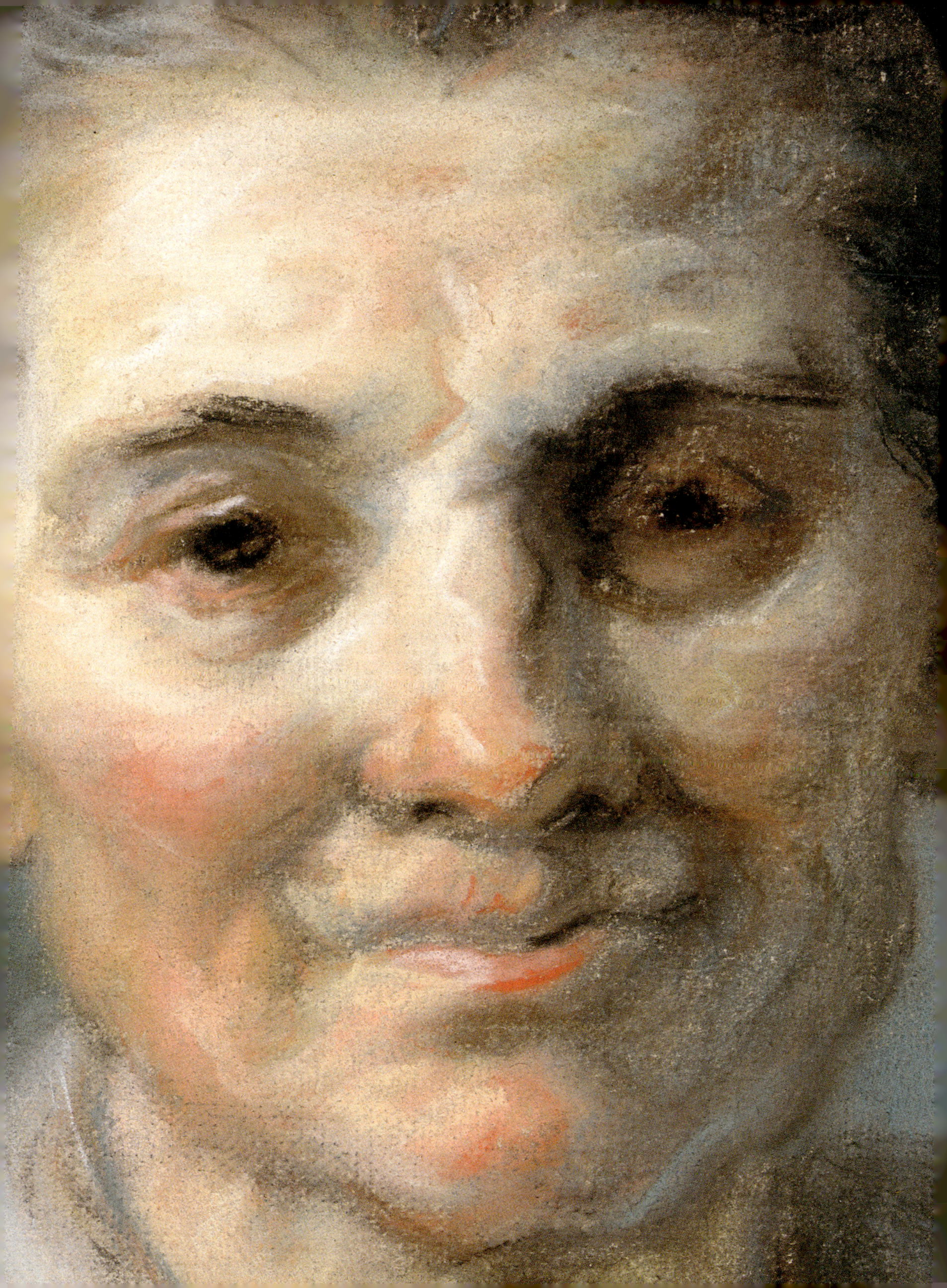

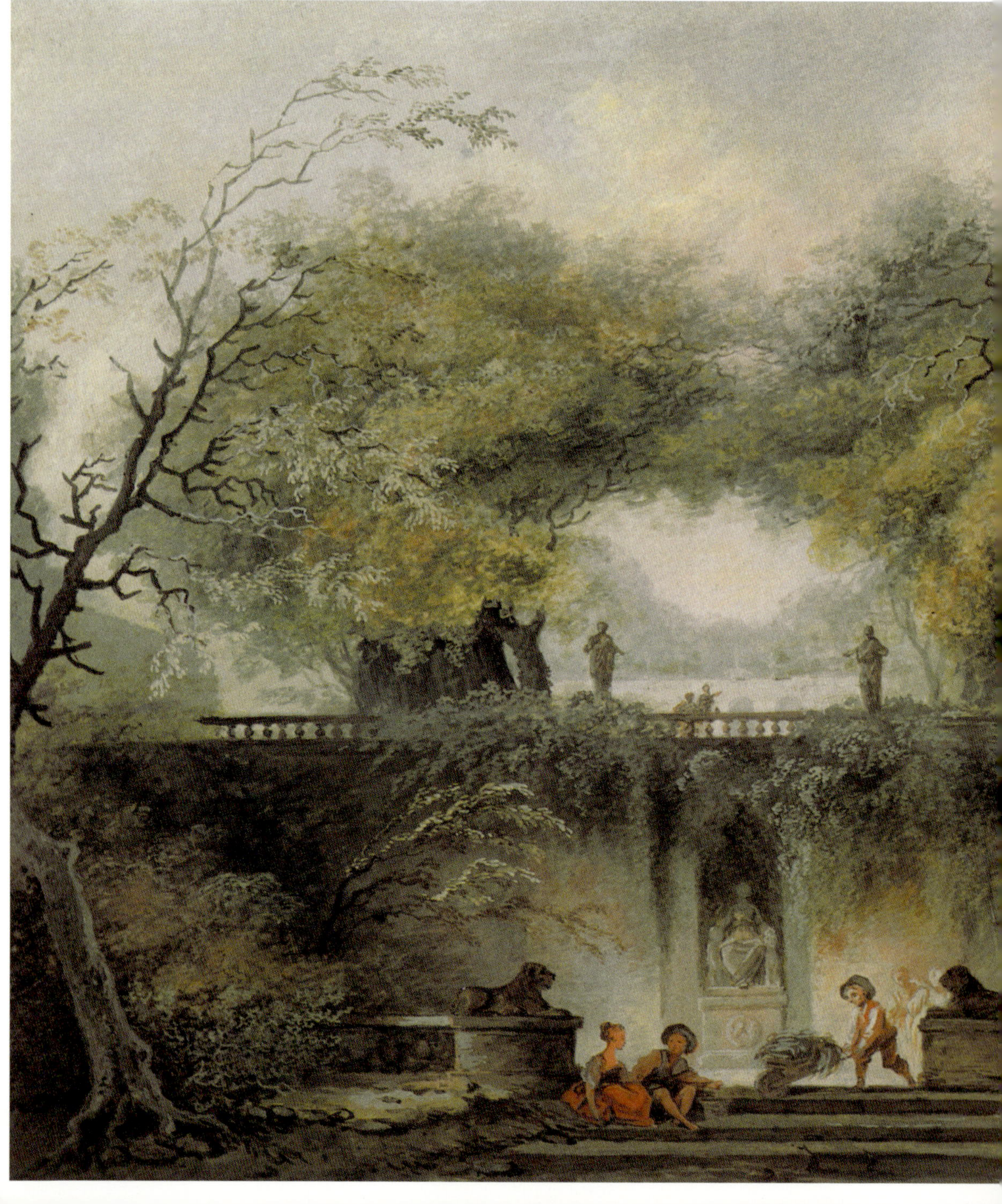

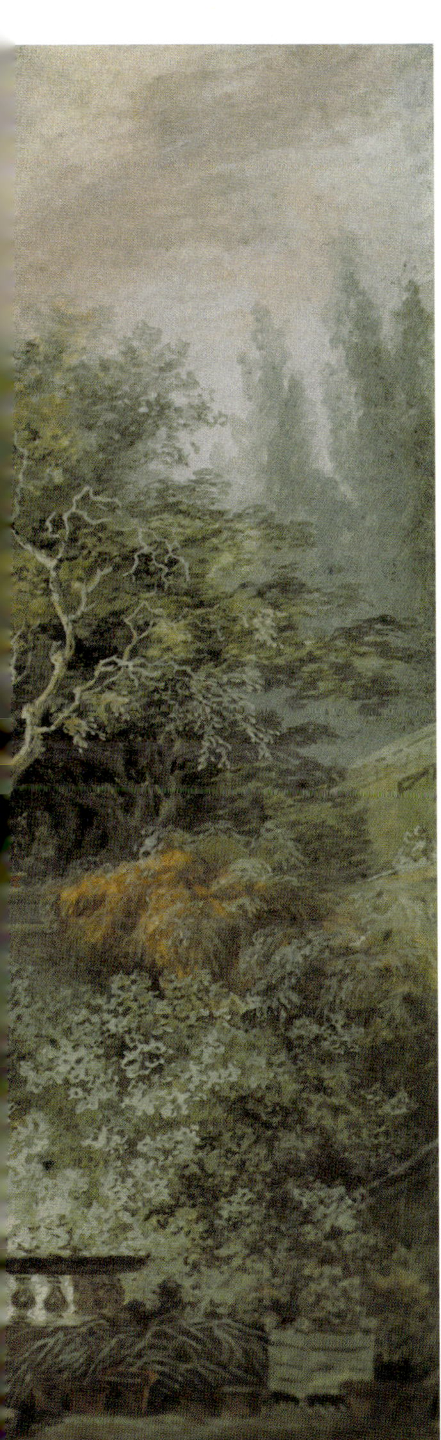

The Gardens of the Villa d'Este,
c. 1765 ?, gouache on vellum, 19.7 x 24.2 cm
New York, The Pierpont Morgan Library.

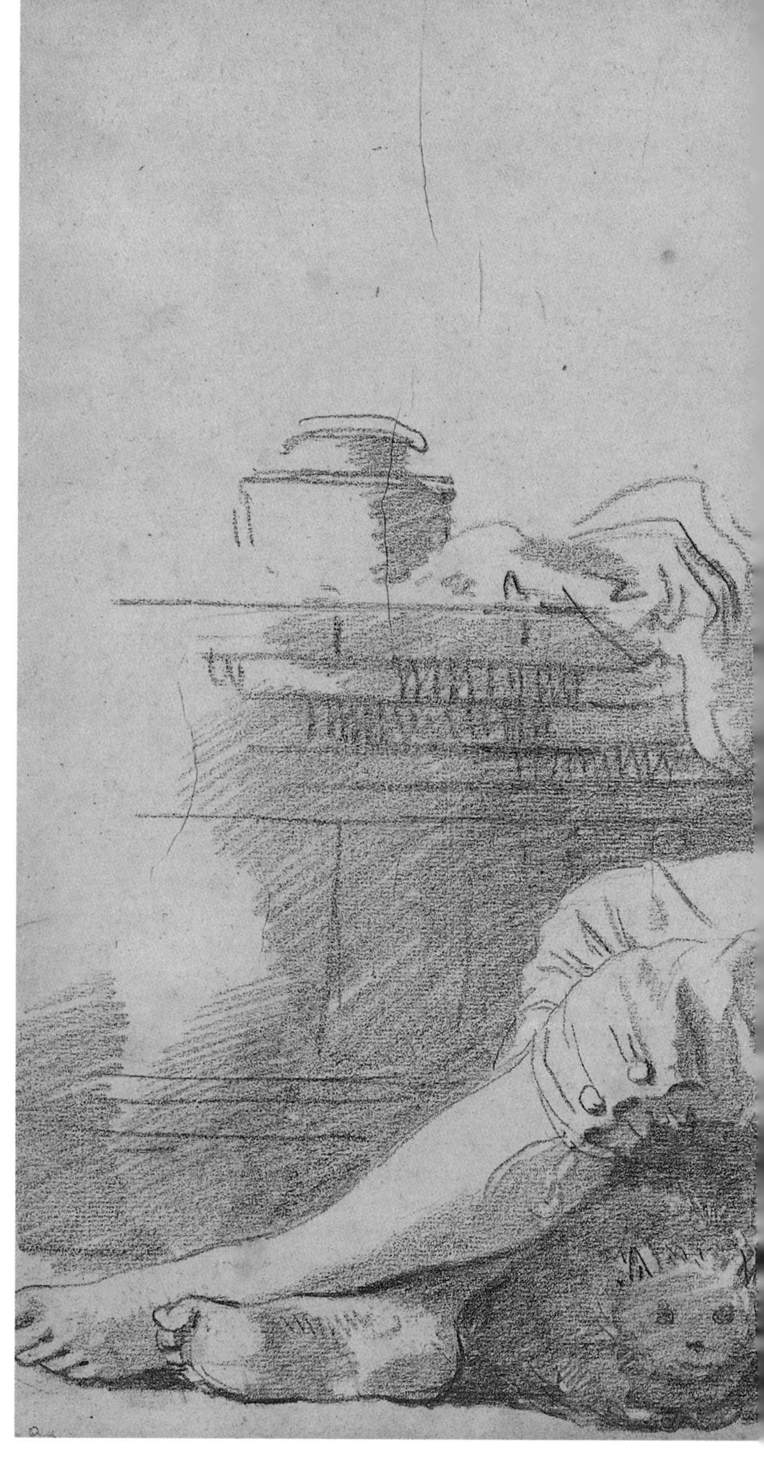

Child with a Cat,

c. 1770-74, red chalk, 35.6 x 49.1 cm

Paris, Musée du Louvre.

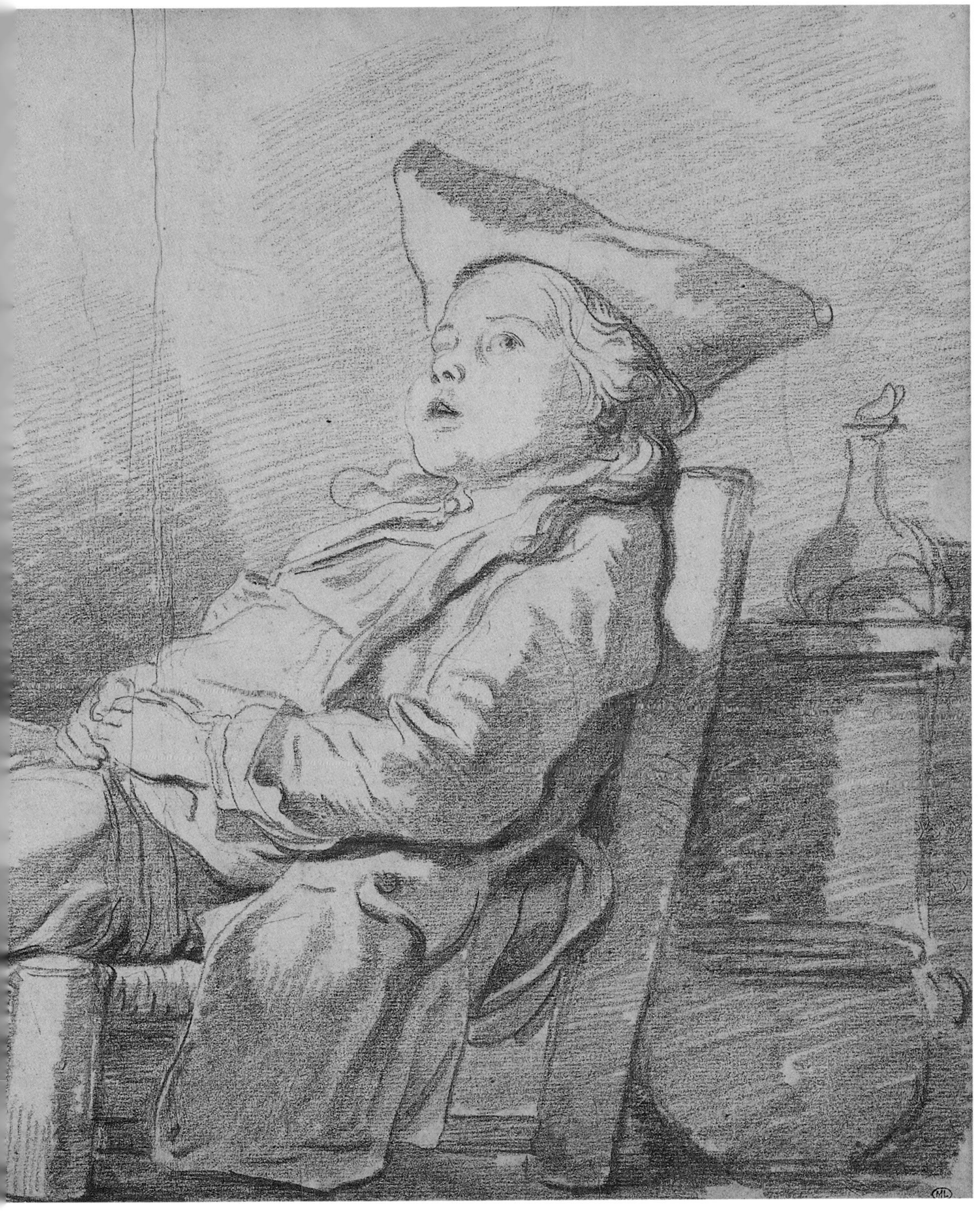

Fragonard and Marguerite Gérard,
The Swaddled Cat
1778, etching, 22.8 x 17 cm
Grasse, Musée des Beaux-Arts.

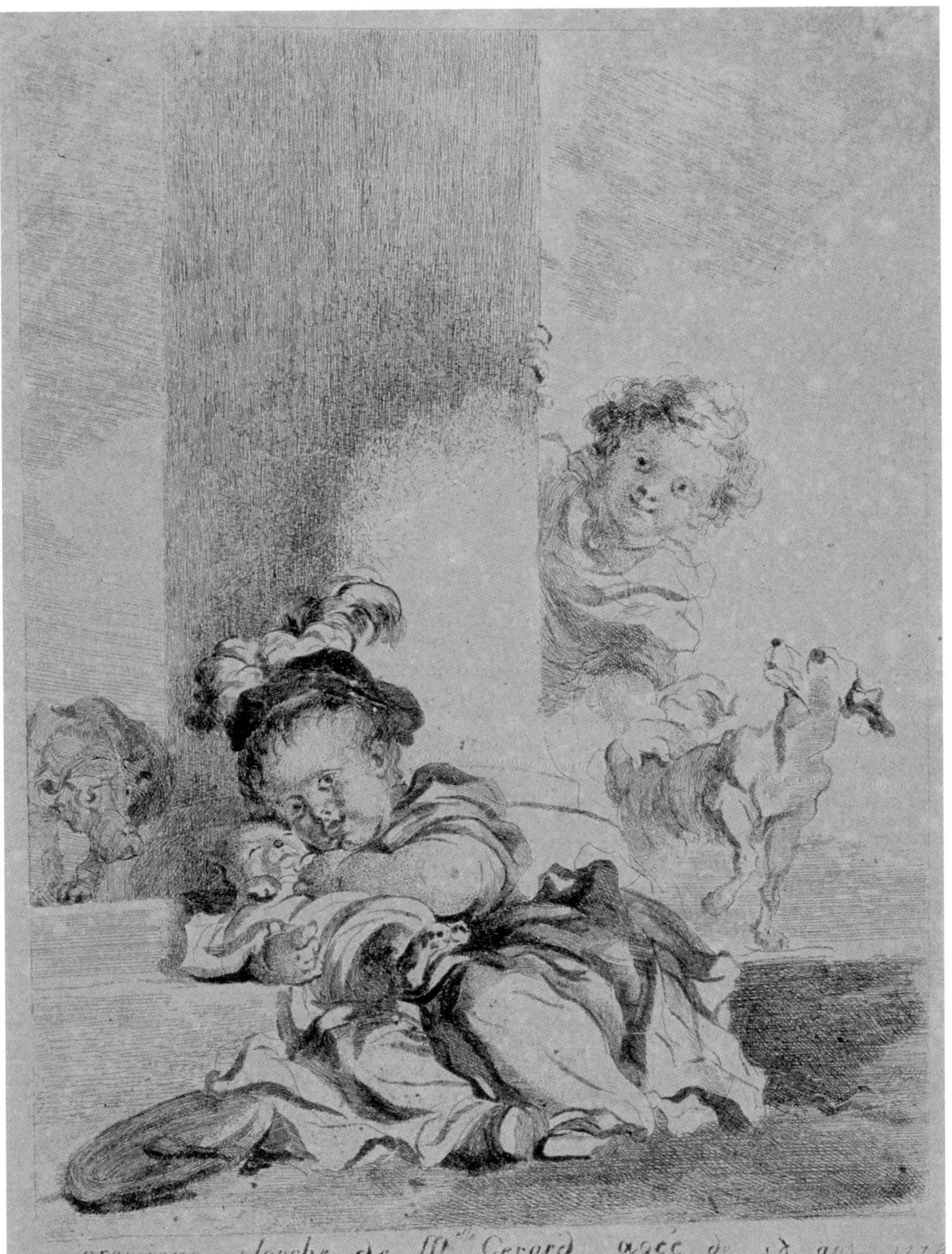
premiere planche de Mlle Gerard agée de 18 ans 1778

VII
Last

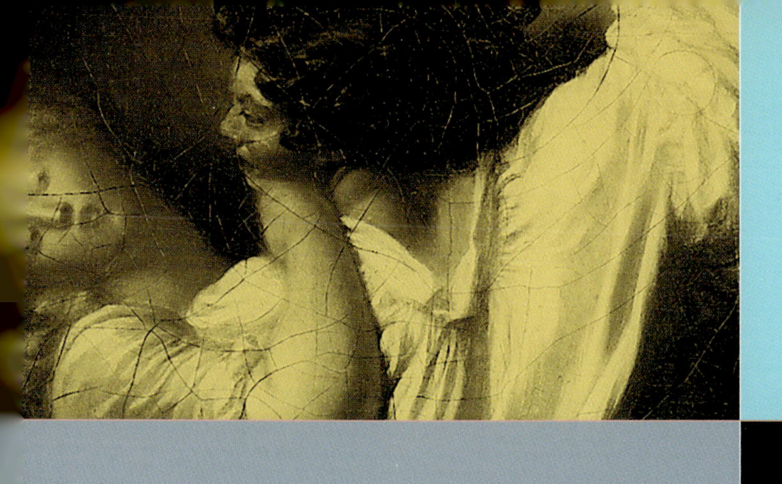

Sparks

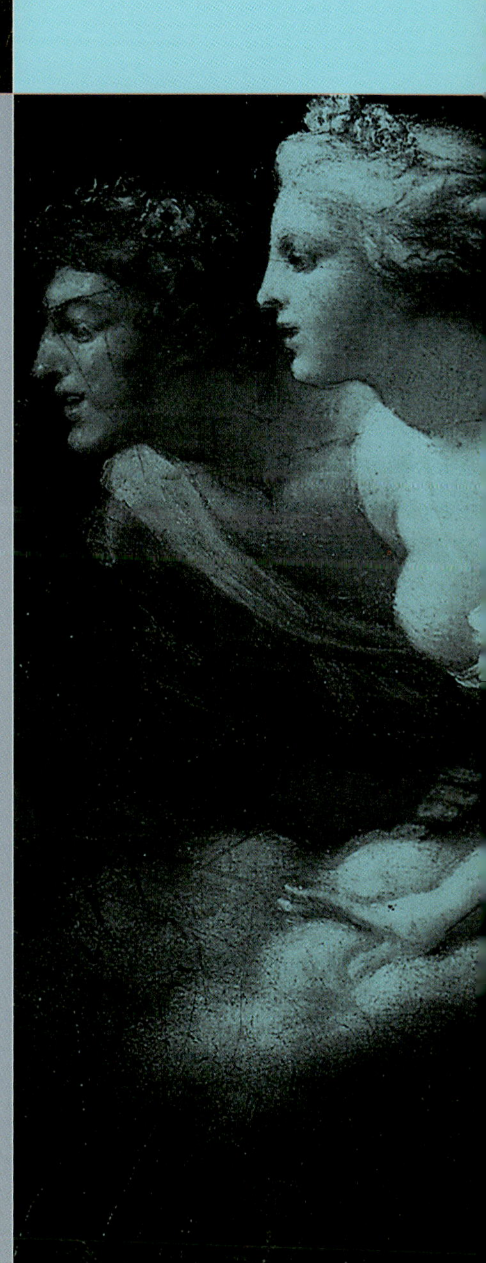

We recall that Fragonard returned from his second trip to Italy in September 1774, coming via Germany. The quarrel with Bergeret and the subsequent legal battle over payment for the drawings seem not to have fazed him in the least: on the contrary, the number of works that can be dated to the ten years following his return indicate that he had thrown himself back into his work with fresh energy. The unfinished projects and rejected commissions were no more than bad memories, with a whole new field of possibilities opening up: Fragonard's batteries had been recharged by contact with the old masters, bringing new life to his art. This did not mean, however, that he had abandoned his favorite subjects: those genre scenes of childhood mischievousness and family happiness had lost none of their appeal for him, together with portraits of children and teenagers dressed up, according to a custom of the time, as Savoyards accompanied by tame marmots. The repertoire still included, of course, those pretty, coquettish women elegantly caught on circular and oval canvases; and the landscapes, either in the manner of the Dutch masters or drawing their inspiration from the parks and residences of his clients. For example, it is generally agreed today that the second half of the 1770s saw the painting of the five large landscapes mentioned earlier, which adorned Marchal de Sainscy's drawing room.

The Bolt

The long voyage abroad was also followed by a number of religious works using a handsomely Rembrandtesque chiaroscuro. Wreathed in a delicate sfumato, *The Adoration of the Shepherds* breathes new life into one of the old faithfuls of the Christian visual repertoire, while drawing on classical composition in a way that embodies yet again Fragonard's attentive contemplation of the masters. In addition to the Charles Le Brun rendering of the same subject, then in the royal collection, he perhaps had in mind the Benedetto Castiglione version, copied during his visit to Genoa in 1761. But the major reference here is surely Poussin's *Adoration of the Shepherds*, which he had had the opportunity to admire only a few months earlier, in the gallery of the Elector of Saxony, in Dresden.

We have the good fortune to know just who commissioned the Fragonard *Adoration*. The collection of Louis-Gabriel, Marquis de Véri (1722–85) was renowned far and wide both for the quality and quantity of its contemporary French paintings, and for the speed with which it had been put together: most of the works had been acquired over the period 1775–79. At Véri's townhouse on the Rue des Saints-Pères one could admire seascapes by Joseph Vernet, mythological works by Louis-Jean-François Lagrenée, and a large number of genre scenes by the marquis's favorite, Jean-Baptiste Greuze. In addition to the "bourgeois dramas" of which Greuze had the secret—among them *The Father's Curse and The Wicked Son Punished*—Véri owned versions of *The Broken Jug* and the charming *Child Playing with a Dog*, both formerly belonging to Madame Du Barry. The ten Fragonards in the collection also included scenes involving children, but there was more, in the form of two masterpieces in quite a different vein: *The Adoration of the Shepherds* and the even more famous *The Bolt*.

According to Alexandre Lenoir, one of Fragonard's first biographers and someone who had known the artist well, Véri had commissioned a picture "to serve as a pendant" to *The Adoration of the Shepherds*. "Intending a display of genius," the account continues, "[Fragonard] resorted to a bizarre contrast in a daringly passion-filled picture known as *The Bolt*." This assertion—published ten years after the painter's death, it should be remembered—greatly exercised the critics: how to explain an embracing couple in a room in disarray as a pendant to a religious scene? It was thus inferred that the link between the two pictures was the apple on the table to the left of the action: it was a reminder of the forbidden fruit in the Garden of Eden and thus an allusion to Jesus' atonement for Original Sin. A further conjecture played on the then-current issue of sacred as opposed to profane love. These theories remain unconvincing, given the glaring differences between the works: subject, format, style, composition, lighting, tone, movement, and so on. What is clear, however, and not for the first time, that Fragonard was capable of working in different styles at the same period.

Rediscovered in 1974, *The Bolt* has gone on to acquire a renown at least equal to that of *The Swing*. Ten years separate the two, and the contrast is astonishing: here we can gauge the artist's enormous skill in matching style to subject and so achieving a greater richness of meaning. Far from setting out to portray a lover's reverie while layering a generous coat of vegetation over bawdy innuendo, *The Bolt* offers the totally different context and atmosphere of a stark, enclosed setting. A wide, rumpled bed prominently occupies the picture space, with heavy curtains cascading from some unidentifiable point and seemingly echoing, in their elaborate folds, the lines of the couple embracing by the door. The taut muscles of the man, the gestural dynamic, and the violent contrasts of light and shade all combine to suggest tension and desire. In a reversal of the peekaboo intimacy of the earlier canvases, Fragonard here seems to be tilting his scene towards greater depth and gravity. The joyous frolicking of teenagers and the conventional by-play of *The Useless Resistance*—subjects already dealt with more than once—have been supplanted by adult passion. The change is perceptible, too, in the soberness of a palette reduced to powerfully simple harmonies between the rich red of the curtains and the porcelain-smooth, meticulously rendered yellow satin of the dress.

The Nativity, after Castiglione,
1761, black chalk, 28.8 x 19.2 cm
London, The British Museum.

Following pages:
The Adoration of the Shepherds,
c. 1776, oil on canvas, 73 x 93 cm
Paris, Musée du Louvre.

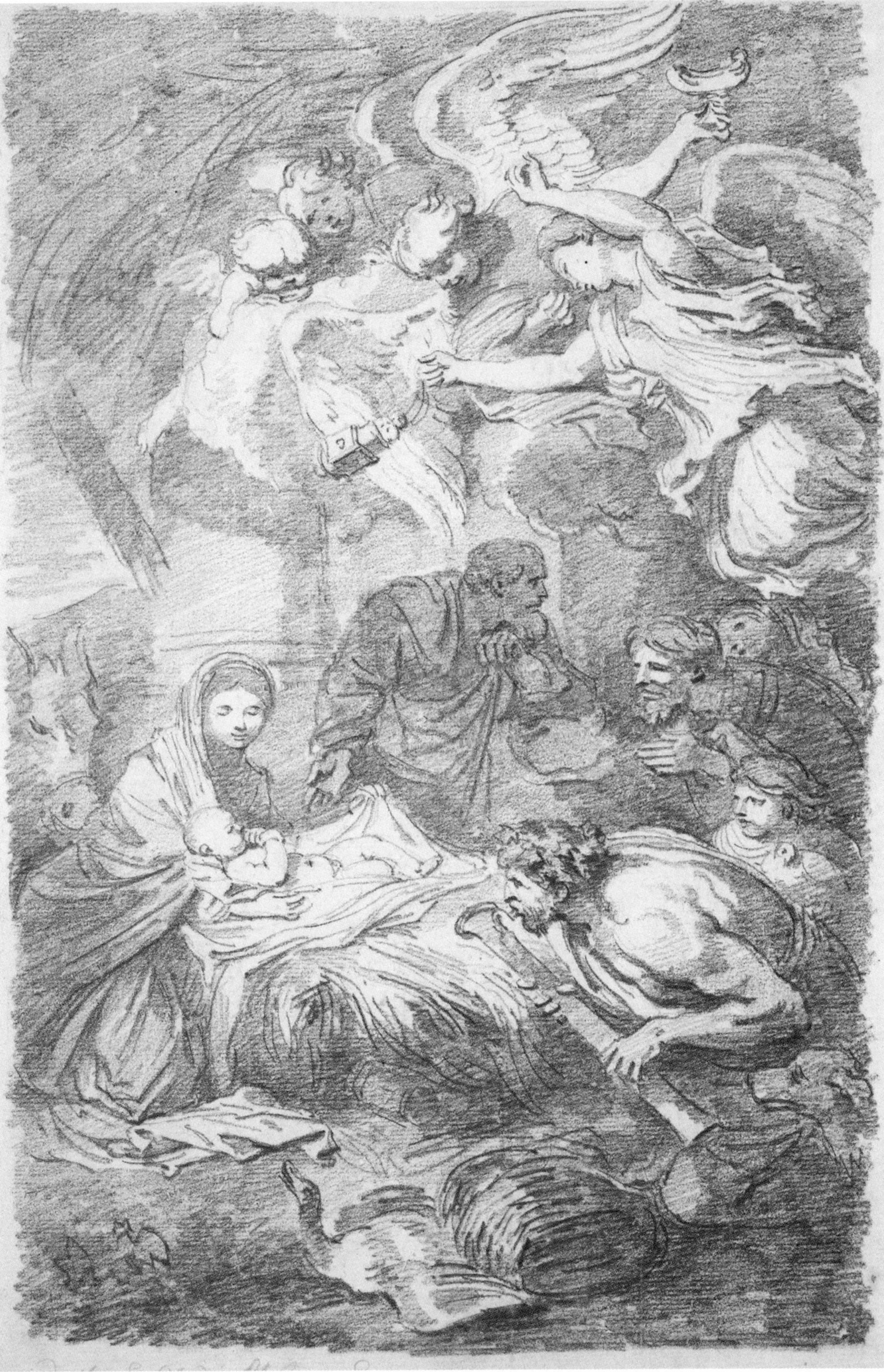

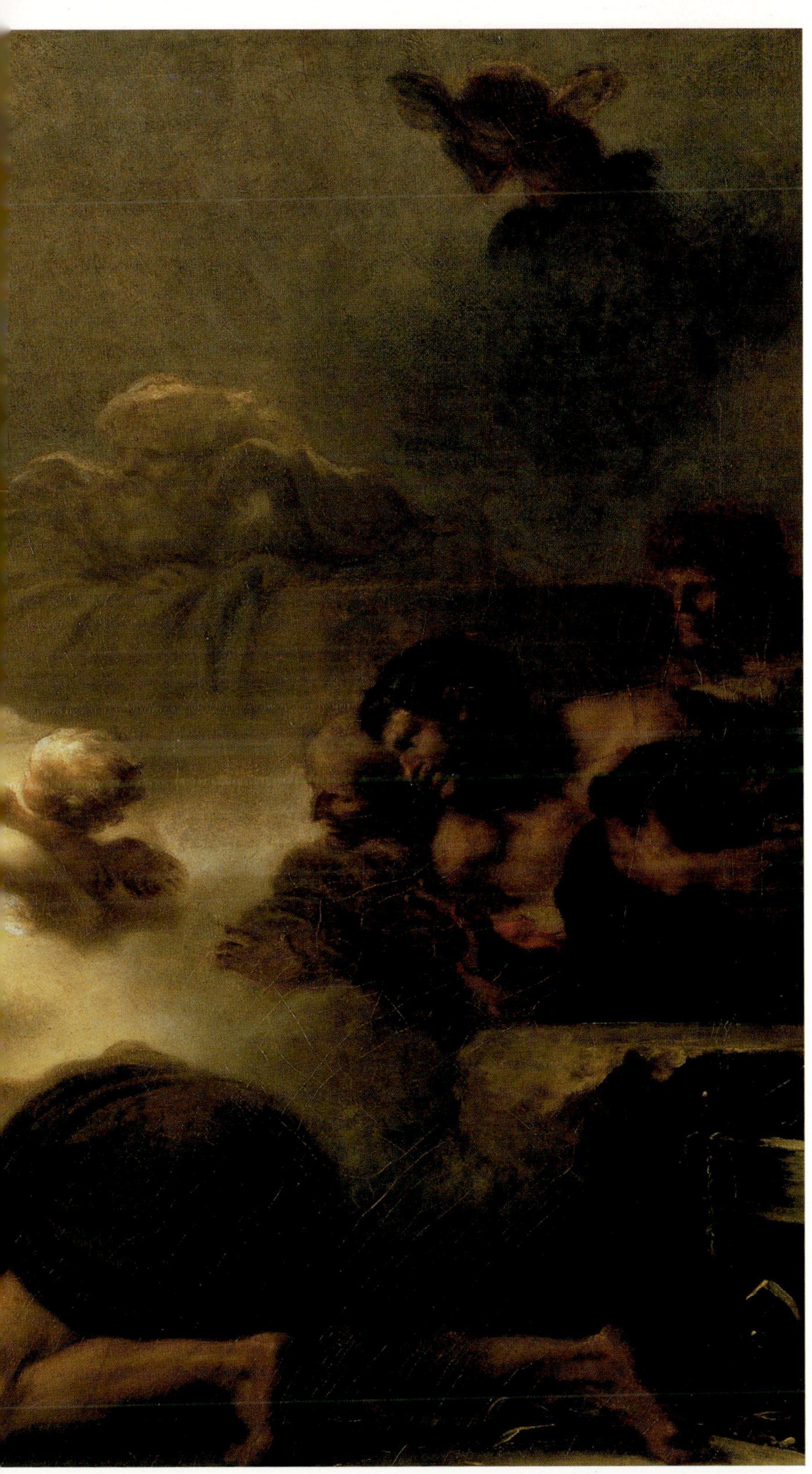

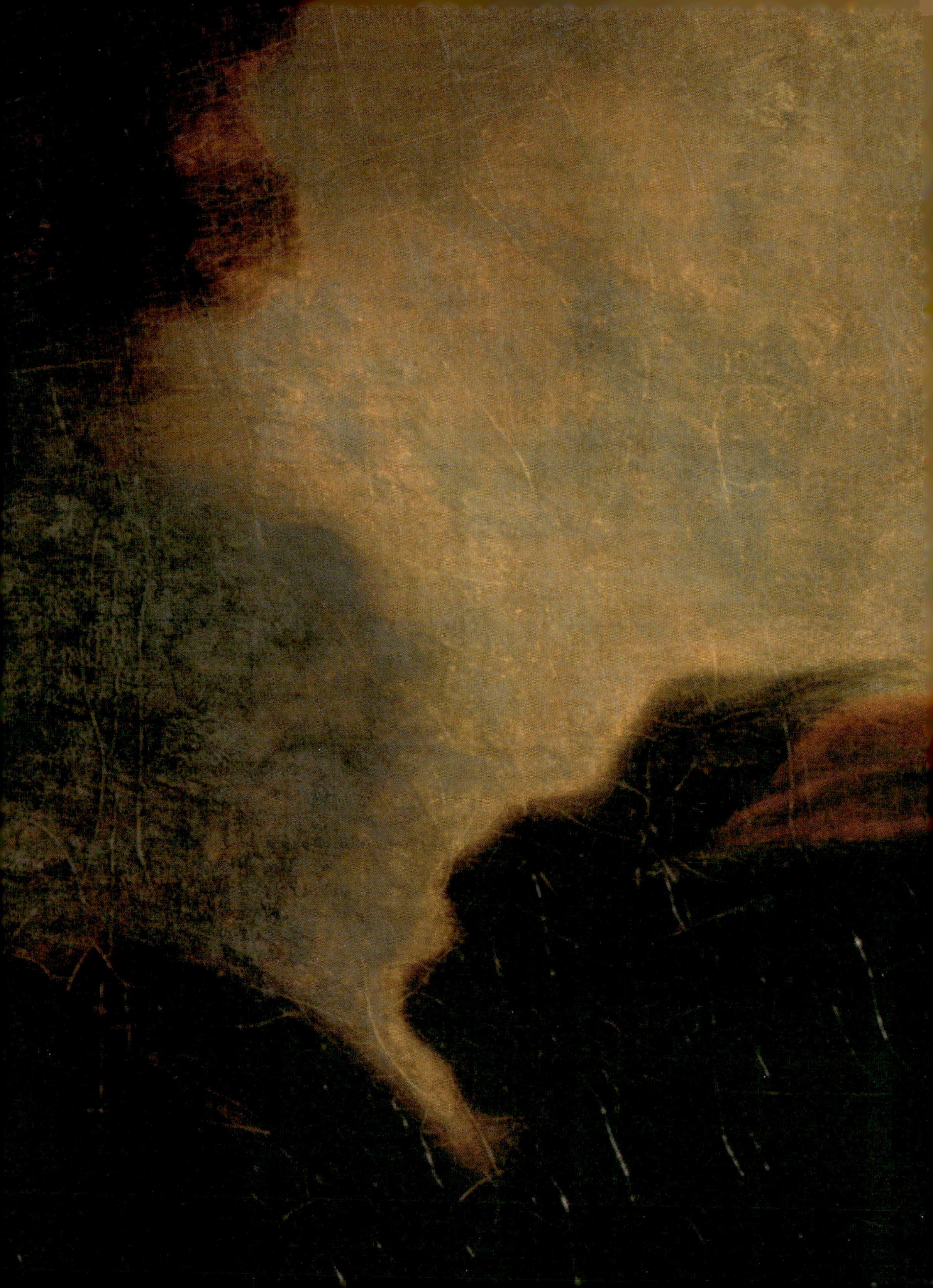

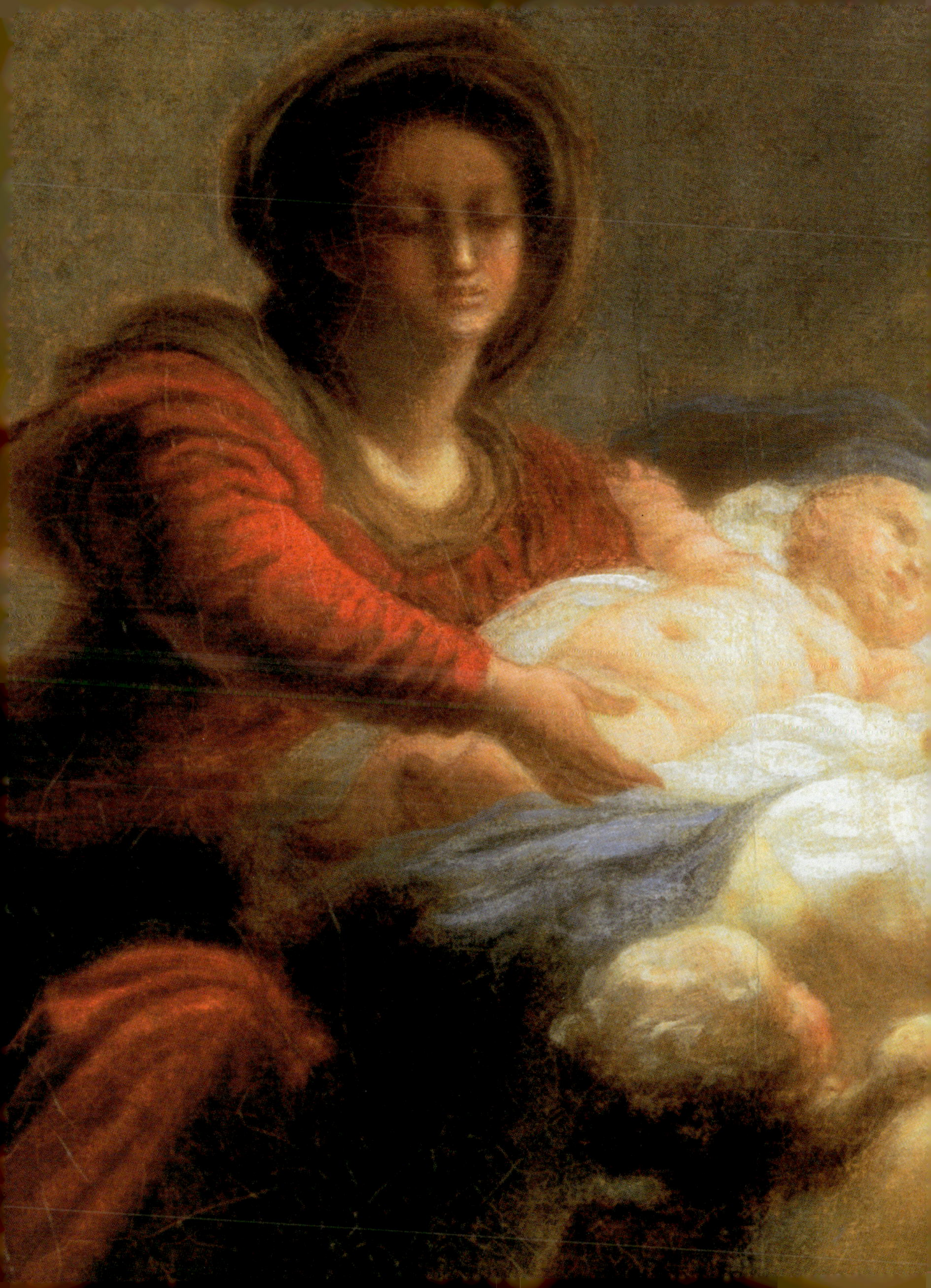

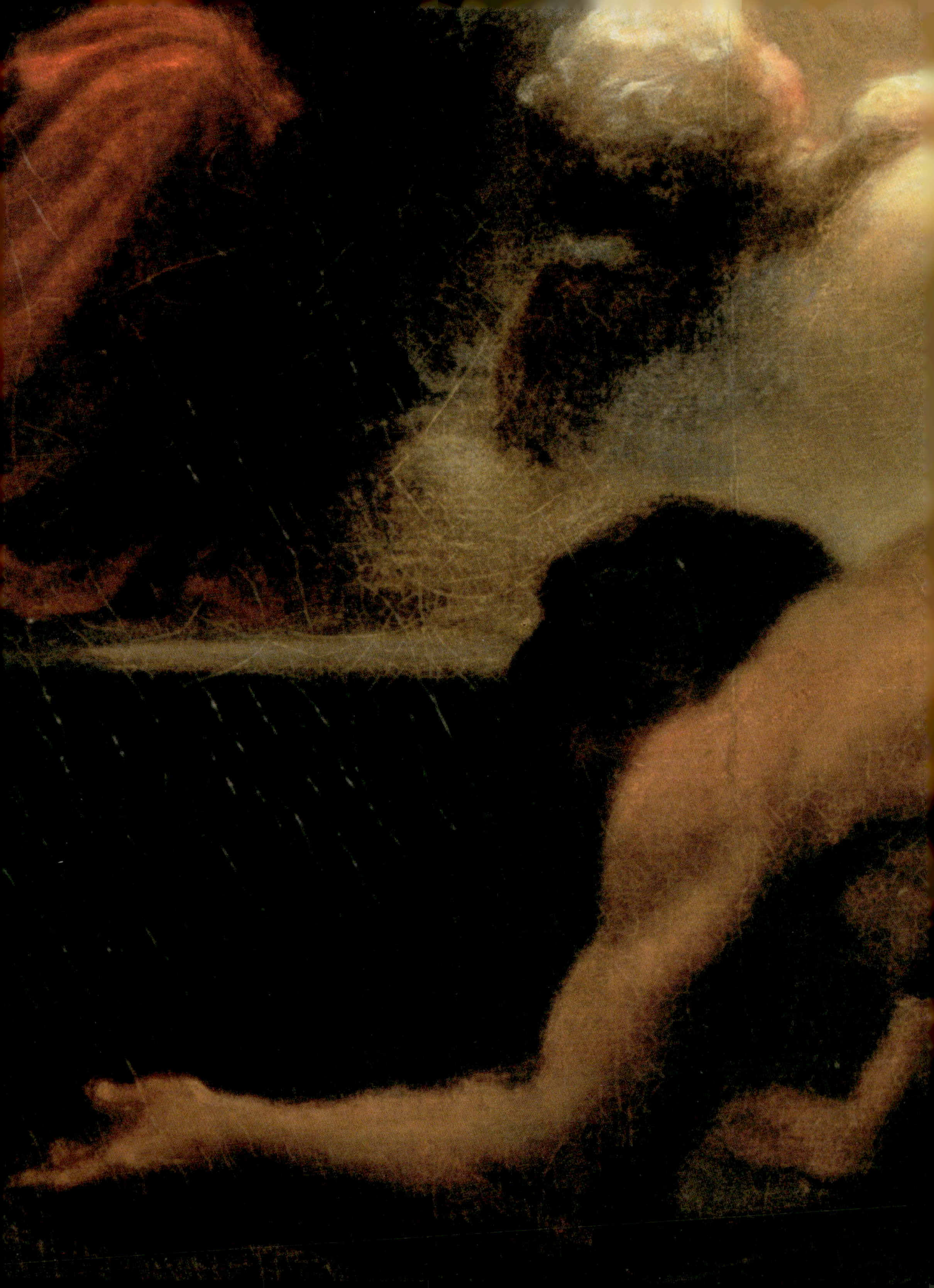

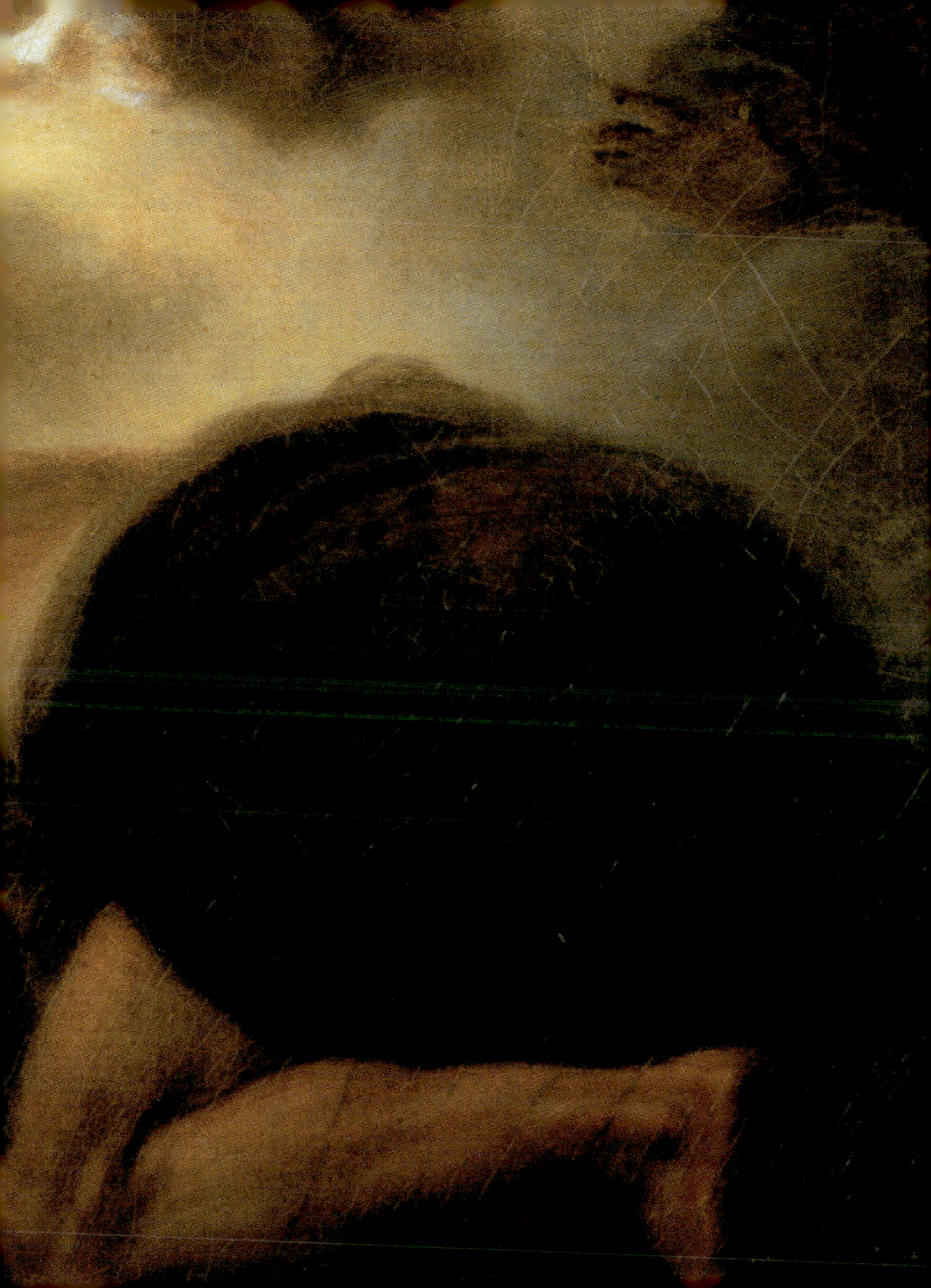

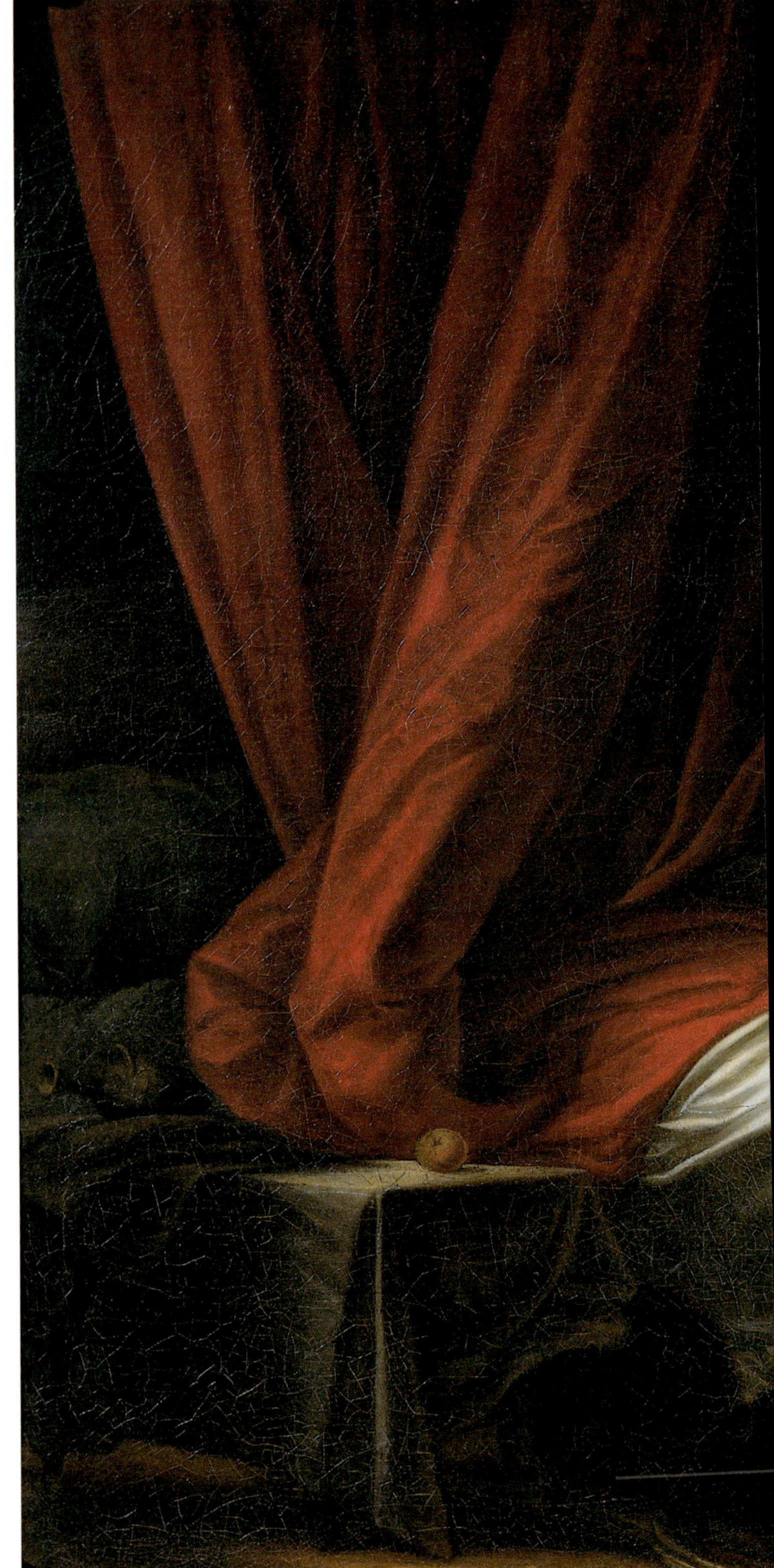

The Bolt,
c. 1777, oil on canvas, 73 x 93 cm
Paris, Musée du Louvre.

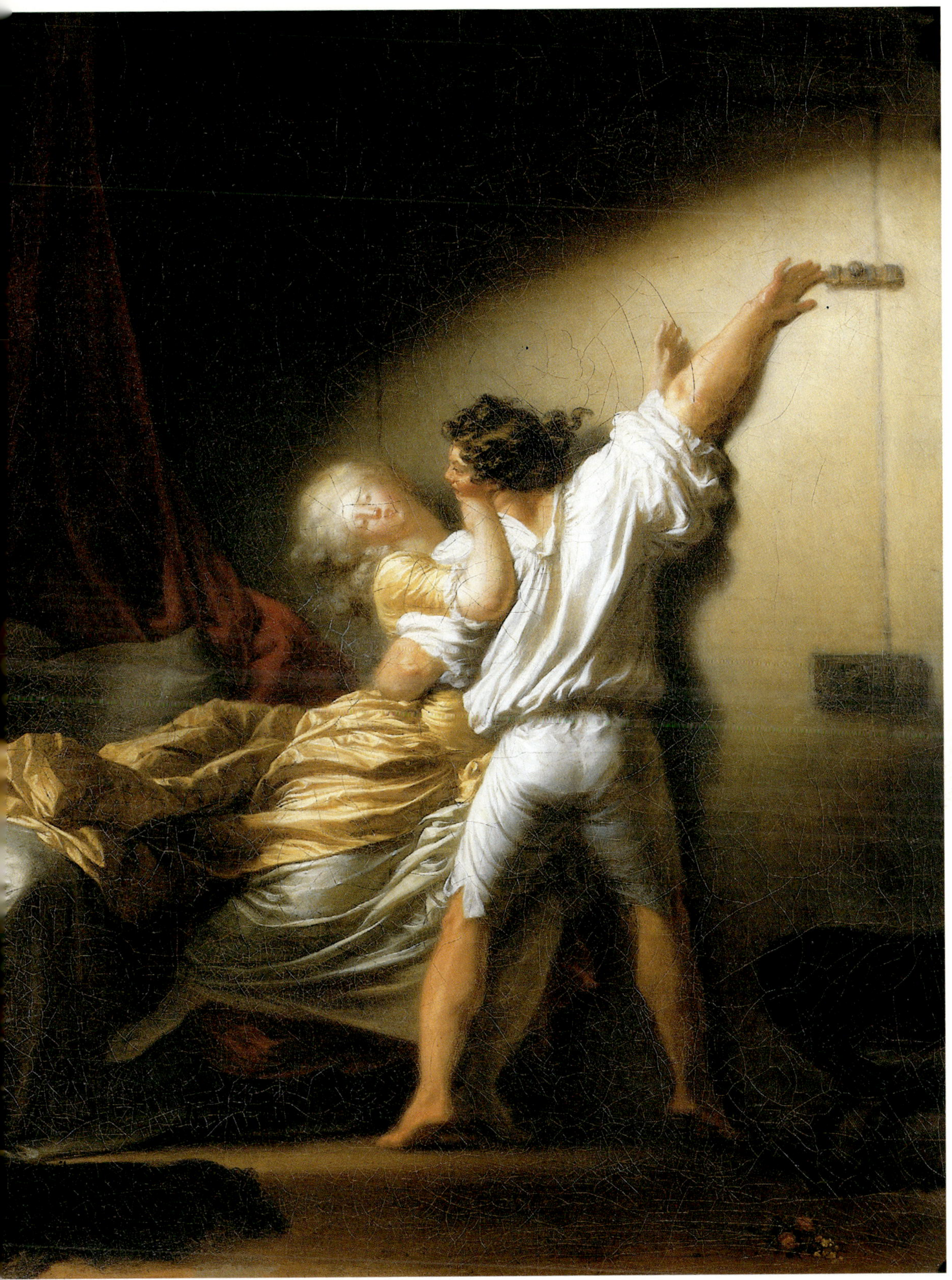

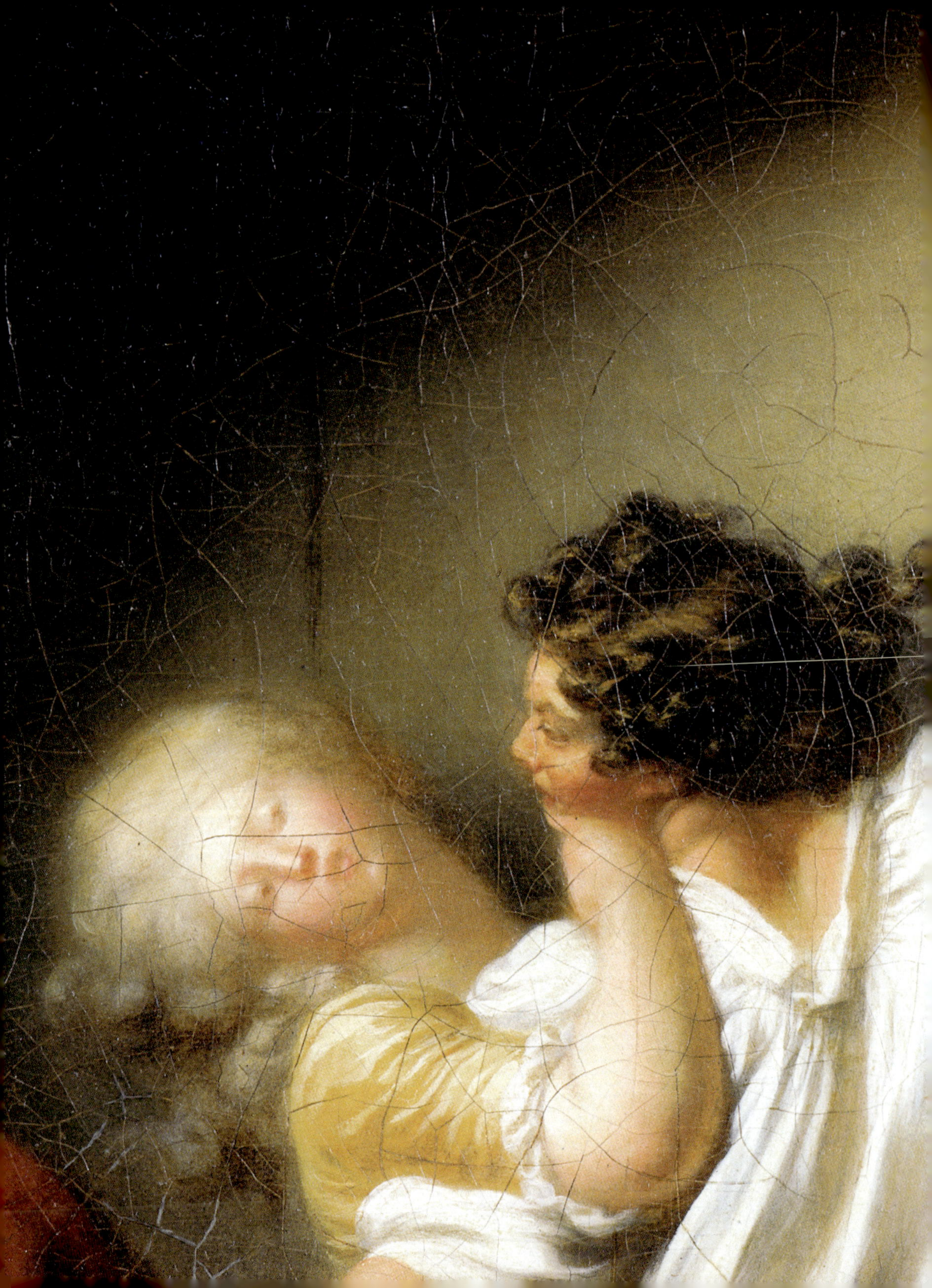

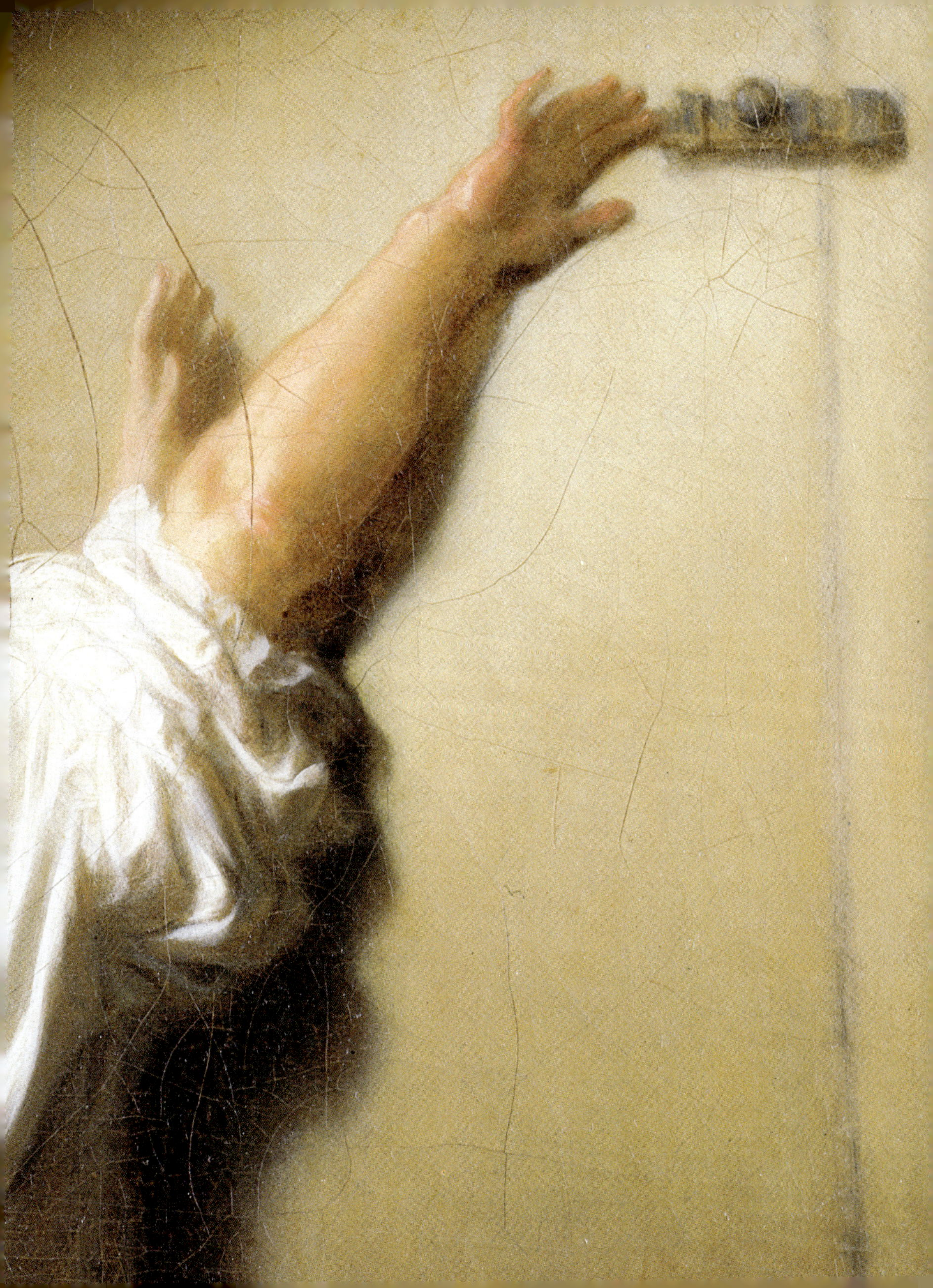

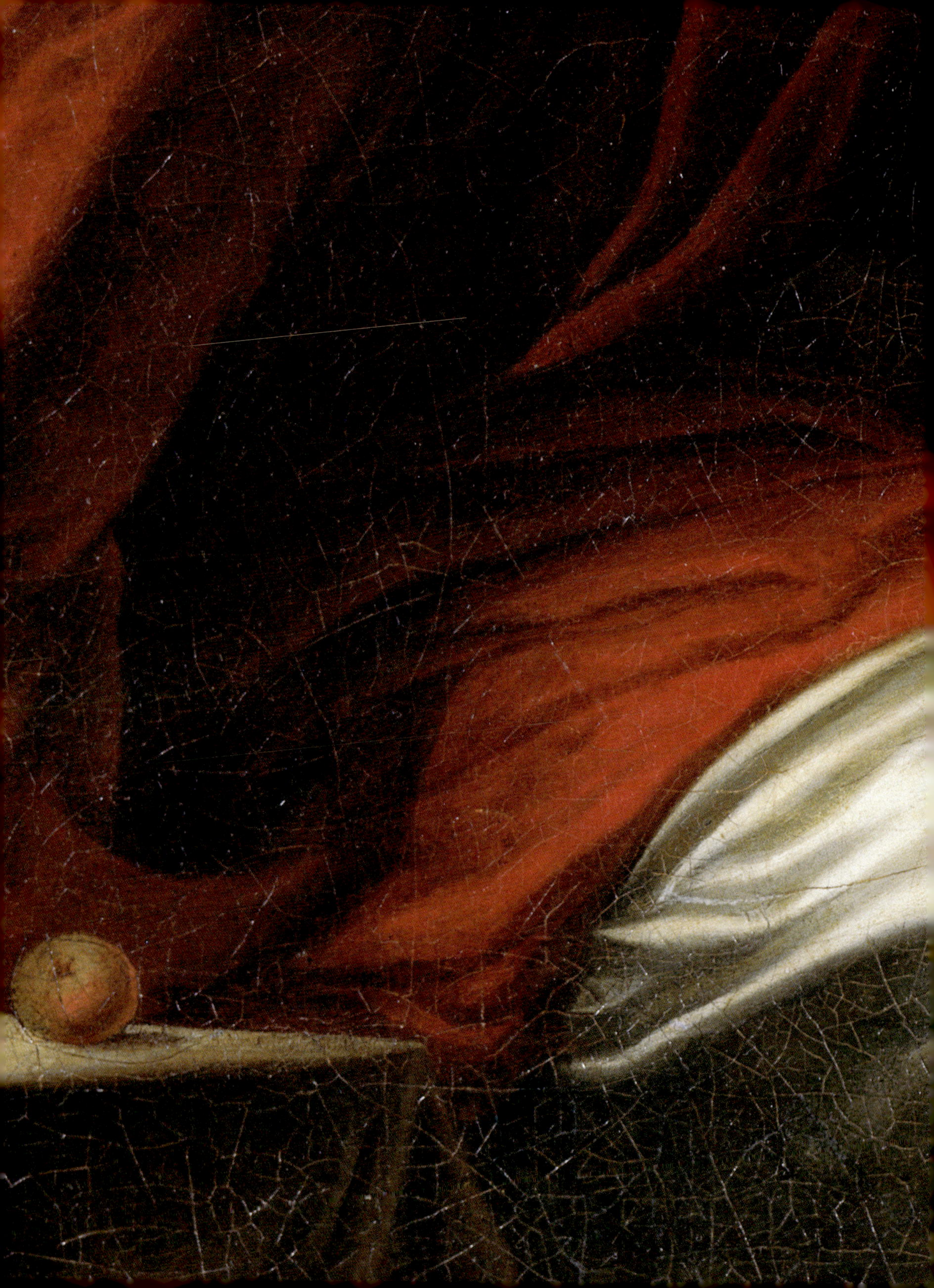

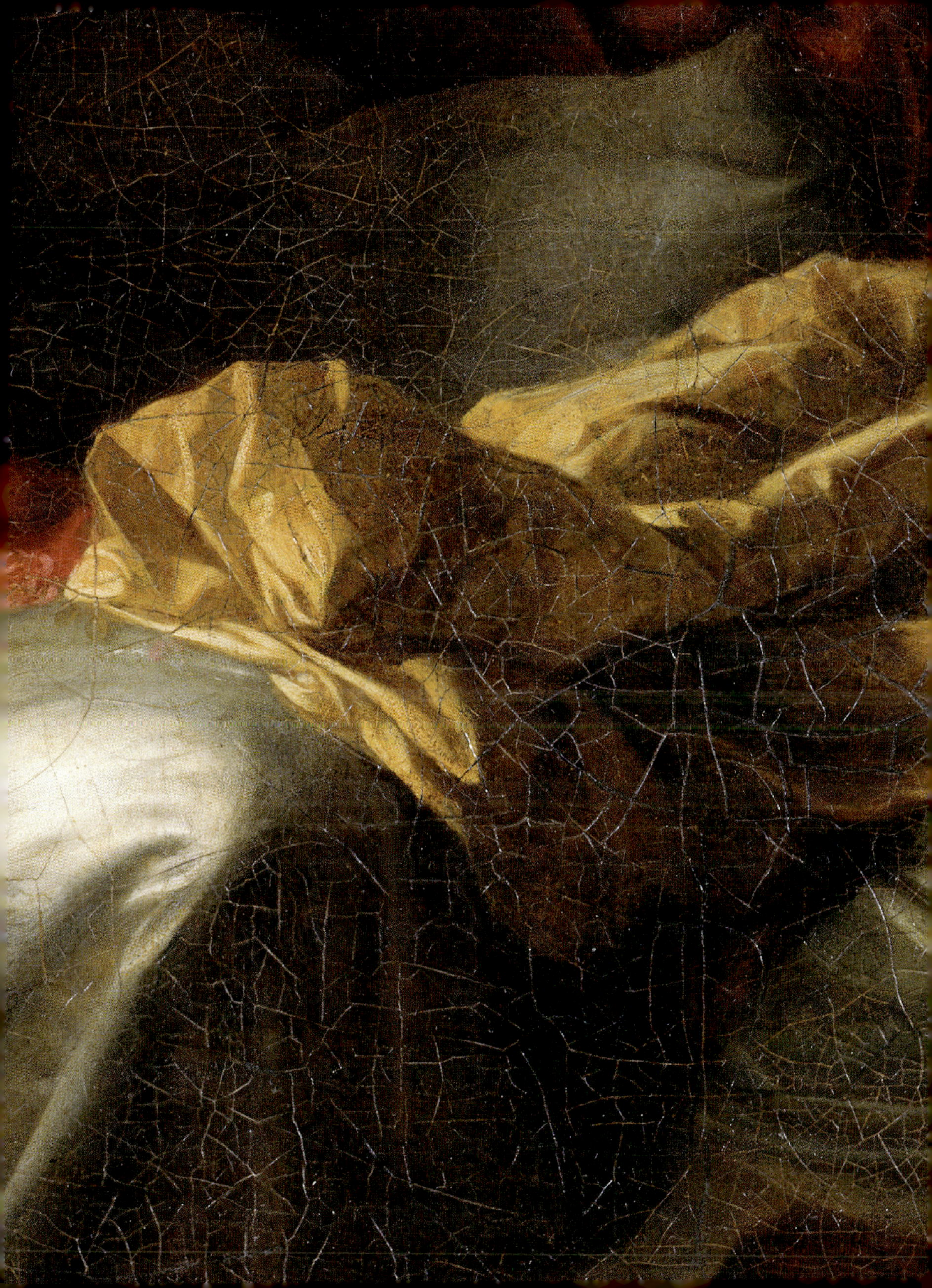

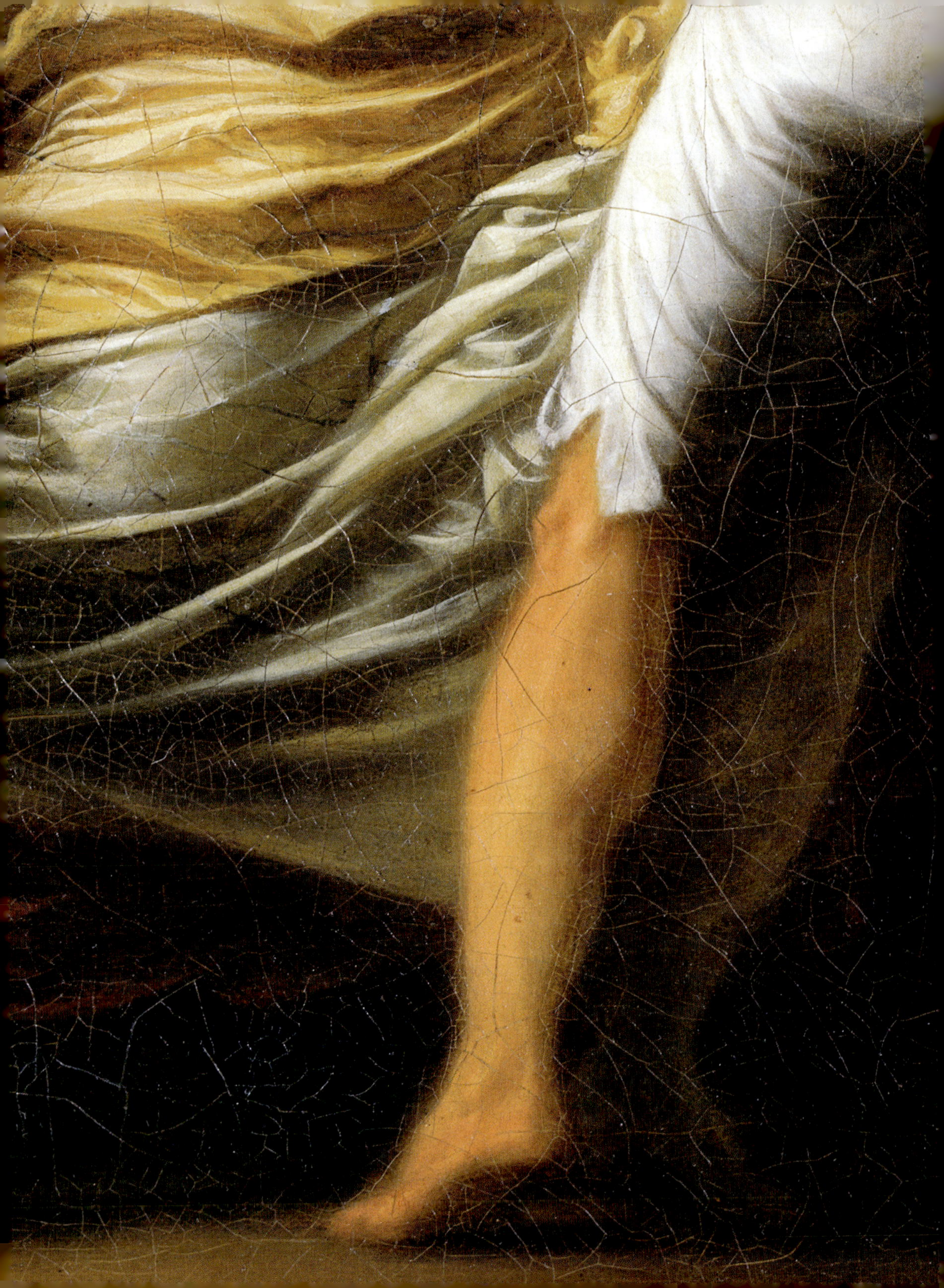

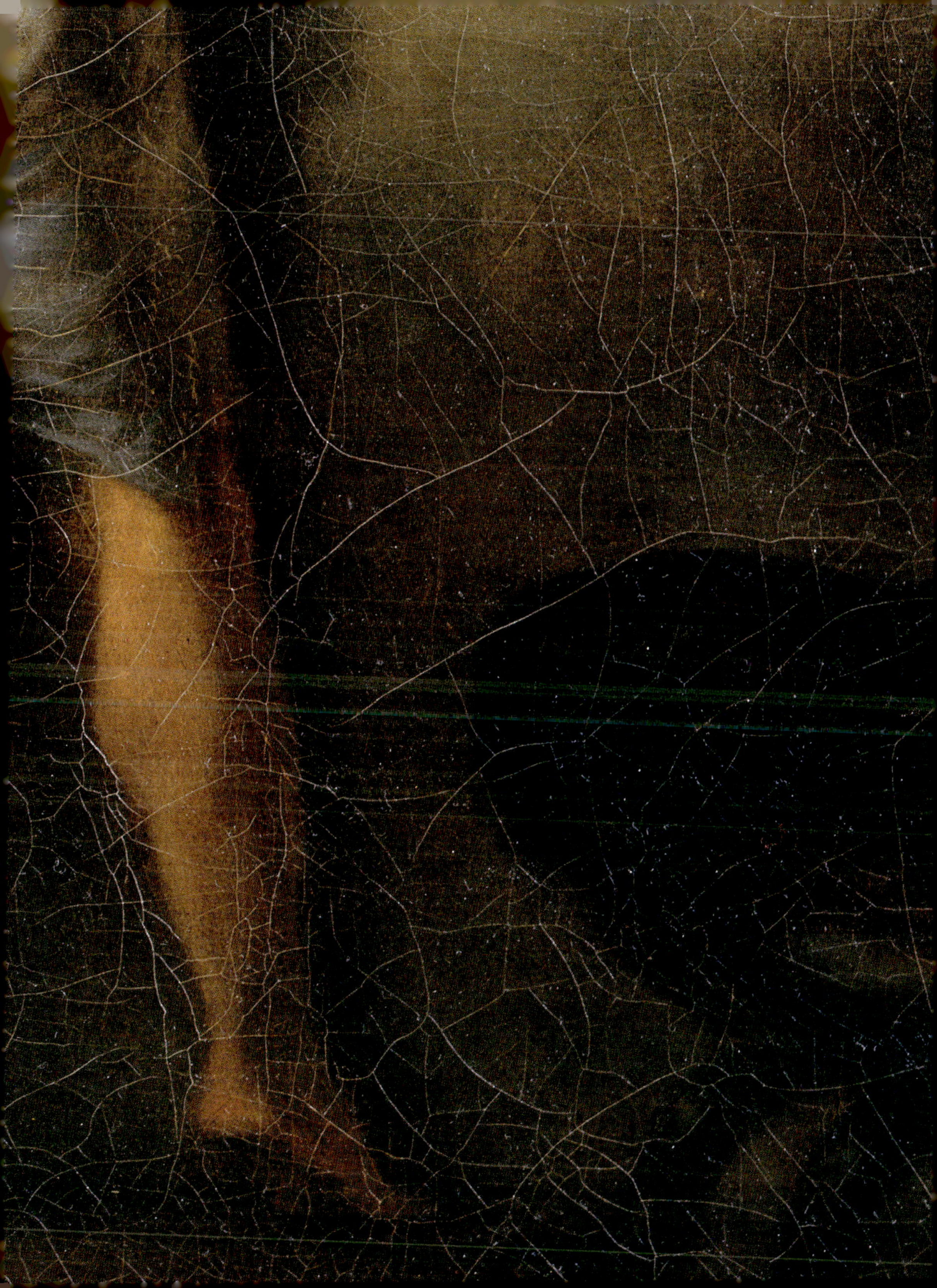

A Celebration of Love

The shift in both form and content was to become more and more apparent, as can be seen in a series of allegories painted in the autumn of the artist's career. In them Fragonard takes on a genre hitherto gone into only superficially, in those overdoors embellished with flying or sleeping *putti*, and in unadventurously classical depictions of the seasons of both nature and the heart. Putting these latter works behind us, we can only admire the way, in the decade leading up to the French Revolution, he further broadened an already enormous range of pet subjects, at the same time moving to a new, symbolic register and far more fertile, more meaningful content.

Nature's Awakening, also known as *The Four Elements Coming to Pay Homage to Beauty*, regrettably disappeared during the Second World War and is now known only through a very old photograph. Converging cupids are seen guiding the elements—represented by doves, an eagle, a lion and a conch shell—towards a statue on whose pedestal we can clearly see the date 1780 in Roman numerals. In that year the artist's family expanded, with the arrival of a son, Alexandre-Evariste, born in Grasse in October. It seems that Fragonard had remained in Paris, his absence being mentioned on the baptismal certificate: he may have been too absorbed in the series of evocatively titled pictures he was then working on: *A Lady Carving Her Name on a Tree* (usually called *Le chiffre d'amour*), *The Vow to Love*, *The Love Vow*, *The Sacrifice of the Rose*, *The Fountain of Love,* and others.

In 1761 Carle Van Loo had already—and he was not the only one of Fragonard's masters to have done so—painted a scene similar to *Nature's Awakening* under the title *Homage to Love*. Visually speaking, these pictures were not entirely new, but the return to the Antique in the second half of the century encouraged a proliferation of works alluding to themes such as loss of virginity and drawing inspiration from Anacreontic poetry: in the 18th century the writings attributed to the Greek poet Anacreon (563-478 BC) had a distinct influence on artists as well as writers. Lagrenée and Greuze, for instance, and the sculptor Simon Boizot had produced scenes showing girls offering flowers to a statue of Cupid, god of Love, or coming to beg him to hear their prayers.

In contrast with the cold, and often mawkish or excessively narrative stuff being turned out by Neoclassically-bound contemporaries, Fragonard construed the erotic symbolism of the rose and the sacrifice in his own way, bringing a matchless lyrical intensity to bear. Not content simply to illustrate some ode or verse, he vied with the Greek writer on the latter's poetic terrain. In a mysterious half-light appropriate to ceremonies of initiation, fair-haired girls approach the altar of Love: sometimes to invoke the god, sometimes—accompanied by Hymen—to sacrifice to him. Eagerness, faintness, unease: their bodies betray all the symptoms of passion, as ineffable, near-monochrome harmonies of brown and gold add drama to the scenes. This oppressive atmosphere finds its culmination in the *Fountain of Love*, in which a couple rushes towards the fountain, the profiles of their ecstatic faces reminiscent of certain antique cameos. Set against a dark, disturbingly opaque background, this so to speak pre-Romantic vision could be taken as premonitory of the storms then brewing in the skies of France.

The Vow to Love,
c. 1785, oil on canvas, 24 x 32.5 cm
Paris, Musée du Louvre.

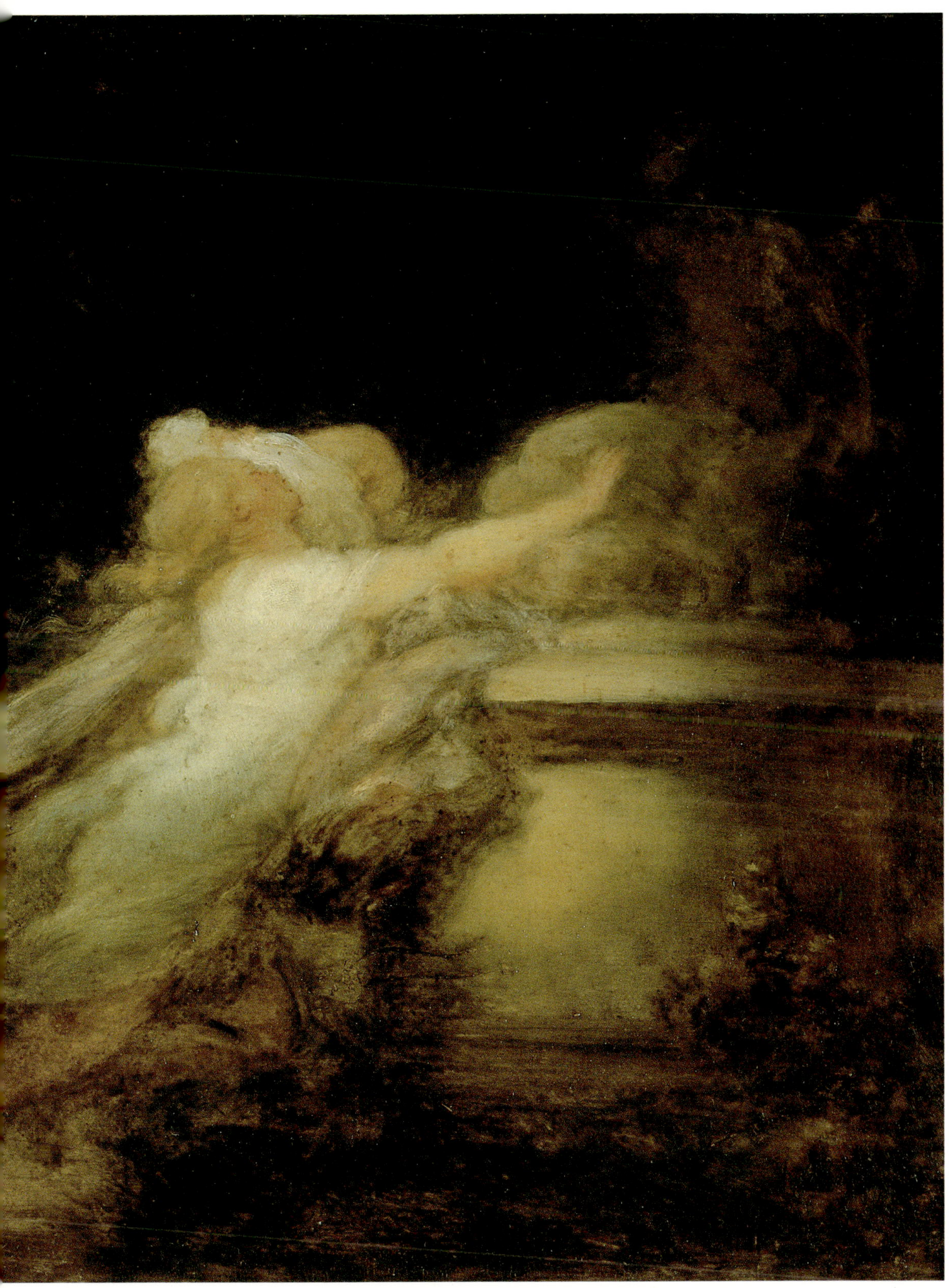

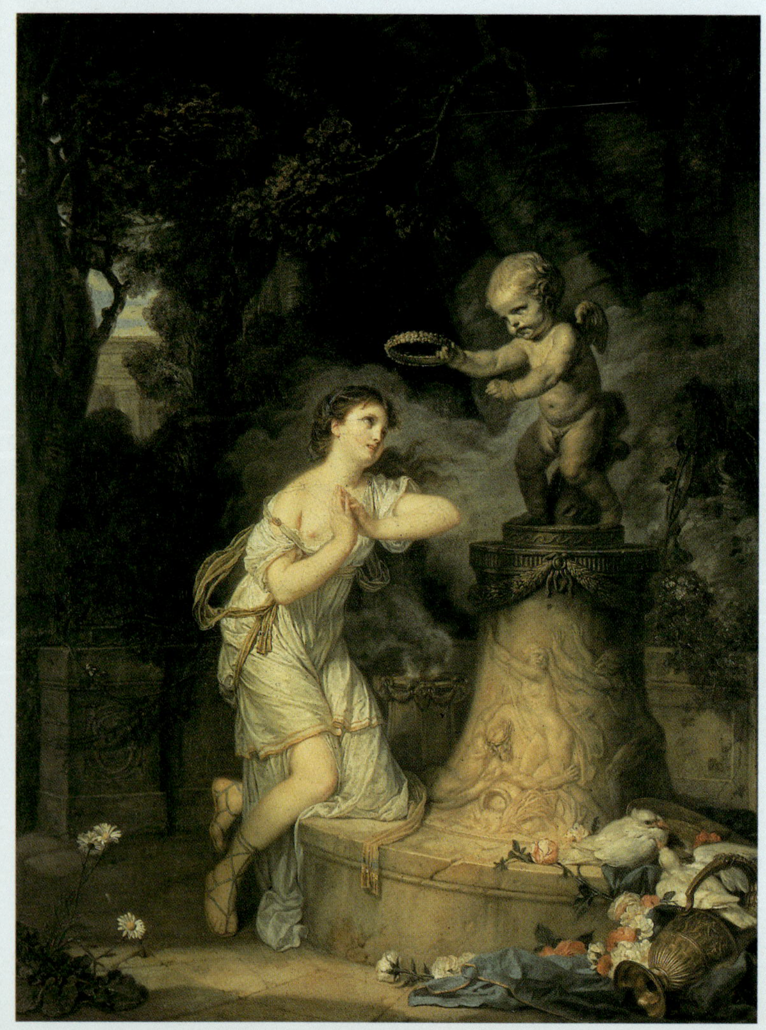

Jean-Baptiste Greuze
The Offering to Love,
1765-1769, oil on canvas, 145.5 x 113 cm
London, Wallace Collection

The Sacrifice of the Rose,
c. 1780-85, bistre wash and watercolor highlights on black chalk, 42.2 x 33.1 cm
Minneapolis, The Minneapolis Institute of Arts.

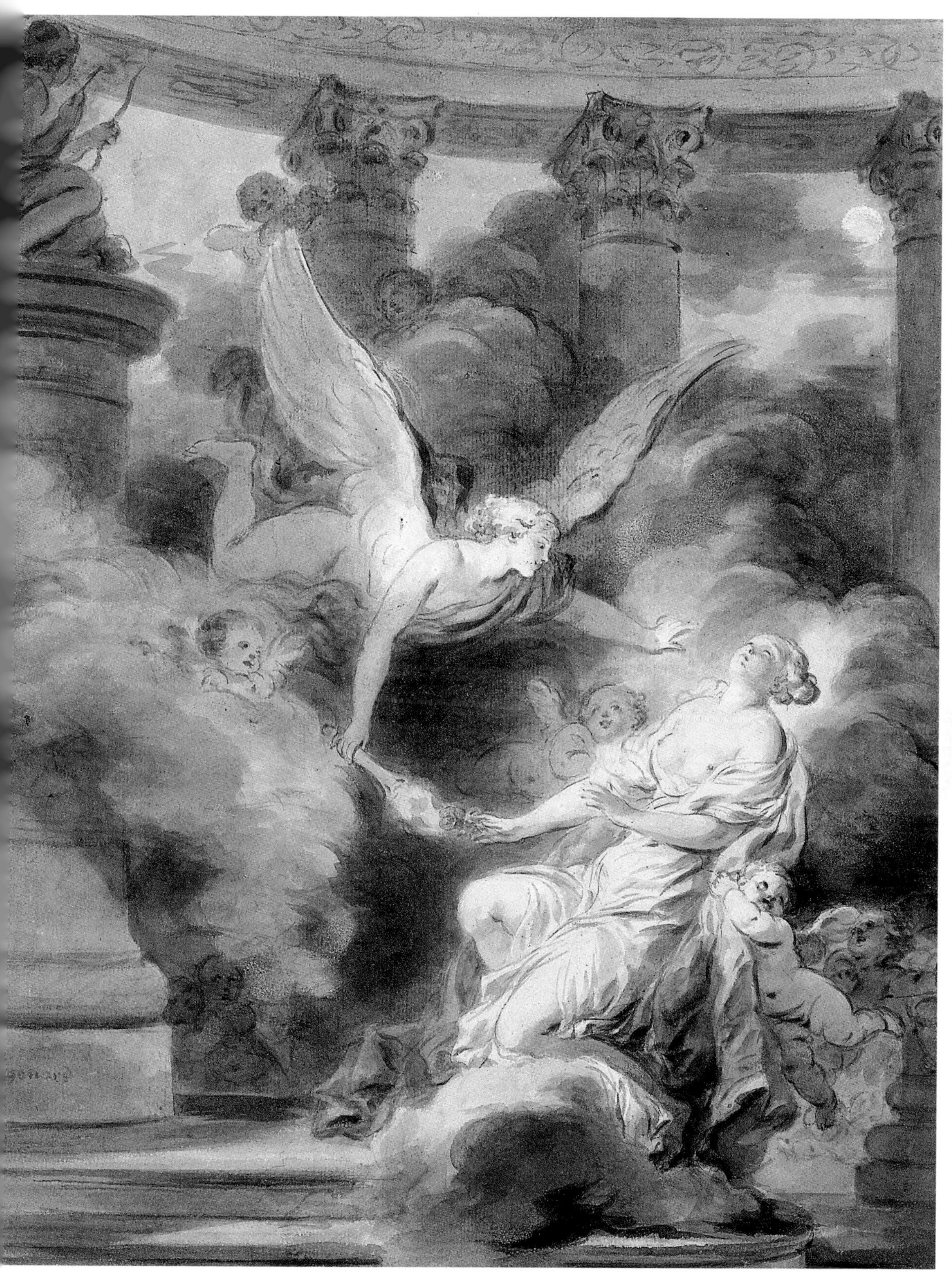

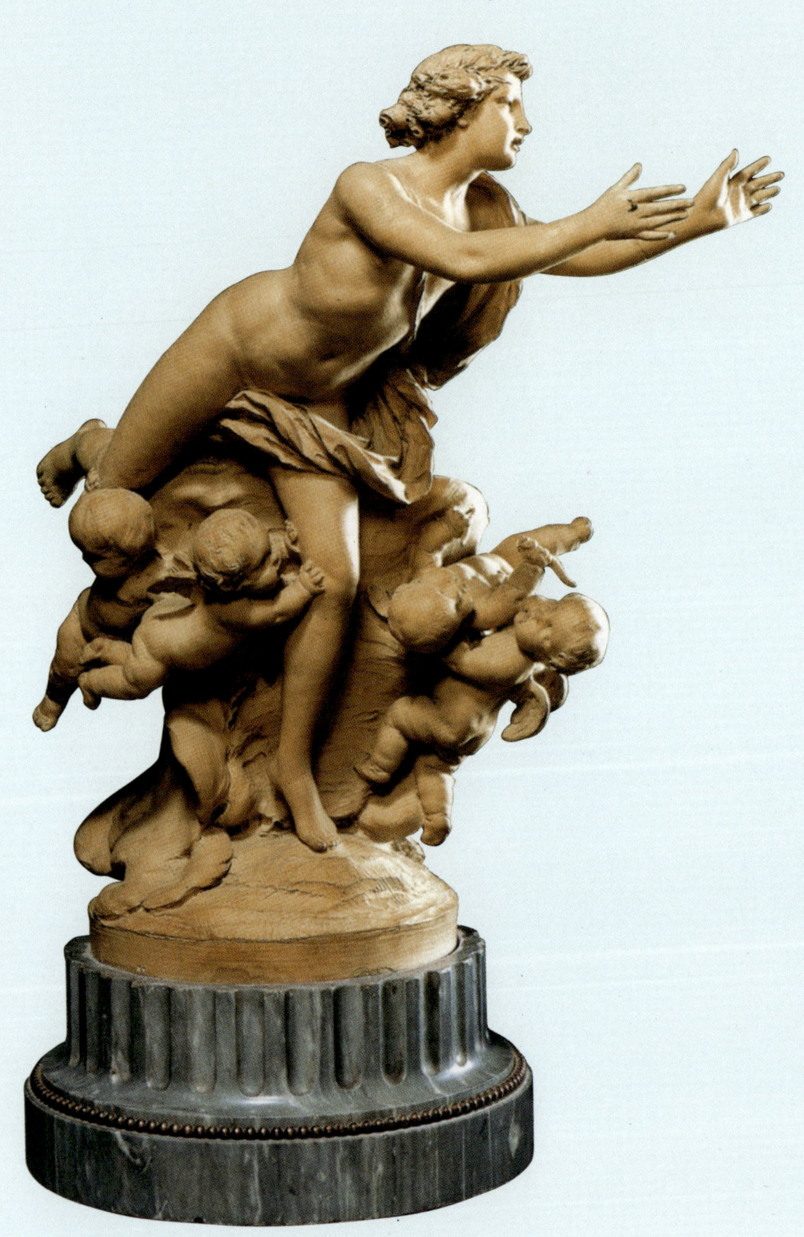

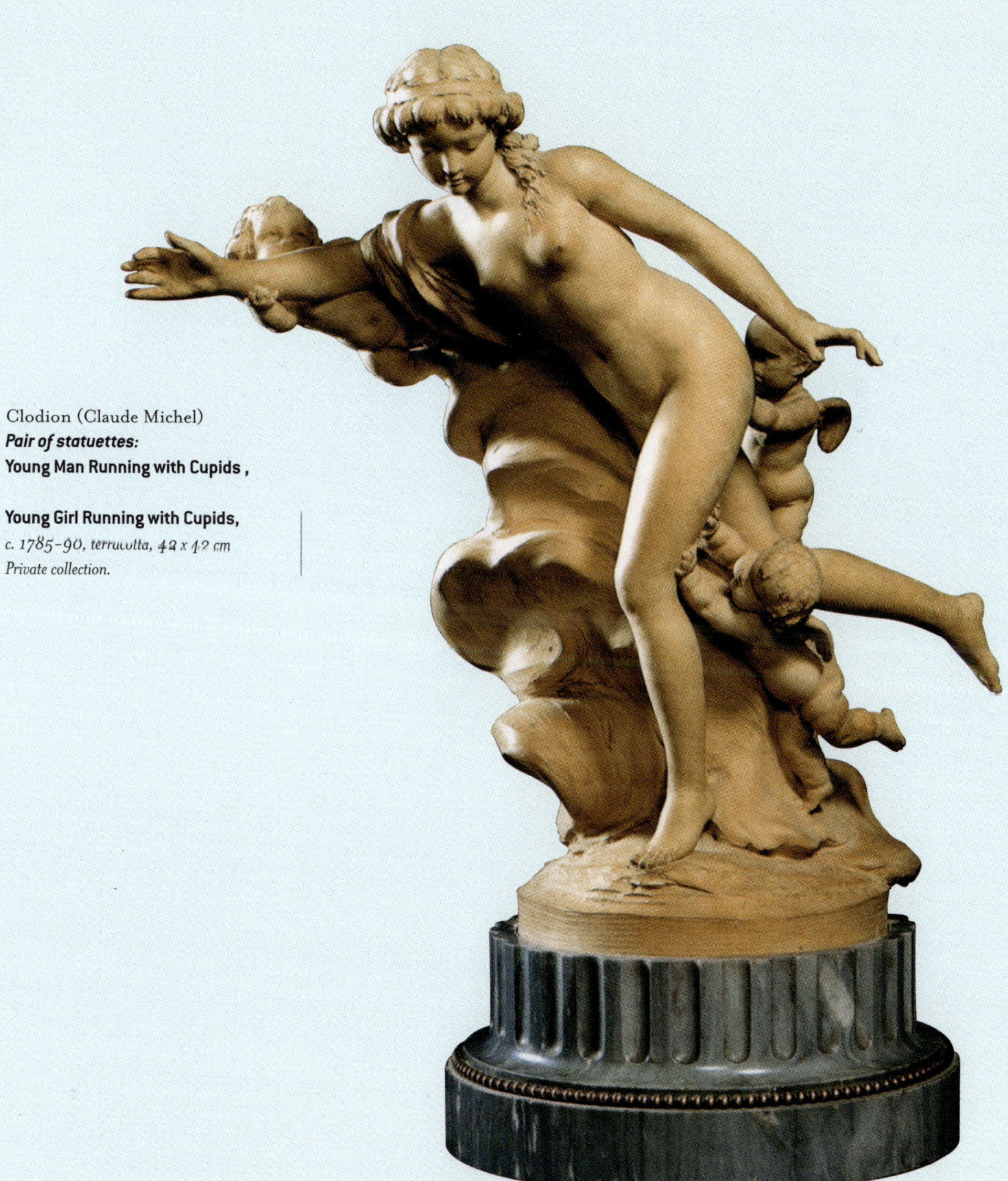

Clodion (Claude Michel)
Pair of statuettes:
Young Man Running with Cupids ,

Young Girl Running with Cupids,
c. 1785-90, terracotta, 42 x 42 cm
Private collection.

Worth mentioning at this point are two works by the sculptor Clodion (1738-1814), listed in an 18th century sale catalogue: "Two handsome groups, one comprising a girl and cupids; the other a boy with groups of cupids going to the fountain of Love." Working from this description, authorities on Clodion have identified two terracotta pieces dating from the late 1780s and now in the Thyssen-Bornemisza Collection. Guided by *putti* as they hasten forward through clouds, these unclothed figures remind us of the Fragonard picture. Nor is this a coincidence, as other works by the sculptor, now lost, were reputedly inspired by the painter. The two artists very probably met in Paris or Rome and worked for the same clients, notably Bergeret. The little *Gimblette* now in the Musée des Arts Décoratifs in Paris is no longer considered an original Clodion, but it may preserve the memory of an earlier, lost work that drew its inspiration from Fragonard's treatments of the same subject. We also know that Clodion's own collection included an engraving after *The Sacrifice of the Rose*.

The Fountain of Love ,
c. 1785, oil on canvas, 63.5 x 50.7 cm
London, Wallace Collection.

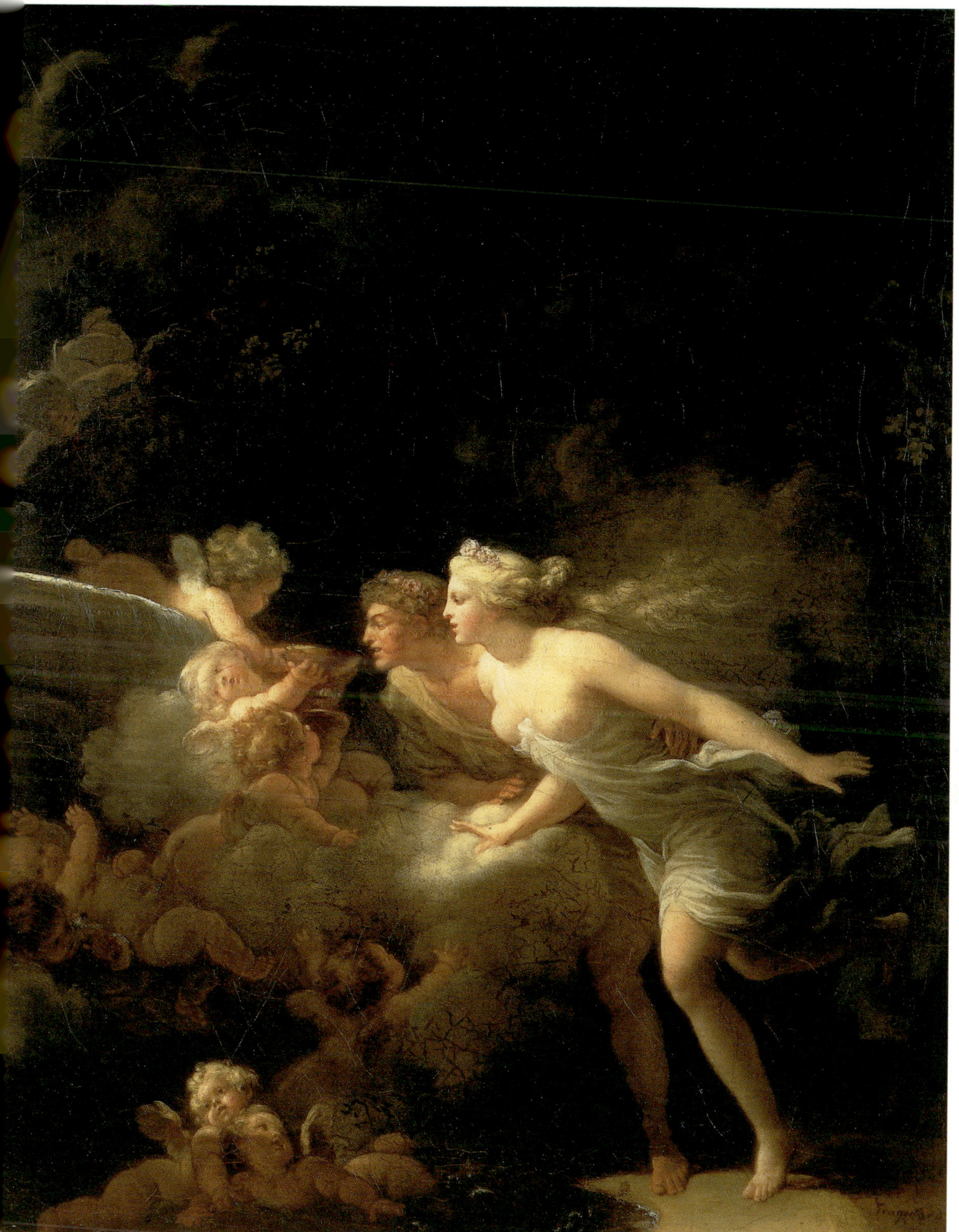

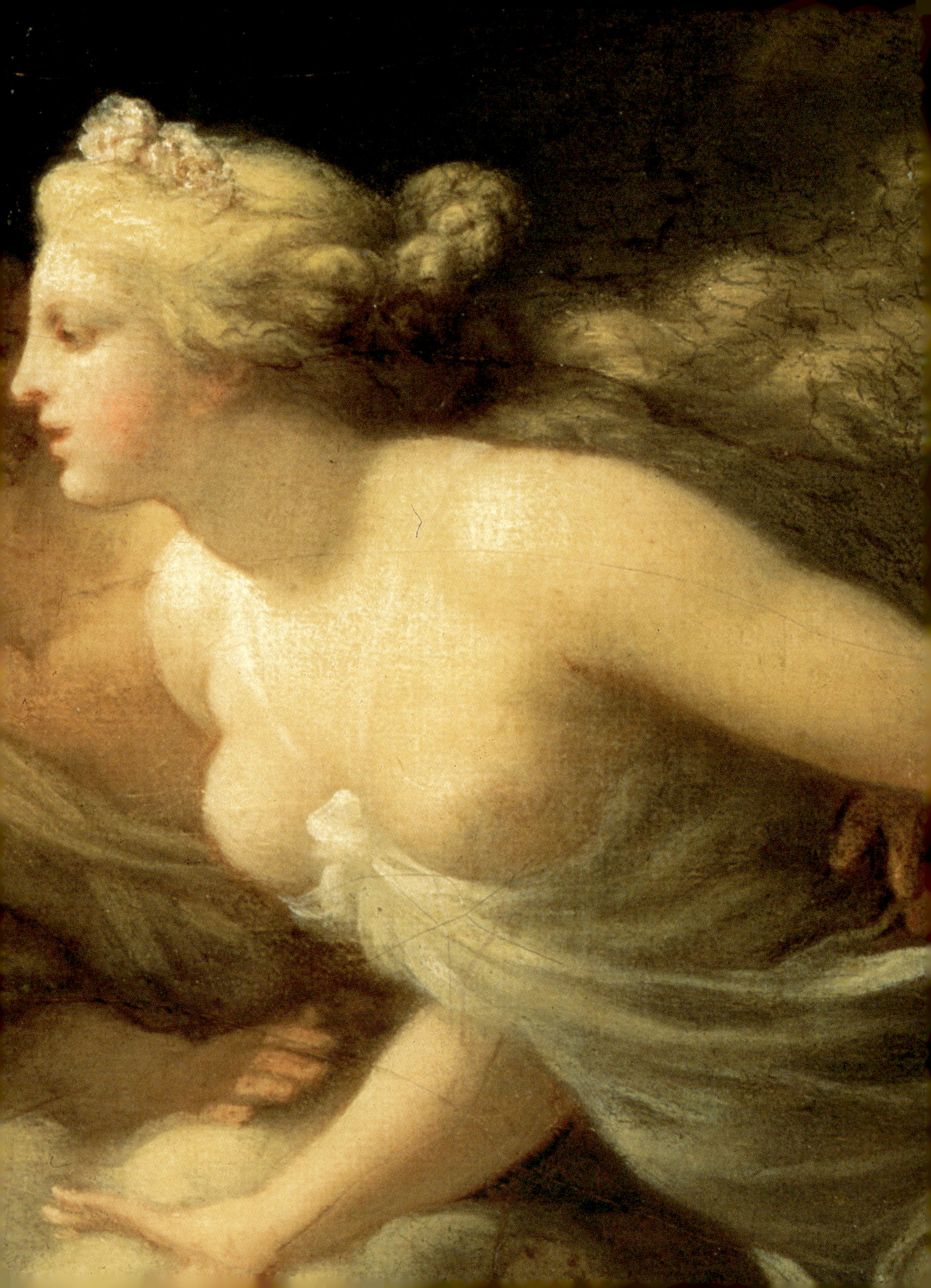

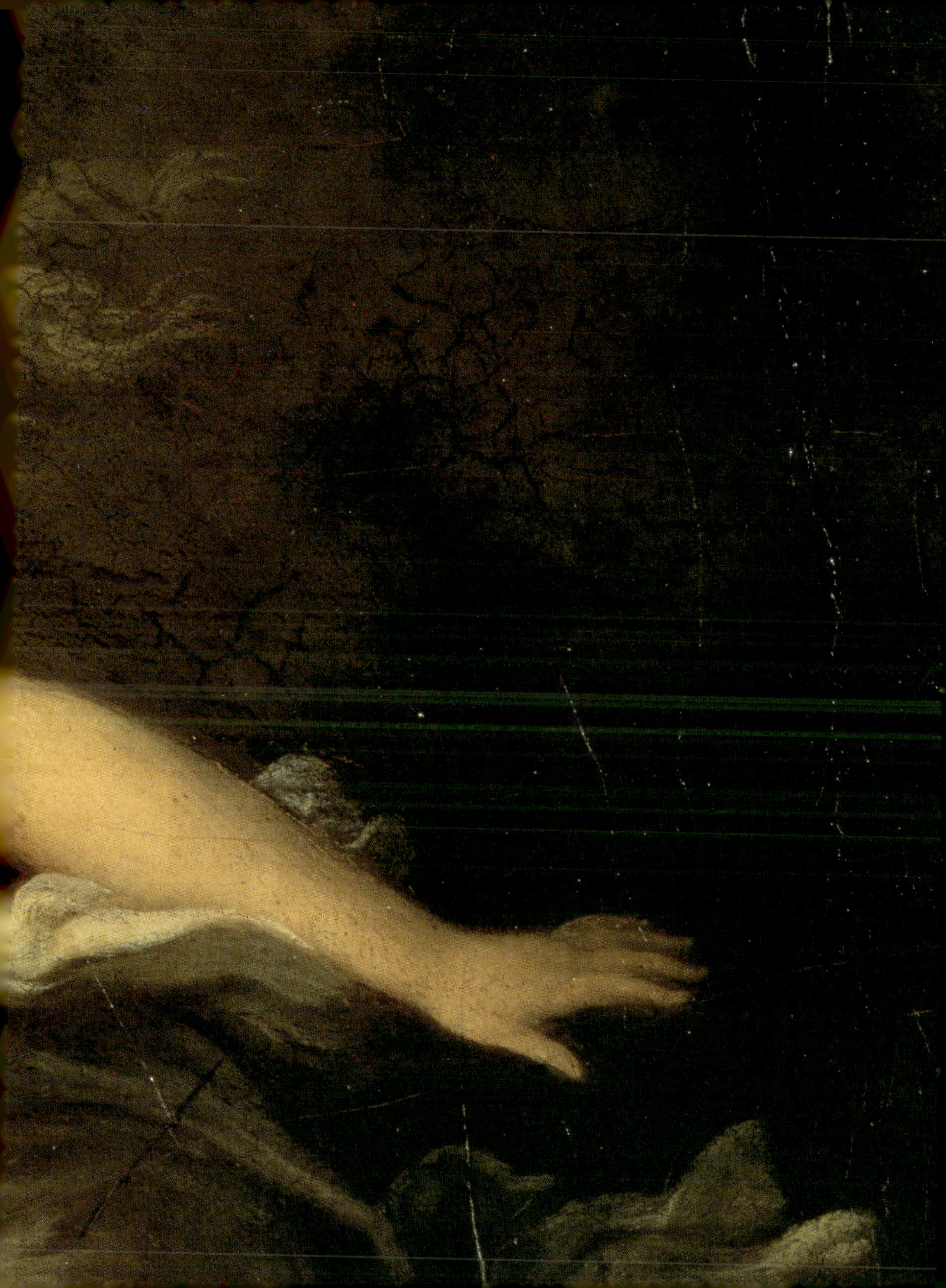

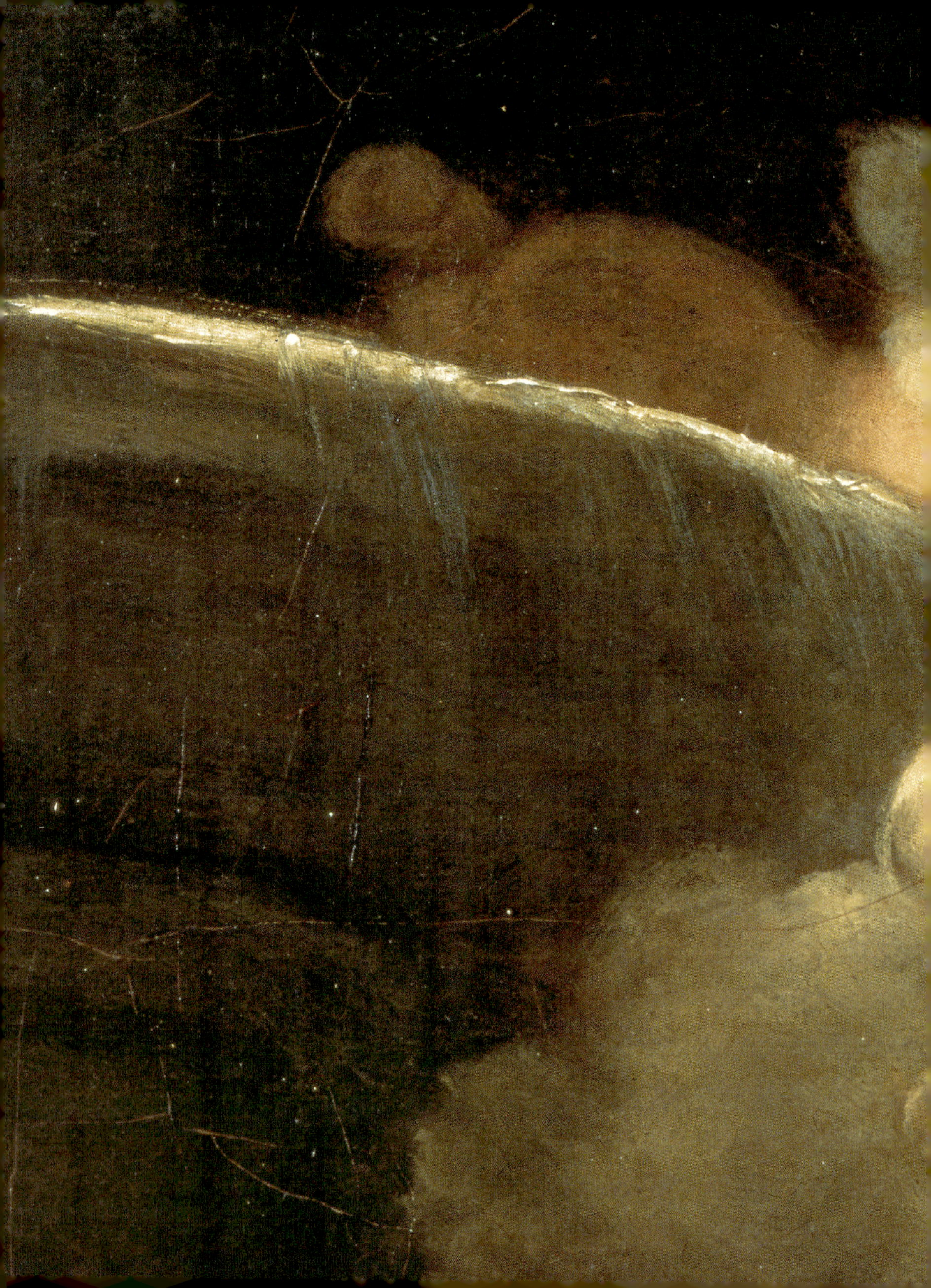

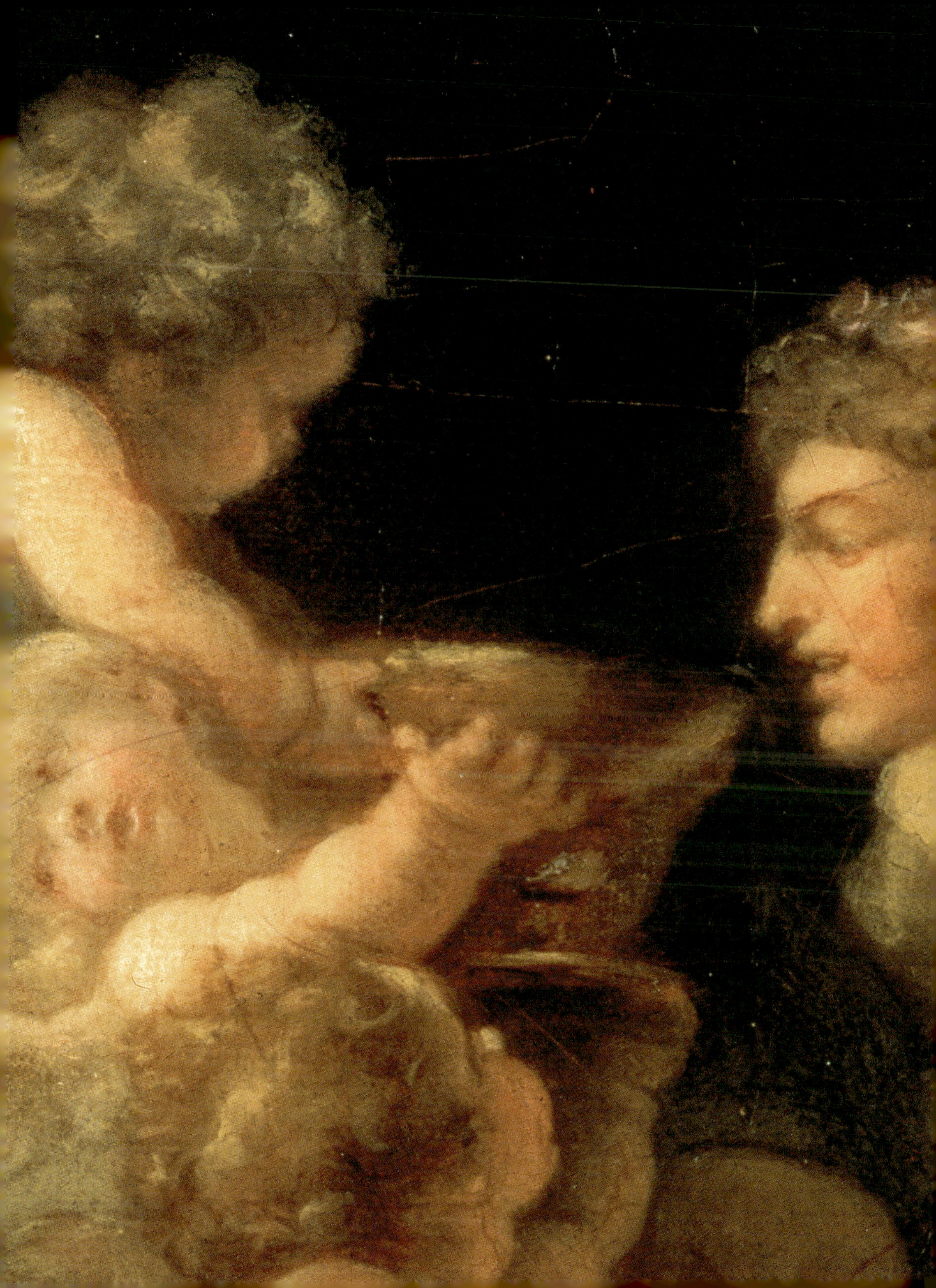

Fragonard and Marguerite

In its choice of literary and poetic subjects, Anacreontic inspiration, originality of approach and links with other artists, Fragonard's art seems always to have been in tune with its time. Yet brilliant as they may have been, these were the last sparks: as we shall see in the next chapter, his decline had set in even before the Revolution. First, however, there remains an entire, still fuzzy aspect of his career to be considered: the nature of his relationship with his young sister-in-law, Marguerite Gérard, and the works they collaborated on. These are tricky issues and a source of heated debate in the context of feminist assessments. Born in 1761 and thus sixteen years younger than Fragonard's wife Marie-Anne, Marguerite seems to have left Grasse after the death of their mother in July 1775, and moved in with the Fragonards—who then had only one child—at the Louvre. It may be that she was brought to Paris to look after little Rosalie, whose health was delicate. Whatever the case, she was to prove far more accomplished an artist than her miniaturist sister. Her brother-in-law was her only known teacher, and the earliest evidence we have of her talents are a few engravings made in 1778 under his eagle eye—and doubtless with his assistance. The pictures she went on to paint in no way belie the blooming of a youthful talent, but the difficulty resides in determining how much credit should go to her and how much to her master.

Was Fragonard, by teaching his sister-in-law engraving, hoping to train someone who would help him get his work into circulation? This is not impossible when we remember that Marie-Anne and Marguerite's brother Henri Gérard (1755–c.1835?), who had come to Paris in 1772, also learnt engraving in Fragonard's studio at the Louvre: his skillfully stippled 1790 engraving of *The Sacrifice of the Rose* would enjoy real popular success. He also made engravings of a number of his sister's paintings and, like other engravers of her work, specified at the bottom of each, "M[arguerite] Gérard pinx[it]." However, certain specialists have seen Fragonard's hand at work in the original paintings, a theory supported by engravings of separate works by the two artists that are highly similar in both style and feeling. Sales catalogues of the time give both names for some of the genre scenes, which were the only type of picture Marguerite Gérard ever painted.

One of the most famous of these still contentious works is a small canvas titled *First Steps* or *The Head Nanny*. Against a backdrop of dense foliage intertwined with rose bush branches, a baby boy takes his first steps, walking towards his mother's outstretched arms as two other women, a governess and an older servant perhaps, tenderly watch his uncertain progress. A preliminary sketch of this scene, certainly the work of Fragonard, would seem to indicate that he was the main force behind the work. Some of the faces—that of the old servant, for example—could be by Fragonard's hand, as could the figure of the child and the use of thick, oily paint in many areas. By contrast the mother, whose dress is treated in great detail—with cool, silvery colors and a host of folds that make her pose somewhat rigid—fits with Marguerite's pronounced taste for the portrayal of fabric. Her style and repertoire were much influenced by the 17th-century Dutch masters: her finely furnished interiors, with young ladies reading or playing the guitar, are reminiscent of the intimist subjects of Gerard Terborch, Gabriel Metsu and Pieter de Hooch, over a century earlier. Like those of the Dutch landscape artists, the works of these painters were very much in vogue at the time, and commanded extremely high prices at auction. Marguerite may have had the opportunity to study them when visiting Lebrun, her dealer, and later produce her own pastiches, faultlessly painted with the tip of the brush. Whatever the case, her work made her the first successful woman genre painter in France.

However, while we sense an underlying Fragonard influence in the look of certain young women—he may have retouched the faces—and in the taste for costumed figures, it has to be said that there is no trace whatever of the master's passion, inventiveness, and wit in these skillfully executed but somewhat repetitive scenes. The affected poses and wealth of descriptive detail that add to their slightly stilted narrative character also single out Marguerite's work, Fragonard's being far more delicately allusive, more timeless. The opposing theory— that these pictures are essentially the work of Fragonard, but a Fragonard in decline, seeking to adapt to current fashion and having trouble holding his brush—does not hold water: Fragonard was only fifty at the time and these paintings, whether the work of two or four hands, date from the same period as the Anacreon-inspired scenes that reveal the still-fertile imagination of an artist in full possession of his means.

We might also wonder whether Fragonard's name had not been added to that of his pupil by engravers and saleroom catalogue writers for purely commercial reasons. This is the point of view of the "Marguerite

Gérard as artist in her own right" school, and it is true that the master's fame could not fail to help get the works onto the circuit and increase their prices. Having no academic training, she was not entitled to show at the Salon in the 1780s and was thus deprived of the recognition associated with the event. It was not until 1799, after the fall of the monarchy had been followed by the suppression of the Academy, that the Salon was thrown open to all artists and the works of "Mademoiselle Gérard" were hung at the Louvre. By then Fragonard was no longer painting. Marguerite was still living with her sister and brother-in-law, communicating with the latter via little notes in a child-like hand, calling him "my good friend" and "my sweet little papa."

Some of these messages are dated 1802. Marguerite was then forty-one and Fragonard seventy. Does the tone of the notes betray, as has been claimed, something other than mere family feeling and friendship between the two artists? The eight surviving fragments of what must have been a larger correspondence seem rather to point to the gratitude and tender affection of a pupil who has spread her wings towards an ageing teacher who also happens to be her brother-in-law. In a reversal of roles, however, it would be Marguerite who took care of Jean-Honoré and gently chided him when necessary. The tone, in fact, is one of inconsequential banter, as proved by the testimony of the artist's son Alexandre-Evariste.

The notes are also interesting in that they convey an unexpected image of Fragonard. Despite the hint of indulgence in his correspondent's manner, and despite her stylistic convolutions and catastrophic spelling, what we find is a touchingly intimate portrait of the master. When asked to tell him of his shortcomings, Marguerite replied, "I see only your loveable nature, that of a child easily upset but easily comforted; a thoroughly temperamental baby. Temperament breeds coquetry; coquetry is very winning when shown the way by wit, and in your case the two always go hand in hand. When my friend asks me to write him something agreeable, I know only one subject—so it is of him I speak... Were it my wish to paint all the joy, gaiety, whimsy, cuddlesomeness and happiness of a child, it is he I should take as my model. Were it my wish to paint the nature, sweetness, kindness, attentiveness and tenderness of friendship, I would yet again take him as the model of the most amiable of philosophers, the most inventive and most gracious of painters, the best of husbands, the most tender, most constant of friends, the most caring and considerate of teachers." And on another occasion she continued: "Should I wish you gaiety, wit, talent, genius, amiability, friends, a lady-friend? You possess all that already. What then am I to wish Monsieur? A few ducats more, and perhaps two or three little daughters to play with, romp with, to tumble and shake and jump with, and to scold the livelong day!"

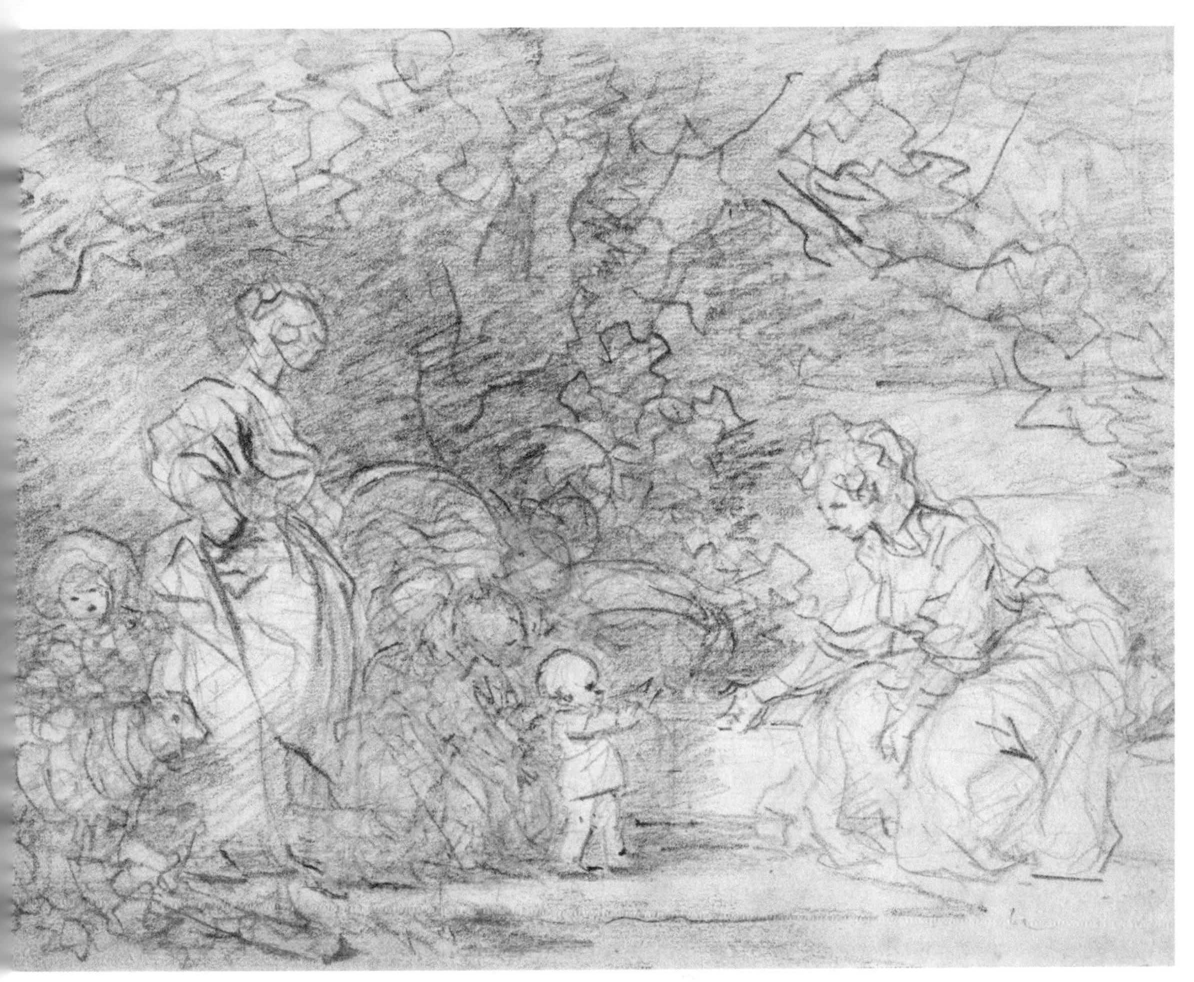

First Steps,

c. 1785, black chalk, 17.1 x 22.5 cm
Cambridge, Fogg Art Museum, Harvard University Art Museums, Isabella Grandin Fund and Marian H. Phinney Fund.

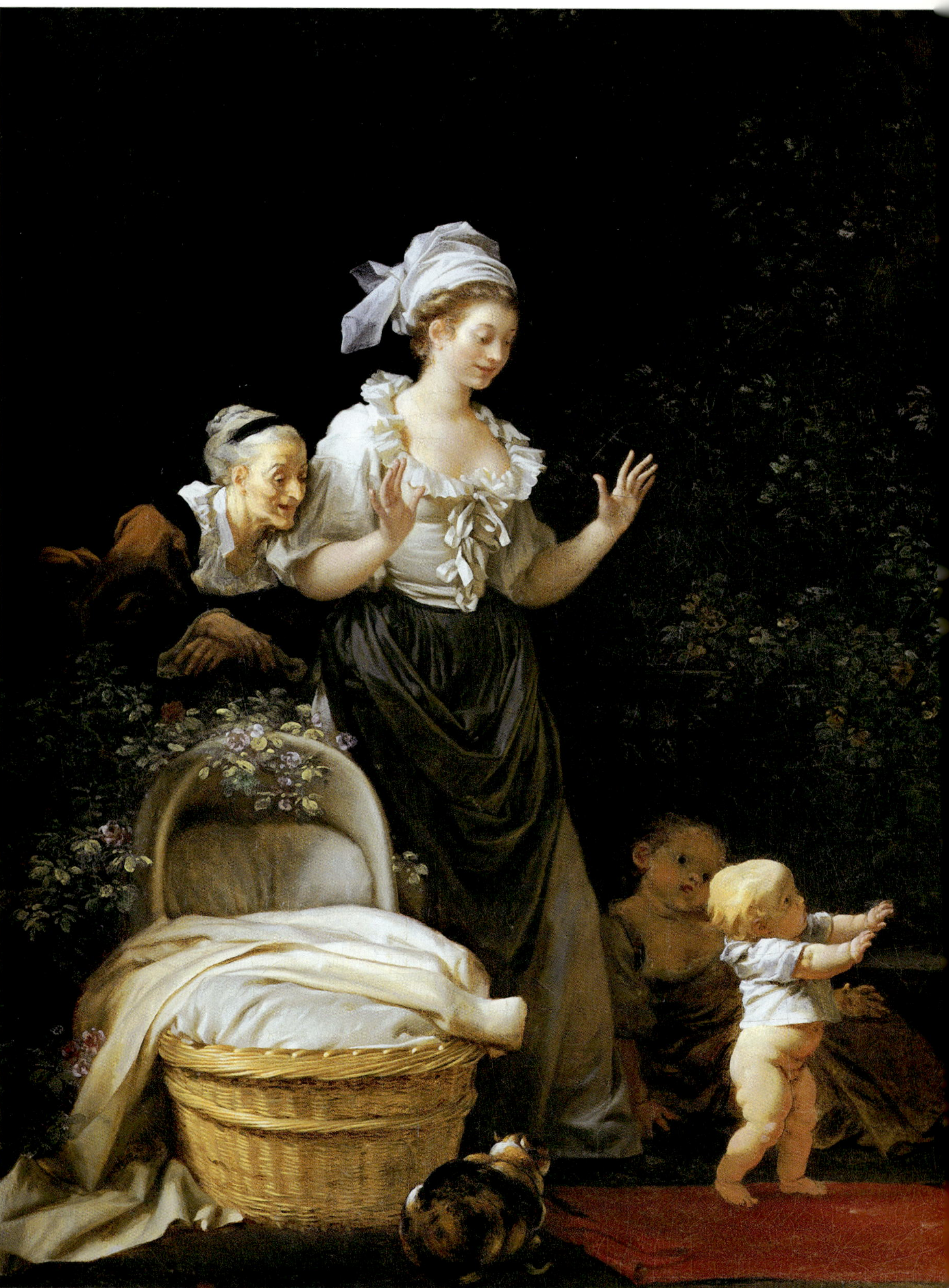

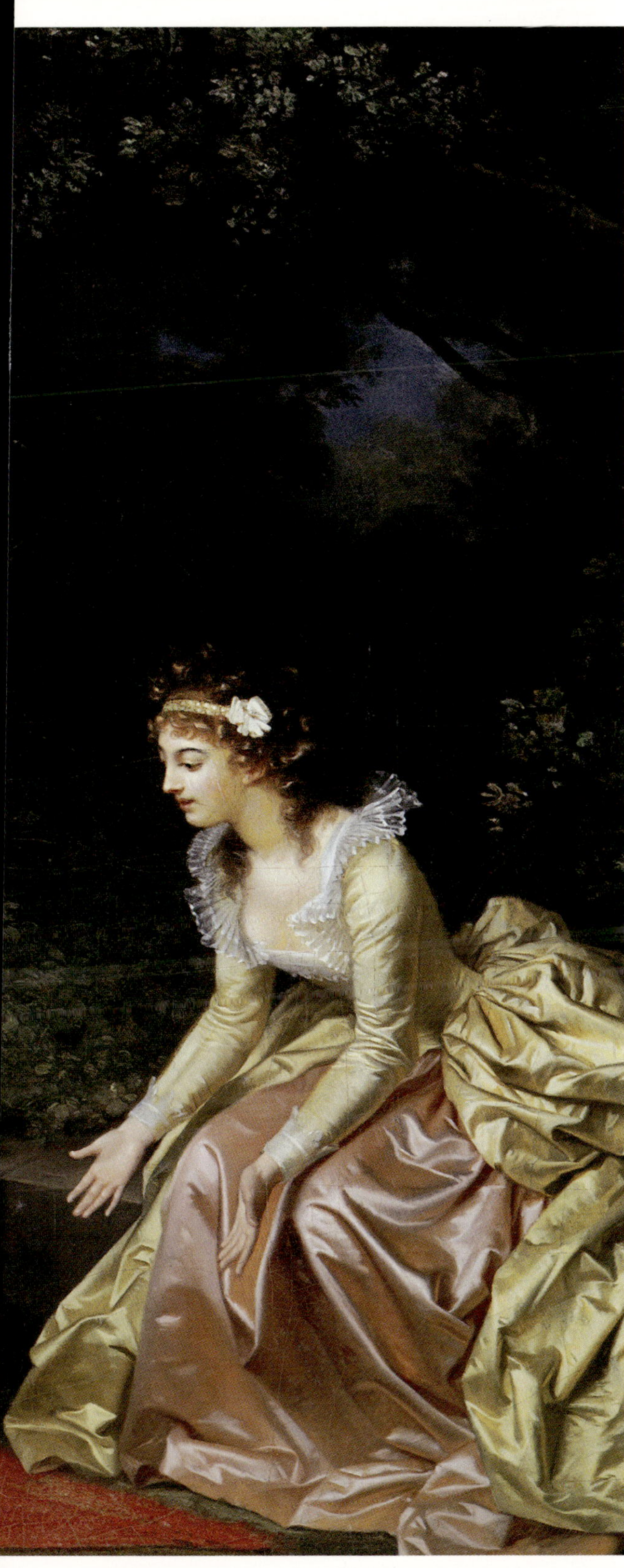

Fragonard and Marguerite Gérard
First Steps,
c. 1785, oil on canvas, 44 x 45 cm
Cambridge, Fogg Art Museum.

VII

Chronicle of an Enc

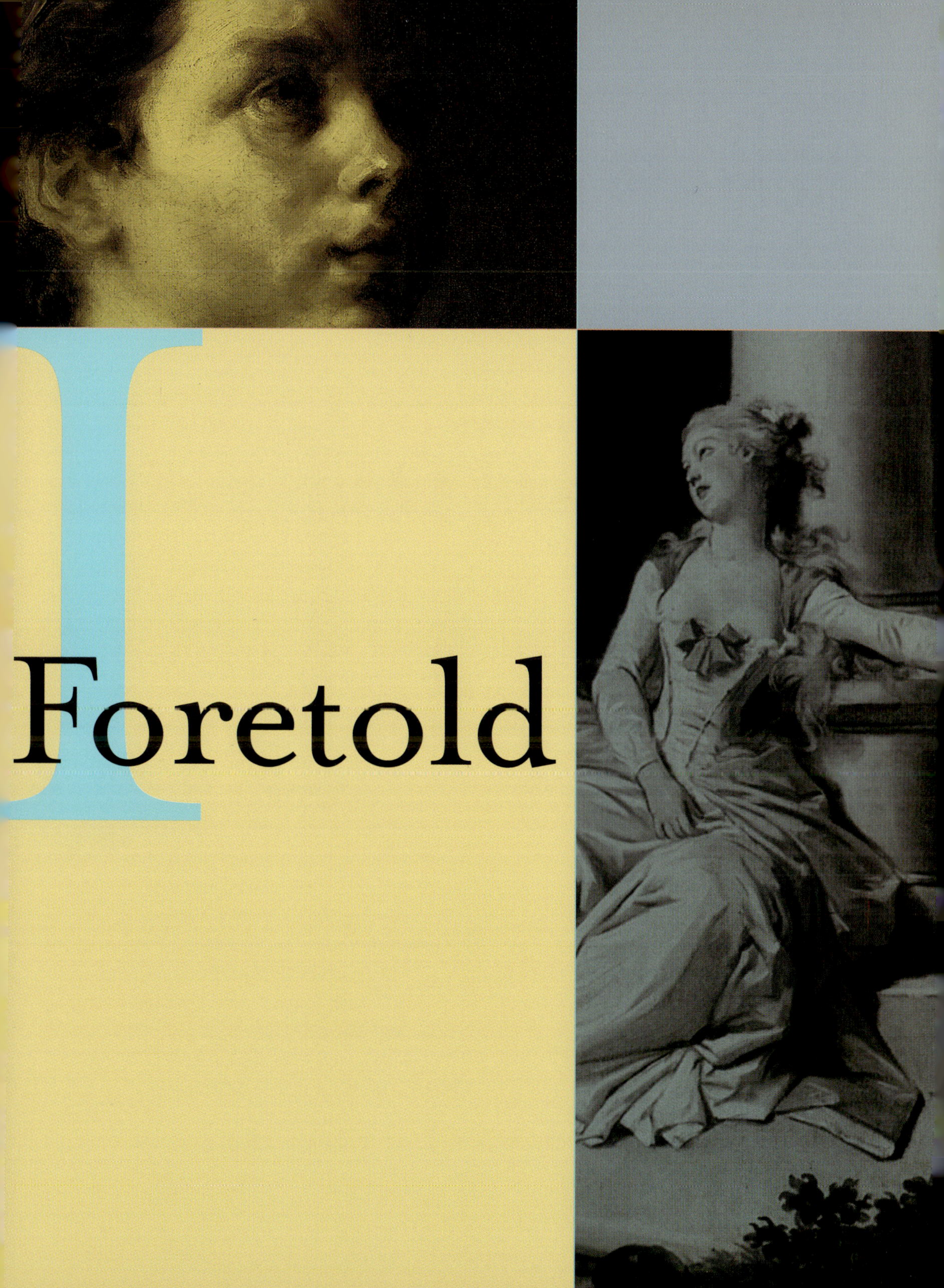

I
Foretold

From Glory to Oblivion

"And suddenly, after all the hullabaloo, everything went quiet around Fragonard. And he and Greuze looked at each other, wondering where it had all disappeared to, and how. For now all eyes were on David and his school."

Thus runs the account provided by Fragonard's grandson Théophile. But is this image—of a career run out of steam, a painter outstripped by the rising generation—to be taken literally?

The year 1785 saw David sweep all before him at the Salon with the compelling mastery of his *Oath of the Horatii*: henceforth the Antique model was the paradigmatic vehicle for moral example. Fragonard, at the time, was only fifty-three. Had he lost the esteem of art lovers? The prices his works commanded at auction are ample proof of the contrary: *The Adoration of the Shepherds*, sold along with the rest of the Marquis de Véri's collection in that same year of 1785, was knocked down for 9 501 livres, a record for a work by a living artist. Théophile relates an edifying anecdote about the respect the painter and his oeuvre inspired: when the name "Jean-Honoré Fragonard" was announced at an auction, "it could be taken by those disposed to hear it that way as 'Honor Fragonard.' And people would state their opinion out loud, saying 'As he so thoroughly deserves.'" A further pointer to his popularity was the fact that engravers continued to reproduce his work until late in the century.

And yet in 1785 there were already those who spoke of him in the past tense: "Monsieur Fragonard, born with enough genius to mold several other artists, seems to me not to have met his obligations regarding nature to the full. Far from following the sublime path of his Art, where the most immense success awaited him, he wandered off down strange by-ways, creating

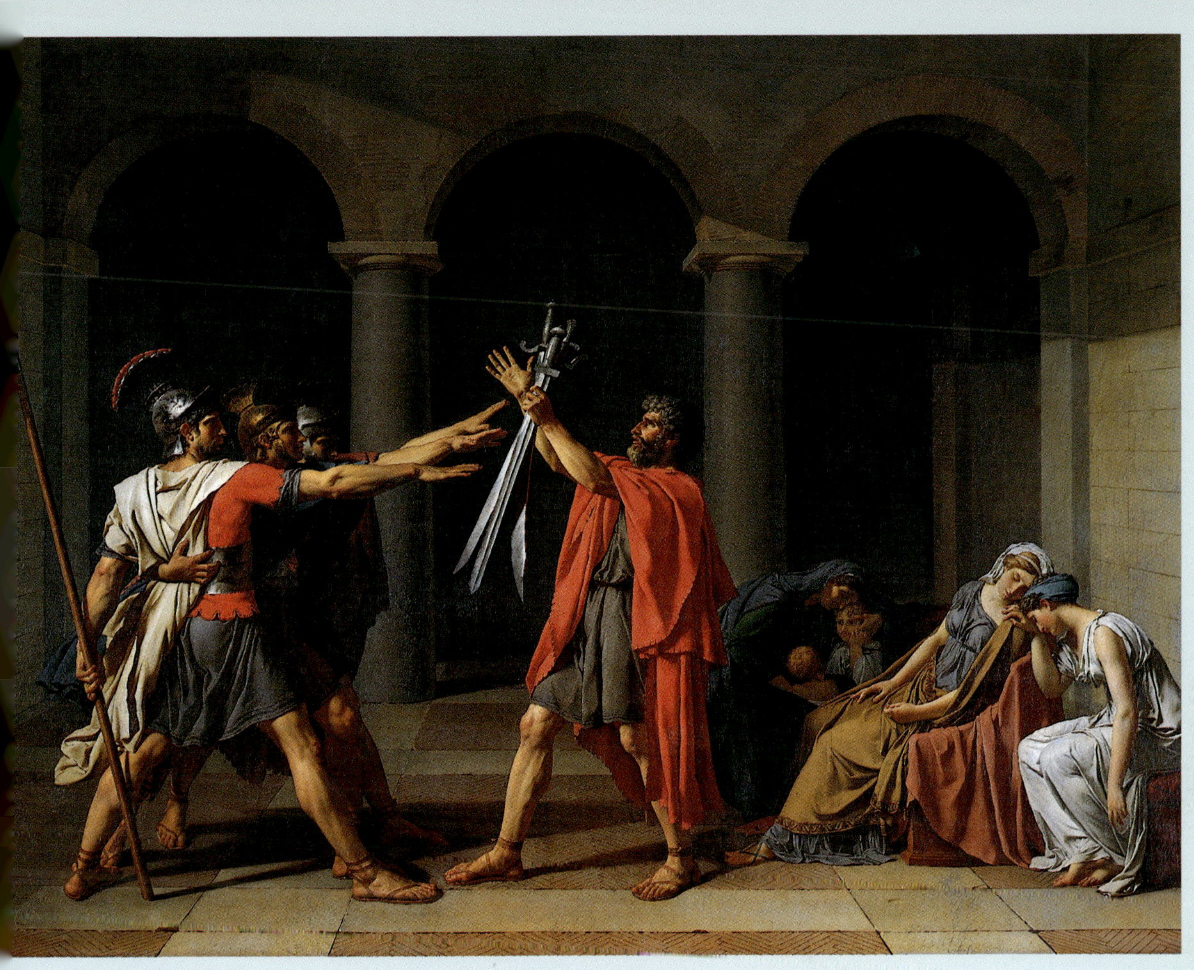

Jacques-Louis David,
The Oath of the Horatii,
1784, oil on canvas, 330 x 425 cm
Paris, Musée du Louvre.

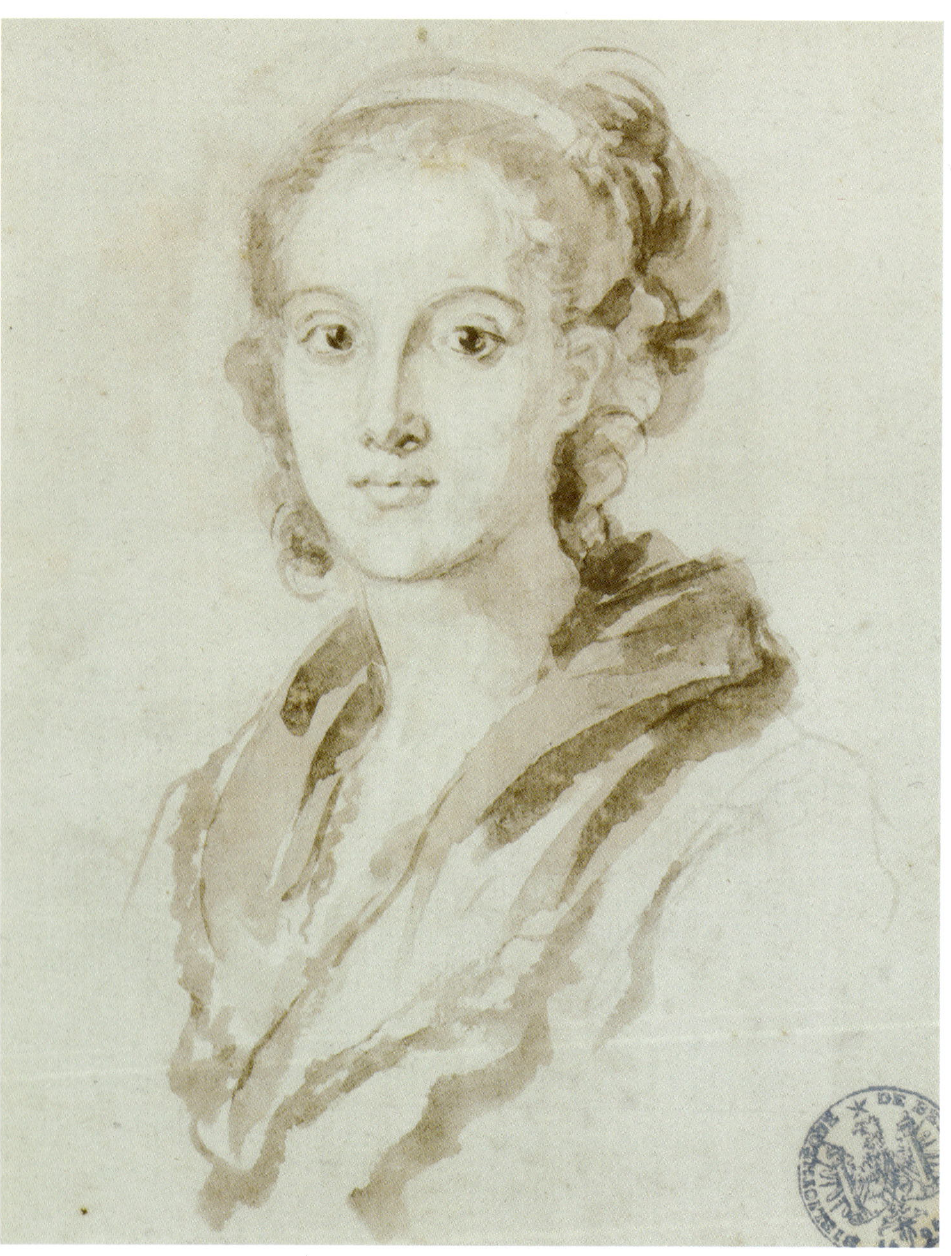

Portrait of Marguerite Gérard,
c. 1780, black chalk and wash, 18.6 x 13 cm
Besançon, Musée des Beaux-Arts.

Young Woman Standing,
c. 1785, red chalk, 33.2 x 22.8
Darmstadt, Hessisches Landesmuseum.

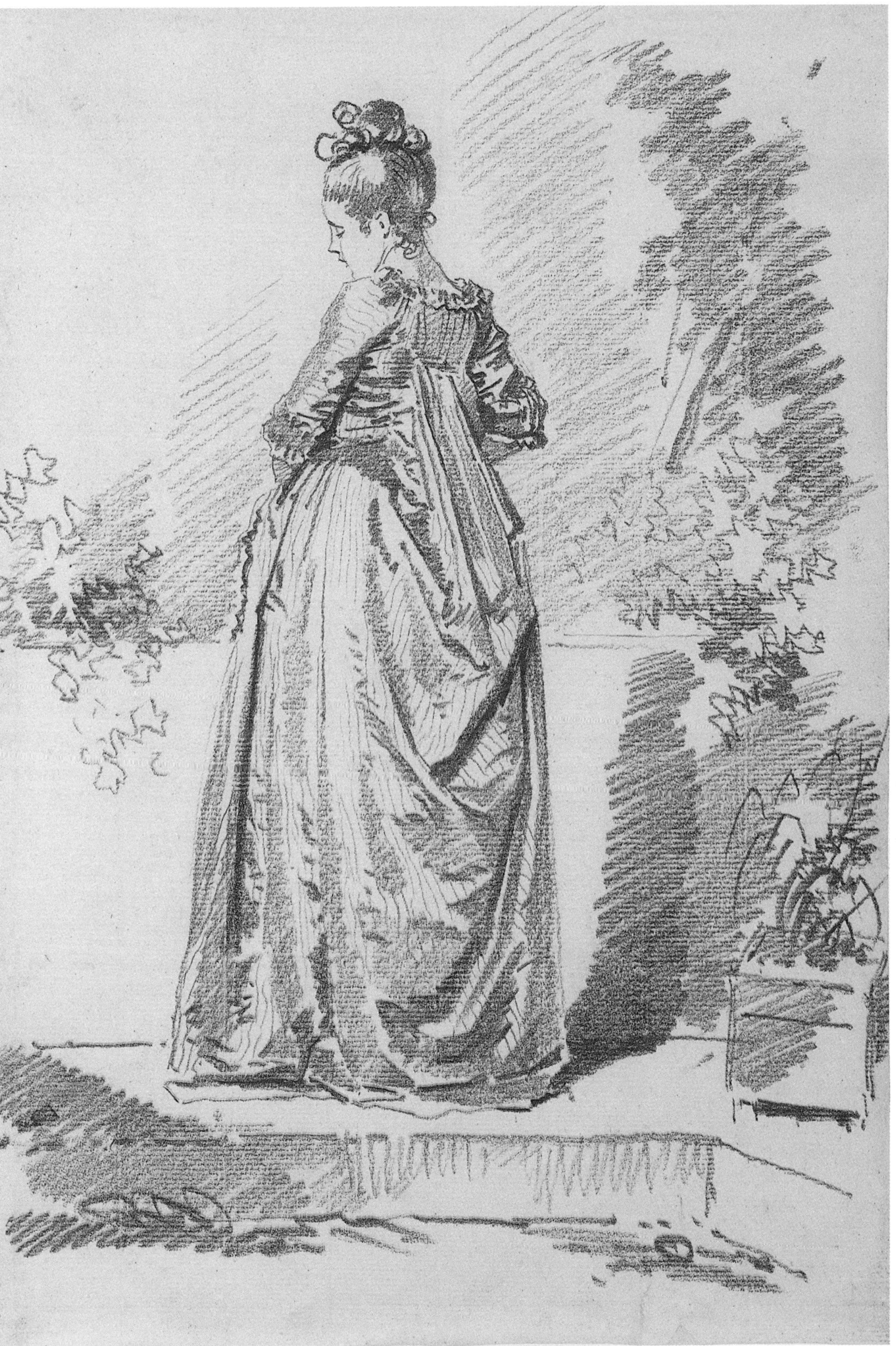

A Young Scholar
c. 1780, oil on canvas, 45.3 x 37.7 cm
London, Wallace Collection .

for himself a style more suited to perfervid imaginings than exact truthfulness. It must be admitted that some of his compositions in this manner have met with well-deserved acclaim; but his ambition was limited to quick, dazzling flashes, despite a genius capable of radiating a greater, more lasting light. His *Callirhoë*, which earned him the approval of the Academy, justifies our reproaches all the more, in that it can be considered a masterpiece of harmony and eloquence. Despite his occasional weaknesses in drawing, it will be a matter of lasting regret that Monsieur Fragonard failed to rise to greater heights."

For someone as subject to doubt and self-questioning as Fragonard, there could be no harsher verdict. Without having exhibited a great deal, he had had to endure his share of criticism, but this time the issue was not one of those exercises in irony the Salon commentators were so good at, striving above all to flaunt their wit at the artist's expense. Even the brilliantly treacherous disparagement of a Diderot was as nothing compared to this anonymous broadside from someone who was so clearly a connoisseur: brief and blunt, the *Discourse on the Current State of Painting* would find a far wider audience than reviews turned out by philosophers for a princely elite. Nor was this simply a hatchet job on a particular picture, or subject, or compositional detail: with terrible succinctness an entire career had been called into question.

Had Fragonard, like the unprofitable servant of the Biblical parable, wasted his talents? Had he been excessively modest and lacking in ambition? Seen in the context of its period, the 1785 commentary is made all the crueler by its pertinence. Despite having all the necessary ability, Fragonard had shrunk from a career as a history painter. In addition, the archives contain references to a number of his students—in 1767 a certain Martin de Cahors, the following year Louis-André Dalbeau, and in 1803 Henry Castel—all of whom remained total unknowns without the least academic success to their names. This tends to confirm the pitiless accusation of the critic, with his reminder of the artist's responsibility: Fragonard did not mold painters; he did not pass his skills on. Marguerite Gérard, aged twenty-four in 1785, was the sole exception. True, she was the artist's sister-in-law, and would never have been able to enter the rigorously all-male Ecole Royale des Elèves Protégés. A particularly gifted student, she was also a source of comfort to her teacher over the twenty years remaining to him.

So there began, in the second half of the 1780s, the long and inexorable decline that ultimately saw Fragonard lay down his brush. The dominance of the Antique style and the spread of Neoclassicism do not explain everything, however: for it was the combination of personal and professional factors, and the effects of the tempest of the French Revolution, that would ultimately see the artist sink into a state of utter despondency.

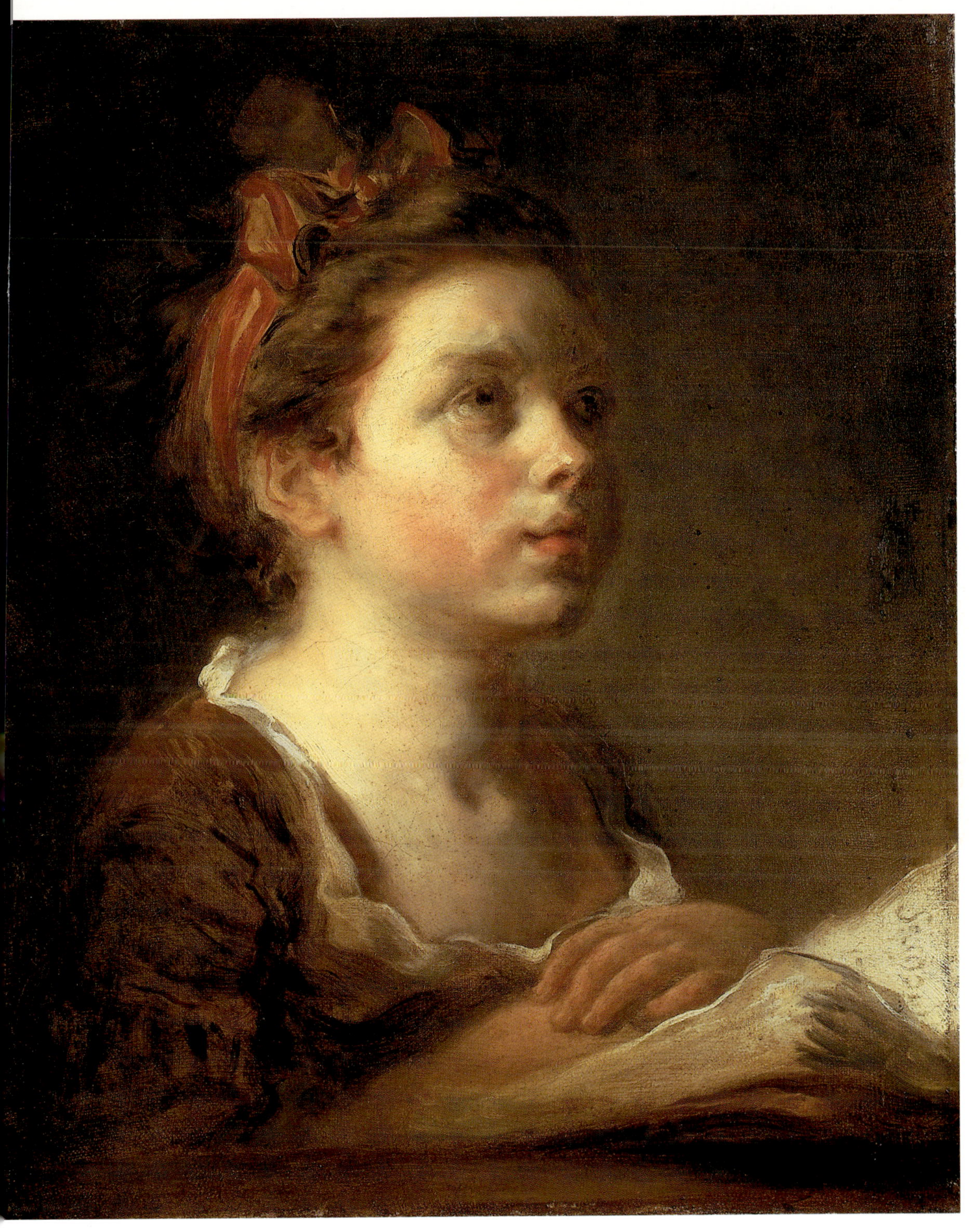

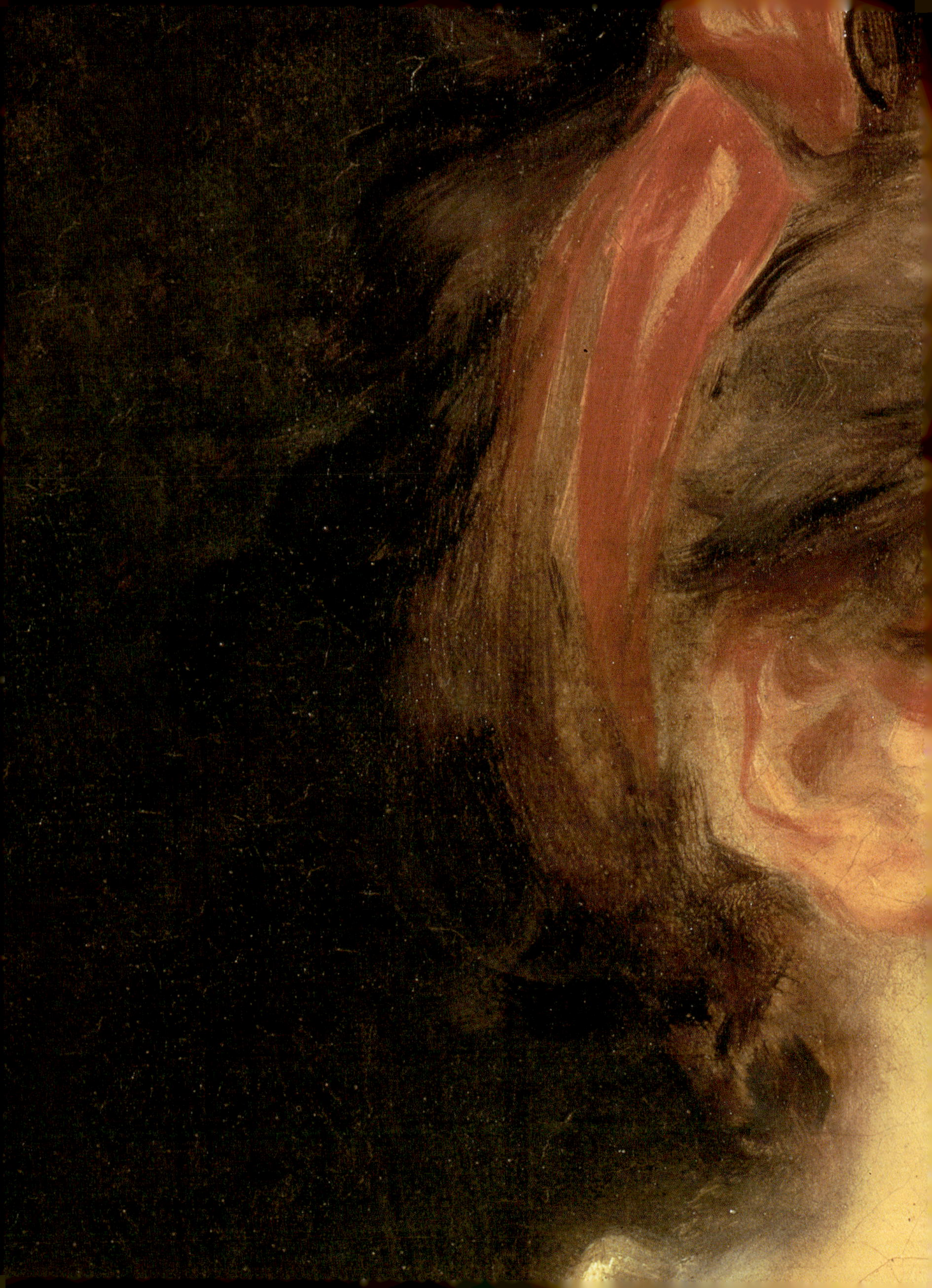

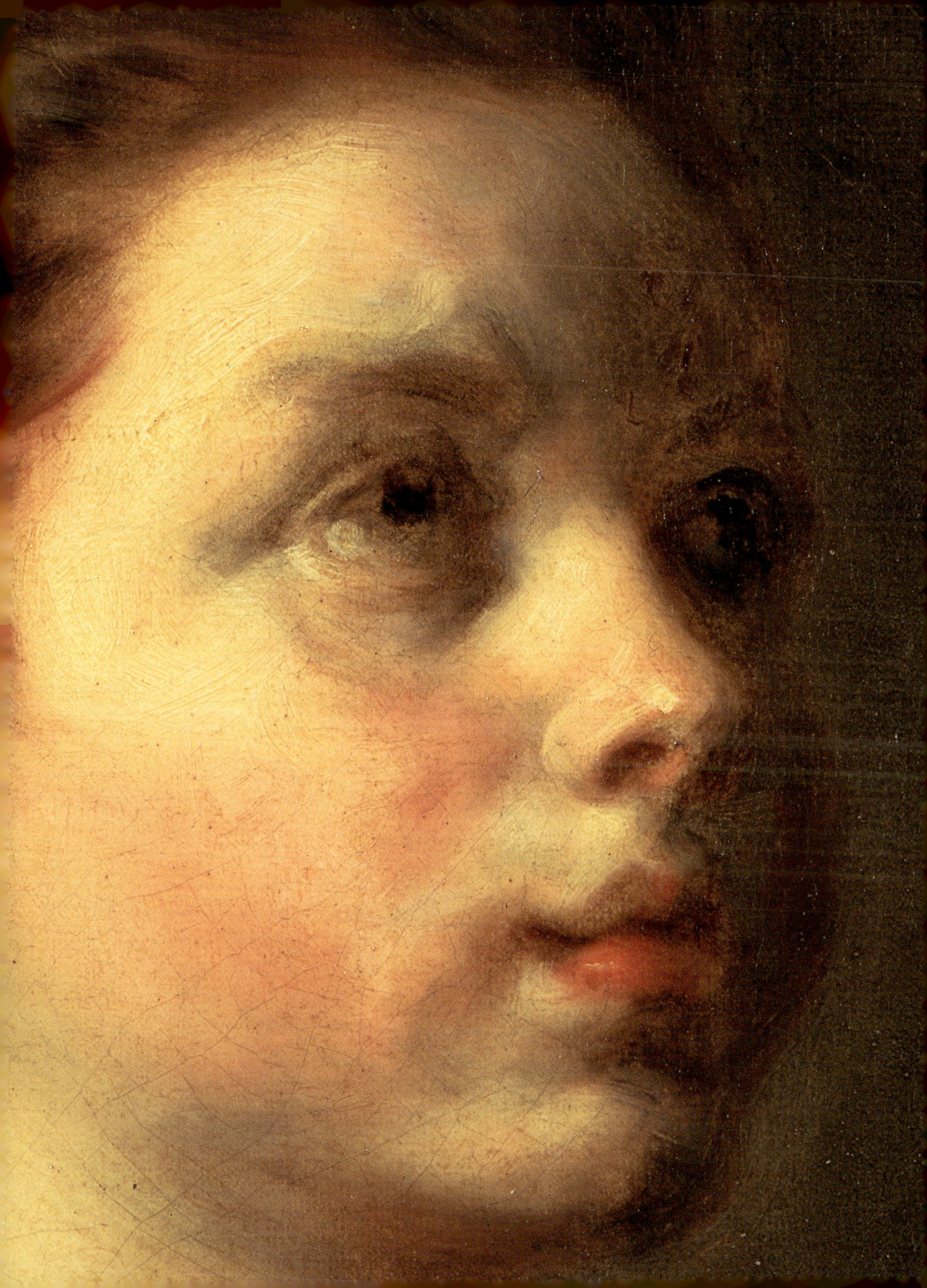

Farewell, Rosalie

The dramatic high point came in 1788. On 8 October Rosalie, the older of Fragonard's daughters, died in the home of the Bergerets, at the Château de Cassan. She was almost nineteen. We know almost nothing about her or about the circumstances of her early death, and although she must have modeled for her father many times, there is no certain likeness of her among his pictures—apart, probably, from a series of simple, pared-down red chalk drawings dated to the period 1785–88. Standing, sitting, or crouching before a fire, the young woman is shown wearing a dress with a silken sheen, and sometimes a crossover mantle with flounced sleeves. The weariness we often see, and the listless pose—sometimes drowsing on a chair, hands crossed in her lap—suggest a fragile constitution.

Deeply affected by the loss of his daughter, Fragonard fell ill himself, and a trip to calmer, more clement climes than Paris seemed indicated. After the taking of the Bastille on 14 July 1789 and the succession of riots that followed, the nobility who were the art buyers of the time began to opt for exile: Madame

Vigée-Lebrun, for example, hastily left for Italy. By contrast others, like Marie-Anne Fragonard and her sister Marguerite, chose to demonstrate their patriotism by joining—along with Jacques-Louis David's wife—the delegation of artists' wives and daughters who donated their jewelry to the National Assembly to pay the public debt. This gesture set the family above all suspicion, but they nonetheless decided to leave for the South. Early in 1790 Fragonard, his wife, their son Alexandre-Evariste, and Marguerite Gérard arrived in Grasse, moving in with a cousin, Alexandre Maubert, a perfume maker whose home is now the Musée-Villa Fragonard. Their stay was to last more than two years.

Cut off from the Paris art scene, Fragonard had the chance to break new ground, as he had done more than once over the previous twenty years; the opportunity to enthuse a public of art lovers far less severe than the critics and still receptive to his work. Yet while this exile—a kind of flight, really—saw him recover physically, it did not provide the energy boost needed to fire up his career again. He did not deign to undertake a commission from the Russian Prince Youssoupoff, organized for him by Greuze in 1789, and as pitiful as it may seem, he devoted most of his time in the South to painting hollyhocks. Having brought with him the canvases painted for the pavilion at Louveciennes, he set them up in his cousin's drawing room and took up once more, in the same spirit, the work rejected by Madame Du Barry seventeen years before. It is worth mentioning in passing that his erstwhile patron was to meet her end on the guillotine on 8 December 1793.

So it was that Fragonard rounded off the series with four high, narrow panels: tall double-flowered hollyhocks for the most part, their dark hearts standing out among the light-colored petals. A fifth canvas, in a format similar to the Louveciennes originals, shows a young woman sitting at the base of a column that culminates in a sundial, a stone sphere ringed by a circle and topped with a *putto* whose arm serves as the gnomon indicating midday. This work has often been interpreted as a postlude to the "gallant" canvases, and the scene of the dreamy young woman titled *Forsaken or Reverie*. Whether or not this reflects Fragonard's intentions is another matter, however, given the sharp contrast between the first four pictures and the nostalgic tone of this one. Whatever the case, this portrayal of a lost happiness was Fragonard's last major work, and we sense in it a sadness never before seen in his work. Aware, perhaps, that his career has come to an end, the artist has let his mood show through in what can be read as an allegory of the passage of time. The chromatic range, all browns and golds, underscores the work's crepuscular, almost funereal character. In this ultimate, melancholic scene, with its soft, autumnal light, might we not see—in the poetic and musical sense—a kind of tomb for the daughter who had been taken from him?

Portrait of a Child (Alexandre-Evariste Fragonard?) *c. 1780-85, black chalk, 34.6 x 24.9 cm, Cambridge, Fogg Art Museum, Harvard University Art Museums, Anonymous Loan in honor of Eunice Williams.*

Marie-Anne Fragonard, **Portrait of a Child (Alexandre-Evariste Fragonard?)** *c. 1785, miniature on ivory, 6.5 x 5.1 cm Paris, Musée du Louvre*

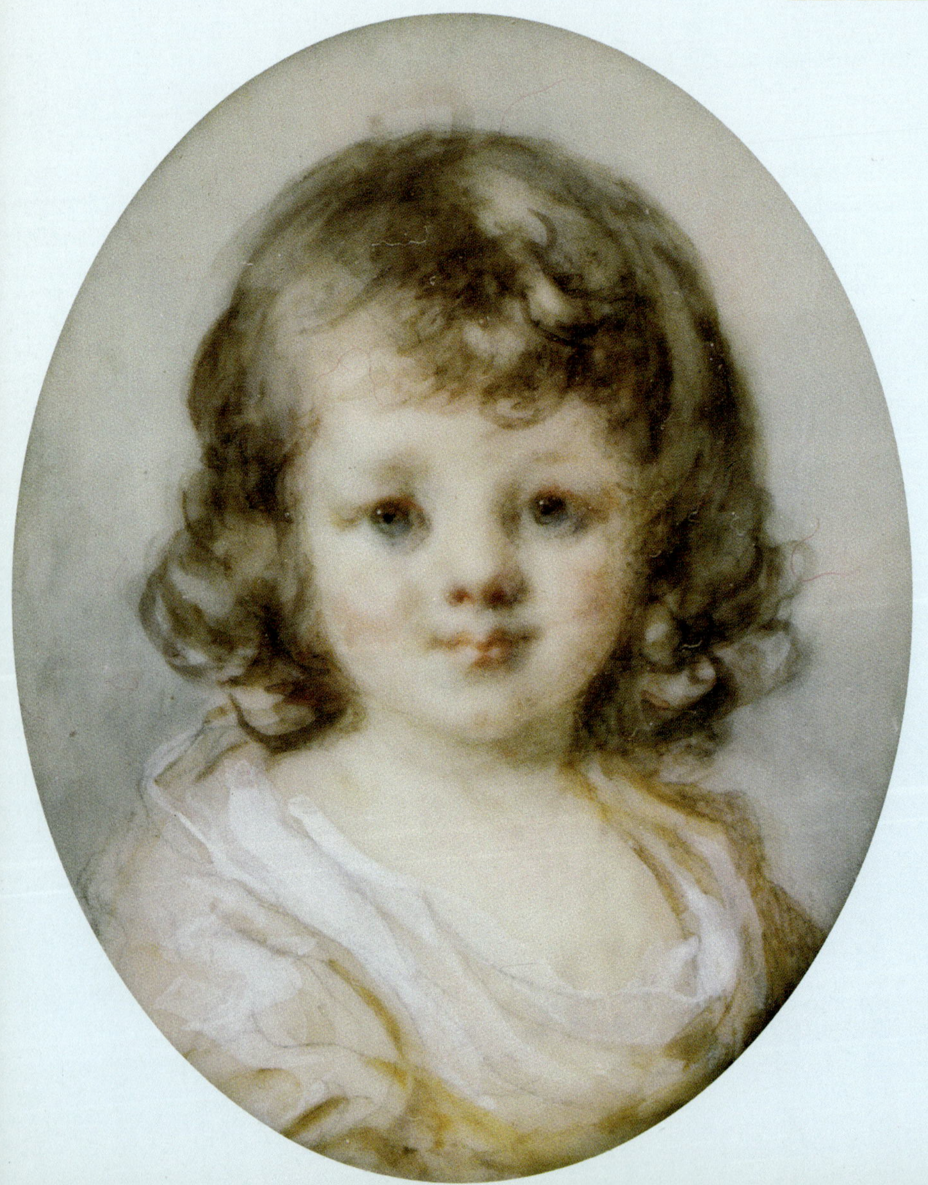

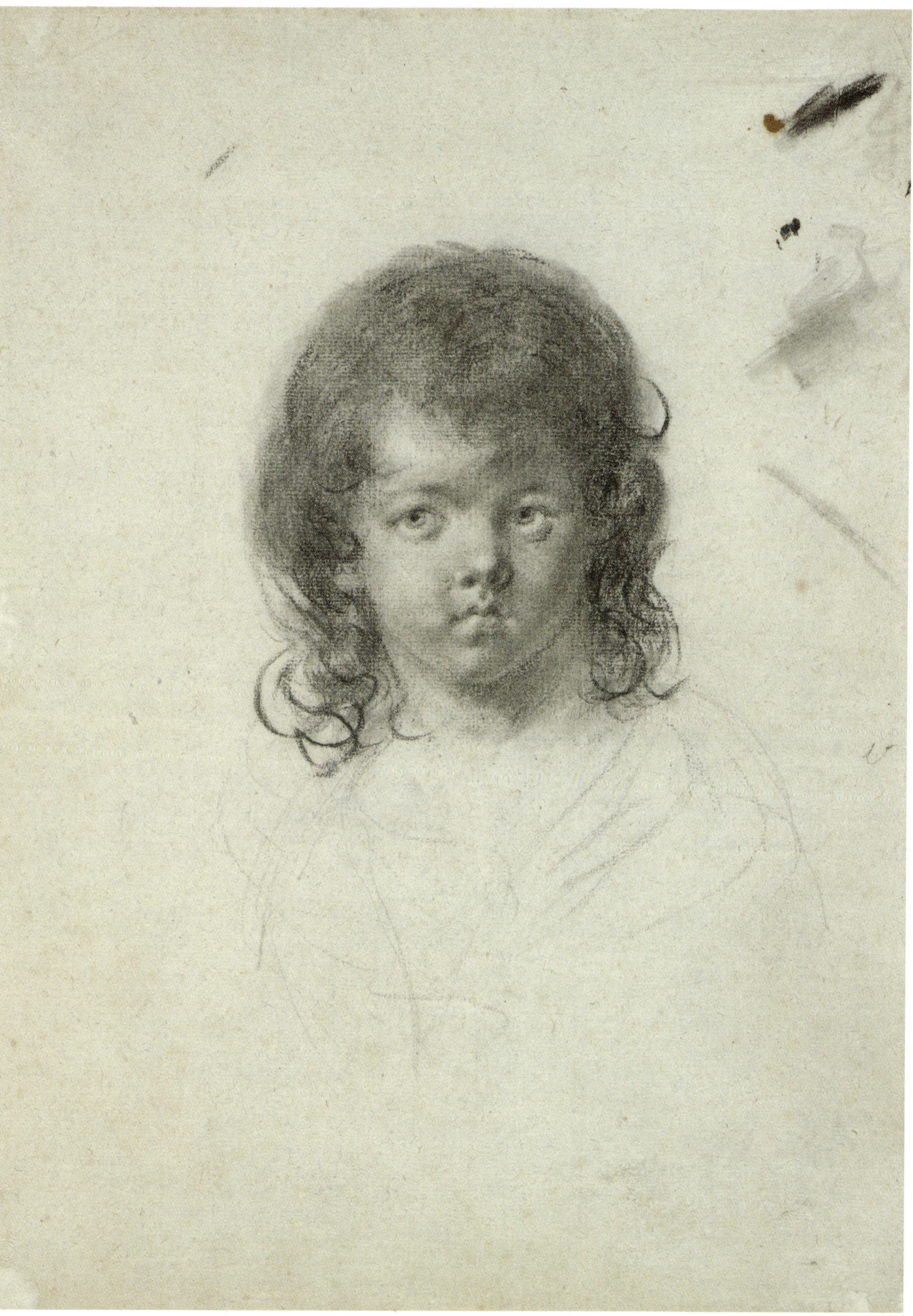

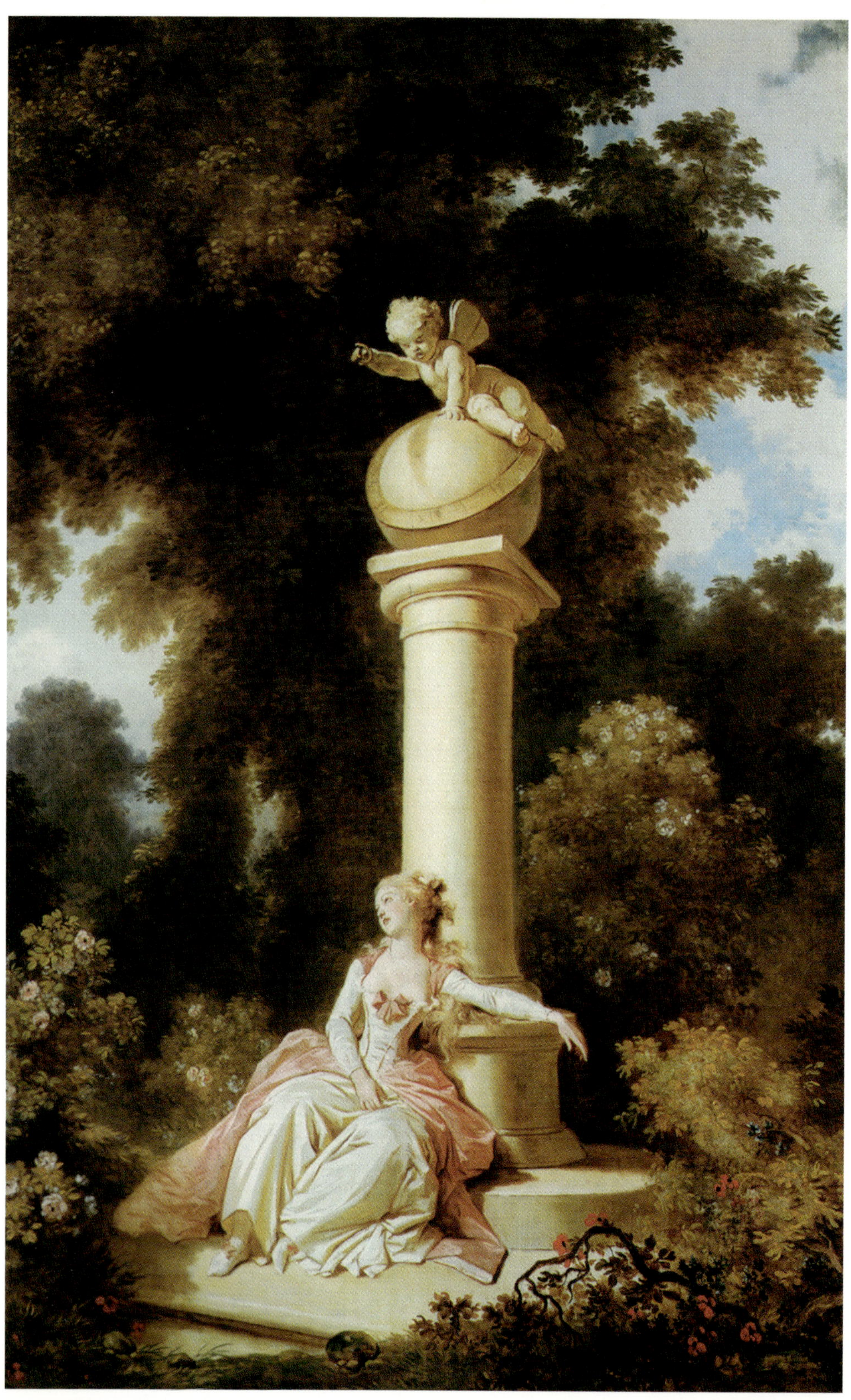

Forsaken,
1790–91, oil on canvas, 318 x 196 cm
New York, The Frick Collection.

Changing Times

When the Fragonards returned to Paris the political situation was no calmer. The opposite, in fact. Instability ruled, and the times were no more propitious for artists. Those friends and clients who had not died—like the Abbé de Saint-Non in 1791—had emigrated. One such was the Duc-Maréchal de Coigny, from whose residence the authorities had taken the sketch for *The Bolt* and a delicious *Cupid Sacrificing His Wings for the Delight of the First Kiss*. The Duc d'Harcourt, who had fled abroad in 1792, would die in England without returning to the park he had had created on his property in Normandy. Others, less fortunate, were arrested and their collections seized before they were tried and executed. This was the case of Charles-Nicolas Duclos-Dufresnoy, guillotined in 1794: at the time of his arrest he was the owner of four Fragonards, among them *The Isle of Love* and *The Fountain of Love*. Another victim of the guillotine was Denis-Pierre-Jean Papillon de La Ferté, Intendant des Menus-Plaisirs, whose collection included the large youthful work *Psyche Shows Her Sisters the Presents She Has Received from Cupid*. Charles-Philibert de Levis-Mirepoix, owner of a *Woman Playing a Hurdy-Gurdy*, met the same fate, as did farmer general Louis-Marie Le Bas de Courmont and chief tax collector Marie-François Ménage de Pressigny, owners respectively of *Girl Making a Dog Dance on Her Bed* and *The Swing*.

Bergeret's son was luckier. Imprisoned on 2 November 1793, he was freed three months later, after the municipality of Isle-Adam had petitioned on his behalf. The architect Ledoux also found himself behind bars on a charge of "aristocracy", but was liberated on 13 January 1795, as was Hubert Robert. Their difficulties were probably due to their connections with the Court and high society, but it is not impossible that David, bent on total personal control of the cultural scene, had played a nasty part in the artistic cleansing campaign.

Apparently the Fragonards had no worries on this score; indeed, they seem to have enjoyed David's protection, and when Alexandre-Evariste was enrolled at the Ecole Royale des Elèves Protégés, he became a student in his atelier. Given that he was not yet twelve, a decision of this magnitude could not have been taken without paternal consent; his father may even have encouraged him in this choice, despite the presumed antagonism between the two camps. While it is true that their work had nothing in common,

Fragonard as Civil Servant

Fragonard and David seem to have held each other in mutual esteem, even if they were not actually on friendly terms. Their acquaintance went back a long way: the younger painter, we recall, had replaced the master as the decorator of Mademoiselle Guimard's drawing room. After receiving the approval of the Academy in 1781, David had become part of the small community of artists living at the Louvre, where he and Fragonard were neighbors. It was he, as a Convention deputy and member of the Comité d'Instruction Publique, who asked Minister for the Interior Roland for a new apartment at the Louvre for Fragonard and "his respectable family" on their return from Grasse. And it was, yet again, David who found Fragonard a niche for his old age as, to quote the former's elegantly laudatory turn of phrase, "guardian of the masterpieces to whose number he had contributed in his youth."

Thus it was that a new career, brief but absorbing, opened up for Fragonard as one of founding curators at the Louvre, which opened its doors to the public on 10 August 1793. The works initially on show in what was then called the Central Museum of the Arts came from the royal collection, their number soon being boosted by confiscations from the estates of *émigrés*—self-exiled aristocrats—and plunder obtained by the Revolutionary army abroad. The new institution was at first run by a commission made up mainly of artists, including the painter Vincent. The following December, however, David lambasted the commission's bad management, the half-hearted patriotism of its members and, among other things, the dangerous clumsiness of the restoration the works were subject to. His solution was a new curatorial body to which his first appointment was a Fragonard recommended as "both connoisseur and great artist." David's arrest in the wake of the fall of Robespierre in the month of Thermidor, Year II—July 1794—seems not to have endangered his appointee. The death of the tyrant led to the throwing-open of the prisons and the liberation of Hubert Robert, who then joined his old friend as co-director of the Louvre. Another companion from that first stay in Rome, the sculptor Pajou, was also invited to join the team.

Regularly president or secretary of the curatorial body, Fragonard seems to have taken his new duties very much to heart, as the minutes recording his activities indicate. Among the questions falling within his domain were opening hours, security, inventorying and cataloguing, guards' wages and uniforms, firewood, and enlargement of the museum within the former palace. Another managerial task, however, was much more in tune with his personal skills: he was charged with taking delivery of old master drawings confiscated in Cologne, the big Rubens from Antwerp, and the Rembrandts from the Stathouder collection in Holland. He spent long hours with the paintings, drawings and sculptures in the different art depots in and around Paris, choosing those worthy of a place in the Louvre; he also inspected the statues in the parks at Versailles, Marly and Choisy, wrote reports on suggested acquisitions, on restorations in progress, and on *émigré* collections—in some of which, as fate would have it, he discovered works by his own hand.

How could he possibly have found time to paint during the years leading up to the very end of the century? Under the Directory an administrative reshuffle saw him removed from his post and entrusted with a mission seemingly even more demanding and unrewarding: a new museum devoted exclusively to the French School was being created at Versailles and he was to supervise the transport of works from Paris, among them his own *Coresus and Callirhoë*. From Versailles he would bring back the works of foreign schools that various monarchs had collected. Thus it was that on 12 August 1797, Leonardo da Vinci's *Mona Lisa* left the Château de Versailles en route for the Louvre, with Fragonard riding shotgun.

Something left unaccomplished

With the dispatch of the ultimate convoy on 25 September 1799, Fragonard was a free man again. This could have been the moment to take up his brush again, but he seems not to have done so, and the house-moving that was forced on him in 1805 could only have aggravated his despondency and hastened his end. Among the fruits of Napoleon's victories were endless additions to the collection at the Louvre; extra space had to be created and proper security provided for works imperiled by their closeness to the living quarters of a host of artists. Accordingly a decree was issued expelling the artists. Greuze would die before the decree took effect, but Fragonard, who was just beginning his seventy-fourth year and had spent more than two thirds of his life inside the Louvre or in the immediate vicinity, had no choice but to pack his bags and vacate his studio. He and his wife found accommodation in the nearby, and then very fashionable, galleries of the Palais Royal, and it was there that he died a few months later, on 22 August 1806—the same year as the libertine

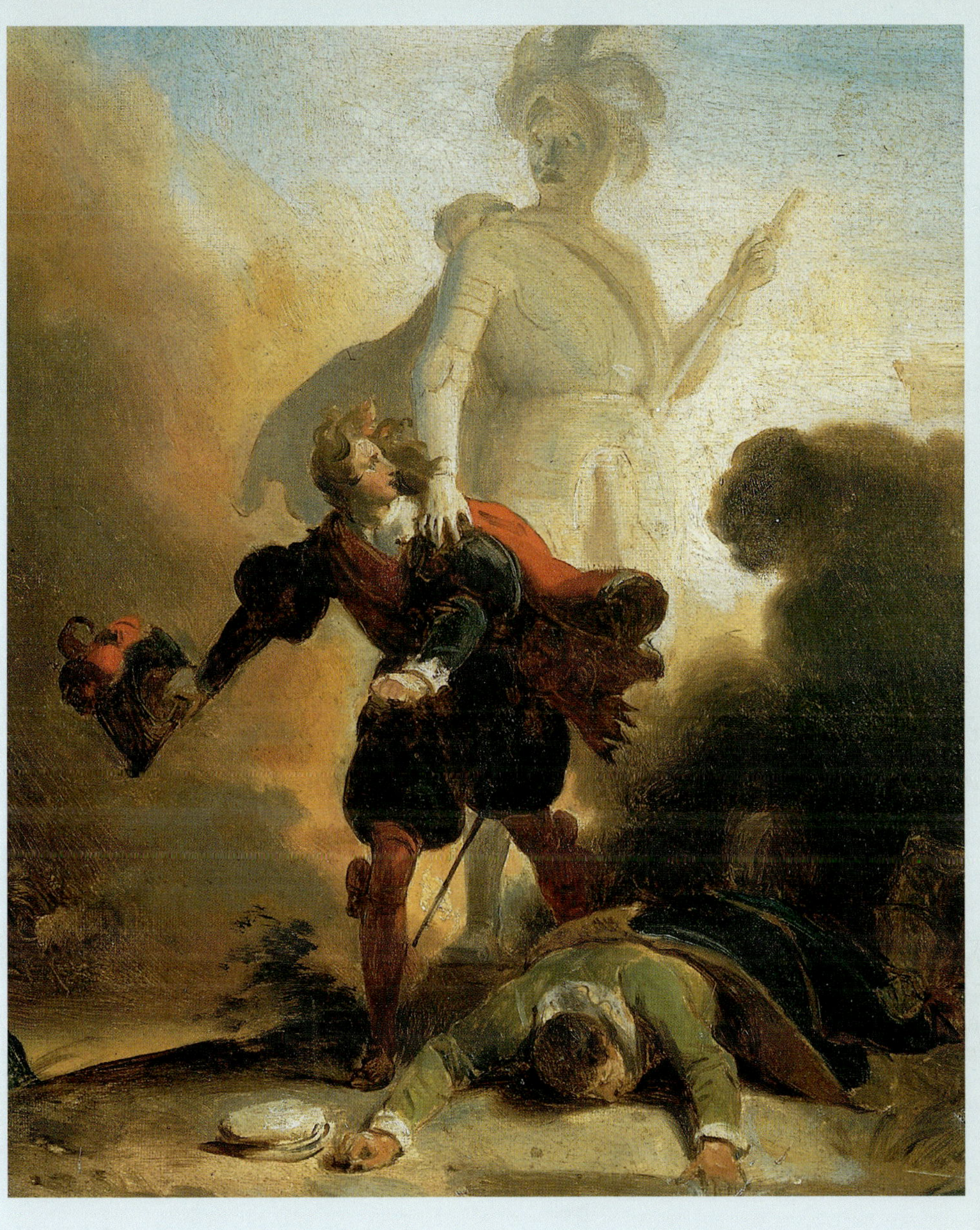

Alexandre-Evariste Fragonard,
Don Juan and the Statue of the Commander,
c. 1825–30, oil on canvas, 38.5 x 32 cm
Strasbourg, Musée des Beaux-Arts.

writer Restif de La Bretonne and the architect Ledoux. Hubert Robert survived him by two years, passing away just after completing his umpteenth imaginary view, a *Project for the Laying-out of the Place de la Concorde with a View of the Arc de Triomphe*.

On the following 15 September the biennial Salon of Living Artists opened to the public. Although he had been showing since age thirteen at a now increasingly popular event, Alexandre-Evariste Fragonard, now twenty-six, presented no works in 1806—but on the walls of the Louvre were three pictures by his aunt Marguerite Gérard. Among them was a genre scene—now unfortunately lost—in which, according to a contemporary commentator, one could recognize Marguerite's former teacher. But it was above all David's pupils who caught the public's eye, with works that created a sensation: the immense *Battle of Aboukir* by Jean-Baptiste Gros (1771–1835), the terrifying *Deluge Scene* by Anne-Louis Girodet (1767–1824) and the fascinating, controversial *Napoleon as Jupiter Enthroned* by Jean-Auguste-Dominique Ingres (1780–1867). It is clear that, even had he been still alive, there would have been no place for Fragonard in the celebration of the Empire and the powers that be that Dominique-Vivant Denon (1734–1825)—Fragonard's friend and associate under the Ancien Régime—was out to force on the arts. Put in charge of the Louvre by Napoleon, Denon had taken over the role of the pre-Revolutionary *Surintendants* to the point of becoming the new "Minister for the Arts". The Academy might have been suppressed, along with its rigid codification of the genres, but other institutions and conventions had taken their place. The Revolution and later the Empire demanded a commitment from artists that left no room for whimsy: the Zeitgeist called for order, the edification of the masses, and the "regeneration" of the arts, seen as having been "corrupted" under the last monarchs.

With his endless play on sundry technical, stylistic and thematic registers, Fragonard was a troubling figure who resisted all attempts at pigeonholing. With his fertile imagination and the incredible diversity of his sources of inspiration, he was as unsettling for the new generation as he had been for his own. Most striking is his ability to move seamlessly from one manner to another, from the intimately amatory to the sweepingly elegiac, from the portrait of an actress to a religious scene. What subjects did he not treat? The still life perhaps: it would certainly have been presumptuous to try to outdo Chardin, but at the same time this painter of movement and the unexpected was little drawn to the portrayal of the inanimate. Nonetheless, certain arresting details prove to us that he was far from insensitive to the poetry of things. Even animals—lumpish oxen, herds of sheep, cats persecuted by playful children, barnyard dogs and drawing-room terriers—caught his eye and appear in all sorts of pictures alone or as secondary figures: we think, for example, of that large bull whose white coat illuminates the entire stable. While never going along with the vogue for chinoiseries, at which Boucher excelled, he did try his hand at fashionable exoticism with some nonchalantly seductive sultanesses. And in each register, while unfailingly, deeply original, he succeeded in capturing the taste and sensibility of his time. Theater, dance, music, literature: different worlds whose resonance, perceptible in his canvases and his drawings, reminds us that he was born at the same time as Beaumarchais and Joseph Haydn.

Fragonard did not die a poor man, but his death went virtually unnoticed. Long gone was the time when the critics took him as a target, and after weathering the accusations of having wasted his time making money, he had become, by the end of his life, a revered patriarch. In the brief notice devoted to his death in the *Journal de Paris*, the author settles for the laconic observation that "The French School has lost in him a justly esteemed painter." He goes on to speak of the work of Alexandre-Evariste, "who promises to uphold the name he bears," and of Marguerite Gérard, who "as Monsieur Fragonard's pupil, is his rival in terms of talent, just as she was, until the last, a steadfast friend to him in his old age."

What emerges from those twenty long years is a kind of sadness, a feeling of something left unaccomplished. This muted end is in sharp contrast with the artist's dazzling career, bright with successes as renowned as his flops and even more so with his painting itself, all vigor and explosions of color. Discreet, indifferent to honors, and fundamentally independent, Fragonard built an oeuvre that ranks among the most varied and innovative in the history of art. An oeuvre which, fallen into oblivion until rediscovered by the Goncourt brothers in the second half of the 19th century, has gone on to become emblematic of its age.

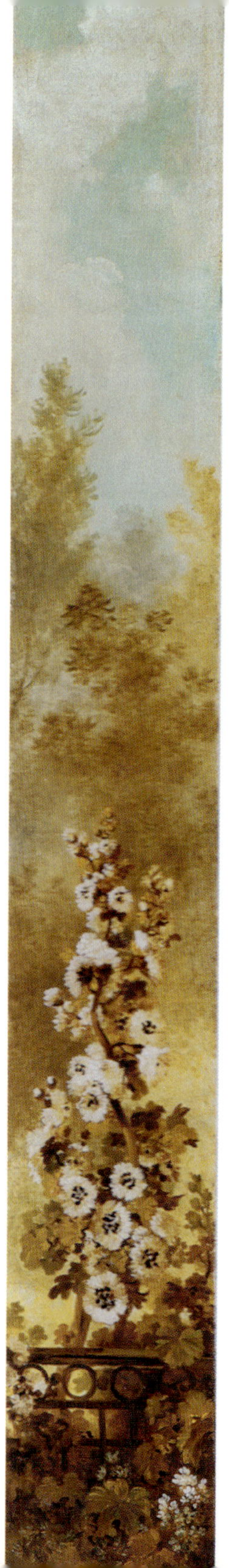
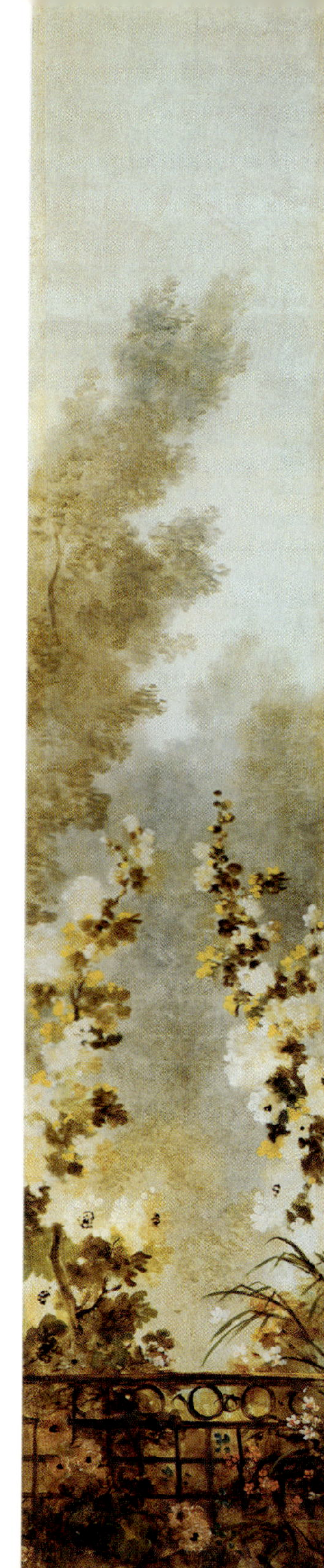

Hollyhocks,
1790–92, oil on canvas, four pannels,
two 318 x 140 cm, two 318 x 63 cm
New York, The Frick Collection.

Index

Chronology

1732: birth of Jean-Honoré Fragonard in Grasse, France (4 April).
1738: the family moves to Paris.
1748-1752: studies under Chardin, then Boucher.
1752: wins the Academy prize with *Jeroboam Sacrificing to Idols*; admitted to the Ecole Royale des Elèves Protégés.
1756: arrives at the French Academy in Rome late in the year; lives there until April 1761, except for a stay in Tivoli during the summer of 1760, and in Naples in March 1761.
1761: returns to France with the Abbé de Saint-Non (April–September), stopping off en route in Florence, Bologna, Venice and elsewhere.
1765: receives Academy approval with *Coresus Sacrifices Himself to Save Callirhoë*. The picture is a great success at the Salon, and Fragonard obtains a studio and lodgings at the Louvre.
1767: his pictures at the Salon, including *Swarm of Cherubs, a Group of Children in the Sky*, disappoint the critics. Probable date of *The Swing*.
1769: marries Marie-Anne Gérard; their daughter Rosalie is born.
Date of *Portrait of M. de La Bretèche*, one of his "fantasy portraits".
1770: Mademoiselle Guimard commissions the decoration of the drawing room in her townhouse on the Rue d'Antin.
1771: Madame Du Barry commissions the *Progress of Love* panels for her pavilion at Louveciennes.
1773-1774: second trip to Italy (October 1773–September 1774), with Bergeret de Grancourt. The return includes stops at Venice, Vienna, Prague, Dresden, Frankfurt, and Strasbourg.
1775: probable date of the arrival at the Louvre lodgings of Marguerite Gérard, the painter's young sister-in-law. She becomes his pupil and artistic associate.
1780: birth of Alexandre-Evariste, Fragonard's son, in Grasse.
1788: death of Fragonard's daughter Rosalie.
1790-1791: the painter and his wife and son live in Grasse.
1793-1800: member of the Commission for the Arts, then curator of the Central Museum of the Arts.
1806: death of Fragonard on 22 August in his new lodgings in the galleries of the Palais Royal.

Akg-images: p. 145.
Aix-en-Provence, musée Granet: p. 54, 69, 70 (detail).
Artephot: p. 33, 200-201, 227.
Bridgeman-Giraudon: cover (detail), p.9, 19, 26, 28, 30, 31 (detail), 39, 40-41 (detail), 45, 49, 50 (detail), 53 up and down (detail), 63, 64-54 (detail), 79, 80-81 (detail), 83, 84-85 (detail), 90-91, 92 (detail), 94-95, 96-97 (detail), 99, 101, 102, 111, 112-113, 114-115 (detail) 128, 129 (detail), 131, 133, 135, 136-137 (detail), 138, 139, 146, 147, 148-149 (detail), 156, 158, 163, 175, 181, 191, 194-195, 196-197 (detail), 198-199 (detail), 203, 207 down (detail), 221, 224, 225, 230, 239, 249.
Bruxelles, Musée royaux des beaux-arts: p. 73 down.
Cambridge, Fogg Art Museum: p. 109, 117.
Private collection: p. 172, 219.
Dominique Genet, Boulogne: p. 213.
Erich Lessing/Akg-images: p. 141, 142-143 (detail), 210.
Frédéric Jaulmes: p. 232.
Leemage: p. 73 up.
Liège, musée d'Armes: p. 37.
London, Victoria & Albert Museum: p. 88-89.
London, National Gallery: p. 127.
Lyon, musée des Beaux-Arts: p. 22, 118, 173.
Montauban, musée Ingres: p. 34-35, 134, 150, 161 bas (detail), 176 up, 178-179, 214, 215, 226, 235.
Musée des Augustins, Toulouse: p. 82.
New York, Frick Collection: p. 217 (detail), 218.
New York, The Metropolitan Museum of Art: p. 75, 124, 159.
Napoléonmuseum Arenenberg: p. 100.
Orléans, musée des Beaux-Arts: p. 15.
Paris, Bibliothèque nationale de France: p. 21 up and down, 32, 60 down, 248.
Paris, École nationale supérieure des beaux-arts: p. 13 down (detail), 27.
Photo Roumagnac: p. 107, 153, 155, 176 down, 251.
Photo courtesy of The National Gallery, London: p. 209.
Paris, Photothèque du musée des Arts décoratifs: p. 57, 60 up.
RMN: p. 13 up (detail), 42, 43 (detail), 46, 61, 76, 103, 104-105 (detail), 125, 132, 151, 161 up (detail), 164, 168-169, 182, 186, 207 up (detail), 231, 236, 238, 241, 242-243 (detail), 244-245 (detail).
RMN/R.G.Ojéda : p. 220.
Studio Basset: p. 170-171.
Washington, National Gallery of Art: p. 121, 122 (detail).

Printed by Grafiche Zanini,
Bologna, Italy,
September 2006.